SEARCHING FOR THE LAST ANGLO-SAXON KING

SEARCHING FOR THE LAST ANGLO-SAXON KING

HAROLD GODWINSON
ENGLAND'S GOLDEN WARRIOR

PAULA LOFTING

PEN & SWORD HISTORY

AN IMPRINT OF PEN & SWORD BOOKS LTD.
YORKSHIRE – PHILADELPHIA

First published in Great Britain in 2025 by
PEN AND SWORD HISTORY
An imprint of
Pen & Sword Books Ltd
Yorkshire – Philadelphia

Copyright © Paula Lofting, 2025

ISBN 978 1 39904 127 0

The right of Paula Lofting to be identified as Author of this work has been asserted by her in accordance with the Copyright, Designs and Patents Act 1988.

A CIP catalogue record for this book is available from the British Library.

All rights reserved. No part of this book may be reproduced, transmitted, downloaded, decompiled or reverse engineered in any form or by any means, electronic or mechanical including photocopying, recording or by any information storage and retrieval system, without permission from the Publisher in writing. No part of this book may be used or reproduced in any manner for the purpose of training artificial intelligence technologies or systems.

Typeset in Times New Roman 9.5/11.5 by
SJmagic DESIGN SERVICES, India.
Printed and bound in the UK by CPI Group (UK) Ltd.

The Publisher's authorised representative in the EU for product safety is Authorised Rep Compliance Ltd., Ground Floor, 71 Lower Baggot Street, Dublin D02 P593, Ireland.
www.arccompliance.com

For a complete list of Pen & Sword titles please contact:
PEN & SWORD BOOKS LIMITED
George House, Units 12 & 13, Beevor Street, Off Pontefract Road,
Barnsley, South Yorkshire, S71 1HN, England
E-mail: enquiries@pen-and-sword.co.uk
Website: www.pen-and-sword.co.uk

or

PEN AND SWORD BOOKS
1950 Lawrence Rd, Havertown, PA 19083, USA
E-mail: uspen-and-sword@casematepublishers.com
Website: www.penandswordbooks.com

Contents

Acknowledgements vii
Foreword viii
Introduction x

PART ONE: ORIGINS AND BLOODLINES

Chapter One	The Godwinson Lineage 1
Chapter Two	Life after Wulfnoth 7
Chapter Three	Forging Alliances 14
Chapter Four	Forging a Dynasty 19
Chapter Five	Royal Relationships and Raising a Family 29

PART TWO: HAROLD

Chapter Six	Son of Fortune 38
Chapter Seven	White Swan 48
Chapter Eight	Swegn 57
Chapter Nine	Storm Winds Gather 66
Chapter Ten	A Small Matter of Succession 80
Chapter Eleven	Return of the Godwinsons 88

PART THREE: EARL OF WESSEX

Chapter Twelve	Conflict and Diplomacy 100
Chapter Thirteen	A Lost Prince and The Invasion That was too Tedious too Tell 111
Chapter Fourteen	Fire and Sword 119
Chapter Fifteen	William and the Crown 127
Chapter Sixteen	Threads to the Past 135
Chapter Seventeen	Tostig 142

PART FOUR: KING

Chapter Eighteen	The Old King Dies	150
Chapter Nineteen	England's Chosen King	157
Chapter Twenty	The Papal Banner	161
Chapter Twenty-one	It Begins	167
Chapter Twenty-two	War in the North	170
Chapter Twenty-three	England is Mine	179
Chapter Twenty-four	Battle for England	185
Chapter Twenty-five	The Killing of Harold, and his Last Resting Place	191

Notes	206
Abbreviations	240
Bibliography	241
Index	247

Acknowledgements

This idea bubbled in my mind for over a year before I decided to give it a go and submit to Pen & Sword books, with encouragement from my good friend, fellow author Sharon Bennett Connolly, whose work I have admired for some time. It has been a long slog and mission since I submitted in January of 2022, and in the main used to writing fiction, I had no idea what I was letting myself in for. Here is a list of the wonderful people who have been with me since I first started this journey and whose advice and assistance has been invaluable to me: first and foremost, the aforementioned Sharon Bennett Connolly whom without a doubt, I could not have done this. She was always there to reassure, guide and advise when at times I felt fraudulent and wondered what I was doing. The discussions we had about Harold were scintillating and stimulating.

The rest, in no particular order, are the Historical Writers Forum admins, Samantha Wilcoxson, Lynn Dawson, Cathie Dunn, Eleanor Swift-hook and Virginia Crow, who were a great support, giving me helpful feedback and encouragement. Stephanie Churchill for her excellent map designs and *Mr. Genealogy*, aka Tony Griggs, for the beautiful family trees. Fellow Anglo-Saxonist, Marie Hilder, who read the first chapters in their infancy and made me work hard, inspiring me to investigate things further. Melissa Speed for her thoughtful advice and feedback. Thanks to Lisl Madeline, who read the MS in its infancy, and Chloe Douglas who shared her thoughts with me on the Hereford chapter. Rob Bayliss, Anna Belfrage, and Carol McGrath for just being there. Jessica Bean and Mitchell Lawrence, my very own beautiful Eadgifu Swanneck and Harold Godwinson. Tricia Gurnett of the King Harold Society, for the wonderful tour of Waltham Abbey. Kevin McKenzie of the Finding Harold Project for sharing his research. Joan Langhorne for the tour of Bosham Church. My son Ron Bassett of REGB_Films for the beautiful images, Matt Bunker for the shieldwall image and my gratitude to English Heritage for allowing me to use the photos taken at Battle Abbey. My best friend forever, Christine Brown for putting up with my scattiness. And I must not forget all the wonderful team at Pen and Sword Publishing for helping me realise my dream of creating a book about my hero, Harold Godwinson.

Much love goes to my daughter and youngest son, Catherine and Connor Wilcox for putting up with my answer to everything: 'Not until I have finished this 'bleeping' book!' Their love is my flame.

Lastly, I would like to share my appreciation with you for Dr. Ann Williams, medievalist and eminently respected historian, for graciously sharing her knowledge and research with me. I will be eternally grateful.

Foreword

If there was to be a competition for the nation's favourite historical period, it would probably be won by the Tudors (who doesn't love a series of nice juicy scandals complete with conspiracies, murders and beheadings?), but I suspect that the runner up would be 1066 and All That. The Norman Conquest doesn't have the same level of scurrilous intrigue, but it does have overweening ambitions, treacherous quislings, catastrophic engagements and traumatic disasters, and of course it can be – and usually is – portrayed as the crucible of English nationality, subjugated to invading upstarts from the continent but gallantly struggling under the Norman Yoke to arise triumphant as 'this blessed plot, this earth, this realm, this England'.

Given the weight placed on the Conquest by modern concepts of identity and ethnicity, it is inevitable that the contemporary view of England and the English in the mid-eleventh century is, to say the least, distorted. For a start, 'England' itself, as a unified kingdom, was barely a hundred years old, and as yet incomplete; large swathes of territory in the north were still disputed ground, subject to the claims of the kings of the English and their neighbours, the kings of Alba ('Scotland' as an entity was barely visible at the time). There were no 'kings of England'; all the monarchs (and this includes the Normans and Angevins' were 'kings of the English', the people, not the place. King Edgar (957-75) in his fourth law-code legislated for 'the whole nation, whether English, or Danish or British, in every part of my dominion' (the 'British' are probably the inhabitants of Cornwall and the areas of Wales which were under English rule).[1] This illustrates a very important point – that those subject to the king of the English were not all 'ethnically' English', Nor indeed were all the Normans 'Norman'. Even in the Duchy itself there were plenty of people who were 'Norman' only in the sense that they owed homage to the Duke, and the army which invaded in 1066 included Bretons, Flemings, Angevins and Poitevins as well as Normans, just as the people standing on the beach were Danish and British as well as various varieties of 'English'. Ethnicity as it is currently defined in the twenty-first century did not exist in the eleventh, and the modern notion of 'Normans' as a group different from and hostile to another group of people defined as 'English' is profoundly anachronistic.

Given these, and other differences between 'now' and 'then', conveying any idea of the history of this remote period is fraught with difficulties, even before we get to the question of sources. There are no diaries and journals, no newspaper articles, no personal reminiscences, no autobiographies, and of course no twitter accounts or facebook pages. Even the texts which look, at first sight, like biographies are actually rather different kettles of fish. What we have is a fragmentary record drawn from chronicles, annals and works of history by named authors, supplemented by some written but non-literary

Foreword

materials, including charters, wills, legal memoranda, law codes and a few documents generated by the royal administration, of which Domesday Book is the most famous. The task of the historian is to collate, analyse and digest all this into some kind of narrative, aided by his fellow-workers in the fields of archaeology, onomastics (place- and personal-name specialists), linguistics and philology (the history of language).

The task is not impossible, but it does make for problems of presentation. Academic histories aim at accuracy of expression and a coverage as complete as possible of all the variables, which must be considered in detail to determine meaning and accuracy. Academic historians also tend to write for each other, rather than for general readers who – understandably – want to know 'what happened and when', a mismatch made worse by the simple fact that much of 'what happened' is now irrecoverable, and can only be guessed at. Bridging the gap between the requirements of academic research and the popular desire for clear information is an art that few possess.

In such circumstances, imaginative literature can bridge the gap. Historical novelists take the few observable facts and weave them into a story, vivid enough to catch the imagination, but still true to what can actually be known. A really good historical novel (Hope Munz's 'Golden Warrior', to which the present work's title pays tribute, is one such) can open the world of the eleventh century in a manner which few academics can achieve. Paula Lofting is an experienced and talented novelist, who has researched the eleventh century for her material and presented it in forms both readable and accurate. This current piece is not a novel but it does employs the art of story-telling and imaginative reconstruction, in tandem with a discussion of the surviving source material and its limitations. This has resulted in a book which can be read with profit by both academics and non-academics. Here is the story, the 'real' story (as far as it can be reconstructed) of Harold II Godwineson, embedded in a thoughtful and well-researched scenario of 'how it might have been'. There are a number of books, academic and 'popular' (and there is nothing wrong with 'popular' if it is done well) on Harold and, since he is one of the perennially interesting characters of English history, there will be more. This is one of the best.

Ann Williams, FSA. FRHS. PhD, Wanstead.

Introduction

Ask most people what the date 1066 means to them and they will say it conjures up the battle in which the Normans defeated the English. More are familiar with William the Conqueror than King Harold Godwinson II and need prompting of Harold's role in the story. Some, when reminded, may recall that he was the chap who was shot with an arrow in the eye. Beyond this, he is mostly relegated to the shadows in English history and is probably less well known than Alfred the Great.

Harold's reign of nine months and nine days was one of the shortest, which partly explains his obscure presence in history. However, Harold's story spans some forty years, and for almost twenty years of his life he played a lead role in the events that led him to become Edward the Confessor's successor, and eventually his death in that same year. He came from a high-profile family who dominated the first half of the eleventh century, their power exceeded even that of the Confessor's when they were at the height of their influence. Their patriarch, Earl Godwin, rose to become the second most important man in the kingdom from obscure origins which are difficult to trace further than his grandfather, Wulfnoth, a Sussex thegn of note.

Though the House of Godwin was not the only famous family of their time, their story shines brighter than those such as the Houses of Leofric, and Siward the Strong and even more so than the House of Bamburgh, an ancient family whose lineage stretched back into the tenth century and earlier. The Godwinsons' story is not just written in the *Anglo-Saxon Chronicles*, John of Worcester, or Norman sources, but is also found in the later chronicles, such as those of Orderic Vitalis, William of Malmesbury, Eadmer, Gaimar, Henry of Huntingdon, and Wace as well as the Scandinavian Sagas. The Godwinsons have also fascinated contemporary and modern historians, like Edward Freeman and Frank Barlow, for decades. However, no Godwinson story can be told without the inclusion of Harold, and no story of Harold can be fully understood without a discussion of his family. This is why I have endeavoured to include the members of this infamous clan as much as possible, notwithstanding the premise that this is Harold's book and not a book solely about the Godwinsons.

People often ask where my interest in Harold Godwinson came from and I tell them it was not so much the man himself who lured me, but the time period that drew me to him. Writing a series about a fictional family set in England in the years leading up to the Battle of Hastings and the Norman Conquest, he naturally cropped up as an important player, so it was necessary to do the research not just to create an authentic historical background, but an authentic Harold Godwinson. And believe me, digging out what I could about the man, was no easy assignment, for there are so many contradicting and contrasting views, even in primary sources. Some are quite insulting, such as the post-Conquest Norman writings of William of Jumièges and William of

Introduction

Poitiers, who are, naturally, completely biased against Harold, referring to him as a tyrannical usurper, murderer, philanderer, and oath breaker. Having to wade through the varying versions of events to choose the most probable, was, at times, problematic, and except for some instances where the choice was straightforward, it was best to present more than one outcome and let the reader make their own choice.

Amongst all the chaos of the sources, the Vita Edwardi is one of the most useful narratives to follow, though not always reliable due to its bias. Commissioned for Harold's sister, Queen Edith, Frank Barlow believed the author to have been the writer, Goscelin, and Tom Licence, Folcard. Both were monks of St. Bertin. The loss of chapter two, thought to have covered the children of Godwin in stronger detail, is sadly missing. Unfortunately, we cannot know for certain who authored the work, but thanks to the afore mentioned historians, candidates have been filtered down to just two, although I refer to the author in this work as anonymous.

The *Anglo-Saxon Chronicles,* are a set of records written in various monasteries around England. The ones used for this work are mainly known as *C,* Abingdon II, *D,* Worcester, *E,* Peterborough/Canterbury, and are written matter-of-factly and succinctly, beside the odd exception, without being overly emotive. Written in the early twelfth century, the *Chronicon ex Chronicis* by the monk, John of Worcester, occasionally referred to as Florence, is much more animated and detailed, sometimes loyal to the Godwinsons, sometimes not. Guy, Bishop of d'Amiens, wrote the earliest of the contemporary sources to describe the killing of Harold, *Carmen de Hastingae Proelio.* Guy and William of Jumièges, who wrote the *Gesta Normanorum Ducum,* are sympathetic to the duke, but William of Poitiers *(Gesta Guillelmi)* absolutely bursts with loathing for Harold and influences later writers such as William of Malmesbury and Henry of Huntingdon. Orderic Vitalis, sympathetic to the English, reviles Harold, and Eadmer, who provides one of the few English views of what happened to Harold in Normandy also treats Harold sympathetically, though still refers to him as a usurper.

The late twelfth-century *Waltham Chronicle* – problematic in that it only survives in thirteenth- and fourteenth-century copies – reveres Harold and upholds him as a great king, though there are inferences to his arrogance being the cause of his downfall. The narrative labours the point that his army was overcome by the higher numbers of Normans. Wace's *Roman de Rou* is naturally favourable to the Normans and the French. Said to have been commissioned for Henry II, it devotes a large section of it to the Norman Conquest and may have relied a lot on oral tradition handed down from eyewitnesses. It does make for an enthralling narrative, especially of the battle, which reads like a novel.

In order to know Harold, one has to study his deeds, the actions and decisions he made in order to have some understanding of his inner workings and his reasoning. Was he driven by the times in which he lived, the politics, the deeds of his family members and those of his enemies? Not forgetting his relationship with King Edward, whom he kept faith with throughout his career as premier earl, the aim of this book is to discover the man who dominated the historical record in the years leading up to 1066.

The sources mentioned are by no means definitive, nor is this book. The main aim is to present Harold as a much of a fully fleshed out personality as the sources allow, and to explore his motivations that drove his decisions. What was the intention of the

Norman sources that villainised him, and raised William to the highest esteem? The concluding chapter does not delve into the fate of Harold Godwinson's siblings, his wives, nor his children, but deals with the myths surrounding his death and last resting place.

There are many aspects relating to Harold Godwinson and the events leading up to the Conquest that I have not been able to include in this work, but I hope to have encompassed the most prominent features. If you would like to read more about this subject, you can find more articles on my website (www.threadstothepast.com).

Part One
ORIGINS AND BLOODLINES

'Godwine Wulfnoðes suna'
the will of Æthelstan, 25 June, 1014

CHAPTER ONE
The Godwinson Lineage

Controversy over the Godwinson's heritage has had historians at odds since scholars Alfred Anscombe and Lundie W. Barlow published their theory that Harold's lineage could be traced to King Aethelwulf in the ninth century.[1] Conflicting ideas have run riot amongst those desiring to provide the last of the great Anglo-Saxon dynasties with a royal heritage which would justify Harold's seizing the throne in 1066 following the death of Edward the Confessor.

In order to make sense of the concept that Harold was descended from the royal House of Wessex, we must explore theories that concern two males named Æthelmær, said to be candidates for Harold's great-grandfather. Frank Barlow briefly discusses one of these Æthelmærs in his work, *The Godwins,* and provides a family tree based on the Anscombe and (Lundie) Barlow theory.[2] The connection depends on the thegn, Wulfnoth Cild (d. c. 1014) who is known to have been Harold Godwinson's grandfather, as being the son of the ealdorman, Æthelmær Cild (d. c. 1015) who was the son of Æthelweard the Historian (d. c. 998). The latter's lineage can be traced back to King Æthelred I (r. 865–871) who was Alfred the Great's brother. However, further examinations of this theory have argued against this. The well-respected historian, Ann Williams, advises that Æthelmær Cild, was of the same generation as Wulfnoth, therefore could not have fathered him. Secondly, the interests of Æthelweard and Æthelmær Cild were concentrated in the areas west of Wessex, whilst Wulfnoth is specifically noted as a 'Sussex thegn'.[3]

The other Æthelmær, whom we shall refer to as Æthelmær Two, was one of several brothers of the infamous ealdorman, Eadric Sreona, whose father was a man called Æthelric (c. late 10thc.). The theory that this particular Æthelmær was the father of Wulfnoth Cild, originated with John of Worcester.[4] But Eadric and his brothers were the sons of Æthelric and not the aforementioned Æthelweard the Historian, said to be the patriarch of the previous Æthelmær Cild, whose pedigree can be traced back to former kings of Wessex. Confused? There is more to come.

We know for certain that Earl Godwin, (d. 1053) is Harold Godwinson's father, and the son of Wulfnoth Cild. Nothing is known of Godwin's mother, but he has been cautiously accredited with possible siblings. One such sibling being the lady Æthelflæd, named in the family tree that Barlow cites in his book.[5] Hubert Grills, in his book about the life of Earl Godwin, discusses an Æthelflæd, owner of land in Buckinghamshire, married to a man named Toki.[6] The estate was gifted to his wife by her father, a man called Wulfnoth, who was connected to Godwin's son, Leofwin, who held the estate thirty years later. This does not confirm, however, that this particular Wulfnoth was the father of Godwin.

The Prosopography of Anglo-Saxon England data base has narrowed down the instances of the name Wulfnoth to sixty-nine individuals, most of whom were moneyers, so identifying this Wulfnoth with Godwin's father is problematic, though the link to Godwin's son Leofwin is intriguing.[7] Grills also mentions the possibility Godwin had a brother, Ælfwig, abbot of New Minster in Winchester. He is said to have died at Hastings and is referred to as an uncle of King Harold's.[8] If true, he would have been an old man to have fought in the battle, so unlikely he was the brother of Godwin. Frank Barlow also doubts this theory; however, it is not inconceivable that he was a brother of Godwin's mother.[9] Since we do not know who she was, we cannot decide on the matter.

It still cannot be proven that the Godwinsons were of royal pedigree despite the evidence produced by A. Anscombe/L. Barlow, and Frank Barlow, and it is unrealistic to assume that the family would not have known and used it to their advantage, especially against King William the Conqueror (r. 1066–1087).[10] It is not impossible that Harold did, and it was supressed by the Normans, but there is no supporting evidence. It also seems unlikely that either of the two Æthelmærs had fathered Wulfnoth. As Ann Williams confirms, Æthelmær Cild, who appears in the royal family's tree, was of the same generation as Wulfnoth. Furthermore, he was from Devonshire. Wulfnoth was referred to as a Sussex thegn by the *E* version of the *Anglo-Saxon Chronicle (ASC)*. Æthelmær number two, can also be discounted because the father of this Æthelmær was called Æthelric and Æthelmær Cild's father was known as Æthelweard. Also, number two does not appear in the royal family tree of Wessex, suggesting that he had no royal heritage at all. He was also of the same generation as Wulfnoth. As it stands, there is nothing to connect either Æthelmær with Wulfnoth, apart from an error made by John of Worcester, which many historians confuse as the same Æthelmær.

In contrast to efforts made to prove Anscombe's and (Lundie) Barlow's theory correct, Peter Rex, in his book on Harold's life, refers to the *Hyde Chronicle* which describes Godwin as a man of low birth. This is not a contemporary source and was written in the thirteenth century for the de Warennes, whose dislike of Godwin is evident.[11]

Alternative stories of a 'lowly' Godwin's rise to fame speak of him as a farmer's boy, who, whilst cow–herding, came across a Dane called Ulf, lost and detached from his men after the Battle of Sherston.[12] Godwin offered to help him and a grateful Ulf took him into his service. These tales have more to do with myth than anything based in reality and do not account for Godwin being left land in Ætheling Æthelstan's will, which we discuss shortly.

Wulfnoth Cild

So, just who was Wulfnoth? And what is the etymology of the term cild?

The paternal grandfather of Harold Godwinson bursts onto the scene under a storm cloud and in serious trouble.[13] We know he was the father of Godwin because both men are mentioned in Ætheling Æthelstan's will as father and son, '*Godwine Wulfnoðes suna*'.[14] *Cild* is the old English word for child, but what is the context here? The meaning is obscure, but it seems that in the late Anglo-Saxon period, it also referred to a male of noble birth. In other words, the son of a lord.[15] Elsewhere, it has been implied that it was a title, not unlike ætheling, but for the lesser of the royal branches.[16] According to Swanton, the title of cild in the late Anglo-Saxon period was used to denote those of high rank and translates this to prince in the year 1009 to Prince Wulfnoth.

Because we cannot identify with certainty a father for Wulfnoth, it is difficult to create a picture of his background, but the title of cild, supports the idea that he was a man of distinction. A thegn called Wulfnoth signed four diplomas between 986–1005. The Wulfnoth in question was not found near the top of the list of those attesting these important documents. The higher up the signature list, the more influential. However, this does not mean he was not an important lord. He may have been away from court a lot because his workload took him elsewhere. Wulfnoth's ten-hide manor of Compton, (known as *Cumtune* in Ætheling Æthelstan's will), is identified as the one in Westbourne Hundred, West Sussex.[17] It was confiscated from Wulfnoth in 1009 and awarded to King Æthelred's eldest son and heir, Ætheling Æthelstan (d. 1014). These lands were close to the manor of Æthelingadene, said to be the land now known as West Dean, in West Sussex.[18] Wulfnoth and his son Godwin may have served Æthelstan locally, overseeing the coastal defences along the shorelines of Sussex and perhaps Kent. This would explain why Wulfnoth was not often at court. It was at Æthelingadene manor that Godwin might well have received weapons training with other youths from the ætheling's retinue.

We know little about Wulfnoth's career at sea, but certainly Godwin and his sons inherited their naval credentials from this man. The fact that he was able to sail competently through storms, may have had something to do with his Sussex connections. The county was known for supplying ships and men for the English fleet.[19] Prior to the year 1008, Æthelred, had hitherto been unable to create an effective policy for the protection of his realm. His main strategy had been to pay off invaders. According to the *E* version of the *ASC*, Æthelred ordered a fleet of ships to be constructed from all over the land, requiring one ship from every 310 hides, and that every 8 hides should provide a helmet and mail coat.[20] The Danes had been targeting Sussex coastal regions over the last two decades,[21] and word had it that a large force of Danish ships led by Thorkell the Tall (*Þorketill inn hávi*), was mustering to mount a summer invasion. The opportunity to provide and lead ships and their crews as part of the nation's largest ever naval force must have been a matter of pride for Wulfnoth. But in 1009, when the great fleet assembled in Sandwich, all the country's hard work would be destroyed in weeks and Wulfnoth disgraced and booted into exile.

At the root of the catastrophe was a dispute between Wulfnoth and a man named Brihtric, who had joint command of the fleet with him. Wulfnoth came highly skilled, Brihtric not so much. They may have already been at odds with each other when they met at the muster in Sandwich, for Brihtric was the brother of Eadric Streona, the king 's son-in-law. Eadric was the king's closest adviser and wanted Æthelred's sons Edward and Alfred by his second wife, Emma of Normandy to succeed him, whereas Wulfnoth supported the æthelings, the sons by the king's first wife, Ælfgifu of York (d. c. 1000), of which he had begat six, though not all of them were alive by this time.[22]

In the *E* version of the *ASC* it was said that Brihtric accused Wulfnoth of treason. Perhaps one too many horns of strong ale had loosened Wulfnoth's tongue, and in an outburst of indignance, he said something he should not have. Brihtric, enraged, seized his opportunity to get rid of his rival. Wulfnoth hastily gathered up his men and ships and left the scene, perhaps recalling what had happened to Ælfhelm of York and his sons, respectively blinded by Brihtric's brother, Eadric. The *E* chronicle reports Wulfnoth ravaging his own coastline. Why would he want to provoke the men he hoped would follow and support him by raiding their homes?[23] Chroniclers were often apt to underplay or exaggerate events. In Wulfnoth's case, he could have been on a foraging mission to collect provisions and items of property before escaping into inevitable exile.

Brihtric now had the opportunity to raise his profile, and so, commandeering eighty ships, he hoped to catch Wulfnoth, dead or alive, and make a name for himself.[24] Unfortunately for Brihtric, his flotilla of eighty ships sailed disastrously headfirst into a storm which reduced them to 'pieces and cast them ashore'.[25] Wulfnoth's skills as a naval commander were exceptionally better than Brihtric's, and he, his men, and his ships avoided the storm by sailing out of its way. But what Wulfnoth was about to do next, out of rage or some strategical reason, was to seal his fate. Wulfnoth turned around and sailed back to spitefully burn what was left of the king's flotilla.[26]

Was it at this point that Wulfnoth considered decanting to the Vikings? By burning what was left of Æthelred's boats, Wulfnoth had also burned his bridges. Was he acting on some deeply rooted anger, railing against the establishment he felt had treated him unjustly? Somewhere during this escapade, he had been deprived of his lands and made outlaw. He had not even been given a fair hearing and so his mindset was bent on revenge. Unfortunately, his actions were treasonous. By depriving the king of so many ships, England's hope of prevailing against the Viking raiders were extinguished. Another more sympathetic chronicler claimed that Wulfnoth was accused unjustly, suggesting he had been wronged.[27]

Wulfnoth's behaviour shows an impulsive streak, though his actions need examining in a wider context. Brihtric and his brothers were the sons of a Mercian called Æthelric.[28] The family were landowners from Shropshire.[29] Eadric, the most important of them is described by John of Worcester as slippery, ambitious, and arrogant. Other brothers were named as Ælfric, Æthelweard, Æthelwine, and Æthelmær, who was the brother mistakenly identified as father of Wulfnoth. Said to have come from humble beginnings, the means by which and how quickly the family rose is unclear, but Eadric's byname being *Streona*, a word meaning 'grasper' or 'aquisitor', suggests that he gained success through 'spurious means.'[30] He was not above stooping to murder to get what he wanted.[31] Because Æthelred's England had not known much peace in more than two decades, the fear caused by annual Viking raids instilled paranoia and jealousy at court. Eadric took advantage of the king's concerns. With trusted royal servants losing their positions, Eadric saw his opportunity to climb higher.[32]

The king's favourite, Wulfgeat, lost his lands on some trumped-up charge, whispered to the king by Eadric. Eadric then had his jealous eye on the noble Ealdorman Ælfhelm. Using the pretence of friendship, the crafty, treacherous Eadric lured the wealthy man to his hall in Shrewsbury. Ælfhelm, accepting the invitation, was welcomed by Streona as guest of honour. After three or four days of feasting, Eadric took him hunting. When all were engaged in the chase, a ruffian of Shrewsbury called Godwin Port-Hund, the local 'dog', bribed by gifts and promises to commit the crime, suddenly sprang from his ambush and assassinated poor Ælfhelm. A short time afterwards, his sons Wulfheah and Ufgeat were on King Æthelred's orders, deprived of sight.[33]

When Æthelred married Emma in 1002, the negotiations stipulated that she be crowned, meaning that any of sons she had would take precedent over his sons by his first wife, Aelfgifu of York.[34] But Æthelred's sons retained their titles of ætheling, and were never set aside. They were, however, drawn into a rift against their father, conceivably by Eadric's machinations, and the court was divided into two factions. Wulfnoth naturally defaulted into the æthelings corner. By the time the spat with

Brihtric occurred, Ælfhelm's murder was still fresh in Wulfnoth's mind. Having been declared outlaw, Wulfnoth was immediately in danger. His crew willingly followed him into exile, and into ensuing piracy.[35] These men were likely elicited locally in Sussex, and knew him well. The *E* chronicle states they were 'enticed'.[36] Since sailors were apt to change sides if there was something better in it for them, the idea of joining Thorkell's Vikings may have seemed more appealing than the end of a Dane's spear. Wulfnoth, however, may have seen a chance for revenge

That Æthelstan was able to later gift the confiscated property of Wulfnoth to his son Godwin in his will, suggests that Godwin was also disinherited. This land grant supports the idea that a close connection existed between Wulfnoth, Godwin, and Æthelstan. Wulfnoth's adherence to Æthelstan's party would account for the enmity between Godwin's father and Brihtric.[37] Wulfnoth was to no longer appear in any documentation following his exile, but what happened to his son, Godwin, when his father was outlawed is a mystery. His diminished status suggests that he was exiled along with Wulfnoth in 1009. Godwin the boy was not heard of again until 1018 when he turns up witnessing in King Cnut's court.

There are those who believe that Godwin had stayed in England, shielded by the sons of Æthelræd.[38] Because we have no visible presence of him in charters or in the chronicles prior to 1014 when he is a beneficiary of Æthelstan's will, it is reasonable to believe he was exiled with Wulfnoth. Godwin, aged between 13 and 16 at the time, was old enough to be complicit in his father's crimes, and would have been in peril if left behind. The blinding of Ælfhelm's sons must have been on Wulfnoth's mind. It would have been an optimistic father who left his son under these conditions. Even under Æthelstan's protection, Godwin would not have been far from Streona's reach.

Wulfnoth needed a plan following his escape from England. He was done with the English court, and they were done with him. But wherever father and son went between the years following 1009, Godwin was to be reconciled with Æthelstan before he died, in time to make it into his will. Wulfnoth Cild was never heard of again, therefore he likely died sometime before 1014.

How Godwin became a Viking

Flanders was to become synonymous with harbouring English exiles, and seemed to be very fond of supporting the Godwinsons in their times of need, except against Normandy during the Conquest. The Godwinsons even went as far as to marry third son Tostig to the daughter of Count Baldwin V. According to the *Ædwardi Vita Regis (Vita)* an 'old alliance' was rekindled in the year of 1051 when Godwin and his family sought Count Baldwin's protection following their expulsion from England.[39] Could the friendship referred to have been one that Wulfnoth and Godwin made subsequent to their exile more than forty years previously?

Thorkell the Tall was said to have been a former chief of the infamous, perhaps mythical, Jomsvikings and a prominent Danish lord. We know he led the raiding army that invaded England in July of 1009. Historian Eric John suggested that Wulfnoth and Godwin joined forces with Thorkell.[40] Hubert Grills, however, refuted the idea, believing that this would have hindered Godwin's entry into Æthelstan's will.[41] However, it is difficult to comprehend that Wulfnoth would have risked leaving Godwin behind with the evil Streona in such a powerful position. Bearing this in mind, it is possible that Wulfnoth, sought the nearest safe harbour for him and his son: Bruges. Perhaps the 'old alliance' the Godwins had with Flanders, started with Count Baldwin IV in 1009.[42] Wulfnoth the sea-lord, might have previously met with the then count of Bruges, Baldwin senior, during one of his trading expeditions. Perhaps after exchanging the goods he had brought with him from England for silver, he mulled over his next move with his friend the count who might have encouraged him to move on to wherever Thorkell's invasion fleet was mustering.

One historian has suggested that the Viking ship army was mustering in Bruges. Another disputes this theory, pointing out that assembly port was more likely to have been Normandy or Scandinavia, as Bruges was not known for harbouring raiding ships. Thorkell the Tall would have happily welcomed Wulfnoth and his twenty ships into his great war fleet later from the entries in the ASC for the year 1009, we know the famous Jomsviking leader invaded that summer, meeting up with another fleet later, commanded by his brother Hemming and another Viking, Eilaf.[43] Imagine the scene as Wulfnoth availed thorkell and his men the tale of how he burned Æthelred's ships to the sound of cheers and raised horns amongst the mead benches.

It was thought that among Thorkell's kith and kin, was a young Cnut, whose fosterage the Danish king, Sweyn Forkbeard (r. 986–1014), had placed in the hands of the prestigious Thorkell.[44] It was customary in the Middle-Ages to give hostages as a promise of sincerity and loyalty. In Edward the Confessor's time, Godwin and his son, Swegn, would later be required to hand over a son each in order to secure their good behaviour, prior to being sent into exile in 1051.[45] Thorkell might have expected this from an Englishman coming into his service to ensure he remained loyal, and had Thorkell been of a mind to like Godwin, he may have come to think of him as a son, especially if Wulfnoth was to expire.[46] If so, it is possible that this was the initial beginnings of a friendship between Godwin and Cnut, explaining their later closeness, and Godwin's fast-tracked rise to fame as Cnut's deputy.[47] If the young son of Wulfnoth was indeed amongst the raiders that sailed to England with Thorkell, he may have done so with his father's ships and men, establishing himself early as a sea-commander. With or without Wulfnoth, it would be hard to say, for we do not know if Wulfnoth was yet deceased, though he was unlikely to have been alive after 1014.

The vanishing of Wulfnoth Cild from the historical record marks the end of his story and the beginning of Godwin's.

CHAPTER TWO

Life after Wulfnoth

Wulfnoth's destruction of the king's navy paved the way for Thorkell's invasion and he ravaged the English countryside from 1009 to 1012.[1] Thorkell, being a Jomsviking, would not have been well disposed toward Forkbeard, which leads some to question the tradition that Sweyn's son, Cnut, was fostered by Thorkell. It may be that they came to some understanding.[2] The behaviour of the Danish king's men and the archbishop of Canterbury's death may have sickened Thorkell, so he and his loyal supporters defected to Æthelred's service with forty-five ships, manned with the best warriors.[3]

Godwin's reunion with the æthelings may have come at this juncture. If Godwin was amongst Thorkell's entourage when he defected to Æthelred, then it stands to reason that Godwin went with him.[4] If we are to acknowledge the closeness between Prince Æthelstan and Wulfnoth, the move may have brought Godwin back into the aethelings' circle. As Wulfnoth's overlord, Æthelstan may have had sympathy with him, though was likely to have been powerless to have helped him at the time of his banishment.

Thorkell's defection to the English king did not last forever. By 1016, he was in the service of Cnut. Æthelred's hatred of the Danes was well known and he and Thorkell may never have been well-matched. Æthelred's sons, too, may well have been suspicious of him and Eadric, no doubt, felt threatened by the powerful Jomsviking. Thorkell's switch to Cnut may have occurred earlier than 1016, sometime after the death of Sweyn Forkbeard. Godwin may have had a difficult decision to make: to stay with the æthelings having rekindled his bond with them, or join Cnut with his mentor, Thorkell. Whatever caused him to stay, we know he was close enough to the æthelings to have received his father's lands in Æthelstan's will.

We have seen how Godwin may have come to be in both camps during the early years of his coming to prominence. The last years of Æthelred's reign may have taught him some lessons in diplomacy that would help him reach and maintain a presence among the powerful whoever he sided with. But what might Godwin's younger years have been like?

We don't know the exact date of Godwin's birth. Barlow dates his birth not much earlier than 993, though he could have been born somewhere between 993–996.[5] In 1018, Cnut was to appoint him as earl in the south. The position required a candidate who was both youthful and experienced in managing personnel and military affairs. Godwin was the ideal fit.[6]

Growing up on his father's estate in Compton in the 990s and early 1000s Godwin would have been exposed to the fear and terror the raids on the south coast caused among his people. Though an child at the time, the horrific raids in 1006 may have had an indelible effect on him. Wulfnoth's use of ships for his role in defending the coast allowed for plenty of opportunities for Godwin to hone his skills at sea. Godwin may have witnessed and earned his sea-legs during some of the raids on the Sussex coast under the tutelage of his father. If Godwin had been born in 993, he certainly would have been old enough by 1006 to have witnessed or been part of a ship defence with his father's sailors.

Wulfnoth's significant role serving under the ætheling, Æthelstan, came with certain privileges and incentives, allowing him to sustain a force of men and ships. This, in part, explains why Brihtric held a grudge against Wulfnoth. Whether these ships were built with money provided by the king, or perhaps funded by a 'ship soke'[7] in which every 310 hides would have to deliver a ship as they did in 1008, is not known.[8] Wulfnoth's actions in the wrangle with Brihtric demonstrate that he considered the ships as his own.

As a young noble, Godwin was expected to train in martial skills from between the ages of 10 and 12 and could have been educated with other sons of local thegns at Æthelstan's manor of Æthelingadene, near his father's estate.[9] His military exploits in Cnut's service, confirm that he had been well taught in weapons and battle strategies. A close relationship formed in Godwin's early years might explain why Æthelstan left him land in his will.

As Wulfnoth's overlord, Æthelstan would have had a vested interest in his well-being, and losing a competent sea-lord would have been a significant blow for the coastal community. Brihtric's disappearance from the narrative suggests some mystery or intrigue surrounded his fate.

Prince Æthelstan died the same day his will was approved by his father on 25 June 1014,[10] but the gift of *Cumtune* may have previously been offered to Godwin to lure him away from Thorkell, then added to the will to make it official. If we believe Godwin had been apprenticed by Thorkell, the æthelings would have welcomed a young warlord with Godwin's skills. Reclaiming his father's lost lands, Godwin found himself with a newfound source of power, a stepping stone to forge his own loyal following. With this in mind, reconnecting with the æthelings he had grown up alongside, appeared not only practical but also enticing.

Towards the end of 1013, when Sweyn had done much damage to the country, devastating England with fire and sword, some of the English thegns and ealdormen submitted to him. And who could blame them? Æthelred's defence of his country had been ineffective. Eventually, Æthelred was forced to abandon his throne to Sweyn, and leaving the æthelings to fend for themselves, he joined his wife and their children at her brother's court in Normandy.[11] At Christmas, Sweyn was elected king by the *witan*, the king's council.

Forkbeard's reign, lasting only forty days, stands as one of the shortest in England. He passed away on 2 February 1014, in Gainsborough.[12] His immediate successor, chosen by his followers, was his son Cnut.[13] However, the English were not in favour of Cnut's rule. Instead, they wished to have Æthelred return, and promptly sent for him.[14] The old king made his way back in the spring, receiving a warm welcome from his people. Discovering that Lindsey, an area of the Danelaw, was mustering to join forces with Cnut, Æthelred was spurred into action, determined to prove himself the sovereign he had promised to be. Swiftly he assembled his troops and galloped towards Lindsey, taking them completely by surprise. As Cnut left his English supporters to Æthelred's mercy, the king's reaction was nothing short of fiery, engulfing their homes in flames.[15]

Æthelstan's will leads us to believe that Godwin campaigned with the æthelings and earned both Æthelstan's and Edmund's respect. The *Vita* tells us that Godwin earned the reputation of a doughty warrior during his early years.[16] Later, in Cnut's service, he was to assist him abroad in the war against the Wends, leading a host of English warriors.[17]

The Fight For England

Little is recorded of the æthelings involvement in their father's affairs, which suggests that they may have disagreed with his policies, acting independently of him. Æthelstan, held the position as England's heir and would have solidified his claim upon his father's return from Normandy.[18] There is evidence to suggest that Edmund did not enjoy his father's favour. His deeds are only documented during the short period when he came to prominence after his brother's demise, inheriting the sword of Offa.[19] It is likely that during their father's sojourn in Normandy, the brothers were forming alliances with their mother's relatives in the north, particularly their cousins Morcar and Sigeferth, the leading thegns of the five boroughs which incorporated Derby, Leicester, Lincoln, Nottingham, Stamford. It is also probable that Godwin was with them when they travelled the country, evading Sweyn's forces and attempting to garner support among the populace for their cause.

The cause of Æthelstan's death remains a mystery. His personal possessions suggest that he was a robust man in his mid-to-late twenties, too young to die of natural causes. Historical chronicles make no mention of any conflicts in which he might have sustained wounds, however we do have the saga of St. Olaf. Though somewhat unreliable due to its thirteenth-century composition, it hints at the æthelings' struggle against residual Danish resistance during their father's stay in Normandy. According to Icelandic historian Snorri Sturluson, Æthelred returned to England from Normandy, joined by a new ally, Óláfr Haraldsson. Óláfr's clever attack on London Bridge against the remaining Danish loyalists to Cnut contributed to the destruction of their naval forces.[20] Some scholars, like Jan Hagland and Bruce Watson, suggest this event occurred in 1014. It may be that during this conflict, Æthelstan sustained an injury that may have ultimately led to his demise.

Æthelstan's loss was a profound tragedy for Edmund. Nonetheless, he found solace in the support of the northern magnates, Sigeferth and Morcar, who recognised him as his father's heir. However, Edmund faced opposition from his brother-in-law, Eadric Streona, who favoured Queen Emma's sons. Streona's policies were abhorrent to the æthelings. Godwin likely harboured resentment toward Streona, the same man who had helped Brihtric bring ruin to Godwin's father.

The prince's northern cousins, Sigeferth and Morcar, were out of favour with the king for having submitted to Sweyn. Undoubtedly their friendship gave Æthelred reason to be discontent, as was Streona. Edmund may have intended reconciling the estranged brothers with the king, and inadvertently caused their tragic demise. In the year 1015, they received invitations to attend the *witenagemót*, (meeting of the *witan*) convened in Oxford.[21] Streona, convinced the king that these two men were untrustworthy. With Æthelred's approval, he lured Sigeferth and Morcar into his private chambers and murdered them.[22] Æthelred exposed his involvement as he confiscated their possessions and incarcerated Sigeferth's wife, Ealdgyth, within the confines of Mąlmesbury Abbey.

The murder of his cousins was another deep wound for Edmund. The strong rapport he and Æthelstan had fostered with the men of the north, lay shattered by that heinous, treacherous act. However, destiny was to intervene, one that Streona had not anticipated. The young ætheling journeyed to Malmesbury, took Sigeferth's widow as his bride, defying his father's objections. With this union, all of Ealdgyth's possessions fell under Edmund's influence. Together, the newlyweds ventured into the Five Boroughs, where Edmund garnered the loyalty of the prominent men. Edmund now stood fortified, better prepared to confront any threat posed by Streona.

Edmund's marriage to Ealdgyth had negative consequences for Cnut. He had been in a union with Sigeferth and Morcar's relative, Ælfgifu of Northampton, the daughter of the murdered Ælfhelm. She was also the sister of Ælfhelm's blinded sons, giving her plenty of reasons to despise Streona. However, Cnut was not in England at this time, having been expelled by Æthelred. Edmund now controlled the northern territory that Cnut's alliance with Ælfgifu had secured for him. With his brother-in-law, Uhtræd, (d. 1016) governing the land beyond the Humber and Ulfketel overseeing East Anglia, Edmund found himself surrounded by supportive allies.

Cnut was said to have loved those who fought unequivocally for Edmund, and hated those who were said to have betrayed him.[23] Godwin, it seems, was in the loyal camp. Streona, however, was in the other.[24] Whilst Æthelred lay sick, Edmund gathered a northern army. Streona did the same in the south. When they came to together to join against the enemy, Edmund, in fear of his life, refused and they parted without a fight.[25] Whilst Edmund was in the north, Cnut came back from Denmark. From Sandwich in Kent, he sailed south along the coast into the mouth of the Frome, blazed a path through Dorset and Wiltshire, and into Somerset. The king lay sick at Cosham and Eadric took this opportunity to switch sides, enticing forty of the king's ships', probably Thorkell with them, and Eadric the evil Grasper, along with the West Saxons, all went over to Cnut.[26]

Edmund's efforts to unite an army against Cnut proved unsuccessful due to deep-seated prejudices and treacheries among various shires, mirroring his father's struggles in the previous decade. The presence of disaffected Danish settlers in England, dating back to the ninth century, is sometimes cited as a factor. However, many of these individuals, often referred to as 'so-called' Danes, were actually of mixed Danish and English heritage and identified themselves as English. For instance, Danes like Tovi the Proud may well have married into an English family and named his son Æthlestan, who also gave his son the name Esegar, the English equivalent of the Scandinavian name Ansgar. Another example is Ulfketel Snillingr, a celebrated Englishman praised in sagas for his bravery and recognised in the *Anglo-Saxon Chronicle* for giving the Danes, by their own admission, their worst swordplay (*worsan handplegan*) experience in England in 1004. Despite his Scandinavian-sounding name, Ulfketel's actions against the Danes highlight his strong connection to his English identity.[27]

In January of 1016, Cnut and his new friend, Eadric, came to England with 160 ships.[28] Edmund's ally and brother-in-law, Uhtræd was deceitfully killed, surprise, surprise, through the engineering of Eadric Streona, now thoroughly embedded in Cnut's camp. Another severe loss for Edmund. Having struggled to get men to rally to him without his father, Edmund rode to London and it so happened that his father passed away on 23 April, 1016.[29] All the councillors and the London Garrison raised him to the kingship 'and he resolutely defended his country for as long as his time was'.[30]

Edmund had managed to gain the acceptance of all the nobles still loyal to the House of Æthelred, but still had a treacherous road ahead of him. But it was not until June when the serious fighting began. Whatever it was that propelled Edmund into such unyielding determination, Edmund was about to blaze a trail that Cnut and Streona had not reckoned with, earning himself the name of 'Ironside' for his courage and determination. At last the previously reluctant English answered the new king's summons, and engaged the Danes in fierce battles at Penselwood, Sherston, London, and Brentwood.[31]

Edmund and his mounted troops pursued the fleeing Danes, savagely cutting them down as they chased them into the heart of Kent and onto the shores of Sheppey. Their unwavering determination led them westward, where an unexpected encounter awaited them in Aylesford—a pivotal moment when the cunning Streona intercepted Edmund. To Edmund's later regret, he naively succumbed to the persuasive charm of Streona, accepting him into his service, despite having been bitten before. The exact words Eadric used to win Edmund's trust remain a mystery, but history judges Edmund's decision harshly. As the *ASC* poignantly notes, 'There was no more ill-fated decision.'[32] But unknowing what was before him, Edmund doggedly pursued Cnut. His indomitable spirit drove him forward, rallying men to his banner in a fervent quest to rid his kingdom of the invading scourge. Finally, in an exciting turn of events, Edmund and his English troops managed to catch up and overtake them, confronting them at 'Ashtree Hill', known as *Assandun*, or *Essendune*.

It was at this battle that the treacherous Grasper was to make his most audacious betrayal to date. He and his contingent of warriors arrived at the site, ostensibly to fight with his English brethren. As the battle raged on, he made the decision to abandon the king, taking the men of the *Magonsæte*, with him. This outrageous act caused a huge void in the English lines. In the chaos that ensued, the Danes were able to take possession of the field of slaughter.[33]

The battle, also known as Ashingdon, was fought on high ground between the Thames and the Crouch estuary in southeast Essex on the 18 October 1016. Many good English chieftains were killed there, including Ulfketel Snillingr of the *worsan handplegan*.[34] Edmund had known his brother-in-law's reputation, why did he fall for the man's deceit? As Hubert Grills suggests, such was his charm he was able to draw men to him with his magnetism alone, despite all the while being in possession of his treacherous reputation.[35]

John of Worcester recounts the battle:

> Both sides fought with all their might, many fell on either side. But the traitor, Eadric Streona, seeing that the ranks of the Danes were wavering, and the English were getting the victory, fled with the *Magonsæte*, the division he commanded, as he had promised Cnut. He deceived his lord, King Edmund, and the English army with his tricks, and gave the victory into the hands of the Danes.[36]
>
> Many good English warriors, 'the chief men of the English race' died at Assandun, but Edmund made it out of there alive. Cnut may have won the battle, but the war was not quite yet over.

Edmund's story did not end here, and of course nor did Godwin's. It is thought that the brave and unyielding king had sustained devastating wounds at Assandun that would eventually lead to his death six weeks after Assandun on 30 November. John of Worcester states that Edmund was keen to continue the fight, but the councillors which included Streona (of all the nerve) urged Edmund to seek peace with his rival. The *Chronicon* stated, that the treacherous Streona and others would not countenance more war.[37]

We have no record of Godwin having been at any of the battles against Cnut, nor can we expect to know what he would have counselled his king. Neither will we ever know how Godwin felt about Streona's betrayal. Undoubtedly, Godwin would have wanted his injured and exhausted king to rest and take some time to recover, especially if he was injured, but the fact that according to John of Worcester he was willing to continue the fight suggests that perhaps he was not. In any case, the two rivals for the English throne did eventually meet on the island of Olney near Deerhurst, and it was agreed, with the involvement of the *witan*, that the two men would divide the kingdom. Cnut, was to rule in the Danelaw and Edmund the whole of Wessex.

The *ASC* says little about Edmund's death, just that he passed away on St. Andrew's Day, and as the *D* and *F* chronicle says, he was buried in Glastonbury with his grandfather Edgar. The lack of detail surrounding Edmund's death gives rise to mystery. His murder is not implausible, however it is also possible that Edmund was overcome with illness, or wounds brought about by the Battle of Assandun that initially were not life-threatening but later became infected. Cnut was said to have mourned Ironside's passing and as previously mentioned, was said to have deeply respected and admired his adversary. There is no solid evidence to say for definite that Cnut had anything to do with Edmund's death. If murder was suspected, fingers would undoubtedly have been aimed directly at Streona, although one historian points to Cnut as the man to have benefitted most from Edmund's death.[38] However, if anyone had the gall to carry out the murder of Edmund, it was Eadric. There can be no doubt that Eadric Streona was involved in the negotiations for territory, knowing that playing off Cnut and Edmund against each other was his only way of staying ahead of the deadly game of chess he had been playing all his life.[39] In Cnut's service, Eadric was to play his last cards, for Cnut was to see him for the false, traitorous wretch he truly was. The scene comes from the *Encomium Emmae Reginae*, commissioned by Queen Emma when she became Cnut's wife, when Eadric dared to ask the new king of England what his reward was to be for deserting Edmund on the battlefield to ensure the victory for Cnut. The king turned on him and said:

> 'Shall you, who have deceived your lord with guile, be capable of being true to me? I will return to you a worthy reward, but I shall do so to the end that deception may not be subsequently to your pleasure', he summoned his commander, Erik, 'Pay this man what he is owed.' Erik indeed raised his axe and cut off his head, so that soldiers might learn from this not to be unfaithful to their lords.[40]

Godwin the Sea-Lord

We cannot know with certainty how Godwin came to be either camp or even if it was possible he was in both or just one. All inquisitive historians can do is look at the evidence, both written and circumstantial, and interpret it in such a way that seems the most credible. The argument that Wulfnoth and Godwin were among the faction who supported the æthelings against Streona who favoured the sons of Emma, provides us with evidence of the enmity between Wulfnoth and Streona's brother. Throughout his career, Streona was to continue the practice of assassination of those who were a threat to him until Cnut exculpated him from this world. Confident he would be able to manipulate the younger sons of Queen Emma, he needed Edmund dead, especially once Æthelred had departed. But he had not factored in Cnut. Edmund was pliable, and easily fooled. Cnut was not. Eadric had to reconfigure his plan to include the Danish leader. Hence, he dismissed any future ideas about young Edward and Alfred, Æthelred's youngest sons with Emma, and threw in his lot with Cnut.

The rivalry with Streona's brother, Brihtric, had much to do with Wulfnoth's downfall. Wulfnoth may have been a major player amongst the æthelings supporters and the question of where Wulfnoth went after he was sentenced to outlawry, and whether or not Godwin went too, has been discussed. It has generally been acknowledged that Godwin, seen as blameless, stayed behind in England. This has a lot to do with Æthelstan's gift of Wulfnoth's estate to Godwin in his will, however, Godwin was, at the time of his father's exile, of an age where he would have been accountable. If we consider that sons might also be implicated in the crimes of the father, as we see later when Godwin was exiled with all his sons in 1051,[41] then it was not likely that the younger Godwin would have been any safer than Ælfhelm's sons had been in 1006.[42] It is, therefore, reasonable to believe that Godwin had journeyed with his father to Bruges where they first forged the original alliance with Count Baldwin and then joined Thorkell's Vikings in the invasion. This theory is reinforced by the mention of the renewal of the 'old friendship' in the *Vita*.[63]

The idea that Godwin held his place in Danish and English society as a Viking sea-lord is also later borne out when he gifts magnificent ships to two of the kings he serves, Harthacnut and possibly Edward, two years later. The gesture is representational of his status as a commander of ships.[43] As said previously, giving hostages was common practice in the medieval period and that rather being taken, captives were 'given'. Wulfnoth's oath to Thorkell if there had been such a thing, would have included hostages, and it is reasonable to expect that he gave his son Godwin over to him. Wulfnoth does not appear to have been alive when the will of Æthelstan was executed. As the land had once belonged to his father, in bequeathing it to Godwin, the prince was pardoning Godwin for his father's crimes, and this was reinforced by Æthelred's approval of the will.

There are also grounds to believe that Godwin, having use of his dead father's ships, sailed in Thorkell's flotilla in the raid on England. Wulfnoth was likely no longer able to assist Thorkell because he had fallen ill or died, leaving the fleet in Godwin's hands. Among Thorkell's followers, the young Godwin would have been surrounded by other strong sea-lords, such as his future brothers-in-law, Eilaf and Ulf, and Thorkell's brother, Hemming. They were for a time to become his family, and with them he would learn the ways of a sea-lord.

And if we want to understand how Godwin might have found his way back from the Norse into the royal court and into the will of the Prince Æthelstan, we only need to look at the defection of Thorkell to Æthelred to see the path lay there. Furthermore, the connection to Thorkell and possibly Cnut, give rise to the implication that the roots of the Danish king's affection for Godwin and their later close friendship, had first sprouted in the years Godwin had spent among the Vikings.

Further proof of Godwin's sea prowess comes in Eadmer of Canterbury's when he narrates that 'Godwin, Earl of Kent was held throughout England to be a great man on both land and sea.'[44]

CHAPTER THREE
Forging Alliances

By 1017 Cnut was now king of all England.[1] One of the first things Cnut did was to sort out his government. Eadric was given Mercia, East Anglia to Thorkell the Tall, Northumbria, Erik (*Eiríkr Hákonarson*), and Wessex, Cnut took for himself. It seemed that Eadric was not the only Englishman found in his camp. Æthelweard, ealdorman of the western provinces, and Beorhtric of Devonshire, Northman, son of Ealdorman Leofwine, were all found guilty of plotting against him and went the same way as the Grasper.[2]

If we agree that Godwin and Cnut were previously together in Thorkell's company, it would not be unreasonable that Thorkell convinced Cnut to take Godwin into his service. Their meeting may have been rather chilly at first, each harbouring mixed emotions. Cnut may have seen Godwin's rejection of the Danes in exchange for his old life among the aethelings, as a betrayal. Suspicious at first, the ice between them may have thawed under Thorkell's mediation, who himself was to have a stormy relationship with Cnut. Of course, we have no solid evidence to back up this theory, nor do we know for certain that Cnut was even fostered by Thorkell. The historian, G.N. Garmonsway, however, claims in his book, *Cnut and His Empire*, that the young Dane had earned his martial prowess on raids with his foster-father, Thorkell, to whom Sweyn had sent his son to be trained.[3] *Encomium* also hints at a close relationship between Cnut and Thorkell in their description of the Battle of Sherston where Thorkell leads the men into battle so that Cnut would not need to fight, declaring that if he were to die, Cnut would be alive to avenge him at a later time.[4]

The emotional state of Godwin in response to the loss of Edmund and his subsequent acceptance of the new regime remains a subject of uncertainty. Whether he possessed any foreknowledge regarding Edmund's assassination orchestrated by Streona, remains speculative. It appears that Godwin displayed a pragmatic approach in swiftly transferring his allegiance from Eadwig, Edmund's brother, to Cnut. However, his choices may have been constrained by circumstance. As a young man bereft of family or a lord, survival took precedence, and the aspirations he had vested in Edmund had been extinguished. Within a society where individuals of the warrior class depended on community affiliations, Godwin's inability to forge a new allegiance risked rendering him akin to the *Wanderer*, perpetually seeking a sense of belonging.[5] If indeed he had previously resided among the Vikings in association with Thorkell, this experience might have facilitated his transition to Cnut's camp. He was at a crossroads and it is plausible that he acquired the acumen to adapt and align with future prevailing currents.

Vita Ædwardi Regis (*Vita*) was created for King Edward the Confessor's wife, Edith, who was also Godwin's daughter. The source, penned by an anonymous author, suggests that Godwin and Cnut had been inseparable. Their closeness led to Godwin holding a prominent position in Cnut's government, surpassing both his English and Danish contemporaries. By 1023, he had become the leader (*dux*) of almost all of Wessex. While the exact start date of the *Vita's* composition is uncertain according to Barlow, it was possibly in the autumn of 1065.[6] Originally, it was to serve as a hagiography for Edith's family. However, after the Conquest, its focus shifted to her relationship with Edward. Edith and the author, whom she commissioned to write the *Vita*, probably aimed to avoid offending the new regime by overly glorifying her brothers. The first chapter of *Vita* begins with Cnut ascending to the throne and praises Godwin as Cnut's most loyal, diligent, and exemplary royal household officer.

The author writes,

> Godwin whom ... was judged by the king himself the most cautious in counsel and the most active in war. He was, too, because of his most equable temperament, most acceptable both to the people and to the king himself; he was incomparable in his tireless application to work, and with pleasing and ready courtesy polite to all. When, however, some fitting business of the kingdom called Cnut to his own people ... Godwin was his inseparable companion the whole journey. Here the king tested more closely his wisdom, here his perseverance, he his courage in war, and here the strength of this nobleman. He also found out how profound he was in eloquence, and what advantage it would be to him in his newly acquired kingdom if he were to bind him more closely to him by means of some fitting reward. Consequently, he admitted the man, whom he had tested in this way for so long, to his council and gave him his sister for his wife.[7]

This passage appears to be referring to the battle on the shores of the Baltic that Godwin was said to have excelled himself against the Wends, a Slavic people who were making the lives of their neighbours' a nightmare. It is clear that Cnut saw the potential in Godwin, but he was not one of his experienced battle-hardened Danes, and for him to have received such a prestigious accolade as an earldom, he must have done something exceedingly daring. Henry of Huntingdon, the twelfth-century historian, places Godwin in this battle in 1020[8], but it was not until after 1022 that Godwin was steadily moving up the signature list. From 1023 onwards, he was signing as the leading earl.[9]

Huntingdon presents a captivating narrative detailing how Godwin left a lasting impression on King Cnut, winning eternal respect from the monarch. He recounts the moment when Cnut and his army encounter the Wendish camp but opt to delay their engagement until the following day. Godwin, leading the English forces, decides to take it upon himself to execute a clandestine night time assault on the enemy. It is possible that Godwin and his men had faced mocking from the Danes regarding their prowess as soldiers. When Cnut awoke the next morning, he discovered that the English had vanished.[10] Suspecting that they had succumbed to the Danes' accusations of cowardice by fleeing or defecting, the king set out to confront the enemy, fuelled by frustration and angry at the absence of the English forces. The Danes stumbled upon the

Wendish camp, only to find it strewn with bloody, lifeless bodies, and plunder amassed by Godwin's English warriors.[11] Instead of berating them, Cnut extolled their valour, bestowing upon them the highest honours. From that moment onward, Cnut regarded the English as equals to his own Danes.[12]

Vita goes on to describe more of Godwin's attributes, such as humility and the capacity to effectively manage those below him, whose disputes required an even-handed arbiter. We are also told that he was revered by the whole country as a 'father'; 'a most beloved man'. Godwin's paternal or maternal ancestry are not mentioned, other than he was 'blessed in his ancestral stock'. Nor does it mention the noble bloodline of his wife, Edith's mother, Gytha. Also omitted is Swegn Godwinson, though he may have been covered in the missing second chapter which is thought to have discussed her siblings. Swegn was her eldest brother, undoubtedly considered the black sheep of the family. Godwin is presented as the founder of four comital bloodlines: Harold, Tostig, Gyrth, and Leofwin, who all held earldoms at some time in their lives. If Edith had wanted to include Swegn, who was dead by the time the work was begun, there would have been five comital lines. Her mother is often referred to, usually as one of the 'parents', but never by name, suggesting Edith had a closer relationship with her father. Cnut, she is proud to have declared, was wholly impressed with Godwin, and this was demonstrated by his rise to earl and 'office bearer'.[13]

Marriage to Gytha

Gytha Thorgilsdottir, was the woman Cnut arranged for Godwin to marry as a reward for his loyalty, hard work, and courage in war. Her father was a Danish magnate, splendidly named Thorgils Sprakaleggr meaning 'strut-leg', or 'fast-leg'.[14] According to Grills, he appears in the thirteenth-century sagas *Fagrskinna,* and the *Morkinskinna* as the father of Gytha.[15] Godwin may have been anywhere between 26 and 29 in 1022 when they were wed following his success in the Baltic and his receipt of the earldom of Wessex. A woman of impeccable pedigree, Gytha is often cited as being Cnut's sister-in-law, when in actual fact she was the sister of Cnut's brother-in-law, Ulf, who had married Cnut's sister Estrid. Gytha has also been wrongly referred to as the sister of her nephew, Swein, who was the son of her brother, Ulf[16] and also inexplicably called Cnut's sister by the author of Queen Edith's *Vita.*[17]

William of Malmesbury tells a tale attributing Gytha with an erroneous reputation as a slave trader. In his account, he paints a peculiar picture of Godwin's marital life, asserting that his first wife was none other than 'Cnut's sister' (Cnut really did have a sister called Gytha). According to Malmesbury, they bore a son, who, while joyfully riding, doing high leaps and prancing, was thrown into the depths of the River Thames and drowned. The mother desperately sought to rescue her son from the river's current, only to meet a grim fate herself. A bolt of lightning struck her down, divine punishment for her involvement in the trade of young girls whom she allegedly shipped off to Denmark in servitude.[18]

It is recorded in later Scandinavian tradition that Cnut may have had around five sisters, the most well-known being Estrid. One of his jarls, Erik, was the husband of his sister Gytha.[19] Where the story of this Gytha's fate came from is unknown, for it is unlikely that this Gytha had been Godwin's first wife whilst she was wed to Erik.

But whatever the case, it is safe to believe that the Gytha who kept slaves was not Godwin's Gytha. Malmesbury, however, shows his own confusion when he reports that Godwin took himself another wife upon the death of this first Gytha, but her name escaped him.[20] Unfortunately for Gytha's reputation, some historians have mistakenly linked Godwin's wife Gytha with the slave trade, for which we have neither solid nor circumstantial fact.

Gytha's father and brothers

Sprakaleggr, was believed to have connections to Sweden through his maternal lineage. His presence resonates within the pages of several thirteenth century sagas, where he is notably recognised as the grandfather of King Harold II of England.[21] Furthermore, Saxo's accounts provide glimpses into his ties with Sweden, recounting how, during dire circumstances, the Danish king embarked on a journey to Scania in Sweden, a land from which his paternal ancestors hailed.[22] In the words of Frank Barlow, Thorgils is a figure of distinction, often described as 'famous'. Legends suggest a mystifying lineage, hinting at a descent from a bear, thereby instilling something of the fantastical into Gytha's ancestry.[23] The name 'Sprakaleggr' evokes a vivid mental image of a confident warrior, striding into the mead hall with an aura reminiscent of a twentieth-century heavy metal icon.

Sprakaleggr's historical context is primarily legend, evoking themes commonly found in the sagas. Therefore, surprisingly, John of Worcester provides us with a link to Cnut's and Gytha's bloodlines. Describing an instance when Swegn Godwinson sought support from his cousin, the chronicler asserts,

> Earl Beorn, son of Swegn's maternal uncle, Danish Earl Ulf, son of Spracalec, who was son of Urso, (Latin for bear), and who was brother of King Sweyn (Forkbeard) pledged to facilitate the reinstatement of Swegn's earldom.[24]

This lineage establishes Gytha and her brothers as second cousins of Cnut.[25] It is possible that this assertion was derived from John of Worcester. Obviously, there are no bears in Gytha's bloodline, but it does add an air of mystique to her family.[26]

Gytha's brothers, Ulf and Eilaf, are both notable figures identified in the *Liber Vitae* of Thorney.[27] Ulf has been characterised as one of the most distinguished supporters of Cnut. According to the *Knyhtlinga* saga, Ulf, Gytha's brother, was the jarl whom Godwin was said to have helped when he became separated from his troops following Battle of Sherston.[28] It is evident that this incident was not how Ulf and Godwin met, but may have been fictionalised in the sagas to explain their friendship.[29] Ulf may have held jurisdiction over a territory in East Anglia under Thorkell before succeeding as earl after the latter's exile. He subsequently assumed the role of regent in Denmark under Cnut's reign, where he assumed responsibility for the welfare of the young prince, Harthacnut (d. 1042). It is during this period that Ulf may have been united in marriage with Estrid, Cnut's sister. The marital status of Eilaf remains unknown; however, he was entrusted with the governance of a territory in the lower west midlands during Cnut's rule. In 1009, Eilaf participated in the Scandinavian invasion of England, leading a fleet alongside Thorkell's brother, Hemming.[30] Tragically, Ulf met his demise under Cnut's orders around 1028.[31] His reputation appears to have been marred by a headstrong, impulsive nature, and was frequently entangled in contentious situations. The jarl came to an end after seemingly leveraging his relationship with his nephew, Harthacnut, conspiring to place the 8-year-old boy on the Danish throne in an attempt to overthrow Cnut.

Though Ulf ended his career and his life on an ignominious note, he was to become a founder of the royal dynasty who were to rule into the fourteenth century, starting with his and Estrid's son Swein, grandson of Sweyn Forkbeard. The couple also gave life to Beorn who died in his prime, murdered by his cousin Swegn Godwinson (d. 1052), son of his aunt Gytha whom had brought him up. Ulf was said to also have had another son named Asbjorn.[32]

There exists a wealth of unexplored evidence far exceeding the scope of this present work. It is patently evident, however, that the genealogical lineage relating to Harold Godwinson's maternal ancestry abounds with enigmatic stories beyond the realm of fantasy. Tales of bears dallying with mortal maidens, resulting in the birth of progeny are not to be taken seriously. Notwithstanding the intriguing nature of such accounts, the precise identities of Harold Godwinson's progenitors on either side of his parental lineage remain shrouded in obscurity, albeit not without a plausible connection to Sweyn Forkbeard and Cnut, potentially traceable through an antecedent named Beorn, son of Harald Bluetooth, father of Thorgils Sprakaleggr and brother of Sweyn Forkbeard (see family tree). Yet, one irrefutable certainty endures: Harold Godwinson was unequivocally not of ursine lineage.

CHAPTER FOUR

Forging a Dynasty

Gytha and Godwin

Gytha may have come to terms with brother Ulf's lamentable fall from grace, and found solace in the belief that his ignoble end had been justified. Even his son, Swein, was to be known by his mother's name, Estrid, rather than his father's. Regardless of this, Godwin and Gytha, continued to have good relations with Cnut, despite the king's hand in Ulf's death. She and Godwin had no qualms in taking in Ulf's sons, to nurture, and bring up at the court of Edward.[1]

We cannot know what Gytha felt about being passed in marriage to an Englishman of a less distinguished lineage. Judging by the amount of progeny they produced, Gytha and Godwin seem to have had a harmonious marriage. She was an excellent match for Godwin and the union was fruitful, with Swegn, the most troublesome of their brood being born first. If Godwin received his prize earldom and wife after impressing Cnut in the Baltic wars, there cannot have been any children until at least 1023. Therefore, Swegn was likely to have been born between 1023 and 1024. Precise birth dates can only be speculated as no one thought to record births the way they did deaths. But by examining the timing of notable events and the signing of charters, it is possible to roughly calculate a person's year of birth to a plausible degree. Harold must have followed somewhere between 1025–1026, and it seems likely that Tostig came not much later than 1028, or 1029, allowing time for Gytha to recover, and the likelihood of Godwin being away from home on official duties.

Edith, whom the *Vita* states was the eldest daughter, may have been born in between Harold and Tostig sometime between 1026 and 1027, making her roughly 18 or 19 when she wed Edward. Of course, she may have been born after Swegn and before Harold making her the second eldest instead of Harold, and giving her a slightly older age for her marriage to the king, Edward the Confessor. These dates are a rough guide only and are presented to give context to the family's narrative. They are not set in stone.

The next of Gytha and Godwin's offspring were Gyrth, Gunhild, Leofwin, and Eadgifu, all born somewhere amid the years of 1030–1037, with the youngest, Wulfnoth, bearing the name of his grandfather, born around 1040. He was thought to have been 12 when he was taken as hostage to Normandy with the archbishop of Canterbury. The reason for choosing the 1030s for their births is because the average age for a first major appointment at this time seemed to be approximately 20-something. Gyrth, next in line, would have been somewhere between 25 or 26 had he been born about 1030, when he was made earl in 1056, a little older, than Swegn and Harold had been, but he'd had to wait for a vacancy to become available. Leofwin received his title in 1058 so could have been born any time after Gyrth but most likely not after 1037 and therefore also in his mid-twenties when he achieved his office of earl.

With Gytha's potential to bear children in 1040, her own birth could have occurred sometime between the years 995 and 1000. Remarkably, she continued to thrive in 1069, staunchly resisting William the Conqueror, a testament to her resilient spirit, campaigning against the invaders whilst possibly in her seventies. It's conceivable that her offspring also inherited her unwavering sense of determination. Regrettably, Gytha's endeavours following the Conquest proved ineffective, and she was forced to end her days in exile.[2]

There have been mentions of the existence of a daughter called, Ælfgifu, who some historians believe to be the mysterious woman on the Bayeux Tapestry. Harold was said to have arranged with Duke William that she should be joined in marriage with a knight of the duke. Ann Williams discounts her in an article written about the women on the spindle side of the Godwinson lineage. She identifies the woman as the sister of a thegn called Harold, who is incorrectly referred to as 'Earl Harold'. An exploration of the Domesday Book discovers land belonging to the thegn Harold that the real Earl Harold did not own.[3] There is also mention of another son, Alfgar, of which there is little evidence for him so can also be dismissed.[4] However, another daughter, Eadgifu, has been revealed. But for a reference of her land, she may never have been discovered, as nothing is recorded of her except in the context of her property. She is identified as, *Eadgiuu fili* [sic] *Goduini comitis*, as it is written in the *Liber Vitae* of New Minster and the land she held in Crewkerne was given her by Earl Godwin.[5] It is hard to place her within the family line-up, but it appears she was dead some time before 1066, and may have been the sister Harold was talking about when responding to William's demand that he send his sister immediately to be wed to the Norman knight promised her. Eadmer, the cleric who wrote from the perspective of the English king regarding his trip to Normandy in 1064, stated that Harold suggested he would send her corpse to fulfil the agreement if the knight was so intent on having her.[6] The sister referred to by William, cannot have been Gunhild, as she was still alive after the conquest, and still alive in St. Omer until she died in1087.

Gytha's position as a daughter of a Scandinavian baron, was useless at protecting her from the whirlwind of scandal that engulfed her in the 1040s. Her son, Swegn, embarked on a rampage of tongue-wagging, proclaiming to anyone who would listen that his true father was not the esteemed Godwin, but rather King Cnut himself. Gytha vehemently refuted these allegations, asserting their falsehood in a solemn oath before a gathering of esteemed noblewomen.[7]

But the intrigue didn't end there; the fates of Cnut and Gytha are mysteriously intertwined with a child's burial in the Holy Trinity Church in Bosham, the heart of the Godwinson's home in Sussex. Legend has it that a daughter of King Cnut tragically drowned in the millrace.[8] It is believed that Bosham had once been a royal residence of Cnut, before he bestowed it upon Godwin as part of his comital lands. If we entertain the notion that both the young girl and Swegn were offspring of Gytha and Cnut, it could shed light on Godwin's meteoric rise to power.[9] To him, a woman of Gytha's breeding, though she bore the stains of disgrace, seemed a small price to pay for a burgeoning empire, a home befitting royalty, and the coveted top position in the hierarchy of influence.

More on Swegn's story in a forthcoming chapter.

Cnut

After the acceptance of the major players in England and his ascension to the throne, Cnut made overtures toward Æthelred's widow, Emma, to be his queen; a move that would further unify the English with the new regime.[10] The *ASC* states 'And there before 1 August, the king ordered the widow of the former King Æthelred, Richard's daughter, to be fetched to him as queen.' His earlier union with Ælfgifu of Northampton had already seen him beget two sons, Swein and Harold, but any sons he had by Emma would have to precede Ælfgifu's.[11] Emma's noble lineage and former queenship meant she out-ranked the northern ealdorman's daughter. The twice crowned queen had far more leverage than Ælfgifu to influence a satisfactory bargain for herself and any offspring she would have with Cnut. She also ensured that her sons by Æthelred were permitted to live peacefully in the care of their uncle, her brother, in Normandy.[12] She and Cnut would go on to have a son and daughter of their own, Harthacnut, later to become king in England (r. 1040–1042) and Gunhildr, queen consort of Germany (r. 1036–38).

In the latter half of Cnut's reign, details about Godwin's activities remain somewhat elusive. However, glimpses from the *Vita* and his prominent role in charter witness lists suggest that he had become Cnut's right-hand man, even surpassing the once favourite, Erik.[13] Around this time, Thorkell was in exile, and it is possible that Gytha's brother, Ulf, assumed the Jomsviking's role in East Anglia. Starting in 1023, Godwin, as premier earl, took on the role of regent whenever Cnut ventured abroad. *Vita* states, Godwin's position among the kingdom's nobles was the highest and he thrived in his authoritative office.[14] Interestingly, Godwin didn't seem to accompany Cnut on his overseas journeys following the 1022 Wendish conflict. This suggests that Cnut relied on Godwin's diplomatic and military prowess to deputize for him while he dealt with rebellions in his Scandinavian realms.[15]

As Cnut's regent, Godwin was able to garner the crucial skills of statecraft, diplomacy, and land management; essential abilities for his sons to acquire if they were to navigate the competitive political landscape. By 1031, Cnut's rule was secure across all his domains, thanks to his loyal governors. This allowed him to travel to Rome, confident that his deputy, Godwin, was willing and able to safeguard England. Cnut had appointed his first wife, Ælfgifu of Northampton, and their son, Swein, (d. 1039) to oversee Norway. Despite his youth, Harthacnut managed Denmark at the age of 12. This freed Cnut to arrange his daughter's marriage to Holy Roman Emperor Conrad's son, Henry III. The marriage, scheduled for 1036, was short-lived as Gunhildr passed away during a trip to Rome in 1038.[16] Ælfgifu and Swein's efforts to win over the Norwegian people eventually weakened, and in 1035, they were driven out by Magnus the Good.[17] Harthacnut provided them with refuge, even offering his half-brother Swein a portion of his kingdom.[18] Swein's death followed shortly, the cause unknown. Ælfgifu returned to England. Her sole hope now lay in supporting her other son, Harold. After Harold Harefoot's death in 1040, Ælfgifu disappears from the historical records.

Cnut's untimely demise in 1035, struck in his late thirties, cutting short a two-decade reign. His departure was to cast a long shadow over England, sowing seeds of discord that would divide the nation. They say kings required many sons, yet the danger lay in the manner of their birth.

Harold Harefoot and Harthacnut

Whilst King Cnut had lain ailing, Godwin took the reins of leadership, with Earl Leofric of Mercia, signing on the witness list in second place.[19] A charter dated 1035 concerns a grant of land to the monks of Sherbourne, and in its expression of hope is the wish that the monks would pray for Cnut's soul that he would enter the kingdom of Heaven despite his sins. It must have been at this time, that Godwin saw to the kingdom's administration until the king's long protracted illness was over and he died, 12 November.[20]

After a period of mourning, Queen Emma settled herself in Winchester with the treasury and the king's household led by Earl Godwin, her 'most loyal man'.[21] Not long after Cnut's funeral the *witan* congregated at Oxford to discuss the succession. Harthacnut's conflict with the formidable Norwegian king, Magnus (r. 1035–1047), obstructed any return to England to promote his claim. Meanwhile, Harold, heavily supported by his mother and their Northern kin, was free to put his case forward in person. Emma, backed by Godwin and the royal huscarls, the king's personal bodyguard, vehemently opposed Harold in favour of Harthacnut, but the cause was futile if he was not there to claim it.[22]

Ælfgifu and Emma were poised for a fierce showdown, defending their sons with all they had. Emma may have been a queen, but she was not above playing dirty, accusing Ælfgifu of slipping the children of a servant girl into her birthing bed—children who were neither Cnut's nor Ælfgifu's. A fiery exchange occurred, and Battle of the Mothers began. But this was a battle Emma was to lose. Harold was overwhelmingly hailed as regent both for himself and his brother.[23]

Imagine having one's parentage unexpectedly disparaged in public. It can only have greatly angered Harefoot. Now unopposed, and ablaze with anger, Harold Harefoot decided he did not want a regency. He wanted the crown all to himself. The very notion of him wearing the crown must have made Emma quiver in fear. Harold sent his men to her. He declared himself as king, and Godwin and his men were powerless to stop him barging their way into the queen's apartments to remove the treasury, which included the regalia Harold would need for his coronation. Fortunately, Emma was not physically molested, and Harold permitted her to stay in her home in Winchester until a plot to overthrow him backfired on her and she was driven out of England in 1037.[24]

It would seem logical that Cnut had intended to leave Harthacnut with Denmark and Harold, England. Godwin's support for Emma may have had nothing to do with loyalty to Cnut, but moreover a strategic move to keep the Danish connection. His change of heart toward Harold, may have developed before he allowed the treasury to be wrested from Emma, concluding that in opposing Harold's election, he was placing himself and his family in jeopardy. Years of tireless effort had cemented his status—land, wealth, power, and an unwavering reputation. Yet, he remained pragmatic, unwilling to gamble everything on the wrong heir. With Northumbria, Mercia, and London all against Harthacnut, the stakes were too high to favour Harefoot.[25] Cnut's failure to clarify the succession mirrors Edward's later catastrophe in 1066 but with a less disastrous outcome. Perhaps Godwin's ambition was to preserve the unity of England rather than let it fall into internal strife. No doubt the years spent witnessing the calamitous fall of a kingdom, torn apart from within, were indelibly etched upon his youthful memories.

The Tragedy of Alfred

Queen Emma's encomiast wrote that Harold Harefoot pleaded with the Archbishop Æthelnoth to consecrate him as king. Æthelnoth, we are told, refused, declaring that as long as a son of Queen Emma lived, he would elevate no other son of Cnut but Harthacnut to the throne and would forever keep his faith to Cnut.[26] He was also said to have forbidden any other bishop to carry out the deed. Harold's threats, pleas of despair, offerings of gifts, failed to sway the archbishop in his resolve. Eventually Harold retreated and developed a pathological hatred toward the church. Those who had supported him were too ashamed to denounce his kingship, having already brought him to the election.[27] According to the *Encomium,* Harold would set dogs on those who entered the church to hear mass, hiding in the glades to give chase when they came out. He was said to lay traps for Emma but her bodyguards protected her, and she was not harmed. But so thwarted, 'Harold started devising schemes with his companions to kill the queen's sons, which 'he would not have been able to effect if not helped by the deceit of fraudulent men'.[28]

Sometime in 1036, Edward and Alfred each received a letter they believed to have been sent to them by their mother.[29] Emma denied that she was aware of the letter's existence. It was a forgery, sent by Harold Harefoot, to lure her sons to England to murder them, though some historians believe she had given up on her youngest son, Harthacnut, and decided to seek out her other sons in order to keep her status as queen dowager.[30]

The letter, the contents of which we get from the *Encomium* itself, is extremely convincing, written in a loving mother's hand, with much resounding empathy for her children. It bid them be aware that with every passing day, the man who deprived them of their inheritance continued to do so. She wanted to know what they were going to do about it, whilst their usurper rode through the country lobbying the nobles with threats and bribes. She begs that one of them should come to her privately and quickly, for men abide them who would rather support a son of Æthelred on the throne than Harold Harefoot. The letter suggests that they reply through the messenger delivering the message and poignantly ends in words that bade them farewell, referring to them as beloved of her heart.[31]

We are told by the author of the *Encomium* that Alfred set out with selected companions which his brother, Edward, was said to have approved of.[32] He travelled first to Flanders, lingering there for a short while, discussing his plan with Count Baldwin. The count offered to send him with some of his men to assist, in case there was any danger, but Alfred was unwilling to do so, and instead took only a handful of men from Boulogne, perhaps from his brother-in-law Count Eustace, (r. c. 1049–1087) by now married to his sister Goda (d. c. 1049 or 1055) [33] The *Encomium* is silent on the exact number of ships that Alfred sailed for England with. De Jumièges, gives the impression of a much larger force than the *Encomium*, stating that Alfred had a substantial military force.[34] John of Worcester gives the number of men he had with him as 600 Norman and Flemish knights. The ætheling landed at Dover and was forced to sail further up the coast, to avoid an ambush. He was met by Earl Godwin, on his way to London to confer with Harold as he had been commanded. Recognising him, Godwin took him under his protection, offering Alfred his oath. He advised Alfred that the best route for him to get to his mother in Winchester would be to go south-west, away from London which was held by men loyal to Harold. In the small town of Guildford, they could rest for the night, Godwin reassured them. Arriving there, Alfred's men were accommodated in smaller groups, in the great hall, barns, and work-sheds, and Alfred was quartered with just a few of his attendants. After entertaining the prince, Godwin suggested Alfred retire for the night and as far as the ætheling was concerned, they would resume their travels to Winchester the next morning.[35]

The *ASC* and John of Worcester similarly reports that when the nobles loyal to Harold heard of this, they were not best pleased.[36] 'Some of the men in power were very indignant at this, (hearing of the arrival of Alfred) being much more devoted to Harold, however unjustly, than to the æthelings: especially, it is said, Earl Godwin. The earl, therefore, arrested Alfred on his road to London to confer with king Harold as he had commanded, and threw him into prison'.[37] The pro-Godwin Canterbury/Peterborough *Anglo-Saxon Chronicles (E)* completely misses out the year of 1035, but puts the death of Cnut in the year 1036 and makes no mention of Alfred's tragic fate. It is quite common for chroniclers to leave out the unsavoury deeds of their patrons. The Abingdon and Worcester chronicles both have similar entries as each other with alliterative verse describing in horrific detail what happened to Alfred and his men.

Quite the contrary to John of Worcester, and the *ASC*, Emma exonerates Godwin from any wrong doing. The *Encomium* appears to infer that instead of detaining the ætheling, the earl dissuaded him away from London and takes him to Guildford to avoid Harold's trap. It seems that Emma believed that Godwin was trying to save Alfred from Harold's clutches.[38] But the earl's rescue attempt was thwarted, for whilst they were sleeping, the Norman and Flemish knights were set upon by the 'abominable' king's henchmen, manacled and humiliated, their weapons removed.[39] Unlike the author of *Encomium*, John of Worcester lays the blame directly with the earl, recording that he took Alfred straight into custody on King Harold's orders. Godwin is also accused of the torture, maiming, blinding, enslaving, and murder of 600 men.[40]

As this heinous crime was happening to his men, Alfred was conveyed alone, under guard, toward London. The ætheling was then brought by water to the Isle of Ely but just as he set foot upon the ship's deck, he was held down and blinded, and death from his wounds must have been a blessing to him. The *Encomium* tells a poignant tale of Alfred's death, and the distressed author claims to tone it down on account of not wishing to cause his mother any further sorrow.[41] The young ætheling was buried in the church at Ely, 'as well befitted him'.[42] Edward appears to have crossed the channel in a separate attempt, landing at Southampton with ships full of armed men.[43] He was with his mother in Winchester when they heard of Alfred's slaughter, and 'she sent back her son, Edward, who remained with her, in all haste to Normandy.'[44]

Hitherto there had been no hint of Godwin being a merciless murderer of men. Unlike Streona, who had no qualms about eliminating human obstacles, Godwin had maintained an honourable reputation thus far. So why would he willingly engage in or oversee such a heinous act? It was an era of dog-eat-dog, and self-preservation couldn't be ruled out, even for someone like Godwin. The brutal manner in which these men met their end resembled the deeds of a young Cnut, evoking memories of the 1014 hostage maiming.[45] Could this bloodlust be ingrained in Harefoot's lineage?

Historian Eric John refutes the idea that Emma had not invited the æthelings to England. He also goes further to say that when it came down to it, Emma's devotion and loyalty was to herself and whichever son could assist her in maintaining her position as dowager.[46] But whatever her relationship with her Norman sons, the brutal death of Alfred must have come as a shock to Emma. If she had lured them to her, she would not have wanted the æthelings to come to any harm. Neither of them was any good to her dead. The *Encomium* claims that she was bereft for the loss of her murdered son, but that she took consolation in his peaceful rest in Heaven. The book reports that 'he was martyred in his innocence, and therefore it is fitting that the might of the innocence be exercised through him. So let Queen Emma rejoice in so great an intercessor, since him who she formerly had as a son on earth, she now has as a patron in the heavens'.

We cannot be certain what exactly Godwin's intentions for Alfred were, or how they affected his relationship with Queen Emma, though later, when she commissioned the *Encomium,* she appears to undoubtedly attribute Alfred's death to Harefoot and his cronies and does not incriminate Godwin.[47] It is possible that Harefoot had lured the brothers to England by writing to them, and it is true, he would have benefitted from both the æthelings' deaths, thus eliminating two of his rivals.

After Alfred's death, Godwin seems to have withdrawn himself from Emma and there appears to have been no support from either of her surviving sons. Suspicion may have fallen on her. It is plausible that in her desperate state she did write such a letter. After all, the *Encomium* postdates Harefoot's death. She had been delusional about their prospects, and any attempt to takeover the crown was badly conceived on her part. If there was any truth in her involvement, it was a scheme that went very badly. No noble would dare to support her now, and believing it provident to plan her future elsewhere, she assembled her household and prepared for exile in Bruges, where Count Baldwin V, offered her refuge, a house suitable for a queen,[48] and guards for her security as well as musical entertainment to while away her days.[49]

Settled regally in her Bruges palace, Emma's focus shifted back to Edward, who had narrowly escaped the same fate as Alfred by sheer luck. She urgently summoned him to leave Normandy and join her. Upon arrival, he listened, and offered no assistance, expressing sympathy for her plight but that he could do nothing, for he had no authority over the English. He promptly rode back home. Emma's plea for aid shows her willingness to call upon her sons, raising suspicions that she may have secretly written to them about her situation in England. Emma, it seems, was a perpetual schemer.

Residing comfortably in her luxurious Flanders abode, courtesy of the count of Flanders, she remained resolute to return to England. Her ambition? To see one of her sons ascend the throne, granting her access to the coveted treasury and lands she had once wielded as queen. Having spent over three and a half decades as a royal consort, embracing a humbler life, proved a formidable challenge. It simply wasn't her nature. Meanwhile, Prince Edward, traumatised by the Alfred affair, stood firmly against her plans, harbouring caution and mistrust.[50]

Eventually, in 1039, enemies, Harthacnut and Magnus of Norway, finally came to an understanding that each would accept each other's sovereignty and agreed that whoever died first, the other would inherit the kingdom of the deceased. Emma now saw her chance. With Edward refusing to contend the English throne, Emma turned to Harthacnut and sent messages abroad advising him of her sorrow over Alfred and the quandary she now found herself in. According to *Encomium,* the young Danish king's ears 'trembled' when he heard of this.[51] Whether his ears trembled or not, we can be certain that Harthacnut was definitely not happy about Alfred's death. Getting together a large fleet of sixty or so ships, he left most of them in an inlet, ready to come to his defence if needed. He then sailed with ten of the ships to Bruges, to meet his mother.[52] There, he was reunited with Emma at last. She had not seen her son for at least sixteen years. Emma had been kept from all her boys for most of their lives and now, unwelcome in Normandy, her husband, one son, and her daughter dead, she cut a tragic figure in her isolation. She was now able to revel the time spent with her favourite son, the youth she had depended on to keep her in the position she had been accustomed to for most of her life. The boy she had last seen at the age of 8 was now a formidable 20-year-old, well-versed in kingship and warfare. Emma undoubtedly celebrated this heart-warming reunion.

In 1040, as spring approached, news came of Harefoot's death. The English council sent for Harthacnut, who was still in Bruges with his mother. It may have been that Harthacnut was reluctant to hurry back, for he may have had some reservations, understandable given what had happened to his brother. He may have been wary of Godwin. It took another delegation to be sent before he set sail just before midsummer, arriving in England with sixty ships, manned with Danish warriors. The English for their part would not have known much of Harthacnut, for he had spent little time in England. There may also have been a reluctance to call him, for they had chosen his half-brother Harold over him.[53] It may have taken his mother some days of frustrating deliberation to persuade him.

But he need not have worried too much for he was jubilantly accepted, but happiness at his arrival was soon to vanish as we shall see shortly. Harthacnut, keen to avenge his brother's death, was about to make a few men's lives miserable. He gathered together the men he believed had a hand in his brother's fate: Aelfric, archbishop of York, Earl Godwin, and men who were the previous king's servants such as Stor, the master of the king's household, his royal steward, Eadric, and Thrond, his executioner and captain of his guards, plus several other men of great rank. Then he ordered them to go to London to dig up the body of Harefoot and had them throw his corpse into the Thames, where later it was pulled out by a fisherman and taken to the Danes who buried it in one of the cemeteries.[54] Later scribes were to describe the former king's corpse as being decapitated.[55]

After this, the nightmare did not stop. It was to continue. According to Grills, Godwin was made the scapegoat for all the ills that had happened to Harthacnut's brother, Alfred, whom he had never met, nor known, and his mother, whose plan to act as regent for him whilst Harthacnut was tied up in Denmark, was thwarted by Godwin's support of Harold.[56] Despite Emma's exoneration of Godwin regarding the death of Alfred, she would not have been able to forgive his desertion. Ælfric, the archbishop of York, accused both Godwin and Bishop Lyfing (d. 1046) of being complicit in Alfred's death. Ælfric's evidence was to stand him in good stead with the new king. Lyfing's see of Worcester, which had been bestowed upon him in plurality with two other sees by Harold Harefoot, was taken away from him and given to Ælfric, but restored back to Lyfing within a year after the king made peace with him.[56]

Harthacnut's thirst for retribution after Alfred's death stemmed more from political motives than fraternal affection. There's no record of Harthacnut ever meeting his half-sibling, Alfred. The formidable Godwin, though, needed chastening. Godwin was summonsed to Harthacnut's court. He was forced to swear under oath that he had merely followed his king's commands when he handed Alfred over to Harold's enforcers. His defence was aided by the realm's most influential figures as oath helpers.[57] In order to win Harthacnut's forgiveness and friendship, Godwin gifted him a great ship, skilfully made with gilded prow, tackle, and eighty hand-picked men, well-clad with helm, armour, and weapons, to sail her.[58]

While Harthacnut initially appeared as a capable ruler, his heavy taxation for ships, 8 marks per rowlock[59] and 12 marks per steersman,[60] weighed heavily even on the wealthier individuals. Consequently, his reign in England lost its lustre, causing his former supporters to lament. But things were about to get worse.

The heavy-handed royal huscarls collecting the crippling taxes caused tempers and feelings to run high. An inevitable strike back was to occur in May of 1040 when two of the king's overbearing officials were chased through Worcester by the suffering townsfolk whose rage after not being able to meet their payments had finally erupted. They were forced to hide in one of the monastery's turrets, but were found, dragged forth, and slain.[61]

Naturally, Harthacnut was furious but waited six months for winter to settle in making matters worse for his already suffering people. He called earls Godwin, Thored, Siward, and Hrani, and a great army with them to slay all the men, and burn the city and lay waste to the whole area, which they did for four days.[62] Many of the townsfolk fled to an island called Bevere, and defended themselves there. The countryfolk, having prior warning, escaped the furore, fled the area, saving their lives. But the king's men returned with great booty, and according to John of Worcester, the king's wrath was slaked.[63]

It was not long after this that Harthacnut died at a wedding, after standing up to toast the bride and groom. He suddenly keeled over and dropped to the floor, unconscious. He died later on 8 June, 1042; he was 23 years old. There is no impression in the chronicles that he was poisoned, though it would hardly be surprising not being England's most popular king.[64] However, Cnut's children were prone to die young.

The subject of who would succeed him was not an issue, for prior to his death, Harthacnut had invited his brother, Edward, to England to help him rule. Edward the Ætheling, whose chances of wearing the crown had always been zero, suddenly found himself propelled onto the world stage as King of England.

Lessons Learned

That Harthacnut had failed to destroy Godwin was not for want of trying, and proved a trial for Godwin, who must have felt the chill of Harthacnut's glare often enough. Despite putting Godwin on trial for Alfred's death, Harthacnut accepted the earl's declaration of innocence assisted by oath helpers. We do not know what Godwin felt about the ravaging of Worcester but later in 1051, he would refuse to carry out the same punishment on the people of Dover, an act that would eventually exile him and the whole of his family.

It seems that the *Vita* was correct in recording that Godwin's best years were the ones he spent as Cnut's premier earl.[65] They were likely to have been his happiest, too. Cnut's absences abroad and Godwin's role as regent gave him the opportunity to entrench himself firmly with a powerful grip on the realm, making alliances with gifts of land, and in turn receiving favours to enforce these agreements. Though he would emerge from the flames like a phoenix, Ætheling Alfred's tragedy, profoundly damaged Godwin's future standing. His efforts to repair the harm made to his reputation would not remove the stain of murder from his character. For Harold, the son that would succeed him as Earl of

Wessex, his father's blunder in the matter of Ætheling Alfred was an important lesson. Harold's exemplary restraint when dealing with those he should have dealt more harshly with, may have been due to the lessons learned by the mistakes of his father, though Harold was not immune to making errors of judgement, the accusation of murder, could not be hung around his shoulders, and it was only after his death that his own reputation was to suffer at the hands of his Norman enemies. Although Harold had not been involved in the Alfred scandal, to the pro-Norman propaganda machine, he was also culpable, despite no evidence, and being a minor at the time.

Godwin's children would have learnt much from him about diplomacy, warfare, statesmanship, and importantly, survival in a world where conspiracy and danger, stood on every corner. He would have shown them the value of creating solid alliances, as he had done with the counts of Flanders, cementing an earlier bond by marrying son Tostig to Judith, the aunt of Matilda, later the wife of William of Normandy. Such friendships served the family well when they were driven into exile in 1051. Godwin's connections in Ireland, notably with the Irish king, Diarmait mac Máel na mBó, Lord of Leinster (d. c. 1051–1072) and Dublin, were to serve two of his sons well. Diarmait was said to have been compassionate toward strangers in need which may explain also why Harold and Leofwin were to seek refuge there whilst the rest of his family had fled England to Flanders.[66]

It was said that Harthacnut himself invited Edward to his ancestral country to help him rule. Emma appeared to be overjoyed as 'here the bond of motherly and brotherly love is of strength indestructible'.[67] According to the *ASC C,* Edward was sworn in as king on arrival, which seems somewhat pre-emptive, however the *E* chronicle states that the people chose Edward as their king before the king was buried.[68] But what were Harthacnut's motives in inviting his brother to England to rule with him? Was it because of the dwindling popularity of his reign?[69] Perhaps it was Emma's suggestion, after all, her Danish son was not so popular with his subjects as she had hoped he would be. The English kings ruled with the consent of the *witan* and the people were not used to the harsh autocratic rule like the one imposed on Denmark. His taxation policies affected even the wealthy. Harthacnut either refused to listen to advice or there was no one willing to challenge him for fear of reprisal. Emma had been consort to two kings over the span of more than a generation, she knew the English people well, and may also have counselled Cnut alongside Godwin to soften his management of them. The *Encomium* places significant emphasis on Harthacnut's invitation to Edward, portraying it as driven by brotherly affection. However, more plausibly, Emma hoped that if Harthacnut was deposed, Edward would ascend the throne, leaving her status as dowager safe and secure.

But as soon as Harthacnut was in his grave, Edward was recognised as king in 1042.

Godwin may have breathed a sigh of relief upon Harthacnut's passing. With Harthacnut gone, Godwin shifted his support towards Edward's claim to the throne. With the power and resources he had amassed so far, his family sprouting like irrepressible weeds, it became clear how, at the peak of his influence in 1051, Edward's hand would be forced to remove this persistent thorn from his side. Nevertheless, Godwin remained kingmaker and never king throughout his life. Edward the Confessor would be the last monarch he helped to crown. However, his son Harold would surpass Godwin's achievements, amassing even greater wealth and influence than his father could have ever imagined.

CHAPTER FIVE
Royal Relationships and Raising a Family

Edward

The new king, Edward, later known as the Confessor, was crowned ten months after the death of his half-brother, Harthacnut, on 3 April, 1043. Having spent many years in Normandy at the court of his mother's brothers, Dukes Richard II (r. 997–1001) and Robert I (r. 1001–1035), in 1042, he was invited by Harthacnut to return to England to rule with him. As mentioned in the previous chapter, this may have been motivated to benefit Emma more than anyone else and it is not known just how much jurisdiction was given if given any. Harthacnut's death could not have come at a more opportune moment for Edward. He was a man who, but for a quirk of fate, should never have been king. Fortunately for him, Cnut had left the country to his successors with a well-ordered, politically stable administration, and the division caused by Cnut's sons, was eventually restabilised by Edward's ascension. It seemed that God, in his divine supremacy, had predestined Edward to be the king that would restore righteousness to the nation, bringing the English to repentance for their sins by his rule.

The new king received widespread celebration, both at home and abroad, especially among important figures. *Vita* describes him, 'living in mercy and ruling with kindness'. He was exceptionally tall, with milk-white hair and beard, full of face in which rosy cheeks shone[1]. His hands were pale, with long, translucent fingers, as we see on the Bayeux Tapestry, the extensive, mysterious embroidery, kept in the Bayeux Cathedral in Normandy.[2] The anonymous author of *Vita* elevated Edward to perfection. He was blessed with an 'unblemished body'. Pleasant, and dignified, he walked with humility, being graciously amenable to everyone, but when provoked, he unleashed a ferocity as 'terrible as a lion'.[3]

Harthacnut's death brought relief to Godwin, but it was short-lived. If anything, Edward was more likely to harbour genuine ill-feelings towards Godwin than his half-sibling had. Employing a familiar tactic, Godwin gifted Edward a splendid ship, just as he had done with Harthacnut.[4] Edward seemed satisfied with this for a while. Later, circumstances would reopen the wound of Alfred's death, but in 1043, it seemed that Godwin had risen from the scandal of Alfred's murder without too much damage. He even felt comfortable enough to offer his daughter, Edith, as wife for the new, half-Norman king. Edward was in his late thirties and had not yet been joined in matrimony with anyone, though his importance in Normandy's political arena had not been inconsequential. Certainly, his cousin Robert, had thought both the æthelings worthy of royal princes and had supported their cause. Edward had signed at least one charter as *Rex Anglorum* in Normandy, though perhaps somewhat prematurely. Some scholars appear to have made much of Edward's unmarried and fruitless status, and later the fact that his marriage to Godwin's daughter, Edith was also childless. Osbert of Clare, who interpolates the *Vita,* refers to him, nauseatingly, as 'a temple of virginity'.[5]

Emma

After Edward's coronation, Emma, begins to withdraw from courtly affairs to her palace in Winchester. While some attributed this to her advancing age and deteriorating health, the reality was quite different. She had seized the royal treasury and brought it with her into her apartments, and from behind locked doors, she was operating as though she were still a central figure in the kingdom. And possibly scheming again.[6]

By now, however, Edward had the measure of his mother. Emma's contributions to Edward's welfare had been rather limited, both during his pre-kingship and subsequent reign. In a decisive move designed to catch Emma off guard, he summoned his trusted earls, Leofric, Godwin, and Siward, and they journeyed in the midst of November from Gloucester to Winchester, as his lords had counselled him to do.[7] For a second time, Emma was stripped of her vast lands, and the royal treasures removed from her grasp. Chronicle *E* further underscores her reluctance to part with the treasures, indicating a steadfast resistance on her part.[8]

Edward's severe actions towards Emma prompts us to consider whether he was justified for his antipathy towards her. It is conceivable that his sentiments were shaped during the tumultuous years of his upbringing when at 13 years old, Emma abandoned him for Cnut. Emma's aversion towards his father, discernible in the *Encomium* where he is noticeably absent, must have been apparent to the young Edward. The sons of Æthelred, are relegated to the background in the *Encomium*, whilst Harthacnut is conspicuous in the limelight.

Edward's calculated actions against Emma, may appear harsh on the surface, but within the context of his upbringing, such perspective sheds light on the familial and political factors that influenced Edward's developmental years and his adult interactions with his mother. Following her humiliation, the queen dowager was consigned to live a frugal life with a much smaller retinue at the manor of *Godbeit* (now known as Godbegot her estate in Winchester). At that time, her friend Stigand, Bishop of East Anglia, who had not long been consecrated, was now divested of office, presumably because he had been advising Emma to the detriment of her son.[9]

But was there more to Edward than a bitter, resentful man, craving the degradation of the mother who had betrayed him with the usurper who stole his crown? Edward was not anointed until Easter, 1043, ten months after Harthacnut's passing. What had caused the delay in his coronation? And what was the current reason for his vitriol toward his mother? In order to gain some insight, we should explore the conflict between the Scandinavian major powers and how they may have influenced Edward's mindset at the time.

Hubert Grills suggests that there were other claimants to Harthacnut's throne. It is possible that the deceased king's cousin, Swein Estridson, also saw himself in line for the English throne.[10] He had been tasked by Harthacnut with leading a naval force against Magnus of Norway who had planted himself in Denmark, breaching the treaty that he and Harthacnut had made in 1039, whilst Harthacnut was still alive and kicking.[11]

Harthacnut may have wanted Swein to be his successor in both Denmark and England. As Adam of Bremen states, he got it straight from Swein himself. Having been repulsed from Denmark by Magnus, Swein arrived back in England to find his king dead and Edward sitting upon Swein's promised throne. Edward, Bremen advises, appeased Swein, by agreeing to make him his heir, even before any children of his own.[12] However, *Vita* describes nothing of the sort. According to the anonymous author, kings everywhere clamoured to send their good wishes on account of his kingship. 'Even the king of the Danes, although separated by the immense distance of the sea… entreated his peace and love, choosing him as a father, submitted himself to him in all things as a son. And by the order of the English king, affirmed this agreement by oath and confirmed it with hostages.'[13] Swein was not to enter England with hostility until some years after the Norman Conquest, which intimates that something indeed passed between Edward and Swein. Exactly what, though, is uncertain.

Bremen and *Vita* contradict each other. *Vita* claims Swein submitted to Edward as a son to his father, with oaths and hostages. Bremen speaks of a scenario set in 1066, but written in the 1070s to strengthen Swein's later claim to the English throne.[14] Swein may have felt that with England under his rule, he would be in a better position to fight Magnus, but when he saw Edward's regal backside was embedded on the throne like a jewel in a ring, he thought it wiser to ask for help with Magnus, rather than stake his right to the throne. But the help was not forthcoming, though he seems to have left England peaceably. He may have felt it would not serve him to fight two battles at once. The folk of England it seemed, desired a return to the bloodline of Wessex, fearing that Swein would draw England into a long war in Scandinavia.[15]

It is possible that Swein's appearance in England at that crucial time, had struck fear in Edward. As a child, he had been in danger himself many a time, and witnessed the psychological traumas his father experienced, being driven out by Sweyn Forkbeard. The memories of these encounters may have motivated Edward to expel some of the Danes who had connections with Danish royalty. Cnut's niece, Gunhildr, the daughter of his sister who had married the king of the Wends, and her sons were expelled.[16] Osgod Clapa, a Danish official who governed part of East Anglia, was exiled in 1046.[17] Æthelstan, son of the Danish standard-bearer, Tovi the Proud, at whose wedding Harthacnut took ill, was stripped of his Waltham estate, inherited from his father, and given to Harold Godwinson. It is quite reasonable to believe that Edward may have been stricken with the same paranoia his father had been afflicted with when he called for the massacre of Danes on St. Brice's Day, forty years before, though not with the same bloodthirsty outcome.

Edward must have expected serious trouble from Magnus when he mustered his fleet at Sandwich that year, and the next. It was a good thing that Swein was keeping Magnus too busy to attempt any invasion, although it may have come as no surprise to Edward to learn that his own mother was offering Magnus support.

The queen dowager, mother of two kings and a short-lived empress, was accused of inciting Magnus to invade, by offering the Norwegian king the treasury she had kept locked up in her house, should he decide to take up the offer.[18] At first, it would seem doubtful, even with Emma's penchant for schemes, that she had been plotting something with Magnus. However, her situation after Harthacnut was no longer tenable to her. Emma's influence in court was dwindling, her prestige counted for very little these days, and it seemed that Edward was not able to fully forgive her shortcomings as a mother. Emma was to claim that she had done all she had to help him, and had only ever done what she could to keep him safe as a child, post Cnut.

From her viewpoint, she had a lot to be resentful for. She had been abandoned and left defenceless by Godwin, who was once her greatest ally, her husband's closest friend and confidante. She had stood by his side through the Alfred tragedy, and he had done nothing to stop Harefoot's men invading her privacy, humiliating her. Now, here he was, conspiring to marry his daughter to Edward, possibly without her consultation. But Godwin wasn't her only resentment. Emma hardly knew her son, and Edward was a man who had grown up deeply aggrieved with his mother, making him difficult for her to manipulate. It may have been possible that he reminded her of her first husband, his father, whom she did not appear to have liked much. Emma's possession of the treasury gave her leverage to control events to her benefit. A plan with Magnus was clutching at straws, perhaps, but Emma had worked hard to ensure her place in the world. For most of her life, she had been queen, or queen mother. Would she go to any lengths to maintain her position?

Edward's treatment of her, though punitive and unforgiving, may have been more about displaying political strength than punishing her for plots and schemes. By handling her with severity, he declared to all, 'I am not weak like my father. I make decisions independently and act on them without the need for counsel', emphasising that his rise to the throne was his own achievement, not his mother's manipulations. He had returned to England under his own merit and as king, he refused to tolerate disrespect, even from his own mother.

Whatever the case, Emma now knew she could no longer rely on anyone, but herself. She was out on a limb for now, but it would not be for long. Edward was soon to restore her lands and her property, dealing with her less harshly, suggesting a reconciliation, though her status would never be what it had been during Cnut's time. She lived a quiet, typical life henceforth, after years fraught with one drama after another, and in 1052 in her early sixties, this remarkable woman passed away.[19]

Edith

From birth, Edith was destined for greatness. Her education at Wilton Abbey honed her skills in prose and verse, and her aptitude for spinning and embroidery.[20] She famously adorned Edward in exquisite garments, embellished with gold and silver thread. Her linguistic talents extended to Irish, French, and Danish, and she spoke them as though they were her mother tongues.[21]

As Godwin's eldest daughter, she likely bore the name Eadgyth in Old English, possibly named after her paternal grandmother, explaining her English name, however we cannot be sure as we have no idea who Godwin's mother was. Some speculate she Anglicised *Gyða* to Eadgyth or adopted the Norman spelling of her name, Edith,[22] when marrying Edward.[23] She even gets a mention in *St. Olaf's Saga* as 'their daughter who married King Edward'.[24] Osbert of Clare, refers to her as having 'ineffable beauty', and also, 'in her graciousness she was inferior to none and superior to everyone'.[25]

Edith stood at the threshold of womanhood, aged between 18 and 20, when she married Edward on Wednesday, 23 January 1045.[26] Though there had long been a service for the queen included in the Edgar ordo of 973, not every woman that a king joined with was consecrated.[27] Take, for instance, Æthelred's first wife, the mysterious Ælfgifu, who remained unadorned by the regal diadem. But Godwin harboured grander ambitions for his beloved daughter, seeking not just to unite her in wedlock with the king but to consecrate her very essence. Her sanctification, the gentle daubing of her head with holy oil, were the symbols of her newfound purity. After the celebrations, the young woman was 'delivered to the royal bridal apartments, with ceremonial rejoicing, anointed by God and crowned with a diadem.'[28]

That Edith and Edward were said to have never known each other carnally, seems to have been a later tradition, whereby Osbert of Clare desired to preserve the idea of Edward's piety and celibacy.[29] William of Malmesbury, writing more than half a century later, suggests it was common knowledge that Edward never once desecrated his purity by having relations with a woman, and hints at his disappointment that he was not able to discover why Edward and Edith were not sexually active.[30] He bemoans the fact he was unable to determine whether or not it was out of dislike for her family or because Edward wanted to remain sexually unsullied. The reference to Edith in the *Vita* conserving the secret of the king's chastity, is a later insertion of Osbert when he was submitting his proposal for Edward's canonisation and wanted to promote the king as less worldly and Godlier.[31] Osbert's initial campaign to have Edward hallowed as a saint failed, but his determination and obsession with Edward's piety and saintliness would not depart him and in 1161 a fresh approach succeeded and the belief that it was out of love for God that Edward and Edith abstained from sexual relations eventually won over the church and Edward was canonised.

Edith herself admitted that her husband treated her like a father would a daughter, suggesting that the relationship was nonsexual. In Edward's deathbed soliloquy, he said, 'May God be gracious to this my wife for the zealous solitude of her service. For she has served me devotedly, and has always stood close by my side like a beloved daughter. And so from the forgiving God may she obtain the reward of eternal happiness.'[32]

But does Edward's and Edith's reputation for celibacy mean that there was no consummation of their marriage at all? There is no evidence to suspect that Edward was as lascivious as the monks of St. Paul had accused his father, Æthelræd.[33] No evidence exists that he ever had mistresses or children born from any union prior to or after he wed Edith. However, piety and religiosity, does not mean that the couple were celibate. Nor does the lack of an heir. The monarch's divine obligation was to secure a rightful heir for both God, under whose banner they governed, and their realm. Edward, naturally, understood what was expected of him. According to *Vita*, after Edward restored his wife's father to favour, a grand procession was dispatched to Wilton's monastery to retrieve the queen and reunite her with her husband in the bedroom[34] Yet, one must ponder whether such regal grandeur was to grace their private chambers ever again, though it is apparent that Edward did, in later years, become fond and appreciative of her.

Emma may have been opposed to her son's union with Edith. It is possible she wanted to thwart the connection with the Godwin clan, proposing a match from the Norman elite to forge alliances outside of Godwin's swelling influence. With Godwin's daughter in bed with Edward, it would be Godwin who would now have the reins of control over Emma's son, and Emma was out in the cold. With two of Godwin's sons and a nephew holding earldoms, and Edith as queen, his power was increasing. Edward may have been willing to relinquish his independence in order to defy his mother out of spite, with Godwin seeming the better option. It is noteworthy that as Edith's presence on the witness lists grew, so Emma disappeared from them.[35]

In accepting Edith as wife, Edward had tied himself to Godwin, just as Cnut had. The new monarch was still in a precarious place, and Godwin's support was vital to Edward in order for him to keep a tight grasp on his kingship. Aside this, it also brought Edward security and the loyalty of his sons, a large clan of potential earls. Post marriage, however, there are hints that Edward might have found Godwin overbearing. The realisation that he was gradually falling under the sway of Wessex may have struck him like a thunderbolt. With the incessant calls for earldoms for his sons, his reliance on them would only deepen. A daunting future lay ahead, which may be why Edward started to turn to his imported Norman supporters who had returned with him to England.

Edward certainly does not appear to have been particularly fond of women. We cannot know what it must have felt like to Edward being abandoned in Normandy, but studies today psychologically show that such childhood trauma can lead to relational problems later in life.[36] Edward's abandonment by his mother could have plausibly played its part in Edward's attitude towards women. It would have made it difficult for him to form any sort of meaningful relationship with women, let alone a wife, especially later in life. He would have been 40 when he wed Edith which meant that she was half his age. He may have found that he had little in common with her unlike the men he surrounded himself with who were mostly learned church men like Bishop Robert Champart. So, in her early twenties, Edith found herself saddled with a man not at all sexually interested in her. That is not to say that the couple did not perform their royal duty, there seems to be no doubt that they did, for why else would Bishop Leofric have been prompted to compose a blessing for a childless king?[37]

Not long into the marriage there were murmurs about her unsuitability as a wife for Edward due to the absence of a child. For a young woman in Edith's position having intimate details of her reproduction ability discussed among courtiers, must have been disturbing. Suggestions that she had failed in her duty to give England an heir and could be divorced on the grounds of being barren were hinted at. But Edward made no move to put her aside, reinforcing the idea that Edward was not one to jump at counsel if he felt it was being forced upon him. However, from 1046 onwards, Edith is no longer found among the lists of witnesses of Edward's royal diplomas, indicating that she might have fallen out of favour with her husband. Or, it could have had something to do with the actions of a certain member of the Godwin family who was about to bring himself and his family into disrepute. She was not to be seen again signing or witnessing charters until 1055.

The Offspring

Living amidst such a lively group of boys, each eager to claim the top spot for attention, surely created occasional chaos. The Godwin household must have brimmed with testosterone, resonating with the sounds of youthful energy. We know of one anecdote where Harold and Tostig were said to have fought at court in front of Edward which suggested they were spoiled and undisciplined. Godwin would have had to have been a strong disciplinarian when he was at home, which may not have been that often, accounting for some of the dysfunction and jealous behaviour amongst the older boys. Gytha would have had needed some hired help: servants, and perhaps a wet nurse or two. The family may also have had weapons instructors, nurses to help bring the children up, and a good *cildemæster* to kickstart their education.

Godwin was by this time extremely wealthy and would have been able to afford good tutors for his sons and daughters. As children of the kingdom's premier family, they would need to be refined and educated, not only academically, but also in diplomacy, deportment, and statesmanship. The boys would have needed to know the art of swordsmanship, weapons, and warfare strategy. The girls would also need to learn languages, sewing and embroidery, verse and poetry, be equipped with a business-like mindset for they would need to know how to run a household and manage the estate's accounts, ensure their many servants were fed, clothed, cared for, and the children of the house reared. It is possible that with Godwin's trade-links the family kept slaves as domestics, most of the rich and wealthy would have, which may have been where Edith learned to speak Irish. The aforementioned story about Godwin's first wife in Malmesbury being a slave trader appears to have been transferred to Gytha by some historians, which is unfortunate for this is incorrect.[38] Though it is not necessarily unlikely that that Gytha may have indeed been involved in the horrific trafficking of women, Malmesbury was referring to Godwin's 'first' wife not his 'second', and it seems improbable that Godwin had a wife before Gytha, especially a sister of Cnut.[39]

Godwin may have kept the eldest of his sons close to him. The younger offspring, might have been entrusted to Edith's care at court, once she was queen.[40] She had charge of many of the nobles' children, where she groomed them for courtly life, seeing to their education in her apartments.[41] Tostig and Gyrth would have been in their teens when Edith ascended to her queenly duties. Although Godwin's relationship with the king was often strained, King Edward does not appear to have had any negative feelings toward his younger brothers-in-law, except for Swegn Godwinson. It is plausible that Tostig enjoyed a closer relationship with his sister, the queen, and her husband, the king, compared to Swegn or Harold. His age likely permitted him to join the court, where he received tutelage alongside other children of noble birth. In contrast, his older brothers had already assumed their lordships in East Anglia a year or two prior to Edith's elevation to throne. The *Vita* regards Harold and Tostig very well and the *Vita Haroldi* speaks of Edward's love for Harold, however according to the *Vita*, the mental well-being of the royal couple deteriorated significantly after Tostig's expulsion in 1065, indicating he later became his favourite of the two brothers.[42]

According to the author, Hubert Grills, all of Ulf and Estrid's sons were born and raised in England.[43] Swein, the eldest of Ulf's sons, was to eventually become ruler of Denmark. As previously mentioned, he had been Harthacnut's *dux*, tasked with the responsibility of the Danish fleet attack on the Norwegian king, Magnus who had helped himself to Denmark in Harthacnut's absence when he claimed the English throne. There was another son, Osbeorn (or Asbeorn). This son may also have been fostered by the Godwinsons along with Beorn, though likely, it is not known for certain. Not long after Harold and Swegn received their earldoms, Beorn, supported by Godwin, was invested in lands close by Harold's and was noted as signing his first charters, S 1008 and S 1010 in 1045.[44] His earldom consisted of London, Hertfordshire, Buckinghamshire and Bedfordshire, and possibly Huntingdonshire and Northampton. It is conceivable that Osbeorn was also given a tract of land to look after. Osbeorn is later exiled after Beorn's death, though it is not clear why. It could be he left voluntarily, either disgusted at his brother's murder or worried for his own safety. In any case he later shows up invited by Ætheling Edgar, and sent by his brother King Swein of Denmark in 1067.[45] Godwin may have convinced Edward that by promoting Gytha's nephews, he was placating any early hostility from Denmark.

Cnut likely insisted on the Danish brothers as hostages to keep their father, Ulf (Cnut's brother-in-law), in check. It is possible that after Cnut's passing, Godwin and Gytha welcomed the brothers into their family, raising them alongside their own children.[46] Beorn, too was possibly at court with the other Godwin boys, but there is evidence to believe that he may have spent some time being mentored by his cousin Swegn Godwinson in his Herefordshire earldom, learning the ropes for his own appointment in 1045.[47] He appears to have had some allegiance to Swegn at one point, a relationship that would cost Beorn his life.

With Alfred's tragic demise casting a shadow on his reputation, Godwin was determined to rebuild his standing within the aristocracy, relying on the ascent of his offspring. In a world where maintaining connections was vital for those in authority, Godwin's sons and daughter in powerful positions, would secure his accustomed comforts. With a wife, numerous dependents to provide for, and fierce competition, promoting his family was an immense endeavour. Godwin's brood absorbed invaluable life skills from their patriarch: resilience, diplomacy, adept handling of challenging individuals, and the art of navigating the turbulent vicissitudes of governments. The earl of Wessex, a true survivor, had thrived under Cnut, yet the comfort he once knew as *sub-regulus* had dissipated with that king's passing. As Cnut's sons ascended the throne, Godwin had faced a more arduous path. As Edward assumed the crown, it was necessary that Godwin position himself as an unwavering advocate for him.

With potential rivals for the English throne lurking, having Godwin as an ally was imperative for Edward. While Godwin may have initially leaned toward his nephew Swein, he likely realised that England longed for the end of Danish rulers and a return to the Cerdic bloodline. Edward was isolated in England following his lengthy exile in Normandy, and desperately desired a formidable ally like Godwin, deploying his sons and nephew to fortify his defences in East Anglia, Hereford, and the heartland counties.

Alfred's death, however, would remain a constant strain on the earl-king relationship. Unlike Godwin's bond with Cnut, there was never a strong connection between him and Edward. Yet, they managed to collaborate effectively for a time—until Swegn Godwinson entered the scene.

Part Two
HAROLD

CHAPTER SIX

Son of Fortune

Earl of East Anglia

Godwin's difficult relationships with Cnut's sons may have left him feeling jittery about working with new-comer to the crown, Edward. He did what he could to advocate for him, and supported him into the throne. The new king seemed to have accepted the earl's oath of innocence regarding Alfred's murder, just as Harthacnut had done, though perhaps more out of political necessity than anything else. Godwin introduced his sons to him, two of whom, Swegn and Harold, were ready for employment. The king had no sons of his own, and appeared to enjoy the company of young men. According to the *Vita,* Harold and Tostig were endowed with charm and elegance and won the king's admiration.[1] The eldest brother, Swegn, not mentioned by name in the *Vita,* was likely to have been the sibling referred to by the anonymous author as a 'gulping monster'.[2] Like most fathers, Godwin had high hopes for his eldest and most troublesome son, Swegn, and could not have imagined in those early days that it would be his second son who would win all the accolades. Sadly, for Godwin, he would not live to see all that Harold accomplished after his death, instead he would live long enough to witness all the havoc Swegn was to cause.

Despite Godwin's previous shortcomings during the reigns of Cnut's sons, he retained the premier slot as *dux Anglorum,* and at this time was still signing charters above any other royal official.[3] In return for his support, Edward promised to allocate important positions for Godwin's sons. Swegn was to win the office of earl of Hereford, Gloucester, Berkshire, and Somerset.[4, 5] East Anglia had been without an official earl since Cnut's reign as the threat from Denmark and Norway had been mitigated with Cnut at the helm of England. Thus, there was no need for a powerful earl to take over from Thorkell the Tall as earl of East Anglia and the region was governed by strong local landowners. But in the 1040s, England was once again at risk, this time from Magnus of Norway. Edward found it prudent to reopen a vacancy in East Anglia and placed Godwin's second son, Harold, as earl. As mentioned in chapter four, we know that Harold was likely to have been born after Swegn, and possibly before or after Edith, so somewhere between 1025–1027. This would make him much younger when he attained office than previously believed by some historians.[6] Shortly after this, Godwin successfully promoted his foster son Beorn, whom Edward invested with lands alongside Harold's lands.[7]

The dominion that Harold entered had once been ruled over by his uncle, Ulf, as well as Thorkell, but had lacked an overlord for several years. The flamboyant Danish staller, Osgod Clapa, a prominent landowner in the area, had been performing the duties of earl without recognition for over two decades.[8] This situation likely strained relations between him and Harold contributing to Osgod's exile in 1046. The decision to favour Godwin's son over Clapa raises questions. If the primary concern was the threat posed by

Magnus, would it not have been wiser to reward the more experienced man? Recognition of Osgod's loyalty might have better aligned him to the king, rather than against him. On the other hand, promoting Harold might have been a calculated move by the king to avoid antagonizing his powerful chief Godwin. Edward's choice may have also been predisposed by a desire to minimise the Danish contingent's influence in England.

Harold's and Swegn's appointments were likely to have ruffled some feathers, especially Earls Leofric of Mercia and Siward of Northumbria. Both had sons aspiring to earldoms. Godwin's sons had found early success without much experience, despite their excellent training, and Swegn's earldom lay within the territory once controlled by Mercia. Leofric might not have opposed the assistance, particularly along the Welsh borders, but would doubtless have preferred it to be his son, Alfgar, who had been patiently awaiting his turn for recognition. With Beorn and Swegn in receipt of ancient Mercian lands to oversee, Harold in East Anglia, and Godwin in Wessex, the entire family had effectively become a buffer zone against Leofric and the boundaries that were once Mercian.

We are able to tell that Harold was in post by 1044, which included Cambridgeshire and parts of Huntingdon as well as Norfolk, Suffolk, and Essex, as he was found witnessing the will of Thurstan as *dux*, dated that year, in which Harold was a beneficiary and received a mark of gold.[9,10] Such gifts were an important part of an ambitious man's income, for it not only added to their wealth, it also brought loyalty from the donor.

If Harold was born no later than 1026 and no earlier than 1024, He could have been as young as 18 or 19 when first settled in East Anglia, and with only a modest retinue, would need to make alliances and friendships with the thegns in each locality. The first thing he would have wanted to do was to familiarise himself with them personally and a tour of his lands to meet the men commended to him was the best way to do so. On his journey, he would come across men and women who sought his patronage, ingratiating themselves with gifts of land to add to the comital estates that came with the occupation. Leading families would have been expected to host him and his retinue on their estates for at least three days throughout the excursion. No doubt, Harold would have to politely negotiate his way through the abundance of females presented to him by their eager relatives as suitable partners for him. It was likely during this tour that Harold set his heart on the wealthy young heiress, known as Eadgifu the Fair, commonly known as Edith Swanneck.

An earl was a warlord, expected to lead a regional army in the defence of the kingdom by land or sea. But he was not just a military commander, Harold would be expected to be an administrator, dispensing justice on the king's behalf, overseeing the collection of king's taxes, handing out writs and witnessing land transfers.[11] He would work alongside the bishop and the shire-reeves, *scīrgerefa,* and may have been lucky enough to have a high-reeve, *hēahgerēfa,* to help him administer his earldom. All writs from the king would be addressed to him and he had the power to act on the king's behalf as he saw fit. On top of this, his duties included attending the king certain times of the year, such as Easter and Pentecost, Christmas and any other time that the king summonsed him.[12] In reward for his hard work he would receive the third penny from the profits of justice in a hundred or a shire.[13]

As well as the third penny, land was the most valuable commodity anyone could possess. Not only was it a way of sustaining one's family, it was also a means of obtaining household retainers, and the patronage of other wealthy men. Land brought revenue into a man's coffers as well as bringing in money for the king. The more estates one had the more tenants one could employ to work it, and in return, the tenants received land for themselves. Men who owned land freely from their lord were known as sokemen, a term used mostly in the Danelaw, in which the regions of Harold's jurisdiction lay. Soke appears to have originated in early Anglo-Saxon law and had its connotations in seeking justice.[14] The terms *sacu,* sake, and *socn,* to seek, literally mean the act of seeking justice for one's sake – or cause. Later, the terms were used in the context of land ownership and that the lord who owned the land would have the right to hold a court.[15] 'Sake and soke' was first documented in a charter of King Eadwig's granting land to Archbishop Osketel of York.[16]

The pre-conquest system was decidedly complex, and terminology was not always consistent. For example, one category of estate common in the north but rare in the south, was where a large number of villages were grouped around a central manorial property owned by the lord. The land held by some of these villagers might actually be held by another landholder within the estate. In the Domesday Book we often see Latin phrases such as *potuit recedere quo uoluit*, meaning, 'he could go where he liked', and the implication was that the person concerned owed personal fealty to the lord named, but the land belonged to him and not to his lord. That land, however, might still be burdened with services and dues to whoever held the soke and probably not the lord to whom the holder was commended to.[17] F.M. Stenton points out that the villages that belonged to an estate where the owner had sake and soke, were subjected to the private court of the lord and would be expected to attend regularly or when summonsed.[18]

A man who was half Danish like Harold might not have expected any trouble from the people who resided in his lands. After all, living in the Danelaw, they would surely support being ruled by one of their kind. Many historians of the nineteenth and twentieth centuries seemed taken by the idea that the people of East Anglia saw themselves as Danes. But did they? The Danelaw originated with the invasions of the Great Heathen Army but was not officially termed Danelaw until the eleventh century, when a Danish King Cnut sat on the throne of England.[19] Their laws, although very similar to the West Saxons, were enshrined in the language and customs of Scandinavia.[20] However, there are grounds to believe that the inhabitants of these regions had come to see themselves as an integrated population. In most contemporary texts, the people in the east Midland region of the Danelaw are declared as 'the east Mercians'. As for the people of East Anglia, the account of Ealdorman Ulfketel Snilling's campaigns against the Danish invaders in the early eleventh century do not suggest any idea of kinship with the invading Danes, despite Ulfketel and his adversary, Thorkell, both bearing names of Norse origin. In Ulfketel's time, more than a century had passed since the first Scandinavian intruders had assimilated with the local populace. By the time of Harold's appointment, they had been integrating for a century and a half in some cases. The following quote from the *ASC* 1004, refers to the Battle of Thetford when the 'Flower of East Anglia were slaughtered there', indicating that these young men of 'Danish' descent perceived themselves as East Anglian English. The Danish Danes, as they themselves admitted, 'never met worse hand-fighting (*wyrsan hand plegan*) in England than Ulfketel dealt to them'. Even in the face of defeat, they were loyal to their king and countrymen.

When Harold took up his post he would have immediately inherited the lands that had once belonged to this Ulfketel Snilling. Additionally, Harold received the lands in Colne, Essex which had belonged to Ealdorman Byrhtnoth of Maldon fame, and later transferred to the old ealdorman's wife. One of Earl Harold's early tasks in the role of earl would have been the unpleasant job of overseeing the expulsion of Gunhildr, Cnut's niece, ordered to leave England with her two young sons. She had been widowed some years before, when her husband, Hakon, one of Cnut's deputies, had been ship-wrecked on his way to England to collect her and fetch her to their new home in Norway. Probably not one of Harold's finest moments, but a job that was expected of him or those who worked for him.

Apart from the aforementioned mark of gold from Thurstan, a whole estate in Fritton, Norfolk, was bequeathed him by the lady Wulfgyth. In a short time, Harold had gone from the landless son of an earl to a wealthy young landowner, responsible for a great swathe of countryside, with thousands of men and women entrusted to him. A great responsibility for a youth.

Harold's acquisition of Waltham came through a stroke of luck with the confiscation of lands and titles, and the possible exiling of Æthelstan, a king's staller, son of Tovi the Proud, the aforementioned standard-bearer.[21] It is not certain why Æthelstan had his lands confiscated. The author of the Waltham Chronicle started in the late twelfth century, stated that he lacked his father's astuteness and wisdom, and lost many of his possessions including Waltham. This appears to have occurred around the same time as, Osgod Clapa, whose daughter, Gytha, had married Æthelstan's father, Tovi, was also exiled. It is possible that Æthelstan may have left England with his stepmother's father. Instead of the land falling to Æthelstan's own son, Esegar (Ansgar) the Staller missing (d. 1085) it was awarded to Harold. Whether or not this caused animosity between Harold and Esegar is not known, but he supported Harold at Hastings, more than twenty years later. Edward did not seem to have concerns about Æthelstan's son, Esegar, whom he appointed to Æthelstan's offices of Portreeve of London and Sheriff of Middlesex.

Harold's income needed to allow for his upkeep and to help him cover the costs of raising armies, and maintaining his own household. An earl would expect to have a personal bodyguard as well as his own *heorðwerod*, the huscarls that would serve as his personal battalion. An earl was also expected to dress according to his status with jewels and golden arm rings to give as rewards to those who served him well. The gifts of property endowed upon him by those who wished to have his patronage would have been for his personal use, and to keep beyond his post as earl, separate from the comital lands commended to him. Soon he would need a wife to see to his apparel to ensure that he was finely dressed in the latest fashion and to raise children who would later keep him in the comforts he had become accustomed to, just as *he* now helped to keep his father in power and wealth.

Osgod Clapa

The East Anglians were an integrated community of Danes and Anglians, with the core of the original Danish immigrants, settling in the ninth century. But there had also been another settling of Scandinavians in Cnut's time, who, like Osgod Clapa, still looked to their old homeland with nostalgia. The ports of Norwich and Ipswich was where traders from across the sea in Scandinavia and elsewhere, such as the Rhineland in Germany, selling wine, and buying textiles from the locals.[22]

In 1044, Edward mustered a fleet of thirty-five ships at Sandwich after rumours abound of the threat from Magnus of Norway.[23] Harold was likely to be there as would be his father, and Swegn, too, if he could get away from the issues on the Welsh border. Both Godwin's sons were trained seamen. Their father was one of the most competent sailors in England whose familial origins appear to be from a seafaring family. However, this threat did not materialise. Magnus was busy elsewhere, locked in a conflict with Swein Estridson over who ruled Denmark.

In the summer of the next year, 1045, Edward, newly married to Godwin's daughter, Edith, gathered the largest ship army 'ever to be seen in this land'.[24] Chronicle *D* clearly states that the reason was another threat from Magnus but reports that the war in Denmark prevented him from coming.[25]

Meanwhile, Osgod found himself increasingly marginalised by King Edward. It must have been greatly frustrating to be pushed further down the witness list, and thegns who would typically sign after him were now signing ahead of him.[26] Osgod's byname of Clapa meant 'coarse' and indicates he had rough manners, which may not have done him any favours.[27] It did not help that Harold's landless brothers, Tostig and Leofwin, were also signing as nobles, whilst Osgod had been downgraded from the list of nobles to a mere thegn.[28] His downfall may have been due to his provocative nature, and his flamboyant attire. He made a point of wearing gold arm rings and furs, and wore a flashy gilt inlaid axe over his shoulder in the manner of the Danish nobility.[29] The following anecdote suggests that by dressing nobly, Osgod was not only parading his Danish heritage before the king, but also his noble status. On a visit to Bury St. Edmund with his attendants, Edward was engrossed in conversation with the monks inside the church while Osgod and his companions enjoyed a meal. However, Osgod, having consumed a considerable amount of alcohol, entered the church forgetting to remove his axe. Tying himself in knots to unsling it, he stumbled and collapsed. Edward ordered the monks to attend him, and he ended up with paralysis in his hands.

In the middle of winter, 1046, Osgod was exiled, perhaps due to vociferous objections against his diminished role in Edward's court. There may have been other reasons why he was removed, but he was obviously miffed by the changing circumstances in the earldom. Not only had he been replaced by a much younger model, he had been demoted in rank. Already known to have a tendency for being uncouth, the whole situation may have evoked some inherent belligerence in him. Edward may have been led to believe by Osgod's behaviour that a plot to overthrow him for Swein Estridson was on the cards, which led him to be suspicious of the Danes. Whatever the reason, Clapa spent that winter with another exile, Swegn Godwinson, in Bruges. Later after some activity in 1049, Clapa was to lose a number of his ships in a storm off the east coast of Essex after a raid by his men acting independently of him.[30] Osgod crossed to Denmark where he appears to have died 'suddenly' in his bed later in 1054.[31] It must have been a devastating way to have ended his career in exile after years of loyal service to the crown. Whether or not Harold had direct input in Osgod's downfall, the chronicles do not to say, but as earl, he would have had to oversee the eviction just as he had done with Lady Gunhildr.

Harold the Youth

The *Vita Haroldi*, written c. 1205, is the one chronicle we have solely written about Harold. It was preserved at Waltham Abbey in honour of their original patron, Harold himself. Its late existence is problematic, however the unknown author could have had access, as the author of the *Waltham Chronicle* did, to earlier documents and local tradition. Although the text focusses mainly on Harold's adventures after the Battle of Hastings, the first four chapters give us some insight into his earlier years when he was a young man and almost died from apoplexy. After chapter four, and following Hastings, the *Haroldi* disappears into the realm of fantasy, claiming that Harold survived the battle and is brought back to health by a Saracen woman in Winchester where she concealed him for two years. After unsuccessfully seeking help from the Saxons (Germans) and the Danes,[32] the reconstituted persona of Harold Godwinson realises his cause is lost and eventually spends the last of his years as a hermit. The chapters are written in no particular chronological order starting with an introductory passage which describes Harold as a 'king most illustrious and lawfully crowned'. It then goes on to mention Harold's parentage. It is the nature of scribes of this time to rarely refer to women, but where they do, it is seldom by name. Godwin is mentioned by name. Gytha is merely, 'a sister of Canute, King of the English', followed by Harold's relationship as brother to the 'revered Queen whom the King and most holy confessor Edward had married'.[33]

Not even the queen was known by her name, albeit she was revered.

The author of the *Haroldi* praises King Edward and Queen Edith, and refers to their marriage as being 'short of consummation', preserving the flower of their maidenhood. However, it is clear that at this time, the Godwinsons were smeared with the 'mark of treason and other crimes'.[34] The author continues with a story that makes Cnut appear weak and easily rattled. Fearful of how Godwin was rising through deceit, Cnut settles on an idea to try and rid himself of him, and sends Godwin to Denmark on a task involving the delivery of letters. Curious, Godwin opens the letters and finds that they are orders to kill him, and he replaces the letter with one that tells the recipient that he should be welcomed warmly and given Cnut's sister to wife. This turned out to be a good move for both men, as Cnut comes to realise that Godwin's calculating nature would come in useful in his administration and that he would make a prudent minister!

So, having made good with Cnut, Godwin found himself on bad terms with Cnut's successor having used treachery to destroy, King Harthacnut's brother (Alfred). The author asserts that there were those who would use Godwin's wrong doings to bring Harold to ruin, suggesting that he 'certainly gained a greater victory in that he overcame and rid himself of the self-same vice to which he was born and reared'.[35]

Moving on to chapter two, the story of Harold's illness and recovery is far more plausible than the first chapter and there could be some truth to it. It begins with Harold and Tostig's devastation of Wales, which is corroborated in other sources, but happened over a decade later when he was in his late thirties. Harold's achievements in Wales is discussed later. First, let us look at the severe illness that struck him whilst a young man.

The anonymous author speaks of Harold as the best, most uprightness of young men in the land. Nonetheless, he was struck with a stroke, causing what physicians called a paralysis, said to have been delivered by the hand of God. The text implies that Harold would receive spiritual reward if he overcame it, 'a remedy for his soul', now, and for any future wounds. The author of the *Haroldi* describes the affliction as that which 'forsakes a man's body' and causes it to forget its ability to function.[36] Thus, as Harold lay very ill, unable to move the parts of him rendered useless and weak, hearts were heavy with grief, including the king who loved him.[37] The chronicler refers to Edward's wariness of Harold's family, stating that of all of them, Harold was dearer than any others; the best of a bad sort. Edward made available his own physicians to attend him. Again, the chronicler draws the reader's attention to the spiritual context of the problem, proclaiming that the Almighty's will cannot be put aside by the power of man.[38] That Edward loved Harold like a son is corroborated by a later chronicler, Snorri Sturluson.[39]

Somehow, the sad news of Harold's predicament reached the ears of the Holy Roman Emperor, Henry III referred to in the *Haroldi,* as king of the Alemanni, and he sent a physician called Ailard, whom it was said that God had entrusted with great skill at healing the sick.[40] We are not told how Henry came to know about Harold's illness, but we learn that Henry and Edward were 'akin' to one another through marriage. for Henry's father, Henry II, had married Edward's half-sister Gunhildr, who died when Edward was still exiled in Normandy and unlikely to ever have met. It is possible that Edward and Henry III, may have met when Edward attended courtly events. Apparently, united in affection and friendship, both Emperor Henry and Henry, King of France had attended Edward's coronation. The emperor may have felt empathy upon hearing of Edward's distress for Harold. As the *Haroldi* reported, Henry hastened to send his own talented physician, Ailard (also known as Master Adelard of Uhtrecht) to his dear friend, the king of England. The friendship may have deepened when, in 1049, Henry called upon Edward to assist him in his troubles with Count Baldwin V.[41]

The learned Ailard, a native of Liege and student of Uhtrecht, arrived in Waltham where Harold was being cared for, and examined the young earl carefully. He realised that he, like Edward's other physicians, was unable to help him, despite devoting every attention to him. And seeing that Harold's illness was one of divine intervention rather than cause of the physical, the physician, who was also qualified as a scholar, a spiritual cause needed a spiritual remedy.[42]

Keeping within the theme of otherworldly the author tells us that those attending Harold, advised Ailard of the life size stone figure of the crucified Jesus Christ that Tovi the Proud had discovered in the ground on an estate in Somerset and brought by divine providence, to the church at Waltham. Tovi was said to have been in such awe of the stone cross, he had used his own sword to gird it and his wife Gytha had adorned its figure of Christ in gold and precious stones, all made of 'marvellous workmanship' with her own jewellery. She had also ordered a gemstone to be embedded within it to provide light for those on watch.[43]

It was to this artefact that Ailard recommended Harold pray if he wanted to live, persuading him to put his hope in God from whom salvation comes if one puts their trust in 'Him'. Harold was carried to the place where the stone cross was kept and 'prayed with great earnestness that the guardians of the place, whose duty it was to minister at the health-giving symbol would deign to obtain for him by their hearty prayers pardons for his sins and alleviations of his sufferings; in a word, health for both the inner and the outer man. Nor was the mercy of the Saviour long in wanting to him who asked for health with a faith unfeigned for soon the pain and weakness of his body grew less; but as he became stronger his love for the observances of the Holy Cross wonderfully increased'.[44] Thus in a short while, Harold was restored to perfect health and vowed to devote the rest of his life to the Holy Cross of Waltham. Later he would rebuild the church there, a magnificent church that would outshine the old one. This new church of the Holy Cross was to become his life's joy, but he would not see it consecrated until 1060, five years before Edward's new church of Westminster.

Appearance and Character

Numerous imaginative ideals of Harold exist, with the most prevalent being the Victorian portrayal of Anglo-Saxon men. The Herculean physique of a Marvel character comes to mind. Robust and war-like, they are incongruously donned with winged helmets and steel breastplates. Their muscular brawny arms wield formidable axes. While some aspects may seem anachronistic, like the plate armour, it's essential to consider the bias that is inherent in many sources. Some paint Harold in a positive light, while others cast him negatively, influencing the pendulum's swing for and against him.[45]

Contemporary portraits of people from this era are scarce, making it challenging to precisely visualise Harold's appearance. However, *Haroldi,* though written 140 years after he lived, describes him as robust, astute, and keen, with a formidable prowess in combat. He was also 'well-practised in endless fatigues', evidenced by his lightning mounted charge into Wales of Christmas 1062, to attack King Gruffudd's palace of Rhuddlan, and also his forced march north to fight Hardrada followed by the journey south shortly after, to face William of Normandy on the Sussex coast.[46] For a man approaching his forties this was no easy feat, and gives weight to the idea that the huscarls were well-disciplined, well trained, and amazingly fit. The fact that this was done on horseback, does not mitigate the stamina needed for, as anyone who rides knows, a long time in the saddle can be pretty tiring. One source claimed: 'he was the best rider of either the old, or the new time'.[47]

Orderic Vitalis, writing in the first half of the twelfth century, refers to Harold as, 'very tall and handsome, remarkable for his physical strength, his courage and eloquence, his ready jests and acts of valour'. The latter is supported by the Bayeux Tapestry in the scene where, crossing the River Couesnon, Harold rescues two men from quicksand, giving credence to the *Vita's* mention of his strength. As for his 'ready jests', we have two examples: the first during an exchange with Duke William before they did battle, that Harold was willing to hand over his dead sister's body to be wed to a Norman knight,[48] and the second was Harold's offer of 7 feet of ground for Harald Hardrada, seeing that he was a very tall man.[49]

The *Waltham Chronicle* describes him as a fine soldier, tall of stature, incredibly strong, and more handsome than all the leading men in the land. The interesting aspect of this source is its late representation, having been written by an ex-canon of the church in the late eleven hundreds, before the collegiate was dissolved and became an Augustinian priory. However, despite having been the church's first historian, he seems to have been able seems to put together a collective history from the available charters that had been archived and oral traditions.[50]

The Bayeux Tapestry is one of two early representations of Harold, the other his coin minted the year he died, with his thick manly neck and large dominant nose. The tapestry, or rather, embroidery, shows him a slim figure, with light-coloured hair and moustache, which is sometimes drawn in black. The 224-foot-long wall hanging was made by various embroiderers which means that the images are never exactly the same, but the main characters are usually distinctly recognisable. Duke William, is represented with clean-shaven features and a monk-like hairstyle, cut long from the crown, combed forward to his ears and then shaved closely at the back of his head, whereas Harold's hair is not shaved at the back and appears to reach his nape. The idea that the Bayeux Tapestry can be trusted as an accurate representation of Harold's looks is somewhat sketchy, as we do not know exactly what year following the conquest the frieze was made, nor do we know if any of the artists had ever met him. Though it is possible that they had, we have nothing to collaborate it. In the scene where Harold is crowned, he is given strong, masculine features, a square jaw and prominent chin. His is a finely shaped nose under which he proudly sports his moustache. This is decidedly the clearest view of his face, but again, it is not something we can rely on as a true likeness but something rather more figurative.[51]

Ian Walker states, that Harold himself would have approved of the masculine and warlike impression.[52]

The *Vita* also refers to Harold's strength of body and mind which seems to be the standard for a panegyric. He was a 'second Judas Maccabeus' and a true friend to his countrymen. Patience and mercy, and kindness to men of good will, are followed by the usual trope that when threatened by evil doers, he would have the face of a lion![53] Comparing Harold with his brother Tostig, both are pronounced as distinctly handsome, graceful, and similar in strength and both equally brave. But in reporting on stature, we might find the author more trustworthy, for height was objective unlike someone's facial aspects, in the eye of the beholder. The *Vita* states that Harold was the taller of the two, but makes no comment of Tostig's height.[54]

As an aside, Harald Hardrada was said to have quipped to Tostig as Harold rode out to parley in the prelude to the Battle of Stamford Bridge, 'Your brother stood tall in his stirrups for such a little man'. Hardrada was said to have been especially tall. It was at Stamford that Harold himself remarked about Hardrada's height when offering more than the usual 6 feet used to bury someone.[55]

Siblings

To unearth the essence of Harold's character, we should delve into the intricate web of his family bonds. We can only speculate about Harold's childhood, but hints of a tumultuous upbringing in a sprawling dysfunctional family will emerge as we probe their family's trials and tribulations. Any impressions we get about the rest of the children of Godwin and Gytha are subtly embedded within the chronicles and often have to be dug for to find. But they are there if we look closely, though not for each of them, but for some. Clues to the dynamics of this powerful family can be found within the narrative, such as the competitiveness between the older sons of the family and the friction between Harold and Swegn, and later, Harold and Tostig.

Harold's easy-going and mildness of nature was tested to the bounds with his brothers. But there was a limit to his easy forbearance and when it came to it, Harold was able to turn his back robustly as we shall see. His relationship with Swegn was not likely to have been close, though whether or not they had developed a fondness as children we cannot know. If they had, it must have been fragile, for it easily deteriorated when Swegn embarks on his rampage of sexually inappropriate behaviour, murder, and self-destruction. The author of *Vita* attempts to treat Godwin's family respectfully whilst at the same time doing his best to make them distinct from the perfect all Anglo-Saxon family. This is shown in the passage where the author explains that no one could possibly accuse Godwin of not schooling his children well, that rash behaviour or flippancy could never be attributed to Harold, nor Tostig, nor anyone else brought up under Godwin's tutelage. Tostig himself was endowed with very great restraint – and here comes the 'but' – occasionally he was a little over-zealous in attacking evil with a bold, determined, constancy of mind.

Among his many siblings, Harold was probably closest with Leofwin, and was likely to have had an affection for his youngest sister, Gunhild, presenting her with a saint's stole he had obtained during his travels in Ireland.[56] Gunhild held her Surrey estate from him, and one, possibly two, of her manors in Somerset were adjacent to properties he held there.[57] In the year 1044, both Leofwin and Gunhild were still in their childhood. During the tumultuous period of exile in 1051–1052, Leofwin was with Harold as they sought refuge from Edward's wrath in Ireland. The partnership hints that Harold might have been grooming his younger brother for a future role as an earl.

It is possible that he developed a long-lasting affinity with Gunhild, just as an older brother might cherish a younger sibling. He knew her well enough to know that the mantle of St. Brigid would be something that his little sister's religious nature would appreciate. Certainly, he named his own daughter after her. Later, Gunhild would become a nun in St. Omer and died there after the Norman Conquest in 1087.

His relationship with his sister, the queen, seems to have been one of mutual respect rather than love. Her actions, however, show more of a fondness toward Tostig than Harold, one of which was to have a man executed on Tostig's behalf,[58] and according to William of Poitiers, the Norman writer, Edith was scathing of her brother Harold during the Conquest of England.

It must have been difficult for Harold's parents to have kept all the children in check when they were growing up, and even as grown men. If Godwin spent long evenings by the hearth lecturing his offspring on the importance of family bonds and blood ties, some of them cannot have listened well. But if you could not trust your family, then who could you? And coming from Godwin's perspective of having grown up in varying different 'families' it was understandable that he would want to bring his children up to value familial affiliations first and foremost, and that dependence on one another was of great importance in a world rife with backstabbing. In future chapters, we shall see how Godwin's absence in his son's lives may have been sorely missed in this somewhat dysfunctional family.

CHAPTER SEVEN
White Swan

Her Name Was Eadgifu

Harold's first wife and lifelong companion was the owner of vast lands in East Anglia and beyond, so it was likely to have been during Harold's initial tenure as earl that they crossed paths and were handfasted. I've refrained from using her more commonly recognised name, Edith, bestowed erroneously upon her by the author of the *Waltham Chronicle*.[1] Eadgifu's connection to the cartulary of St. Benet's Holme in Norfolk, where she was benefactor, is preserved under the epithet 'Eadgifu Swanneck'.[2] Richard Sharpe supports the notion that 'Eadgifu Swanneck' was her true name, dispelling earlier misconceptions that mistakenly referred to her as Edith the Rich, or Edith the Fair (Eadgyth), a distinctly different name from Eadgifu.[3]

In the Domesday Book, she is identified by the Latin rendition of her name, *Edeva pulchra, dives*, signifying respectively, 'beautiful' and 'rich', respectively. She is alternatively referred to as Edith, Eadgyth, and Eadgifu, but it is important to note that these names do not share a common etymology and convey entirely distinct meanings. Thus, one cannot be considered a derivative of the other, contrary to widespread assumptions.[4] Most Old English names are constructed from two distinct components. In Eadgifu's case, *Ead,* meaning wealth or good fortune, and *gifu,* the second element in her name, corresponds to 'gift' in Old English. Therefore, her name could be interpreted as Fortune's Gift. Eadgyth, on the other hand, Fortune's Battle, is a totally different name altogether. So, from here, out of respect for her, we will use her real name, 'Eadgifu'.

In exploring the identity of Eadgifu, it is worth ruling out who she wasn't. Bill Flint in his book, *Edith the Fair, Visionary of Walsingham*, identifies 'Edith the Fair', wife of Harold Godwinson, as the Lady of Walsingham, also referred to as Rychold. He claims that her parents were Thorkell the Tall, and Wulfhild, supposedly Æthelred's daughter. It is not even certain that Æthelred had a daughter of this name.[5] Through a ballad by the fifteenth-century printer Richard Pynson, it was thought that the founding of the Marian Shrine of Walsingham, dated to 1061, was the work of a noble widow called Richeldis. The name meant rich in virtue.[6] According to Roman and Anglo-Catholic tradition, she was Richeldis Faverches, a devout, prayerful lady who, in 1061, had a vision in which she was taken by the Virgin Mary to Nazareth and shown the house where Gabriel had announced the news of Jesus' birth. Mary asked Richeldis see to it that a replica of the house was built in Walsingham, and promised that whoever sought her aid there would not go away empty-handed. Richeldis was a Saxon noblewoman, said to have been married to the Lord of Walsingham who died and left her with a son, Geoffrey. Known for her compassion and care for those around her, she was also devoted to the Virgin Mary. Her son was believed to have joined in the crusade in the middle-east, having inherited his mother's immense love of God.[7]

Historian J.C. Dickinson has proposed that the date of the foundation was somewhere in the 1130s.[8] Flint challenged this dating, claiming it as 1061. Furthermore, he claims that the former date was based on poor evidence.[9] The confusion and choice of 1061 may have had something to do with the similarity of 'Walsingham' and 'Waltham', also associated with a religious miracle. The eminent historian Harriet Leyser agrees with Dickinson that Richeldis Faverches flourished in the 1130s and a date for her death is put at 1145. She also states that the family are not mentioned in the Domesday Book, making it difficult to agree with Flint that she was the woman that Harold married.

Suggestions have been made that Eadgifu may have been the daughter of the woman, Wulfgyth, who left Harold the estate of Fritton in her will in 1046.[10] However, the daughter that is named in the will was known as Ealdgyth, another entirely different woman from Eadgifu, and with a different name, different spelling, and different meaning. According to Ann Williams, none of the estates in Wulfgyth's will interconnect with the lands of Eadgifu the Fair. Eadgifu was more likely to have been related to Ordgar, the sheriff of Cambridgeshire.[11] This theory is based on the distribution of lands held by Ordgar, Eadgifu, and Harold, in which Ordgar was named as Harold's man. Eadgifu and Ordgar both had interests in two tenements so it is plausible that she might have been his daughter.[12] If Eadgifu was the sheriff's daughter, then she would be a useful link for Harold to the local government in his first earldom, not only because of her land but also her kin. Some of her estates in Suffolk were also mutually linked with Harold's, and three of her manors in Cambridgeshire were held by Godwin Cild, recorded as her 'man', and probably the couple's eldest son, giving grounds that Edith the Fair and Eadgifu the Rich were the same woman.[13]

The tale of Gunhild, daughter of Harold and Eadgifu Swanneck, reinforces the connection between all three. Gunhild emerged as the only offspring to be left behind in the diaspora of Harold's surviving kin, following the turbulent events of the Norman Conquest. During this upheaval, Gunhild was placed within the confines of Wilton convent with her Aunt Edith, the previous queen, and her father's sister. Gunhild's life was to take a remarkable turn as she became either the victim of abduction or a willing participant in an elopement with a Breton count named Alan Rufus, aptly known as 'the Red'. Rufus, a steadfast companion of William of Normandy, had been granted lands in Cambridgeshire that had been in the possession of her mother. It seems that this count orchestrated the removal of Gunhild from Wilton, undertaking this course of action knowing that Gunhild was the daughter of the deceased King Harold and his wife, Eadgifu, seeking to bolster his claim on her mother's lands through their alliance.[14]

Marriage

Harold seems to have chosen Eadgifu first and foremost for the benefits he would receive being married to a wealthy heiress, but he was to stay true to her throughout most of their lives, indicating that it was a long-lasting love. It is possible they remained together even when he became king and married Aldith (Ealdgyth), the sister of the northern earls Edwin and Morcar, a marriage alliance that would gain him the loyalty of her brothers, Edwin and Morcar, the sons of Alfgar of Mercia.[15] Unlike Harold's marriage to Aldith, he and Eadgifu had been married in the *more Danico*, the old tradition of hand-fastening, commonly used by the nobility in the eleventh century. Although the church frowned upon it, the marriage was looked upon as lawful and any children of the union were entitled to the same rights as those born to a couple whose union had received religious benediction.[16] Both Cnut's sons by Ælfgifu of Northampton had been able to take up kingships despite being born of this type of union.[17] Such a marriage meant that an important young man starting out in his career, could make alliances with a woman from a powerful family, giving himself a solid base to support his lordship over a dominion. Later, when his power was consolidated, he would be able to look to new alliances, a 'real' marriage recognised by the church, such as Cnut made when he married Emma of Normandy. Cnut does not seem to have put Ælfgifu aside despite his marriage to Emma. These arrangements were to become illegal with the coming regime change, even though William himself was the result of his father's affair with a woman considered of low birth.

Because of the change in the laws on marriage and the stricter clerical regime set up by the conquerors, Eadgifu was mentioned retrospectively at times as *concubina Heraldi* insinuating that she was Harold's mistress, and not married by church law.

An unidentified woman, denoted as *quaedum conqubina Heraldi*, is documented in the Domesday records as the proprietor of four houses situated in Canterbury. This property could be attributed to Eadgifu, albeit subject to uncertainty, given that all of her other estates were situated north of the River Thames.[18] Conversely, Domesday registers few individuals bearing the name 'Harold'. This prompts an inquiry into whether Eadgifu Swanneck possessed a collection of dwellings in Canterbury. Alternatively, we should contemplate the possibility of a distinct individual, with Harold possibly having a past, later, or parallel relationship with another woman, alongside Eadgifu.

It is not evidenced in any contemporary English sources that Harold was a promiscuous man. It is only in Norman propaganda that such claims are made without providing evidence.[19] However, the *Haroldi* mentions him being given to the Godwinsons' proclivity to vice in his early years before his stroke, but we must tread carefully, for this is written more than a century later than he lived.[20] In any case, it is not impossible that this could have been a woman he had formed a relationship with in his teens, before he became earl of East Anglia. Given his striking appearance and high status as a lord, it would not be surprising for him to have had other romantic entanglements beyond his official commitments.[21]

Eadgifu's lands were numerous, making her very wealthy indeed. As Harold's wife, she brought £366 to their joint capital.[22] In 1066 her lands amounted to 280 hides and 450 acres worth £520 pounds. Twenty-nine men and three women were commended to her. Her men would lend military service to Harold out of loyalty to their lady as the soke holder over their lands, thus making her invaluable to him as a wife.[23] In return, Harold would provide her with protection for herself and her lands.[24] Harold's connection to East Anglia stayed with him throughout his life, even after becoming earl of Wessex. He was still holding lands in Essex, Norfolk, Suffolk, Huntingdon, and Cambridgeshire when he died. These were lands granted by Edward to maintain his status as earl, and would have brought many men to him.[25] It is likely they were with him at Hastings.

Eadgifu was rich enough to employ two goldsmiths, Grimbald and Wulfwin.[26] The former held land from her that he could neither sell nor grant in Cambridgeshire, and Thorney Abbey owns an eleventh-century gospel book thought to have belonged to

Eadgifu which is inscribed with a note that suggests that Wulfwin had donated the gold used to decorate the binding. She was also recorded as a benefactress of St. Benet Holme.[27]

Eadgifu's marriage to Harold appears to have been as fruitful as was loving. She bore him six surviving children, and it was said that one seventh child died in early infancy and was buried in Canterbury Cathedral.[28] The *Waltham Chronicle* notes that she knew him intimately – better than anyone else – implying that their union was also a marriage of mutual love.[29] *Haroldi* reaffirms by stating, 'she loved him exceedingly, and had known him well'.[30] She may have been present in the hours preceding Battle Hastings as well as in the aftermath although it is alleged that the canons of Harold's collegiate at Waltham had been unable to find their lord's body amongst the mangled wreck of bodies and had returned to Waltham to bring her to help find him. The veracity of the *Waltham Chronicle*'s narrative as to how Harold's body was discovered in the carnage a couple of days later is difficult to confirm. No earlier contemporary sources correlate with it, but it is popular tradition.

We know the names of Harold's children as follows, Godwin, Edmund, Magnus, Gytha, Gunhild, Ulf.[31] If Harold met and married Eadgifu in the early days of becoming earl of East Anglia, Godwin, the eldest of their brood, could have been born as early as 1045–1046. Then subsequent children were likely born after that in varying stages over the next ten or so years. Except for his two eldest sons, Godwin and Edmund, whose names are English in origin, his remaining four children were endowed with Danish names.[32] It is clear that Godwin was likely to have been named for his grandfather, and his son Edmund may have been in honour of the king that Godwin had served prior to Cnut. His third son was called Magnus, not a common name until the first king of that name, Magnus the Good of Norway and for a time, Denmark. Proceeding him, it becomes very popular. It would seem unlikely that they would name a son after the man who harried their cousin off his throne, though his appellation of 'the Good' signifies that he had some decent qualities. The youngest son Ulf was no doubt named for Harold's uncle, his mother's brother, so may have been chosen to appease Gytha. Young Ulf may have been no older than 6 or 7 when his father died at the Battle of Hastings. He was to join his uncle Wulfnoth as a guest of William the Conqueror, but released after his death, unlike Wulfnoth, who was freed then tragically rearrested by the new king William Rufus.

The girls' names were also Danish. Gytha, his eldest daughter, was named for her grandmother, and Gunhild perhaps after Harold's sister, whom he was close to. As we have already touched on, Godwin Cild was the only landholder known of the couple's children in 1066. No doubt Harold would have prepared his sons for a life in office, seeing to it they were trained in military arts as well. We see later these skills are put to use after the conquest and although not successful, they demonstrated they could coordinate and recruit fighting men to at least attempt to retrieve their father's throne. Eadgifu and Harold's daughters go on to have colourful and adventurous lives. Gunhild we have already discussed, is carried off by a Breton lord, and Gytha finds herself in Eastern Europe, Married to Prince Vladimir II Monomakh, beginning a new Anglo-Rus dynasty.

Establishing a Collegiate and New Church

Harold and Eadgifu are thought to have made their home together at Nazeing, where local tradition has it that Eadgifu was brought up.[33] They may also have spent a lot of their time together in Harold's manor of Waltham, known as Waltham Abbey today. It is situated just outside of northeast London in Essex. Nazeing is not much more than 5 miles, from Waltham. There had also been a hunting lodge that was part of Tovi the Proud's manor and his son, Æthelstan's after him. When Harold became Earl of East Anglia, the lodge became his. It may have been there, at the lodge where he fell with the illness that almost killed him. Harold vowed to make restitution for his life by rebuilding the old church of the Holy Rood, where he had prayed to be restored to health.[34] The story of Harold's illness is only accounted for in the *Haroldi*. Harold's struggle and recovery are probably the most plausible passage in the document. The rest of the book is somewhat imaginative and obviously fantastical. This passage explains why Harold chose the church of the Holy Cross as his major project and why he lavished so many gifts upon it. He 'raised walls with lofty columns, interlacing arcades and a roof lined with lead'.[35] He also increased the staff of canons from two to twelve, and appointed a schoolteacher, Master Adelard, and a dean, Wulfwin. Adelard can be identified as the Lothringian, Ailard of Uhtrecht, sent by the Holy Roman Emperor, to cure Harold of his paralysis.[36] The fact that there is a clear connection between Ailard and Adelard, gives credence to the story of the earl's illness and recovery. And the earlier story that he was the physician who had advised Harold to pray for his life explains how he came to be part of the staff of Harold's collegiate in Waltham.

The *Haroldi* does not give a date for Harold's affliction, but talks of him being a 'vigorous young man'. It is likely to have happened when Harold was earl of East Anglia as evidence is recorded that he was in the flower of his youth, and whilst ill, appears to have been cared for at Waltham, suggesting it occurred anywhere from 1044 onwards. The timeline in the chronicles are slightly erratic in the 1040s, and he is not singled out to have been anywhere in particular until 1049.

As mentioned previously Edward summonsed the fleet to Sandwich in the years 1044 and 1045.[37] No doubt, Edward would have required his leading earls' naval skills, including Godwin, Swegn, Harold, and their cousin Beorn. There were no call outs for the ship army in 1046 or 1047, so it could be assumed that Harold's illness occurred somewhere between those years. In 1048 there was some action with raiders in Essex. Harold is not named in the *ASC* that year. The raiders, Lothen and Yrling, sold their booty of English gold, silver, and slaves in Flanders.[38] Chronicle *C* for that year states that Sandwich and the Isle of Wight was raided, and 'the best of men were killed there'. The king and the 'earls' then went out after them in their ships. Frustratingly we do not know what happened after that and we do not know which earls went with the king and the ship army.[39] Chronicle *D* does not mention the attack on Sandwich or the Isle of Wight. Instead, in 1047 we are told that Swein of Denmark sends an urgent plea for aid to repel Magnus of Norway, and is refused. In 1048, Swein sends for help again, this time against Harald Sigurdson (Hardrada), who is now the new king of Norway, after the death of his uncle, Magnus.[40]

It seems possible that Harold's illness could have occurred during any time in the aforementioned years. The timing, however, might depend on when King Edward's friendship with the Emperor, had deepened. Did it coincide with his sending the physician to help treat Harold? Incidentally, it was in 1049, that Edward entered into an alliance with Emperor Henry III of the Roman Empire, who had gathered a great army against Baldwin V of Flanders. Baldwin was accused of rebelling and breaking down the palace at Nijmegen, and committing other offences against the emperor.[41] Edward appears to have been eager to help and sent the Godwinsons to join a naval blockade with Swein of Denmark to prevent Baldwin escaping Henry's great land army.

The situation between Baldwin and the emperor soon came to an end and peace was restored. By this time, Swegn Godwinson was seriously in the bad books after kidnapping the abbess of Leominster, and keeping her with him for some months before he freed her. For this heinous crime, he was sent packing by his father. Swegn knew when to pick his moments, and returned like a prodigal son to beg forgiveness and ask favours of the king. To Harold's and Beorn's dismay, he pleaded with the king for the land he had once owned that was now in their possession.

When Harold and Beorn were summoned before Edward, they refused to support Swegn, making it very clear they would not give up any land of Swegn's that the king had given them in his absence. Edward realises he has no choice but to dismiss Swegn, and told him to sort it out with them. Harold makes himself scarce, avoiding any awkward, embarrassing scenes between him and his wayward brother. Beorn on the other hand, allows himself to be manipulated by the wayward Swegn, and agrees to go with him to entreat Edward to change his mind. But this turned out to be a big mistake for Beorn, for courtesy of Swegn, he ends up dead. Of course, the black-sheep of the family claimed it was an accident, and to prove it, he had buried Beorn in an unmarked grave. The exact sort of thing one does if one is innocent, right?

Beorn's murder was to cause the Godwin family great strain. Harold's stroke may have been induced by a brother who was a defiler of nuns, a kin killer, and a general bad boy. The consequent search and exhumation of his beloved cousin and reburial of his body could have seriously affected Harold. If he had become ill late in 1049, or early 1050, he would still have been youthful enough to be the 'vigorous young man' referred to in the *Haroldi*. And the timing of events correlates with the idea that it might have been out of thanks for Edward's naval assistance that Emperor Henry sent Ailard to help heal the sick Harold, whom Edward loved dearly.[42]

Strokes were not at all uncommon in these times, and at least five are recorded in this generation. King Harthacnut, Osgod Clapa, Earl Godwin, his son, Harold, and King Edward himself all suffered. Physicians clearly knew about these attacks that caused paralysis, and the effect on the body and mind. Being fit and having age on his side, must have helped Harold heal, however stress can increase blood pressure even in the fittest. The blood vessels become weaker and the risk of a stroke higher.

The *Waltham Chronicle*, states that Harold was at the height of his power when he decided to found his collegiate to show his gratitude to God for his recovery.[43] With this in mind, we could tentatively propose a date around late 1049 to 1050 for his illness. The healing may have lasted months before he had recovered fully and was back fighting fit to face the coming storm of 1051. However, we cannot conceivably rule out the date of his illness as being anywhere between 1044 and 1051, but the events prior to and proceeding Beorn's death, may conceivably have contributed to the stress that possibly induced Harold's stroke.

Harold was as devoted to the Holy Cross as Tovi the Proud had been.[44] His creation of a collegiate of secular canons began a new phase in the church's history. He based his idea on a community centre of education, where priests could live close to the populace they served. The priests would hold their revenue in common and share a refectory close to their church. They would live by a regulated rule drawn up for their guidance begun on the Continent in the eighth century.[45] The rule was disseminated via the council of Aix-la-Chapelle of 816 but England lay outside the regions that it affected, so it was little used. However, there was a copy of an adapted and enlarged *Regula* which was kept at Winchester, translated and used more extensively throughout England in the eleventh century to control secular clergy.[46]

Harold may also have visited Lorraine when he was abroad and travelling around the Continent, coming into contact with some of the churches who were using the enlarged *Regula* and whose discipline he was said to have greatly admired. Therefore, it is understandable that he wanted to instil the principles of the code into his own enterprise and it was from Lorraine that he recruited some of his canons. It was not uncommon for great land magnates to want to fund a religious foundation. Around the same time that Harold began building Waltham, King Edward was also rebuilding the church at Westminster as his memorial and resting place. Perhaps Harold, not wanting to seem as though he was competing with the king, thought to create something almost as worthy but with a difference, and in expanding the collegiate, he was providing a training ground for priests and clerics, who would not only serve him personally, but the parish communities too.

The chronicler gives us the names of some of the clerics, each of whom were paid a prebend of 40 shillings a year. There was a dean and twelve canons. They included the aforementioned schoolmaster, Adelard, who had studied in Uhtrecht. Harold may have been impressed when the Lothringian cared for him throughout his recovery and invited him to establish the regulations similar to the rule in Lothringia for Waltham. The dean was named Wulwin, which was sometimes written as Unwin. His ownership of estates diverged from that of certain other canons due to his distinct responsibility for the provision of hospitality. Some of these estates he held from Harold himself.[47] Another was Turkill who died when he was 80 or 90 in 1125. Two more canons are named from Harold's time, Osgod Cnoppe and Æthelric Cildemæster who went with Harold to Hastings.

The *Regula*, we are told by the *Waltham Chronicle*, insisted on a communal life with the canons dining and sleeping together in dormitories, though they might be allowed, bishop permitting, to live in houses, *despositos mansions*, within the church precincts.[48] Meat was included in the food allowance which was provided for from the several farms that surrounded Waltham. Values such as faith, love, and chastity were encouraged, and the leaders of the community were expected to lead by example as the local bishop's representative.[49] Although the canons might be given houses in the precinct, women were not officially permitted into the enclosure at any time. But rules as we know, are meant to be broken and often were. By the mid-eleventh century, the marriage of clerics had become widespread. Even Master Adelard had a son called Peter, and he didn't do that by himself. When something is legislated against, it generally means it was a thing, and Peter was proof that marriage among the clergy was present in the community.[50]

The canons were to be sufficiently knowledgeable in the gospels. Their duties were to instruct the community in divine law and reading law: *lex divina; lectio divina.* The rule demanded good behaviour; conduct was to be orderly and reverent, especially during the services of the church, such as when singing the psalms. A disciplinary code was also supplied. This included verbal reproach, minor physical chastisement, or harsher penances. Frustratingly we don't know the details. For those who committed more serious disobediences, we know that there were severe punishments: deprivation, flogging, or even worse, excommunication.[51] To be excommunicated was to be cut off from the community you lived in, losing your religious privileges. The fear that you could die without the last rites and absolution, buried in unhallowed ground, would have been the worst anathema ever to a believer.

As a patron of the collegiate, Harold would have had a say in how the school was run and most likely held regular inspections when home. The dean and the schoolmaster, and canons, however, were the ones in charge. They would have prided themselves in running a tight ship. Though, where the married canons were concerned, Harold may have been lenient. The lands endowed to the church itself were plenty enough to pay for the upkeep of the canons and the schoolboys as well as giving arms to the poor.[52] According to the foundation church's charter given to them by King Edward in 1062, Tovi the Proud had already endowed upon them a closely populated group of estates carved out of the forest of Waltham: Loughton, Alderton, and Kelvedon, documented as *Chenlevedene,* in old English, and should not be confused with the Essex Kelvedons which belonged to Westminster. Outliers, Lambeth and Hitchen, were manors that Æthelstan had lost and were endowed upon Harold.[53] Harold would go on to donate a total of thirteen estates to the new establishment worth £43 a year.[54] He also donated rich gifts, many of which he brought back from his trip abroad to St. Omer and to Rome in 1056. There were many chalices, candlesticks, censers, crosses, richly embroidered vestments, and twelve statues of the apostles to support the front of a golden altar with lions to support the rear. Watkiss and Chibnall explain in their translation of the *Waltham Chronicle* in more depth how the lands and the manors were organised to provide for the religious community of the collegiate. It is worth reading.

Boys could enter the collegiate at Waltham at the age of 5 as the anonymous author of the chronicle in 1124 had done. Once the pupils had finished their education, they could take priestly vows at the age of 21 as did Adelard's son. Peter was also to become a school master like his father. Many books were stocked in the library, and went back to the early days of the collegiate's foundation. Certainly, some of the books on medicine were attributed to Adelard as well as a commentary on Quintilian. If Harold wanted to have an exciting adventurous read, there were also other volumes such as Vergil's *Aenied* and a substantial number of books by Ovid among other writers such as Horace. According to the author, the daily regime was strong discipline for the boys who were required to walk, stand, read, and sing in a becoming, dignified manner. It is poignant, though, that he remembered his time as a child at Waltham as a happy time. He speaks of Wulwin the Dean, who must have been a young man when appointed, and schoolmasters, Adelard, and his son Peter. He talks of the elderly sacristan, Turkill, whose tales of 1066 he recounted, including a story of when the head of Jesus on the Holy Cross was said to have bowed.

Waltham was not the only church that Harold had an interest in. A great man would need to curry favour with the church as a whole, as his contemporaries, earls Leofric, Odda, and Siward had also done. Not only was it necessary to show piety, it was absolutely vital that one atoned for one's sins, and being a serial benefactor of churches was one way of getting into Heaven. Some of the religious foundations that Harold patronised were Durham Cathedral, for whom the clerks recorded an obit in their *liber vitae,* and Peterborough Abbey who recalled his patronage fondly. He and his father were also known to have campaigned against Bishop Herman from drawing Malmesbury Abbey into his diocese of Ramsbury as his seat.

Many well-to-do English women were renowned for their embroidery skills. It is pleasant to imagine that Eadgifu and her eldest daughter Gytha, spent many nights, creating her husband's war-banner, made with gold thread and embedded with jewels. Eadgifu may also have contributed to the making of the canon's vestments and other valuable textiles lavished upon the Church of the Holy Cross. As Harold's wife, living nearby in Nazeing, she certainly had an interest in contributing to such an important institution, considering that had it not been for the powers of the Holy Cross and God's divine intervention, she might have lost her husband to the paralysis illness. Her association with Waltham and its canons after Harold's death at the Battle of Hastings, shows that they were familiar with her and she them. She would have been grateful to have their assistance in bringing back her beloved Harold's body to Waltham, the place they both shared, and where they had once both felt safe together.

CHAPTER EIGHT

Swegn

Careless Whispers

No biography about any Godwinson could ever be complete without a chapter on Swegn. Not only was he integral to their story, he also played an important role in the background of the Norman Conquest. Swegn was quite active in the years leading up to the 1050s, but not in a positive way. Rather more black sheep of the family than shining star, his activities had an immense effect on Godwin's power, triggering the mechanism that would lead to the end of Anglo-Saxon England. Not only is Swegn's story entertaining, it brings home to us that the people who lived a thousand years ago were emotional beings no different from us. They loved, laughed, wept, and raged, and took risks in the same way as we do today. It also shines a spotlight on the fluctuating power of medieval kings who were not the all-powerful autonomous rulers people think they were. Often only as strong as their councillors allowed them to be, respect had to be earned. The issue here for Edward was that he was isolated, unlike Godwin, who was surrounded by his own flesh and blood. Collectively, their land and wealth combined with his made him the most powerful landowner in England.

Swegn, firstborn son of Godwin and Gytha, received his earldom in around 1043. Born somewhere around 1023 or 1024, his age at this time was 19 or 20. He signed his first royal charter as earl in 1044 and signed consistently from there on, indicating he was at court often before 1046 when his career nosedived. He signed once more in 1050, but only after a series of events that contributed to him being outlawed, declared *niðing*, and exiled again.[1] If John of Worcester was correct that Swegn's great-grandfather was Urso/Beorn, the brother of Cnut's father, Sweyn Forkbeard, he may have been named for his great uncle.[2] The thing about Swegn was that whilst all his siblings seem to be leading exemplary lives, Swegn definitely was not. The *Vita* hints that he was the 'gulping monster'.[3] How else would you describe the anti-social, narcissistic tearaway in your family, the eleventh-century equivalent of a modern-day gangster? Had he been alive today, he would probably have ended up serving time in Wandsworth for murder, kidnap, rape, and probably drug dealing.

Grills refers to him as having inherited a wild streak from his Scandinavian heritage and compares his impulsivity with that of his Uncle Ulf, who, like Swegn, seems to have had trouble controlling himself.[4] On the other hand, he does bear a striking similarity to his hot-headed English grandfather, Wulfnoth. The author who coined the phrase 'gulping monster', does not mention him by name, unless he was dealt with in the missing chapter ii, which is thought to have focused on the children of Godwin.[5] The original author's poem that follows Osbert St. Clare's insertion on page 15, speaks about the 'four guarantors of England's peace' with Edith first and foremost among them, 'gem-like on the kingdom's breast', leading her siblings, out into the realm to 'stir the earth's recess and nourish the estate of men and beasts', all as one from the same womb. These four 'ample streams' can only be the first of the brothers, excluding Swegn the black sheep. They are described as one, working together for the good of the land. Then 'one part' of the 'one' is depicted as climbing the skies to the heavens and there nurtures its 'race's hope in a treetop nest'. The other 'part' becomes a 'gulping monster' seeking the depths, attacking its 'parent trunk'.[6] Barlow clarifies the mystery of this passage in the *Vita*, and identifies the gulping monster as Swegn.[7] The rest of the poem is ambiguous, it's passage, difficult to discern. The meaning may allude to Swegn's abduction and rape of an abbess and his begetting a child upon her and also the murder of Beorn, his cousin. We shall not know for certain its secret.[8]

Regardless of Edith's reservations about her troublesome brother, at some juncture in his tumultuous life, Swegn demonstrated that he possessed the capability to conduct himself as reasonably as anyone else. At least he did what was needed to gain the respect that would see him sashay into his first appointment as earl. Swegn inherently leaned toward his mother's Scandinavian roots, alienating himself from his English roots. He was certainly adept at seafaring, as was his father and had been given charge of a fleet Edward had mustered by Edward in 1045 against an anticipated invasion by Magnus of Norway. The expected assault turned out to be a no-show, thanks to his cousin Swein Estridson, who had been keeping Magnus busy in Denmark.

Swegn Godwinson may have had another string to his bow, moving in the realms of trade, he may have sold both innate objects and human merchandise. Bristol lay in his sphere of influence, and he may have taken advantage of the slave trade to increase his income. Though there is no evidence of any of the family being involved in trafficking people, during the crisis of 1051, he was to offer his brothers Harold and Leofwin a ship already rigged to escape to Ireland where he may have had links to markets in Dublin.[9]

Swegn's preference for his Scandinavian roots emerged at an early age. Rumours about Swegn's parentage appear to have arisen not long after Cnut's death when as an adolescent he may have first heard them.[10] Such a rumour would have come as a huge shock to a young impressionable lad stumbling across careless whispers spoken in the shadows. Whatever the circumstances, these sad revelations could not have come at a worse time for a youngster trying to find his way in the world and a period of pre-teen tantrums and pubescent acting out may have proceeded. Hopefully, a gradual, none-too-painful, settling down period arrived, inspired by the loving reassurance of his parents. It must have been with great relief to his family that Swegn was able to turn things around. However, unknown to everyone, these events were a mere prelude to the troubles that lay ahead.

Denies Parentage

Being invested with such a key role as the new lord of Hereford, Somerset, Gloucestershire, Oxfordshire, and Berkshire, Swegn grew in confidence – and, unfortunately, arrogance. His earldom contained the parts of Wessex often disputed over by Mercia, the latter shire mentioned above being the birthplace of Alfred the Great.[11] Gloucester, formed from the tribes of Magonsæte and Hwicce, had previously been sub kingdoms of Mercia. It is likely that Leofric, earl of Mercia, was not particularly happy about Swegn's takeover of the lands that had once come under his jurisdiction. It was a difficult area to manage because of the constant incursions by the Welsh, hence Cnut had appointed such lords as Eilaf, Hakon, and Hrani under Leofric. By this time, Eilaf and Hakon were gone. Leofric was probably expecting his experienced son, Alfgar, to be appointed to the lands they had vacated. Earl Leofric, however, was a member of Mercian nobility, and not one to make a public spectacle of himself. He does not seem to have openly objected to Swegn's advancement over Alfgar.

It is conceivable that Swegn did not initially receive the full extent of the area he would eventually come to manage. As Uncle Eilaf's lands lay in the region Swegn inherited, it is possible, that he was sent to him for fostering as a boy, earmarking him for a piece of land to manage under the tutelage of his uncle. But Eilaf did not hang around for long after Harold Harefoot became king, and Swegn's foster-ship may have transferred to Hrani, who was then earl of Hereford. It may be that initially, Swegn was given the jurisdiction that had belonged to Hrani on his demise, somewhere in the early 1040s.[12] This would have prepared him for his future career as an earl.

By 1043, Swegn was in full possession of the shires of Hereford, Gloucester, Somerset, Berkshire and Oxford, inherited from the Danish earls. Having kept out of trouble, everything seemed to be going swimmingly until something triggered Swegn to repeat the allegation of his mother's infidelity.[13]

Hemming's cartulary is a combination of charters that reveal despoilers of the church in Worcester in the eleventh century. It gives us a glimpse of Swegn's character and conjures up scenes of a young, impressionable Swegn, egged on by a group of young males, possibly the sons of Cnut's Danish landowners. Clutching their mead horns they gather round him. Swegn, a lofty, gangly-limbed, long-haired youth, smiles arrogantly and boasts, 'I swear to you, it is true. I *am* the son of Cnut.' The alehouse rings with raucous laughter as the self-styled son of the old king, impiously regales his friends with a story of his mother's love affair with the Danish king. Cnut, he assures them, could not keep his hands off her. In a series of lustful trysts, the result is a child, Swegn. After several rounds of tongue-loosening mead, and goaded by his companions, he hinted to the young men he hopes to impress that it is *he* who should be king and not the old fool currently on the throne;[14] a treasonous statement, worthy of execution.

Naturally when Gytha heard of this, she was not amused. Incensed by her son's behaviour, she denied his lies on oath before a council of noble women that both she and Godwin were Swegn's natural parents.[15] Swegn's strategy to endear himself to the young men commended to him might have worked, but he seems to have become obsessed with his new identity.[16] There may have been rumours when they were both young that Gytha was the young Danish king's lover. Of course, there is every likelihood this was not true, but like many rumours of a similar trend, people find reasons to believe them – the 'no smoke without fire trope'. The aforementioned story of the daughter born in 1012 and drowned in 1020 appears to have preceded the finding of the child in the coffin buried under the altar. There is no proof that this child was related to Cnut or Gytha. We only have the legend and the possibility that the coffin contained the child who was said to have drowned at Bosham and was Cnut's daughter. It does not necessarily follow that Swegn was also Cnut's son. However, it is often difficult once started, to stop rumours from spreading and if it was known that Gytha and Cnut did indeed have a daughter who died before she met Godwin, then it would have been difficult for members of the community to ignore rumours that Swegn was Cnut's son.

Other historians have stated that this could have been anti-Godwin sentiment, possibly used by the Normans to discredit Harold Godwinson at the time of the Conquest. But this also brings up the question that if this was so, surely Harold would have been the son at the centre of the scandal and not Swegn?[17] There are many ways anyone might have heard the gossip. A flippant remark that Swegn resembled Cnut more than he did Godwin possibly followed by another casually spun line that he *was* rather unlike the other Godwin children, therefore the rumours must be true. There are plenty of scenarios to invent if one is imaginative enough. Perhaps Cnut lodged Gytha in Bosham with his daughter because he needed a quiet hideaway for his mistress and child – somewhere he could meet with her and no one might ever know? Whatever the case, it may have been no more than hearsay, but whatever the story, it was enough to have convinced Swegn, and once in his head and out of his big, boastful mouth, it got him the attention he craved.

Despite his mother's denial and his father's continued support of him, there were, according to Frank Barlow, certain aspects that pointed positively to him being the son of Cnut. His name, for example, ran in Cnut's family; his behaviour among the Godwinsons was that of an outsider; his exclusion from the *Vita*.[18] Barlow also adds that if Cnut had been Gytha's lover, it explains the favours granted to Godwin and his speedy rise to fame.[19]

Lie or no lie, the situation cannot have sat easily with Gytha. Her son accused her of adultery with the former king, blackening her name and insinuating her husband was a cuckold. But would she have admitted it if the tale was true? It seems reasonable enough to believe that innocent or not, she was unlikely to have admitted to being guilty, even on oath. There was always the confessional to absolve one's lie. If one was wealthy enough, then souls could be saved by paying the right amount to the church.

But there is one theory that we should explore, for if Cnut, wanting to promote a loyal and competent man, and at the same time, rid himself of a difficult issue, Godwin may have been the perfect fall guy. Cnut already had two demanding women in his life, would he have been able to cope with one more? Did he approach Godwin and make him an offer too good to refuse, and was a pregnant bride a small enough price to pay for lands and wealth beyond Godwin's imagining? It is possible that Godwin did not know she was pregnant with Cnut's child. His love for Swegn never wavered no matter what the boy did. He had brought Swegn up as his own, and whether the lad was his or not, his actions concerning Swegn are those of a loving father. On the other hand, perhaps he *did* know, and had entered into a deal with Cnut. He would have to accept that there maybe those who would wonder about his first-born's parentage and was willing to bring Swegn up as his own child. Pride, then, would likely have been a factor in his attitude toward Swegn. As Barlow states, eager minds can never determine the truth. But we can speculate.

Gytha's dirty washing aired in public must have been difficult for the whole family. Edith, as queen, may have been the most embarrassed by it. That there must have been tension between mother and daughter shows when her name is also omitted from the *Vita*. Harold, quiet on the subject, later showed his disgust for Swegn when he refused to give him his land back. But how did he feel about Godwin's rampant support of the errant Swegn when he had so defamed him? How did he feel as he resided in his own earldom, playing the dutiful son, knowing that his brother was getting away with such hideous behaviour against his father for whom the sun shone out of Swegn's backside? The clues may come later.

Abducts an Abbess

Despite his outburst about his parentage and all things considered, a summary of Swegn's first three years in office, seems to show that he did remarkably well.[20] He managed his territories and attended court without so much as putting a foot wrong… Until 1046.

Earlier it was mentioned that something triggered this behaviour and although pure speculation, it may have had something to do with a love that was either denied, thwarted, or unrequited. John of Worcester gives us a hint of this when he reports that Swegn had wanted to marry Eadgifu, the abbess of Leominster, whom he debauched for a year.[21] He does not say anymore on the matter and gives little context to the statement. No other chronicle mentions him wanting to marry her or that he kept her for a year, rather that he kept her for as long as it suited him, then let her go.[22] The idea that Swegn was the sort of chap that could fall head over in heels in love doesn't necessarily fit the image we have of Swegn in the chronicles. Through his deeds, it is much easier to picture a wild Viking type, taking advantage of any beautiful woman he could lay his lascivious hands on. Of course, it may not have had anything to do with love, but more to do with getting those same dirty digits on the abbey's extensive lands, as if he did not already have enough with several counties under his control. But if Eadgifu was an abbess who had taken vows of chastity, what made Swegn imagine he could permissibly marry her?

Ann William's explains the distinction between how a Benedictine house and that of a minster, were run. The two houses were rather different. Leominster was not Benedictine. Minster clergy were often married, though usually it was male clergy married to laywomen. This was very much frowned upon by the church hierarchy, especially the Benedictines who were connected with the king. Minsters were commonly linked to influential local families, who inserted their own kin to manage them. This is likely the case with Eadgifu, though we have no idea which important family she was connected to. Many minsters collapsed during the tenth and eleventh centuries as their communities dwindled. Such defunct houses of religion were picked up by the bishops of Worcester. In other cases, the lands would revert to the lay patrons, which is possibly what happened at Leominster. If Eadgifu was a member of the patronal family, put in office by her kin to manage their investment, Swegn marriage to her would put the lands at his disposal.[23]

Based on this evidence, it is not impossible that Swegn and Eadgifu had met prior to the incident and may have had a previous dalliance. Eadgifu may have been fostered in Godwin and Gytha's household, and perhaps that was how they met. A suitor of Swegn's rank would have needed to ask permission from the king. It could be that the couple had asked if they could marry, but Eadgifu's family, having inside knowledge of Swegn's character, may have forbidden it and sent her to the abbey to keep her away from him.

Swegn was not the first noble youth to have abducted a nun. Æthelwold, youngest son of King Æthelred I, had abducted and married a nun in 899 against the wishes of the king and the bishops. Like Eadgifu, she was a nun of a minster, namely Wimborne. This may have been to strengthen his claim to the throne, but who she was is not known.[24] King Edgar also seems to have had a penchant for nuns, two perhaps, cousins Wulfhilde and Wulfthryth, the former having to escape his charms through the abbey sewer and the latter who did not escape. She became the mother of his daughter Edith and the young, murdered Edward the Martyr.[25]

The story goes that whilst Eadgifu was cloistered away in her minster, carrying out her duties as the abbess, Gruffudd ap Rhydderch, King of the Deheubarth, had been raiding Swegn's borders for some time and Swegn, on behalf of his own king, had been ordered to act decisively against him.[26] Swegn may have known that Gruffudd ap Llywelyn, King of Gwynedd, had ambitions to be king of all of Wales, and Gruffudd ap Rhydderch was a powerful lord that needed dealing with if he was ever to achieve his desire. Joining forces with Gwynedd made perfect sense. It was not unusual for the English Marcher lords to collaborate with the Welsh to rid themselves of their mutual enemies.

The raid into Deheubarth was more of a success for Swegn than it probably was for Gruffudd ap Llywelyn, who had hoped to slaughter Rhydderch so he could take Deheubarth for himself. The incursion into South Wales that took place in 1046, did not see the end of Rhydderch, that would come later. Nonetheless, it showed him the power of Gwynedd's might, and Swegn's lands benefited from giving the Welsh a good kicking.[27]

Swegn returning home with his warriors, elated, full of bravado, and trailing cartloads of loot, passed by the village of Leominster.[28] Perhaps memories of a girl he once loved pricked at his heart, which was often hard as stone, but on this occasion, soft as melted butter? Did he think of Eadgifu, who he had once been set on marrying? Was his resolve determined by the realisation that he was doing the king's bidding and yet not permitted the girl he wanted as his just reward? Perhaps drunk on pillaged mead, the resentment grew until he made up his mind to call at the abbey and take what he deserved.

Problem was, he picked the wrong abbey, for it was none other than Earl Leofric, and his wife, Godgifu, who patronised the abbey. No doubt this was not pleasing to Leofric, whose son was overlooked for Swegn.[29] But Swegn did not give a fig who the abbey's patrons were and what was to follow would set the whole of his family on a course that would have disastrous consequences for the future.

Only the Abingdon version of the *ASC* gives us an account of the event:

> Here Earl Swein went into Wales, and Gruffudd, the northern king, (of Gwynedd) together with him, and he was granted hostages. Then when he was on his way home, he commanded that the abbess in Leominster be brought to him, and kept her as long as it suited him, and after let her travel home.[30]

Abbess Eadgifu does not appear to have figured in any other narrative of the time until her kidnap.[31] As the daughter of nobility, it was common for wealthy families to promise their daughters to the church. The abbey's lands were quite extensive as eminent historian Sharon Bennett Connolly explains: Swegn, unhappy that his income was not sufficient enough for his needs, thought to expand his lands by wedding her.[32]

Ann Williams, also agrees that it was possible that Swegn wanted to benefit from attaining control of her lands.[33]

In what order Swegn had asked permission to marry her, before or after he had kidnapped and seduced her, is not known, but the outcome was that Edward refused him.[34] The information we have from both the *ASC* and *Chronicle ex Chronicis* is that, suddenly, out of the blue, Swegn Godwinson took it upon himself to abduct a religious woman on a whim. His actions may have been impulsive, for he must have known that his rash actions were not going to impress anyone, least of all the king, and then as an afterthought, he made his application to marry her. Of course, Edward said no, he was pious enough to understand that as an abbess she was already married to Christ and could not be wrought asunder from her vocation.

Swegn, however, might well have been impetuous, but he was not stupid. It seems more likely that he and Eadgifu had known each other prior to her abduction, and that they had already been denied marriage. Taking all this into account, it makes more sense that her kidnap was much more than an opportunistic act of madness. John of Worcester seems to have believed that the young earl loved her enough to risk his life and his earldom for her.[35] Some were not as empathetic to Swegn as John of Worcester was. Hemming stated that Eadgifu was forcibly kept against her will, which is also the version that we also read in the *ASC*. It should be noted that Hemming was writing forty years after the event and Worcester some sixty plus years later than that.

The chronicles disagree with how long Swegn hung on to Eadgifu. Hemming stated that Swegn kept her for a year before allowing her to travel home, and that he let her go due to the threat of excommunication by bishops Lyfing and Eadsige.[36] This is, however, problematic, as Lyfing was dead by March 1046, before the raid on Deheubarth with Gruffudd ap Llywelyn and Eadsige was out of action at the time through illness.[37] Knowing what we do of Swegn, it is hard to imagine that he would let a little thing like excommunication stop him. Nonetheless, Swegn understood he was going to have to let her go at some point but to have kept her for a year does not seem logical bearing in mind he was to spend the winter of 1046/47 with Baldwin V in Bruges and the following summer in Denmark with his cousin, King Swein.

Whatever the time scale, it was long enough to get her with child. The general consensus among historians agree that a boy named Hakon was the son of the illicit union between Swegn and the abbess of Leominster. No other woman is linked to him in the chronicles. Hakon was said to have been the member of the Godwinson family held as hostage in Normandy.[38] Another theory states that there was another Hakon identified as Swegn's son. The timing of Eadgifu's abduction appears to fit events more so than the other Hakon, who would have been too old to have been the son of Swegn.[39]

Considering Hemming was wrong about the bishops who were supposed to have threatened Swegn with excommunication, there is no reason to believe he was right about the length of time Swegn held on to her. However, if Eadgifu did go to Bruges with him, and was with him until he sailed for Denmark in the summer, it is possible that he left her behind in Flanders and arranged for her to be brought back to England by members of his family. There with Gytha at Bosham, she could have spent the rest of her pregnancy until the birth of her child.

Eadgifu's abbey was dissolved sometime after 1066. What happened to the abbess after her return to the monastery and its dissolution we cannot be sure, but the Domesday survey speaks of an abbess who had once overseen Leominster during the reign of Edward, living on land that was still part of Leominster's estate. 'For the nuns belonging to the manor of Leominster, for the abbess 1 free hide Fencote. The abbess held it herself before 1066. Queen Eadgyth held the manor of Leominster of 80 hides.' Other historians have agreed this was likely to have been the same Eadgifu as there is no other abbess of Leominster recorded in Edward's reign.[40]

Cousin Swein

Meanwhile, Gytha's nephew, Swein of Denmark, had thrown in his claim to the Danish crown, but the Danes plumped for Magnus instead. Disappointed but not defeated, Swein Estridson decided to submit to the king of Norway along with his countrymen.[41] Though obviously pleased with this result, Magnus thought to test his loyalty by making him jarl of Denmark.[42] Swein was not like his impetuous namesake Swegn Godwinson, he knew when to pick his battles. Now that he was in a position of power in Denmark, he saw his chance and audaciously took the Danish crown at Viborg during an assembly of free men where important political decisions were made.

It was not long before an angry Magnus was on his way to Denmark, baying for Swein's blood. Swein fled to Sweden, where his cousin, Ánundr, was king.[43] Whilst at the Swedish court, Swein joined forces with Harald Sigurdson, Magnus' uncle.[44] Magnus sensibly broke up this alliance by offering Harald half his kingdom. Swein was left severely in the lurch. A year later, the determined Swein returned with a fleet raised in Skåne. Magnus was fighting the Slavs, as Swein sailed into Denmark with his new fleet. As soon as Magnus could, he headed for Denmark, where he defeated Swein, and punished the disloyal Danes by burning their lands.[45]

Whilst his cousin Swegn Godwinson was engineering his own self-destruction in England, Swein realised he was in a precarious position having to fight both combined forces of Magnus and Harald. Godwin distracted himself from his errant son's problems by wholeheartedly supporting his wife's nephew, suggesting to the *witan*, England should send fifty ships to Denmark's aid. Godwin must have been the only one who felt it was in England's best interests to keep Swein afloat, for his battle with Magnus was what was keeping him from attacking England.[46] But Earl Leofric, leading the council, opposed it, and King Edward agreed.[47]

His cousin's predicament came at a fortunate moment for Swegn Godwinson, for his days in England were numbered, and wanting to intervene before Edward exacted some severe punishment on his son sent Swegn to Baldwin V of Flanders, with money to fund a fleet of ships and crews to assist his cousin in Denmark. In Bruges he spent the winter doing as his father suggested, gathering ships and *lithsmen* to sail with him to Denmark to join his cousin's fight against Magnus. Whilst in Bruges, who should also appear with the same idea? Osgod Clapa. Osgod would have undoubtedly made a good drinking partner whilst they wintered in Bruges.

Denmark

Swein Estridson must have looked forward to the arrival of Swegn and Osgod Clapa with their contingent of Flemish mercenaries, however, there was a terrible cold spell in the new year.[48] This was to hold up Swegn's and Osgod's expedition to Denmark and it was not until the summer before the two men could come to Estridson's aid. Unfortunately, when it did come, their arrival was too late. Magnus had defeated Swein's forces and driven him back to Skåne.[49] Shortly afterwards in October 1047, Magnus died. This was fortunate for Swein, for Magnus held his opponent in high esteem. He was said to have confided in his step-brother, Thor, that Swein should succeed him in Denmark, not his uncle Harald, though the latter should have Norway.[50] Harald was accepted in Norway and offered a treaty of peace to Edward in return for not intervening in his conflict with Swein. Despite his nephew's wishes, Harald was not giving up on Denmark.[51]

Swein was enthusiastically proclaimed king by the Danes in Zealand and in Viborg in Jutland, and immediately found himself again threatened by Harald who quickly resumed hostilities.[52] In 1048, Estridson resumes his entreaties for help from the English and again, Uncle Godwin failed to avert rejection. Harald's peace treaty with Edward had been a sneaky move on the Norwegian ruler's part.[53] Edward now had a good excuse for refusing anymore future requests from Swein. Edward's fears about Swein may also have deepened. Should Swein ever succeed in beating off Harald, Edward may have seen him as a threat. The young Dane was of Swein Forkbeard's bloodline and was English born. Some might say he had a strong claim. Edward deliberated with his advisors and agreed that England should not be drawn into a costly foreign fight.

Swegn Godwinson seems to have found a place where he was wanted for a while, with his cousin in Denmark helping him fight Harald Sigurdson. Things in the northern European sphere were about to change in 1049 that would complicate things for Swegn and Osgod. When conflict broke out on the Continent, Estridson and Edward became allies of Henry III against Baldwin of Flanders. Both responded to Henry's call for assistance in the North Sea, and the king of the Danes swore on oath to become the emperor's vassal, therefore under Henry's protection.[54] This must have had an impact on Harald of Norway, for now at least. If he was to attack the new state of the Holy Roman Empire, it was possible he would feel the full weight of the emperor's might on him.

Estridson's oath to the emperor had improved his situation, but Swegn's had worsened. He had gathered a ship army of Flemings with the help of his friend Baldwin, whose family had ties of friendship with his own that went back to the days of Swegn's grandfather Wulfnoth and Baldwin's own father and namesake, Baldwin IV. Swegn is noted in the *ASC* as returning to England in 1049 after he had 'ruined himself with the Danes'.[55] This turn of phrase suggests that Swegn had caused some other scandal in Denmark, however it is more likely that his position there was now untenable due to the fact that his paymaster, cousin Swein, was now an enemy of his patron, Baldwin. Osgod was likely to have been in the same position and it is doubtful the Flemish mercenaries brought to Denmark with them to fight for Swein, would want to stay.

So the saga of Swegn Godwinson, the gulping monster and black-sheep of the family does not end here, in fact we are only halfway through the scandalous tale of Swegn Godwinson and the affect it had on the whole family, for what Swegn did next was to set England on a path that would eventually bring about the end of Anglo-Saxon monarchy.

CHAPTER NINE

Storm Winds Gather

Harold and Beorn were to benefit greatly from Swegn's absence. King Edward saw fit to share his lands between them, augmenting their own substantially with a portion each of Swegn's. It was another reason to irritate Leofric and Alfgar. But in 1049, Swegn was back with a small fleet he'd accrued in Denmark, possibly a mix of Flemings, Danish, and Englishmen who had followed him into exile. According to the *ASC*, he 'ruined himself' in Denmark, but give no detail. Perhaps he fell out with Swein by refusing to fight for him against Baldwin who had helped him out during his banishment, bearing in mind he may have had Flemings on board with him. Alternatively, he could have gone to Baldwin, but then he risked destroying any chance of worming his way back into Edward's favour whose relationship with Baldwin was not amicable.[1]

Sometime around the end of June, beginning of July 1049, Swegn and his seven ships, sailed into Bosham.[2] The estate had a fine, natural harbour, and was the safest place to hide and moor a small fleet.[3] He'd been away for almost three years, and hoped that dust had settled over the incident with Eadgifu. Perhaps greeted frostily by his mother, he met the son he had fathered on the hapless nun for the first time. Eadgifu, however, had gone back to her abbey. It is not hard to imagine a fraught homecoming for him. Things had no doubt been a lot calmer in the Godwinson household without Swegn. Certainly, Gytha must have had reservations, as Godwin was not there to keep him in check, for he had spent the first part of the summer with the king in Sandwich, where Edward had assembled forty-two ships. The conflict with Baldwin had come to an end, and had been a game of scare tactics, with the emperor and his allies marching on Bruges and Edward, building a reputation as a competent sea commander, conducting manoeuvres to prevent Baldwin from escaping.[4] Edward's sea-faring activities in the chronicles, though not detailed, show a competent leader who was very much at home with the fleet.

Swegn left his ships at Bosham and travelled over land to find the king in Sandwich.[5] Gaining himself an audience, the wayward Godwinson humbled himself and begged Edward for land to maintain himself. Chronicle *E* states that he 'makes peace with the king and was promised all of which he formally possessed'. It is possible the king was willing to accept him back into the fold, as his effective alliance with Gruffudd ap Llywelyn had been a buffer against the incursions of Gruffudd ap Rhydderch over the border.[6] The problem was Harold and Beorn. They had made it quite clear that they were not prepared to give back anything of Swegn's that had been given to them by the king. There was no love lost there for the wayward brother and the consensus of the chronicles was that Edward had no choice but to ask him to leave. He was given four days to get back to his ships.⁷ The *C* chronicle is harsh toward Swegn and intimated that he had premeditated malice.

The *E* chronicle reports that no sooner was Swegn on his way than thirty-six ship loads of Hiberno-Norse, appeared in the River Usk and raided Deheubarth.⁸ Gruffudd ap Rhydderch, rather than be their victim, joined forces with them, suggesting they help him invade England. Together they stormed into Gloucestershire, burning down Tidenham.⁹ On the other side of England, after the conflict with Baldwin was over, Godwin sailed from Sandwich to Pevensey with forty-two ships commanded by Harold and Tostig.¹⁰ Although *C* and *D* do not mention the Irish raid on Wales, they report that messengers inform the king that Osgod Clapa lay with twenty-nine ships at an Island north of Bruges. Edward had just disbanded the Mercian ships, and now, expecting an attack from Osgod, Edward calls back as many ships he could and set them at the 'North Mouth' in East Kent.¹¹

As there often is, there are disparities between the chronicles. Curiously, *E* talks about the western raids but does not mention the incursion by Osgod and both *C* and *D* fail to mention the attacks from Ireland. *E* curiously mentions that Earl Beorn came and took over Harold's command. This may have been because Edward had allowed the Mercian *lithsmen* to go home and sent Harold into the Wantsum to guard his east coast against the exiled Osgod.¹² When Osgod got wind of Harold's presence in Essex, he took six of his twenty-nine ships to Bruges to deposit his wife there, and the rest went to raid in Eadulf's Nest.¹³ John of Worcester states that he took 6 of his ships, 'turned back and went to Denmark'. The rest, hit a strong wind on their return, destroying all but four of the ships and drowning many of their crews.¹⁴ Osgod is not heard of again until his death is recorded in the year for 1054.¹⁵

Meanwhile, Godwin, Tostig, Beorn, and the Wessex fleet, were weather-bound at Pevensey. Without any help from Edward's fleet, and no earl to lead them, Bishop Ealdred took on martial responsibility for the southwestern provinces and gathered the *fyrds* of Hereford and Gloucester to oppose the Hiberno-Norse and the Welsh. But among these troops gathered by the bishop, were Welshmen who were supposedly loyal to the English. These crafty Welsh betrayed them by letting Gruffudd know where they were.¹⁶ Ambushing them very early in the morning of the 29 July, they killed many 'good men'. Bishop Ealdred managed to escape with those who survived, realising that a strong, warlike commander such as Swegn Godwinson was what was needed to keep the area safe from Rhydderch's increasing encroachment of English lands.¹⁷

Back in Pevensey, two days after the strong winds that had stopped Godwin and Beorn's progress west, Swegn turned up unexpectedly and spoke with his father. How Godwin responded to his son's sudden appearance is not known. What they discussed is not known either, though *C* hints that Godwin and Swegn were plotting against Beorn. After speaking with his father, Swegn then approached Beorn to see if he would ride as his companion to Sandwich to plead with the king once more.¹⁸ Considering Beorn had only recently refused to support him, he must have been reluctant, but eventually agreed. After all, he had known his cousin all his life, and knew that Swegn could be unstable at times. That day, something about Swegn's demeanour must have worried him, so he took with him three of his companions.

Somewhere along the way, Swegn turned them around, suggesting they go to his ships at Bosham first, rather than to where the king was. He claimed that he was worried that his crews would abandon him if he did not return soon. Beorn was apprehensive, confused, and hesitant, but once more put his faith in the fact that they were kinsmen. At Bosham, Swegn tried to persuade Beorn to go on board his ship with him. Beorn refused. Swegn then ordered him bound and thrown into a rowing boat. He was taken out to Swegn's ship, and forced aboard against his will. Hoisting their sail, they then put out around the coast to Axmouth. The *C* chronicle states that Beorn was conveyed to Dartmouth and there said to have met his death, and 'buried deep'.[19]

What Swegn's intentions had been with Beorn on ship has never been made clear. John of Worcester states that Swegn cunningly asked Beorn to travel with him to Sandwich to plead for him to the king.[20] Chronicles *D* and *E* are not as harsh as *C* which suggests that Godwin was implicit in Beorn's death. Adam of Bremen adds fuel to the theory that Godwin was plotting to destroy Swein Estridson's chances of claiming the English throne by doing away with his supporters in England. Coupled with the fact that it was also Bremen's belief that Edward had made Swein his heir, the theory is interesting if not compelling.[21]

It seems implausible that Godwin would advise Swegn to murder his cousin. Godwin appears to have thought of Beorn as a son, bringing him up with his own boys, doing much to advance his career. His killing would serve neither Swegn nor Godwin anything useful. Beorn was well liked by the king. Godwin was more likely to have advised Swegn to ask Beorn for support rather than kill him. No doubt Swegn could be persuasive when he wanted, playing the victim to accrue sympathy. But his erratic behaviour on the journey must have unsettled Beorn, rousing his suspicions to the point that when they arrived at Bosham, he had endured enough.

The three companions that Beorn took with him were left on shore so they could not interfere. Worried for his safety, they sent word to Harold who left what he was doing to search for Beorn. Harold was able to locate Beorn's body, dug it up, brought him to Winchester, and gave him a prince's burial next to his Uncle Cnut.[22]

ASC D continues in more detail. After Beorn's death, Swegn's men mutinied, leaving him with only two vessels and their crews. Hastings local militia captured two of his ships and had the crews put to death before bringing the ships to Edward at Sandwich. Then at an assembly of elite huscarls the king had Swegn officially declared a *niðing*. It must have been an awkward experience for Harold, having to witness his brother being denounced.[23] It would be difficult for Swegn to come back from such a situation. This adopted Scandinavian term of abuse was absorbed into English use from Scandinavian settlers and meant that a person who was given the status of *niðing* was nothing more than a vile coward, an outlaw to be killed on sight. The *wergild* laws were laid down to ensure that the victim's kin were allotted justice, and the family of the culprit shared the shame and was liable for restitution as much as the perpetrator. It was also the obligation of the victim's family to demand justice.[24] With this in mind, it is hard to imagine what Swegn had to gain from killing him – Beorn was not only his cousin, but also the brother of the king of Denmark. Retribution would be a high price financially, physically, and socially. But this was Swegn Godwinson: impulsive, impetuous, and imprudent. Nothing about Swegn ever made sense. Some have thought it was an accident and that Swegn had no intention of killing his cousin. If he had intended to kill him, he could have done so at Bosham and not waited until he had got him miles out to sea. Both Hubert Grills and Tom Licence suggest that Swegn was going to hold him as a hostage.[25] The fact that he left the other men on shore as witnesses to his capture, indicates a lack of intention to kill his cousin. The most favourable scenario is that when Beorn was brought on board a heated argument got out of hand, ending with his death. Swegn may have been trying to coerce Beorn into declaring an oath of loyalty to him, thinking this would put him in better stead with the king. When he wouldn't swear, Swegn snapped and killed him. It is also possible that Beorn was killed unintentionally in a struggle.

After his crime, Swegn realised his number was up, but he was not going easily. After burying Beorn's body in a church grave, he fled to Flanders where once again, Baldwin gave him sanctuary.[26] Harold's refusal to support Swegn must surely have dismayed Godwin, who had forgiven the prodigal son and wanted him reinstated. He may even have blamed Harold for Beorn's death; after all, if Harold had agreed to help Swegn, the incident with Beorn would not have happened. This attitude would have driven a Swegn-sized wedge between Harold and Godwin which is why, perhaps, later in 1050, Harold appears to be silent when Bishop Ealdred returned with him from Flanders. Was Godwin trying to make up for Swegn's troubled childhood by making sure he was there to fight his corner every time he needed him? Was Godwin motivated by guilt for not being Swegn's biological father, and having lied to him about his true parentage? Or was he simply doing for Swegn what he would have done for any of his children? Sadly, we shall never know.

The Calm

Swegn was now living miserably in Bruges under Baldwin's protection, constantly looking over his shoulder in case he should bump into a disgruntled member of Beorn's Danish family.[27] Swegn had plenty of time to ruminate on his murderous rampage and reflect on his bad behaviour. Back in England, the death of Beorn must have strained relationships with Denmark, leaving Godwin's dreams of an Anglo-Dane alliance well and truly in pieces. Could he ever look his nephew, the Danish king, in the eyes again?

Not only does Harold seem to have distanced himself from his brother's behaviour, but also his father, who was still pushing for Swegn's re-instatement. Harold had acted quickly in searching for Beorn, hoping to find him alive. His actions sent a message to all that he was disgusted with Swegn and wanted nothing to do with him.

The year of '49 was not yet over but it was at least peaceful with Count Baldwin V of Flanders having signed an agreement with the Holy German Emperor Henry III. William of Normandy had sought an alliance with Baldwin of Flanders by seeking to marry his daughter, Mathilde. At the synod, Pope Leo forbade this marriage.[28] He also criticised the marriage of Eustace of Boulogne to Goda, Edward's sister, though on what grounds it is not specified.[29] It appears that Eustace had taken the pope's criticism to heart and Goda was said to have returned to England around 1049, bringing her youngest son, Ralph, by her first husband, Drogo de Mantes. Goda seemed to have lived quietly upon her return to England on lands given for her use by her brother. Historians have been at odds with the date of her death for which 1047 has been mentioned as well as 1056. Her husband Eustace married again in 1049 to Ida of Lorraine.[30]

Despite the incursions that occurred in that year of 1049, Edward and his advisors started to think about getting rid of the foreign standing fleet which had cost the country a pretty penny since arriving with Harthacnut. It was at the mid-lent council that they discussed paying off nine of the fourteen ships and keep the rest on a year's contract only.[31] They still kept the regional ships that were commanded locally.[32] It was Earl Leofric of Mercia who had led the *witan* against sending out ship-aid to Swein in Denmark and it was likely he would have agreed to defund the standing fleet now there was no longer a threat to England's shores. She had been groaning under the burdensome yoke of the *heregeld* since Edward's father had introduced it forty years previously. Godwin, for whom the sea had been the mainstay of his wealth and power, was probably astounded by Edward's dismissal of the fleet which had been at his disposal at times when it was needed, but seems to have acquiesced as he was more concerned with winning the king over in the matter of son Swegn's return, an act that would seem even more extraordinary than the loss of the fleet.

Swegn Returns

John of Worcester stated that Swegn had remained in Flanders until Bishop Ealdred brought him back and 'reconciled him with the king'.[33] The *ASC* does not mention Ealdred, but John's narrative fits the idea that he may have stopped in Bruges on the way back from the synod of Rome in 1050. Ealdred's motivation for doing so would no doubt have been to solve the issue of the safety of the Marcher Lands along England's borders with Wales.[34] The bishop of Hereford, Æthelstan II, had been blind for seven years and so the defence of the town fell to Ealdred who was currently the bishop of Worcester. Whatever anyone thought of the wayward, Swegn, he was an effective warlord. Ealdred's persuasive skills were successful, and the king was convinced to have Swegn back.

Swegn, according to Ealdred, was now a contrite, remorseful man, who had, before the bishop would agree to bring him back, confessed his sins with full and honest regret.[35] Swegn had also revealed to the the bishop his intention of making a pilgrimage to the Holy City of Jerusalem to atone for his sins. One can imagine a few eyebrows raised in response to that piece of news as well as the appearance of a few flying pigs. Edward reinstated Swegn in the West Country, also setting his nephew Ralph and his fellow Norman retainers, Osbern Pentecost, Hugh, and Richard FitzScrob to build castles in Hereford.[36] Soon, not surprisingly, Swegn would be at odds with them.

Harold was no doubt astonished by the king's approval of Swegn's return and must have wondered what his unruly brother had to do to be removed permanently. It wasn't murder or the rape of a nun, that was clear. Perhaps Harold had been persuaded by his father to show a united front as a family, for there were other problems brewing at court with Godwin unwittingly cultivating himself a new enemy in the shape of the new archbishop of Canterbury, Robert Champart. If we are to agree that this may have been the time when Harold experienced his stroke, it could have been that he was lying too ill at Waltham unable to object to Swegn's reinstatement.

Robert Champart

Archbishop Eadsige of Canterbury had been ill for some time and had passed away in 1050. Canterbury was the highest see in England and Eadsige had been in the seat for twelve years. As Canterbury was now part of Godwin's jurisdiction, the earl took an active interest in its wellbeing, ensuring that during Eadsige's illness, he had someone act for him. In 1048, Eadsige had to come out of retirement and return to his duties, as Siward, his temporary replacement also fell ill and not long after passed away.[37] This left a vacancy and it had been common practice that the monks of the cathedral of Canterbury would nominate their choice to the king. This time their nomination just so happened to be a relative of Godwin's, a man called Æthelric.[38] In what way they were related it is not known, but Godwin was keen to advocate for his kinsman. Edward on the other hand, had other ideas.

In 1051, sometime during the mid-Lent *witenagemót*, Edward shocked everyone by announcing that his good friend and favourite, Robert Champart, had been elevated to the role of archbishop of Canterbury.[39] Godwin and the monks of Christ Church were furious. A robust discussion about Champart's lack of qualifications compared to Æthelric's broke out in the volatile atmosphere of the council chamber. Æthelric had been brought up in the cathedral priory since a child and was a competent, hard-working officer who was highly regarded by the monastic chapter.[40] But it was no use. Edward's mind was made up.

Robert Champart, or Robert de Jumièges, as he was also known, became the first Norman archbishop of Canterbury. The *Vita* instructs us that he came to England in Edward's entourage.[41] Previously he had been abbot of Jumièges, and before that he was a prior at the Abbey St. Ouen in Rouen. Edward appointed him as Bishop of London in 1044.[42] With his close friend and advisor in the highest ecclesiastic see in England, Edward had effectively created for himself a buffer between him and the Godwinsons, giving Edward a powerful devotee to call on if he needed support against Godwin. At this point, Edward would not have been happy with a kinsman of Godwin's in that role, no matter how clever or pious the man was. The whole debacle of Swegn, Godwin advocating for a connection with Denmark, and demanding earldoms for his various sons and kinsmen had jaded Edward. Godwin always got what he wanted, but this time it was to be the last; his precious, murdering, rapist son, was reinstated. The king's respect for Ealdred persuaded him to allow Swegn back in office, but relationships with the Godwinsons would no longer be convivial. Even his wife was on the way down, and had not signed any royal diplomas since 1046.[43]

But it was not just Godwin that Edward was trying to break free of. Edward's confidence was growing, and he was doing his best to make his way as king in his own right. Some believed that he was now under Champart's thumb. Malmesbury held that Robert had a magnetic influence over the king, and it was said by one chronicler that if Robert said a crow was white, Edward would have believed him.[44] But he would soon prove them wrong when his newly appointed archbishop refused to consecrate Spearhafoc, (Sparrowhawk) as bishop of London.

The tale goes that Edward's goldsmith, Spearhafoc, appointed as bishop of London in Robert's stead, had been supplied by Edward with enough gold to commission him to make a beautiful imperial crown, which was probably indicative of how Edward was coming to see himself. Upon Robert's return from Rome where he had gone to receive his pallium, Edward suggested he consecrate the goldsmith as the new bishop of London, but Robert declined, stating that Pope Leo had forbidden him due to an accusation of simony. If Spearhafoc had bought the London Bishopric, then the pope can only have found out about it from Champart himself. Edward was not happy. He was not going to back down and insisted that his new Bishop of London stay in his position, which he did throughout the spring, summer, and autumn.[45]

Robert Champart was soon to turn his attentions on reform toward Harold's father. His dislike of Godwin was so malevolent, deeply rooted from the moment he stepped onto English soil and met the man. Godwin's manipulation of Edward was no doubt distasteful to the archbishop, who craved control of Edward himself. Champart started to investigate Godwin's church properties, and his questioning of the earl was to bring the two men to each other's throats.

As the *Vita* tells it, many good things and bad were done by Robert's counsel in the kingdom with varying result. According to Edith's scribe, using his position as archbishop, Champart intruded 'more than was necessary in directing the course of the royal councils and acts; so much so that through his assiduous communication with him, the king began to neglect more useful advice'. It was also implied that because of Robert's poor guidance, the king offended quite a number of the nobles of his kingdom, 'disturbing the peace of the realm'.[46] Having satisfied his ambition of attaining the highest honour possible, the new archbishop 'began to provoke and oppose the earl with all his strength and might'.[47]

The feud became a vendetta in which Robert set about the destruction of Godwin with as much determination as he administered his role as archbishop of Canterbury. First, he accused the earl of acquiring land that belonged to Christ Church. We are reminded by Grills in his book about Earl Godwine, that Eadsige had turned to Godwin in his time of illness for help. It may be that Eadsige had gifted Godwin some land in return for his assistance. The acquisition of church lands was not something peculiar to the Godwinsons either. Leofric and his wife, Godgifu, known as Lady Godiva, his brothers Godwin and Edwin, his nephew Ælfwine and even his young grandsons Edwin and Morcar do not pass scrutiny when it came to acquiring lands.[48] Siward, earl of Northumbria, and his son Waltheof also were accused of cheating the abbey of Peterborough. Even the pious king and queen were not innocent, having attained the lands of Leominster and Berkley as their own.[49]

In the case that Robert brought against Godwin, the *Vita* concedes that the bishop held the right of it, but we are not told what the outcome of the land disputes were. Rather, however, the book concentrates more on Godwin's reaction to the barbs fired at him by Champart. The archbishop hurled accusations at the earl that he had injured him by invading his episcopal lands and keeping them for his own use.[50] Godwin, we are told by the author of the *Vita,* endures the abuse peaceably and waits patiently for things to die down. In the meantime, we are advised that

Godwin's servants are not happy with the treatment measured out to him by the archbishop and would have attacked the archbishop with terrible insults if Godwin had not forthrightly forbidden them.[51]

It seems that Godwin played a clever game, for his conciliatory inaction probably made him look more like the good guy than Robert did with his mad ranting and raving.[52] Edward refused to make Godwin give back the encroached upon lands. Robert was furious and upped his game. According to the *Vita*, Robert began his operation to annihilate Godwin. And so, the devious archbishop convinced the king that Godwin had been guilty of the crime of murder against his brother, Alfred, and was now plotting to end the life of himself. Robert continued to press upon Edward the veracity of this matter, and eventually the king was to 'give more credence to this than was right'.[53]

Eustace of Boulogne

Eustace of Boulogne, also known as aux Grenons, or Eustace with Moustaches, was the ruler of the county of Boulogne. He was not on the best terms with Baldwin nor William of Normandy, though he was to fight on the duke's side in 1066. Eustace was also Edward's brother-in-law, the once husband of his sister Goda whom he had been forced to repudiate in 1049, and was unlikely to have been well-disposed toward Godwin as he had supplied Alfred, Edward's brother, with men from Boulogne on his tragic trip to England in 1037. This was a factor that may well have some bearing on the next phase that was to lead to the invasion in 1066.

At some point in 1051, Godwin successfully negotiated the marriage of his third-born son Tostig to the half-sister of Baldwin V, Judith. This would have strengthened the old alliance with Flanders that Godwin's father had started with in 1009 with Baldwin IV and it was just as well, because it would not be long before they needed it.[54] According to the *Vita*, the events that lead to the family's exile began on the evening of Tostig and Judith's wedding.[55] Baldwin had been stacking up allies. Given that the emperor and he had renewed hostilities, Baldwin hurriedly negotiated three weddings in quick succession. The first was in 1049, uniting Flanders with Hainaut by marrying his son, Baldwin to the widow of Herman de Mons. Baldwin's daughter Mathilde had been promised to William of Normandy around 1049/50 and despite the pope's opposition, the wedding had gone ahead anyway.

Judith was related to Edward through her mother, Eleanor. If Baldwin thought that by marrying her to a son of the leading earl in England was a way in with Edward, he was sadly mistaken, for the Godwinson's fortunes were about to go very awry.

It is not known whether or not Edward had given permission to Godwin for Tostig's marriage to Judith, but it is doubtful that he would have been happy about Godwin entering into a union by marriage with his enemy. Despite Champart's attempts to bring Godwin down, the earl was still standing, and Edward may have begun to wonder who was king in England. Robert may have intuitively picked up on Edward's irritation at Tostig's marriage to Baldwin's sister and found Edward suddenly more pervious to deadly whisperings about the death of Alfred.

The *Vita* especially believed that the archbishop was plotting against Godwin, but exonerates Edward from any involvement, as naturally he would, given that he was writing the book on behalf of the queen. He puts the blame for what happens next on Robert but leaves out the Dover incident and Eustace of Boulogne's part in it and concentrates on Champart's accusation of Alfred's murder. We find the absent evidence in other sources such as the *ASC* and John of Worcester. *C* mentions it briefly without any detail of the Dover incident, making the statement that the family was put to flight adding only that Godwin escapes to Bruges with three of his sons and Harold and Leofwin to Ireland. *E* and *D* discuss Dover in more detail, as folows.

Eustace of Boulogne makes a sudden appearance in England, his arrival from across the sea coinciding with the feud that was going on between Edward's leading earl and his archbishop. This came soon after Archbishop Robert returned from Rome, St. Peter's feast, 29 June.[56] Frustratingly, the chroniclers leave us to our imaginations, stating only that the count visited Edward, spoke with him about what he wanted, then went homeward. They stopped at Canterbury, and he and his men had a meal before heading back to Dover where they intended to stay overnight and embark for home the next day. The *E* chronicler makes a point of stating that before they arrived at Dover, they stopped and put their mail on, as though expecting trouble. As they entered the town, they started making demands on the householders to give them lodging. When one of the householders refused, Eustace's man wounded him. The householder retaliated and ended up killing him.[57] The chronicle then states that when Eustace heard of this, he mounted his horse and rode to the house where his man was killed, entered the home, and killed the culprit at his own hearth. The French then went on a rampage, killing nineteen people and wounding several others.[58] Eustace escaped with a 'few' of his men, suggesting that he lost quite a fair amount himself. He travelled with haste back to the king and told a 'one-sided story' leaving out the fact it was his men who drew the first blood.[59]

The *D* Chronicle, giving a slightly more balanced account, states that 'great harm was done there on either side with horse and weapons'.[60] John of Worcester describes the attack far more colourfully:

> His (Eustace) soldiers, while they were bluntly and indiscreetly inquiring for lodgings, killed one of the townsmen. A neighbour of his witnessing this, slew one of the soldiers in revenge. At this the count and his followers were much enraged, and put many men and women to the sword, trampling their babes and children under their horses' hoofs. But seeing the townsmen flocking together to resist them, they made their escape, like cowards, with some difficulty, and leaving seven of their number slain, they fled to king Edward, who was then at Gloucester.[61]

The purpose of Eustace's visit was, as we have seen, only known by Edward and those privy to the meeting. The clue might have something to do with his stop in Canterbury, at the home of the Archbishop Robert, where it was said that Eustace had a meal on the way to Dover from the court of the king. Had the two men already met abroad in Boulogne on the archbishop's journey back from collecting his pallium in Rome? Had they discussed their mutual dislike of Godwin and Edward and Edith's childless marriage? And why did they put on their armour *before* entering Dover if they were merely innocently seeking lodgings for the night?

On the face of it, it appears straight forward. Eustace comes from across the sea, with no apparent purpose other than to visit his former brother-in-law the king of England.

He and his entourage, of which there were a tidy few, came with horses, armour, and weapons. They spoke with the king, and all seemed well, then they travelled back toward Dover where they had left their transport, stopping to have dinner in Canterbury on the way back. After this, they headed for Dover, and paused to put on their mail and arm up before entering the burgh. It is clear that whatever they had in mind; they were expecting trouble. The whole episode bears the hall marks of a plot.

The King's Wrath

Meanwhile, Edward had invited his nephew Ralph and some of his French friends to build a castle in Herefordshire, which lay in Swegn's province.[62] Swegn, as we know, did not need much provocation and conflict with Ralph was inevitable, for the French were inflicting 'every injury and insult upon the king's men thereabouts'.[63] Whether or not these events in Hereford and Dover were concurrently connected, we cannot be certain, however, the *E* chronicle stresses both events, and it seems were clearly aimed at demoralising lands owned by two members of the Godwin family.

Upon hearing Eustace's breathless complaints after his ride back to the court at Gloucester, an irate Edward summoned Godwin to him and demanded that for the crime of an unprovoked attack against his guests, he punished the people of Dover by razing the market town to the ground. This was the second time that Godwin had been ordered to destroy a town and this time was having none of it, for it was abhorrent to him to harm one of his own provinces.[64] This enraged the king who provided Eustace with an escort so they could pass unharmed through Godwin's earldom, and called an emergency *witenagemót*, the meeting of the council, for the 8 September. In the meantime, Godwin, called the burgesses of Dover to him and listened to what they had to say. The French, it seemed, had got to the king before they could put their side. Godwin became concerned that Edward was plotting something against him and sent messages to Swegn and Harold to meet him at Beverstone in Gloucestershire, and to bring with them many men, so they could travel safely to the council. The *E* and *D* Chronicles differ in tone. *E* appears to be showing the Godwins as the peaceful side, wrongly accused, merely seeking a solution to the issue and to put right any insult perceived. *D* and John of Worcester show them as the more forceful, stating that all three earls brought a great, countless army from all over their earldoms, armed and ready for war against the king if Eustace, his men, and those Frenchmen from the castle, were not transferred to their custody for justice.[65] John of Worcester reports that Godwin 'took it badly' that such an event should have happened in his region and was moved by great anger to gather a colossal army, demanding that Eustace and all his associates, plus the men of Boulogne who were 'holding the castle on the cliff top in Canterbury' be handed over to them.[66] The scribe of Worcester seems to have confused the castle with Hereford Castle built by Ralph de Mantes. Dover Castle was not built until after the Conquest.

A week before the meeting was set to convene,[67] the Godwinsons were advised that should they attend the council, Earls Siward and Leofric would take measures against them. Upon hearing this, although it was abhorrent to them, the Godwinsons reluctantly arrayed themselves as ready for battle.[68] Ralph, according to the *D* chronicle, was called out and also mentions that Siward and Leofric turned up with too few men, but as soon as they realised the urgency of the situation, they sent for more men from the north to support them.[69]

John of Worcester tells us that the terrified king trembled, not knowing what to do, but when he saw the armies of Leofric and Siward riding into Gloucester, enflamed and ready to fight for him, he was emboldened, and sent messages stating that he refused to hand over the French.[70] But as Leofric observed the size of the men facing each other on both sides, from all the nation, he thought it a folly to 'embark on a war with his compatriots'.[71]

Both the *ASC* and John of Worcester conclude that all involved needed to reconvene at a later date to give time for the tension to dissipate to a level of equanimity, realising that to enter into a civil war at that time would make England vulnerable to their enemies abroad. Harold was forced into a difficult position. Who should he support? The king or his father?[72] In this case, contrary to when he chose to not support Swegn, he opts to choose his bloodline.

On the advice, of his earls led by Leofric, Edward calls for another full council-meeting in London on 24 September, requesting that Godwin and Swegn should bring hostages to the next meeting.[73] John of Worcester also mentions that hostages were exchanged on both sides, however, Godwin's repeated requests for hostages in return are denied in *E*. It seems disingenuous to imagine that Edward – the king – would have given hostages to Godwin whom he was determined to bring to heel.[74]

Once in London, the king arranged for the militias of the home counties to be called out north and south of the Thames. The *E* chronicle describes it as 'quite the best (army) there ever was'. In the meantime, Harold and his family travelled to his father's manor in Southwark. When the time came, he and Godwin were summoned to court, but Swegn was excluded, and advised he was outlawed. Neither chronicle gives an explanation. It can only be assumed it was due to conditions placed on him for his good behaviour, negotiated by Bishop Ealdred on Swegn's return the year before. Fearing the worse, Godwin sent to the king asking for safe conduct and an exchange of hostages so they could come and go from the assembly safely. The king ignored the request and instead demanded that he resign all the thegns that were commended to both of them. Father and son did as they were commanded without complaint. The *D* chronicle mentions that Godwin had many men from all over Wessex, and that they began to desert him, worried that the situation was about to escalate into a civil war nobody wanted.[75] Messengers went back and forth across the bridge over the Thames where Godwin had arrayed his men on the south bank, and the king on the north. Edward demanded that they come to the council with twelve men, the number of men needed to swear on his behalf to prove him innocent of any wrong-doing. By ordering this, Edward was instigating trial-by-ordeal and Godwin, still apprehensive for their safety, repeated his request to be given safe-conduct and hostages so he might go without fear to clear himself of the charges. Godwin agreed to hand over his youngest son, Wulfnoth, and his grandson, Hakon, who were respectively around 12 and 5 years old. To the earl's fury, Edward handed over no hostages in return. Interestingly, Harold was not required to hand over his own hostage, which suggests that Edward did not view him as much of a threat as his father or Swegn. We know from the *Vita Haroldi* that he was much loved by Edward.[76] However, it may be that the sons of Harold were not at court or in the vicinity whilst it is likely the other two were.

Then Edward dropped the bombshell. Having refused Godwin's last request for hostages, Edward demanded that the troublesome Godwins leave the country. At least he had the grace to grant them five days protection to arrange their journey.[77] However, the *D* Chronicle relates that after all the thegns had been handed over to the king and Swegn had been outlawed, Godwin made the tactical decision to leave by night. He saw the way it was going and like his father before him, made the decision to flee before it was too late. The king summonsed the council again and declared Godwin and his sons outlawed. According to *Vita,* messengers had been sent across the bridge at Southwark to let the king know that Godwin was willing in every way to satisfy him that he was innocent of any wrongdoing. Bishop Stigand, who was mediating, managed to get a temporary 'ceasefire' so Godwin could counsel with his men.[78] The *Vita*'s account of the showdown in London is far more emotionally charged than the *ASC*. Archbishop Robert instigated the decision that the king came to by standing 'fiercely in the way of the earl'.[79] Tom Licence suggests that the king's fury with Godwin may have had something to do with Godwin's hypocrisy. After all, he had been able to act on the orders of Harold Harefoot, but when it came to it, not for Edward.[80] The king's decision to outlaw Godwin and his five sons was delivered by a 'sorrowful' Stigand, apparently weeping 'abundantly'. Godwin's only hope for the king's peace was 'when, and only when, he gave him back his brother alive with all his men and their possessions intact which had been taken from them'. Seeing his case was impossible, the earl 'pushed away the table in front of him… and mounting his horse rode hard for Bosham on Sea.'[81] John of Worcester reports that they readied a ship and gathered as much treasure as they could and steered her toward Bruges to seek refuge from that old friend of theirs, Count Baldwin.[82] Departing with them was also Tostig and Gyrth, and Tostig's newly-wed wife, Judith, who must have wondered about the family she had married into.[83]

Being driven into exile was not enough punishment for the archbishop, and he called for a 'large force' to pursue the earl and to slay him should he be caught within the boundaries of the kingdom. The fact that Godwin was not killed, sent him into a 'frenzy' and convinced Edward that he should banish Edith too.[84]

Earl Harold and Leofwin, travelled with haste to Bristol where Swegn had readied a ship for himself. Swegn, it seemed, had experienced an epiphany, and decided to sail with his father and mother to Bruges, perhaps with the idea that he would from there, travel to Jerusalem to atone for his sins. The brothers raced to the dock. Edward sent Bishop Ealdred, then bishop of London, in pursuit of them to stop them from boarding the ship.[85] The source ambiguously claims 'but they could not, or would not' (Ealdred and his men). What the king intended to happen to them must have been in line with what the king, according to *Vita* had for Godwin, but we cannot be certain whether they were to be brought back for execution or to be kept in custody. Whatever the aim, Ealdred could not bring himself to carry it out and let them go.

There was no hint that Edward was aware of any plot to cause the downfall of Godwin, or the furore that emerged as a consequence of Eustace's behaviour in Dover, nonetheless, there are instances that point toward a secret meeting between Eustace and Champart meeting both prior and after Eustace's visit with the king. If this was so, the conspiracy seems to have worked far beyond what they had imagined. It is quite possible that Eustace and his men had not expected such fervent reactions from the insulted townsmen.

Edward's anger at what happened in Dover, his lack of consideration for the people of the burgh shows a completely different side to the gentle, noble king as we have come to read about in the *Vita*. The problem appears to have been that neither the king nor Godwin were prepared to meet on the other's terms. Edward wanted to assert himself and bend Godwin to his will. The Dover incident may have triggered memories of what happened to Ælfhelm and his sons, and the treachery his father had faced was probably still vivid in his mind. For months he had been forced to stand by whilst a campaign to have him removed from power was waged against him. He could feel himself getting closer to the boiling pot than ever. It may have been that in Godwin's mind, Champart took on the identity of Streona and it must have terrified him as it had his father, that his sons would end up the way of Ælfhelm's.

Whilst Godwin trembled beneath the prospect of violence against his family, Champart was drip-feeding lies in Edward's ear, that Godwin was planning to deal with him in the same way he had dealt with his brother. It is within the *Vita's* narrative that we will find what might have been going on in the king's mind. Despite his fury in all its glory, Edward does seem to have desired an end to the dispute in a legal and dignified manner, and this is likely to have been where Champart needed to improve his strategy. Drawing on the death of Alfred, and Godwin's part in it, the archbishop goaded Edward into believing that Godwin, having done away with Alfred, was planning to do the same to him, adding the right amount of dramatic spice to inspire Edward to be more forceful against Godwin.[86]

Edward and Godwin's relationship, though not a shining example of friendship, had always been one of goodwill, solidified by the marriage of the king and Godwin's daughter. It looked as though he had forgiven Godwin's role in Alfred's death, and accepted his plea that he was simply acting on Harefoot's orders as any dutiful soldier would.[87] That Godwin was powerful, may have made it harder for Harthacnut to severely punish Godwin for the death of his half-brother, though not beyond his means as king. It is, however, important to remember that his position upon arrival in England was tenuous, being an unknown entity to the people of England. Nonetheless, the earl's gift of a beautiful ship, worth far more in monetary terms than Alfred's wergild, quickly placated Harthacnut. During Edward's days as Harthacnut's associate, he seems to have become trusting enough of Godwin to turn to him for guidance in those early days of his own succession. Would Edward have done so if he had really believed that Godwin been involved in Alfred's terrible torture and death?

For the next five years at least, their working relationship went well, with the advancements of Godwin's sons, and a daughter in the king's bed; at least until Swegn's bad behaviour impacted negatively on their relationship. By 1051, Edward's patience was running out with the Godwinsons. Did Edward now feel resentful toward Godwin for having foisted upon him, Swegn, seducer of nuns, trickster, and murderer. As said previously, the king seemed to have genuinely thought well of Harold. That Harold was now tainted by his association with his father and brother meant that he too would be outlawed as the rest of Godwin's sons were also.

The Archbishop's Madness

It was clear that even with Godwin outlawed, Champart was not going to stop. The writer of the *Vita*, claims that the archbishop had been driven to madness in his hatred for Godwin.[88] Being thwarted in his attempt to capture the earl, Champart turned his attentions to ridding Edward of his queen.[89] Shortly after her father's escape, Edith, was stripped of all her possessions and property and was sent in disgrace to Edward's sister at Wherwell nunnery in Hampshire with just one handmaid.[90] John of Worcester tells us that she was repudiated out of Edward's anger against her father.[91]

The *Vita* is more sympathetic to the queen. From Edith's viewpoint, it was Robert who had manipulated the king into getting rid of the whole family. In his 'frenzy' the archbishop was determined to see that not one member of the Godwin family was left by the side of the king. That even Edith, the queen, was separated from her husband exposed the extent of the hatred the archbishop had for the family, for it is clear, according to Edith, that Champart had well and truly poisoned her husband against them. Via the author, we are advised that the queen was sent away to ride out the storm until the crisis of that autumn had settled.[92] With great emotion and in contrast to the *ASC*, it was to the monastery of Wilton she was sent, where she had been educated as a child. Leaving the court with honours and an imperial retinue, 'but with grief in her heart', she entered the convent she had been brought up in, 'where for almost a year in prayer and tears she awaited the day of salvation'.[93]

The rise of this great earl had taken many years, and everything he had achieved was gone in a moment. The maelstrom that had brought Godwin and his family to their knees had started with Swegn, had reached its peak by 1051, and ended in such shocking, unexpected circumstances.[94]

CHAPTER TEN
A Small Matter of Succession

The Visit

The *D* chronicle is the only version of the *ASC* that mentions the visit by 'Earl William' (duke of Normandy) which followed the Godwinsons' ruin and exile in 1051.[1] He was said to have arrived from beyond the sea with a 'great troop of Frenchmen, and the king received him and as many of his companions as suited him, and let him go again'.

A similar record of this can be found in Symeon of Durham[2] and John of Worcester elaborates that the king entertained William and his friends and when it was time to return home, sent them on their way with plenty of valuable gifts.[3] 12th century, Norman writer, Wace, also records the visit without dating it, and states 'William was generous, and the strangers who knew him, cherished him much. He was very gentle and courteous, therefore king Edward loved him well; great indeed was their love, each holding the other his lord. The duke went to see Edward and know his mind; and having crossed over into England, Edward received him with great honour, and gave him many dogs and birds, and whatever other good and fair gifts he could find, that became a man of high degree. He did not tarry long, but returned into Normandy; for he was engaged with the Bretons, who were at that time disturbing him'.[4]

The Norman writers made much of the relationship between Edward and William as though they had an everlasting, undying friendship, forged when Edward was in exile. Wace employs such phrases such as, 'each holding the other his lord', to emphasise their closeness. This rather grandiose statement can only be considered a post conquest ploy, in order to hammer home that William's invasion of England was justified.[5] They are keen to portray William as Edward's close kinsman, that he knew the young duke well, and thought him the worthiest of all to be his heir. But until that meeting, if we are to believe it did indeed take place, the two men had hardly ever seen one another, if at all.

Edward had been 13 years old in 1016, when he made his final departure from England and travelled to Normandy for the last time. In 1035 when Edward was in his early thirties and had been living as an exile in Normandy for nineteen years, his second cousin, William, aged 7, became the duke of Normandy. William had been brought up by his mother's family, remaining in their care for most of his early adolescence. It is doubtful that Edward would have had time to forge any sort of bond with his uncle's son in the time he had known him. The boy was a mere adolescent in 1041, when Edward left Normandy and sailed for England, never to return.

But the opportunity arose in the year of 1051 for Edward to invite his cousin to visit. The threat of Godwin still loomed across the sea, and Champart still whispered in his ear about the succession and lack of an heir. Edward may have thought it advantageous to shore up his defences on the coast with one more ally. The business with the Godwinsons had been traumatic and psychologically waring, but without them, he may have started to feel alone, and perhaps, irritated by Champart's nagging. He might even have missed Edith's fussing, and her brothers' boisterous presence at court. And when all was said and done, Godwin had been like a father to Edward and Godwin's sons, his younger brothers. Feeling the loss, Edward may have looked back to fonder times in Normandy. He had grown up with his cousin, the deceased Robert, the new Duke William's father. The idea of having a close friendship with the son of the man who had been so kind to him, must have seemed appealing.

Some think that it was unlikely that William had the time to come to England, however examining the situation on the Continent, it was not totally impossible. Wace purports that he did come, but it was not for long, as he and the king of France were mutually engaged against Geoffrey Martell of Anjou, although Wace suggested it was the Bretons, not the Angevins who was troubling him.[6]

We can imagine the scenario of the duke's visit to England. Seeing the young William, Edward may have been reminded of the closeness between him and William's father. Feeling nostalgic and desiring a less lonely existence, the king endeavoured to instil a sense of kinship within his cousin. He may have established with him a brief friendship in the fleeting time he was in England. William, no doubt asked about his great aunt Emma, and enquired if she might join them. Emma, now in her sixties and eager to oblige, may have felt she had much to discuss with her great nephew over dinner, regaling him of her resentments toward Godwin. Not only had Godwin betrayed her, but he had also been involved in her son, Alfred's captivity and death. It is likely William was already informed of the way the Godwinsons had treated the king recently, this extra piece of evidence may have confirmed in William's mind that the Godwins were a thoroughly nasty lot. No wonder cousin Edward had wanted rid of them. The man who presided over this terrible family had also been the man who had supported the regime who had kept his cousin's throne from him for so many years. Of course, Emma would stay silent on her marriage to Cnut, which had forced Edward into exile. We cannot know, unfortunately, what was said and what was not on this visit, for there is no detailed record of the conversation. The facts, however, are open to conjecture, and this is obviously mine.

It can be argued that Edward's objective in inviting William to visit at this time was to win him over as an ally against any Flanders-backed Godwinson return, not to offer him the crown as William is said to have claimed.[7] Edward may have been pleased at the large force William had brought with him to England, for it would send a strong message to the Godwinsons and to any of their supporters in England, that Edward had the backing of both Normandy and Boulogne. Both shared the Continental coastline with Godwin's protector, Baldwin, and could, if necessary, create a 1049-style blockade against them. If Edward could negotiate a deal with William, he would be able to call upon both parties for assistance, giving him some security and peace of mind. Of course, William would need to tread carefully if asked to go against his father-in-law, Baldwin. However, there was no reason why the duke and Baldwin should not come to some arrangement that meant both sides could still act protectively toward their allies, without compromising the relationship between themselves.[8]

We cannot be certain what William may have made of all this, but the question of the succession may also have been raised. We will discuss this later. For now, as Wace suggests, Edward made sure his cousin was laden with hounds, birds, and other 'fair gifts', so we can only assume, that whatever happened, everyone was happy when it was time to leave.

The Norman Sources

In order to make sense of what happened in 1051, the Norman sources need to be studied in the context of whether or not the succession was discussed prior to Harold's visit to Normandy in 1064, and who with. No Norman sources prior to 1066 mention the visit, and just as important, none mention that Edward wanted him to be his successor.

Firstly, let us take a look at the *Carmen de Haestingae Proelio* by Guy of Amiens, the bishop of that place. It was Orderic Vitalis, an Anglo-Norman monk, who identified Guy as being the author of an unnamed poem about Senlac (Battle of Hastings) reviling Harold and praising William.[9] It was not until much later until 1826, that a German archivist came across the poem hidden between two manuscripts in the library of Brussells.[10] The *Carmen* was written in the first few months of 1067, and is probably the earliest account we have of the battle in support William's invasion.[11] Guy states that on the eve of battle, the duke, having heard Harold's message demanding he leave his kingdom immediately, sent an envoy to Harold with this reply:

> Fitting greetings O king, from the duke, whom you are forcing unjustly to do wrong. And this is so, because as many bear witness – and the duke himself maintains – King Edward with the assent of his people and the advice of his people and the advice of his nobles promised and decreed that William should be his heir, and you supported him. The ring and sword granted him, and, as you know, sent to him through you, stand witness to this...[12]

This is the basis upon which William and the Normans literally make their claim. Strangely, though, the *Carmen* does not mention any visit to England where Edward and William discussed the succession.

William of Jumièges, writing after Guy in 1070, also in support of the conquest, was the composer of the *Gesta Normannorum Ducum* (The Deeds of the Dukes of Normandy). He had initially finished this chronicle in 1060 which he had started in the 1050s, based on that of an earlier writing by Dudo of Saint-Quentin. When Duke William became king of England, Jumièges brought his *Gesta* up to the year 1070. He was not aware of the visit to England either, but makes available circumstantial evidence that Edward and William communicated about the succession and that Edward also sent Archbishop Robert to William to confer that he should take the crown upon Edward's demise. None of this, however is dated.[13] Sometime later, in the 1070s, William of Poitiers revised Jumièges' work with embellishments, adding that Robert brought with him the sons of Godwin and Swegn as hostages as proof of Edward's commitment to him.[14] Jumièges does not mention the hostages and Poitiers makes no mention of William's visit to his cousin Edward in 1051. Both are out of kilter with Guy of Amiens who simply mentions that it was Harold who came with sword and ring to confirm Edward's wishes.

Tom Licence examined the writings of these scribes and explored Poitiers' deviation from the earlier source of Jumièges and its relation to the *Carmen de Hastingae Proelio*. As we have already mentioned, Guy has Edward sending Harold to him with the gifts of a ring and sword. Historians mostly agree that Harold's visit to Normandy took place in 1064. The Norman sources claim that Harold was purposely sent by Edward to Normandy to confirm on his behalf, the earlier pledge made to him through Archbishop Robert. We see this on the Bayeux Tapestry. And we also have an account by Eadmer which tells the story of Harold's trip to Normandy from the English perspective also matching the Bayeux Tapestry. Eadmer's account will be discussed in chapter fifteen.

The *Carmen* is the earliest and first recorded mention of the promise and the only contemporary one that refers to Harold as the messenger. As we have no other evidence that Harold had travelled to Normandy more than once, we must accept that this was the occasion that Guy is referring to. Therefore, it is worthy to note that the first account in support of William's invasion and subsequent conquest, included no visit by the duke in 1051 to England, and no discussion about the succession until Harold arrived on William's doorstep thirteen years later. This visit in 1064 took place only three years before Guy of Amiens writes his *Carmen* and was at its freshest in the minds of everyone involved.

Poitiers, however, contradicts *Carmen* by replacing Harold's ring and sword with the hostages brought to Normandy by Archbishop Robert which, if we accept, was somewhere between 1051/1052. We know that the hostages were in Normandy when Harold visited there in 1064. In that case, Poitiers must have heard about the hostages from another source other than Jumièges. Like Guy, Jumièges does not mention the hostages at all, suggesting he followed Guy's narrative. It has been proposed that Poitiers, desiring to reinforce his benefactor's claim that Edward had appointed him his heir, felt that the story of the hostages was a far more solid argument than the sword and ring, despite these items being symbolic of kingly regalia.[15] However, a hostage pledge could be seen as a firm commitment that Edward was staying true to his word, and that he had the backing of his number one earl of that time, Godwin. Whether or not Poitiers truly believed that Robert Champart took the hostages with Edward's agreement, nonetheless, it was used as Norman propaganda after the Conquest to impress upon any doubters that William had the right in the eyes of God to invade and take what he perceived to be his.

On the face of it, if Edward had offered the crown to William, he undoubtedly would have made certain that anyone and everyone would have known about it.[16]

The King's Marriage Problem

After the Godwinson's had fled England, Edward had to deal with the issue of a barren queen. The author of the *Vita* had been at great pains to present Edward's marriage to Edith as a vision of marital harmony. But this seemingly blissful marriage had deteriorated during the time of the crisis, and Edward's contemplation of a permanent separation was revealed. By including this in the narrative, the author of the *Vita* was willing to risk any previous announcements made that all was well within the relationship. Licence suggests that in that case, we should acknowledge the *Vita's* credibility as a source on the matter.[17]

The *Vita* does not mention that Edward was going to remarry. By sending Edith away, the king is clearly showing that he was giving it some thought. The author mitigates the seriousness of her banishment by insisting it was for her own safety and wellbeing, and that she should wait patiently at Wilton, where she had been brought up, for the storm to settle.[18] With this in mind, the author also hints that Edward was perhaps sending her away to appease the archbishop.

Of course, at this time, it was possible that Edward was being harried by his Norman clerics led by the archbishop of Canterbury, to remarry. The only course of action for a king who was putting aside his wife because she was barren, would be to remarry in order to provide the kingdom with an heir. So, it is not beyond the bounds of reality that at the time of William's visit, the succession of the crown was something Edward was indeed thinking about, and may have discussed with the young duke.[19] If he had been exploring divorce, he was slow in setting the legalities in place.

There are two issues here. Edward would have known that it was not in his authority to gift the kingship to anyone he pleased. He needed the endorsement of the *witan*, as had been demonstrated amongst all candidates for the throne throughout the eleventh century. Furthermore, it was usual that the heir would be selected from those designated æthelings, either a son or brother of a king.[20] William of Normandy was none of those things, furthermore, his bloodline did not link him to the House of Cerdic, a fact ignored by the Normans.[21] One is certain, it was never officially announced that Edward had decided to make William his heir. And unquestionably never before 1066.

Was Edward Looking for Another Wife?

Edward seemed to be in no hurry to divorce Edith. During William's English visit, there would be little point in a discussion of marriage within his family. Their bloodlines were too close and any marriages between himself and an accessible kinswoman of William's would have not been permitted by the pope. William himself had no available sisters, and his daughters were not born yet. However, it would not be preposterous to believe that the new archbishop of Canterbury would have wanted to see Edward divorced from the Godwinsons and allied with the Norman nobility instead, making the ties closer between Normandy and England. The probability of this is based on Champart's involvement in the Godwinsons' banishment. The archbishop may also have considered arranging a match with Boulogne. For much of the first half of 1051, he had been telling Edward that Godwin wanted to murder him.[22] Edward's reluctance to divorce Edith may have had to do with the fact that he could, when so desired, be both stubborn and bloody-minded, pushing back against his advisers. It is possible that he found Champart as deplorable as he had found Godwin. He may not have wished to remarry at his age and preferred to find a suitable heir of his blood. One wife had been enough; was it a 'better the devil you know situation'?

Norman sources, imply that Robert Champart arrived in Normandy to convey Edward's wishes to Duke William that he intended to name him heir to the English throne.[23] But the *Vita* claims that the archbishop of Canterbury was pushing for divorce, implying he had engineered Edith's banishment.[24] Edward would only agree to a divorce if he wanted an heir with a new wife. So, one of the aforementioned sources must be mistaken, the issue being that if the archbishop carried Edward's 'promise' to William is proof that Edward desired William as his heir, then the archbishop was going against Edward's policy of either getting himself an heir of his own loins, or one whose blood came from the House of Cerdic. So which strategy was the archbishop trying to apply? What was Champart hoping for? That Edward would remarry, and beget children on a new wife? Or that Edward would forgo the customs of the land and offer the crown to William who was not in any way linked to the royal family of Wessex.

And what did Edward prefer? Edward, aware his duty to England was to provide an acceptable heir, had already tried to get an heir of his own and failed. Was he privy to information that none but himself was aware of? He was a man in his prime by the time he married his much younger wife, whose family were fertile, she should have had no trouble getting pregnant. It couldn't have passed Edward by that he had never sired a child of his own in all the years he had been in exile. Many tend to think of Edward as this chaste and saintly man whose piety forbade him the sins of the flesh. Many of the men with the royal blood of Wessex were known to have been particularly licentious, a trait that Edward appears not to have inherited. It would be unusual if a young man in his position had not had a few fumbles before 40. If so, he may have realised that he was not going to sire a child with Edith or anyone else for that matter and that the best plan was to bring the readymade heir, Edward the Exile, home from abroad.

William's only connection to the crown was that his second cousin Edward, was wearing it. As a Norman, he had no direct blood link to England, and no land or other interests there. Furthermore, Edward knew that he had no right to gift the crown without the say so of the *witan*.[25]

The Blood of Cerdic

At this time, other candidates with much stronger rights to the throne than William had, existed. We do not need to look at Swein Estridson, for it is doubtful Edward or anyone else would ever have considered the Scandinavian bloodline now. There was Walter, Count of Maine, who later died, imprisoned by William in 1061.[26] He and his brother, Ralph de Mantes, were both sons of Edward's sister, Goda. Ralph married a 'Lady Gytha', who may have possibly been the widow of Tovi the Proud, and they had a son, Harold. There was also Gospatric, a great-grandson of Æthelred II. All of these were the progeny of Æthelred's daughters and granddaughters, and although they had the blood of Cerdic running through their veins, they were not the sons of kings and could not automatically be considered as ætheling, which meant 'throne worthy'. Lastly, there were the sons of Edward's half-brother, Edmund Ironside, Edward and Edmund whose bloodline came directly from the male line. Apparently, Edward was still alive and kicking in Hungary and married to a European noble woman called Agnes. He also had a family. Two girls and an infant son who may not have been born yet. Edward the Exile, along with his brother, Edmund, were said to have inherited their father's appetite for martial activities and had made names for themselves in Hungary as knights who supported Andrew, king of Hungary.[27] If Edward was in possession of information about his existence at this time, it appears possible that he would have considered the idea of bringing him to England, especially with Edith still childless. And even if she had managed to produce an heir, it was always a good idea to have a few worthy applicants to choose from, just in case anything went wrong with the first one.

Edward was no longer in his prime and heading for 50. The typical lifespan of a king in medieval times seems to have been around the mid-forties to mid-fifties, so if Edith were to become pregnant at that time, the heir, should it be male, would not be of an age to take the throne when his father died, that is if we stick to the law of averages. It seems to have been an issue with the kings of Wessex. Out of the sons of Aethelwulf, five out of six sons became king of Wessex. His eldest son Æthelstan became king of Kent under his father, but died before him. All of the subsequent kings after Æthelwulf did not have any issue until Æthelræd, his fifth son had two sons who were infants following their father's death, and so, Alfred, the youngest son of Æthelwulf being of age, was elected to take the throne instead of the infant sons of his brother. This was a perfect example of how, having as many heirs as possible in a time of high early death rates, need not be terrible, and could be useful. In the case of King Æthelræd II, he outlived many of his sons, but he still had Edmund (Ironside), Eadwig, Edward, and Alfred left to step into his shoes when he died, though it was only Edmund and Edward who eventually did. A search for Edmund's son, Edward the Exile and his family would prove expedient for England at this time, negating the need to wait for a child to grow up.

Due to complications with the conflict between the Hungarian kingdom and the Holy Roman Empire, it was not until 1054 that Edward was able to send enquiries abroad about Edward the Exile.[28] The decision to launch a delegation led by Bishop Ealdred to find the Exile, demonstrates that Edward was looking for an heir that shared the blood of Wessex. The eventual naming of the Exile's son Edgar as the king's heir begs the question: why would the king reach out to Hungary, if he had already designated William of Normandy as his heir, in 1051? The king would be breaking his own oath.

Edward's Intention

William's visit has been the subject of debate by several historians for years. As David Bates conceded, it could not have been for more than a few days and due to the lack of interest in most of the other contemporary chronicles, it does not appear to have been an official visit with the usual pomp and ceremony expected for something as important as the adoption of an heir to the kingdom.[29] It attracted even less interest in the chronicles than Eustace of Boulogne's trip, with only the *D* chronicle and John of Worcester laying claim to its existence. The Norman chronicles mention it not at all. The most likely scenario appears to be that if the visit did take place, and if the subject of the succession was brought up, it was by William, who was eager to learn what Edward's plans were and perhaps to offer himself as a candidate.[30] Edward may have been taken aback at William's presumptuousness and feeling compromised, searched his mind for a suitable answer that would not upset his guest whose assistance he was hoping for. Was it that William, eager to be considered as heir, and unable to read the room, took Edward's reluctant, bungled reply that he might consider him if no suitable heir appeared in the future, far more seriously than which it was meant.

The interesting thing is that William was never to claim that Edward had ever adopted him as his son, which he would have had to do if William was to be his successor. And never once did William claim himself as the ætheling. Wace's statement that 'there had been much love between them', seems like an overstatement, since William had been a mere youth in adolescence when Edward left for England in 1042.[31] There had been little chance for the two men form any bond of kinship or love.

So just what were Edward's intentions in those initial weeks that Godwin was gone? It would not be unreasonable to think that he had designs on remarrying, but by the time he had explored all available options, it may not have seemed so very attractive a notion. Initially, Edward reacted with rage over Godwin's refusal to bend to his will and may out of spite, stripped Edith of all her treasures and properties, and cast her out, sending her to Wherwell without honours. Other writers have suggested that when he had calmed down somewhat, he no longer wished to look for a new bride, and moved her to childhood home in Wilton, where she knew the sisters and would have better comfort.

It seems that Edward came to the realisation that he would remain childless and that out there across the sea, was an heir with a blood link to the royal House of Wessex, who would meet that criteria.

CHAPTER ELEVEN
Return of the Godwinsons

In Exile

Godwin and Gytha, along with sons, Swegn, Gyrth, Tostig, and Tostig's wife Judith, spent a dark, miserable winter in Bruges at the hospitality of Count Baldwin V. No doubt they worried about the welfare of their other sons, Harold and Leofwin under the protection of Diarmaid mac Máel na mBó, king of Leinster. They may have had word that their ship had been accosted by stormy weather and that there had been much loss of life. But perhaps they had not yet heard that their sons had survived and eventually made it alive to Dublin.[1]

Baldwin's attempt to intervene on behalf of the Godwinsons were ineffective. Edward's dislike of the count may not have helped the situation and Flemish envoys sent on their behalf returned empty-handed. Baldwin's plea to his wife's brother, Henry I of France, urging him to arbitrate with Edward, was also unsuccesful.[2] The author of the *Vita,* is emotional in his description of the reverence shown toward Godwin and his absence from the country, and considered his banishment a catastrophe for the country. Messages were sent abroad from Godwin's supporters advising that should he wish to return, they would be ready to receive him and fight for him, declaring they would die for him. The *Vita* states pointedly that these men openly proclaimed their support for him, hinting that some had followed him into exile. The author also stressed that Godwin's love for the king was such that he sent his own missives to the king, begging to be able to return, go before him, and lawfully purge himself of any wrong doings laid against him.[3]

But the pleas fell on Edward's deaf ears, whose mind was filled with the malice and intrigue of 'evil men'.[4] That aside, Godwin and his sons' exile had wrought changes in the kingdom. There would be a whole set of disgruntled magnates to contend with if he relented and allowed them home. Leofric and his son Alfgar would be none too happy, for Alfgar, who had waited a lengthy amount of time for his own earldom, now had East Anglia, which had been Harold's. Godwin's second son had spent years working hard to build good relationships among the region – and within it was the place where his wife and children had made their home, and where he had survived the illness that nearly took his life. Then there was Osbern Pentecost, a Norman associate of Ralph de Mantes. He now held the lands of Swegn along the marches in Herefordshire and had built the castle called Pentecost, then later Ewyas Harold after Ralph's son.[5] Bishop Ealdred took up a comital role in Gloucestershire and to Odda, Edward's kinsman, a promotion is awarded in Devonshire, Somerset, Dorset, and Cornwall,[6] leaving the rest of Wessex not held by Ralph de Mantes for Edward himself.

Return of the Godwinsons

Godwin's plea for peace was again declined, his only option was to plan his return by force. The once mighty earl resolved to win back his office, his lands, and his place at the king's side.

Harold and Leofwin had arrived in Ireland in the late autumn after a dangerous start, almost having been captured in a terrifying chase to Bristol to be finally let go by a guilt-ridden Bishop Ealdred.[7] They sailed out from the mouth of the River Avon, where they hit severe weather and many men were drowned. Whether or not the men in command of the ship were men that Swegn had employed for the voyage, or Harold's men is not known. They may have been recruited from the Irish or Scandinavian freelance sailors who hung around looking for work in Bristol.

Harold's recent acceptance of Swegn back into the fold may have been out of duty to his father, rather than forgiveness of Swegn himself. It is possible that Harold's errant brother and had connections in Ireland, and perhaps originally Swegn meant to travel with them. Dublin was a great trading destination, the slave industry being one of the major commodities that Swegn was possibly involved in. It is also conceivable that Earl Godwine also had links to Ireland from his days with Cnut.[8] Swegn's change of mind may have been spiritual. Perhaps Bishop Ealdred advised him that now would be a good time for him to go with his parents to Flanders and from there on to Jerusalem to carry out his promise of undertaking the pilgrimage he had promised when Ealdred had brought him back from Bruges. If he was ever to be rehabilitated, atonement might stand him in better stead than not.

The separation of Harold and Leofwin from the rest of the family, may have been indicative of how Harold felt about his father's favouritism toward the black sheep, Swegn. The fact that Harold and Leofwin were together shows a good indication that Leofwin was under Harold's mentorship. Though Harold remained loyal toward his father during the crisis of 1051, it does not necessarily mean that Harold was content with his father's blind defence of his wayward brother, and may have mirrored the situation in which he had grown up in. Godwin's denial of Swegn's inherent selfishness, the excuses he made for his son's violent, homicidal tendencies may have caused Harold to feel excluded from his father's affections. Harold would have been more directly affected by Swegn's behaviour than the others being closer in age. And after all, he had worked hard to build his reputation with Edward as his loyal representative in East Anglia. Edward's care and fondness for Harold when he was ill, demonstrated that the king greatly valued him. Now he was paying the price for Swegn's crimes. Harold must have felt isolated on that trip to Ireland with just a young boy to confide in. It had been Swegn who set the wheel of destruction in motion. Forced to leave behind his wife and his children, it must have played on his mind that his family was now at risk from whatever the vengeful bishop might want to do to them in order to punish him. Harold, no doubt, was determined to fight his way back home, with or perhaps without the father and brother who had cost him dearly.

That Harold was able to endear himself to the Irish king is evidenced when post 1066, the sons of Harold are given shelter in Ireland when they fled in the wake of the Exeter conflict.[9] Diarmaid had been the head of the Úl Chenneslaig and had allied himself in the 1030s with Donnchad mac Gilla Pátraic, the king of the Osraige, to consolidate his own position. Around about the same time, the Hiberno-Norseman, Echmarcash, became king of Dublin. At the time that Harold and Leofwin were under

Diarmaid's protection, Echmarcash was keen to capture the Scandinavian city of Dublin in the Fine Gall. Diarmaid took the city and kingship of Dublin by force in 1052 after some frantic fighting, and it is likely that Harold and Leofwin took part in the attack to repay Diarmaid for his seafaring and military aid when they return to England.[10] For Harold this would have been his first major, armed expedition, whilst Leofwin was to cut his soldierly teeth at the siege of Dublin. The experience both brothers would receive in Ireland would stand them in good stead later.

Back in England

Whilst the Godwin family was in exile, Robert Champart continued to snub the king on the matter of Spearhavoc's consecration. Edward's choice of bishop for London, continued in the post through to autumn. Both men had dug their heels in, neither giving way. Edward seemed determined not to go back to being ruled by anyone. Unfortunately, Archbishop Robert was also of the same mindset and had the support of the papacy behind him. At this rate, Robert was showing signs of becoming Thomas Becket's forerunner, the king was his good friend, but his loyalty was to God and the pope first.

But even Edward knew when he was beaten.[11] By autumn, Edward capitulated and expelled Spearhafoc from his position in London. Spearhafoc responded by permanently disappearing with the jewels commissioned to him by the king to make his new crown.[12] William the Norman, Edward's mass priest, a friend of Champart's, was ordained to Spearhafoc's post, suggesting that the archbishop was doing his best to make way for more Norman clergy to surround the king with.

On 6 March 1052, the old queen Emma died and was buried with her husband Cnut in Winchester. She was probably in her mid-sixties and had seen many changes and dangers in her life that was to end quieter than it had started out. With his mother gone, Edward was now bereft of any direct family in England, and without Edith, Emma had been the only maternal figure he had left. Champart had gotten his way with Spearhafoc, ridding Edward of the chances of a beautiful new crown and had been instrumental in his current isolation from his wife.

In the same year that the dowager queen passed away, the wily Gruffudd ap Rhydderch led his warband on raids through the Wye Valley and into Herefordshire.[13] Rhydderch, King of the Deheubarth, whom Ealdred fought with in 1049, pushed his luck and came almost as far as Leominster where the local levies were waiting for him. The D manuscript also mentions the French were with them, 'from the castle', possibly the men under Ralph de Mantes.[14] The Welsh managed to kill many English and French with some substantial losses of their own.

In the meantime, Edward's thoughts were focussed on the likelihood that Godwin would try to force his way back through hostile means. To combat the threat, the king stationed a flotilla of forty cutters at Sandwich to look out for and waylay Godwin.[15] Without the maritime skills of the Godwinsons and Osgod Clapa, Edward had no experienced sea-commanders and resorted to using his newly appointed western earls, Ralph and Odda. How good these two earls were at managing a fleet of warships is anyone's guess, there is no record of them being involved in any prior seafaring campaign, but the king was soon to find out to his dissatisfaction, the old adage that you don't know what you've got until its gone. With Ralph and Odda out of the way, the Welsh took advantage of Edward's decision to deploy his western earls elsewhere, leaving the military capability of Hereford poorer for their absence.[16]

Fight for Authority

It was just before the feast of midsummer's eve that Godwin felt it was time for him to test the water in England. He had spent the last months since arriving in Bruges making plans for his return, preparations that would have included liaising with friends back home in England. He needed to know what he could expect in terms of real support.[17] Godwin was astute enough to realise that paying lip service was not the same as giving it. It is not clear whether or not Tostig and Gyrth accompanied him on the initial visit, they may have stayed behind in Flanders gaining experience in organising their first military expedition. Swegn was out of the picture also, for he had embarked upon his journey of penitence to Jerusalem. He must have really meant it this time, for he left on foot. Barefoot.[18]

Godwin left the port of Bruges with a large contingent of sea vessels into the Yser.[19] *D* chronicle and the *Vita* gives no details about the ships. John of Worcester refers to a 'few ships'. They arrived in Dungeness on the furthermost tip of southeast Kent a couple of days later on the 22 June. Godwin managed to avoid the detection of the earls Odda and Ralph but when the earls heard of this, they turned the ships out from Sandwich to hunt for them.[20] A substantial land army,[21] probably from the local fyrds and led by one or both of Edward's stallers, Esegar and Bondi, had been put on high alert to defend any land incursion Godwin might make. Apparently, Godwin was warned that the earls and land army were on their way, and instead of engaging them in battle, he sailed away from them toward Pevensey which adds weight to John of Worcester's supposition that he only had a few ships. This was not meant to be a full-scale invasion, but simply the intention to see how much support was going to be available to him.[22]

According to the *E* Chronicle for 1052, a bout of bad weather caused the king's fleet to lose sight of Godwin, and the ships were forced to turn back to Sandwich. Godwin's fleet returned back to Bruges. The *D* Chronicle reported nothing of bad weather, but mentions that whilst Godwin was in Dungeness, he had enticed the Kent and Hastings boatmen and the men of Surrey and Essex to his cause.[23] Chronicle *C* agrees with *D* on Kent and Hastings, but *C* writes Sussex and Surrey, not Essex, which makes more sense considering the latter county's proximity to the king's fleet.[24] On the other hand, Essex was where Harold's jurisdiction had once lain. His wife Eadgifu's lands were also there as well as their home in Waltham, so it is possible that word of the Godwinsons' comeback had reached her and Harold's followers. Though not impossible, Surrey was too far inland to be safely reached from Godwin's base at Dungeness and supportive factions or messengers were at risk of interception by the land army. It is difficult to tell due to the fact that we don't know how much time Godwin had spent in the region before heading to the Isle of Wight, but both the *C*, and *D* chronicles are in accordance that all these men who offered their oaths had declared 'they would live and die' with him.[25]

Edward, not impressed by Odda and Ralph's failure to catch Godwin, recalled the navy back to London. Hearing that Harold was waiting in Ireland with an invasion force, it is possible the king thought the earls would be better employed in their own regions, considering what had recently happened with the Welsh in Herefordshire. Ralph and

Odda's poor performances may have had something to do with the loyalty of the oarsmen whose interests lay with their old master, Godwin. Edward would have wanted to replace them with crews that were better experienced and faithful to their king.[26] But finding new men to sit at the row-locks was not as easy as Edward had hoped. The whole process of recruiting oarsmen delayed the campaign to the point where the king thought it better to abandon it and those who sat there waiting for the rest of the recruits to turn up went home. Whether it was an administration problem or issues with getting pro-Godwinists to fight on the king's side, is not known. Godwin, however, must have had good intelligence working for him, for when he heard that the ship army had gone to pot and the south coast was unprotected, he joyfully hoisted up his sail, and rode the waves to the Isle of Wight. There he was the owner of the manor of Bonchurch which lay nestled in a valley between cliffs and a landslip of rocks along the island's coast. He also owned a small estate called Woolverton and his wife Gytha owned the manor of Wroxall.

The *E* and the *F* versions are similar here. On the Isle of Wight, the *F* version states that Godwin and his men seized all the valuable ships they could get their hands on as well as hostages, suggesting that people there were not necessarily happy to see him.[27] The *E* version does not mention the boats but states that they 'raided so long that the local people paid as much as they charged them (demanded from them); then made their way west (the *F* mistakenly says east) until they came to Portland, and went up there and did whatever harm they could'.

Portland Island, off the southernmost tip of Dorset, was a major royal estate owned by Edward.[28] Godwin was using the standard Middle-ages practice of raiding, burning, and devastating the enemy's land not only to grab provisions, men, and boats, but to show the Godwinsons were back and meant business.

Battle for Lives

At some point, Godwin must have got word to Harold. Coming out of Ireland, with nine ships, Harold and Leofwin burst into the narrative, determined to make their mark in history. The men manning the ships, may have been Hiberno-Norse, recruited with Diarmaid's permission, or they may have been Harold's men who had joined him in Ireland. One standard longship would have been able to hold up to sixty men per ship so there may have been anything around 400 to 600 men with him. A good number for raiding. Some of these men might have also had links to the slave trade for when they arrived along the Somerset coast, they not only killed thirty or more of the thegns who had turned out to oppose them at Porlock, they took cattle, property and men.[29] The *E* chronicle uses the phrase that Harold, 'seized for himself whatever came his way in cattle, and in men and in property'. The men may have been taken to sell in the slave markets, but more likely to have been pressganged into Harold's cause, for he was probably intent on gathering provisions and finding his father, without being hampered with a cargo of slaves.[30]

The manor of Porlock was owned by the affluent thegn, Algar, who may also have held other estates in Somerset to the value of 12,000 acres. Grills describes 500 acres of flat pasture land lying among clusters of woodland.[31] Along the coast a pebble ridge stretched for 3 miles and between it and the village was a marshy area that lay below sea level. Beyond this is some land now that is known as Hell Byes where some shards of swords and other weapons were discovered and may have been the site of the battle there.³² Nearby, to the east of Porlock was the manor of Selworth, held by Harold's sister, the queen. It may have been Selworth that Harold was heading for. The manor, which was 2 miles from Porlock where he had left his ships, being the only place in the area to give them access to land.³³ He was not expecting trouble, for he was only there to acquire provisions for the ongoing journey. The estate he was in had been previously owned by his father, and latterly Swegn. He was probably expecting the men there to have been friendly. Now, it was part of Odda's jurisdiction, and the men, being loyal to Odda were certainly not disposed to Harold. There is also evidence that the local militia were watching the coast, and knew they were coming, for archaeologists have found traces of an encampment stationed a mile and a half west of the current church.³⁴

Having gathered what they needed, Harold and Leofwin made around Land's End to rendezvous with his father in Portland.³⁵ Both *Vita* and John of Worcester elaborate, with the former declaring that the two sons of Godwin came with a large naval force from Ireland, and wasted with sword and fire, the kingdom from its farthest limits to the place where the earl was stationed. This is inconsistent with what all the *ASC* states which was essentially that once the raid on Porlock was over, they sought out their ships and sailed to meet with Godwin. But the author of the *Vita* was embellishing to please the queen, and writes animatedly of the return of Godwin in such exaggerated terms: 'All the eastern and southern English who could manage it met his ship; all came to meet him, I repeat, like children greeting their long-awaited father' and, 'The sea was covered with ships. The sky glittered with the press of weapons. And so, at length, with the soldiers made more resolute by mutual exhortation, they crossed the Kentish sea and with the ships astern in a long line, entered the mouth of the River Thames.'³⁶

Once the Godwinsons were happily reunited with their father and their other brothers, they went together to the Isle of Wight where they collected what had previously been left behind on Godwin's earlier raid. According to the *D* chronicle, no further harm on the island was done after this, except the taking of provisions and the enticement of men from the local population along the coast and across to the mainland. Having gathered more men and ships, the delighted family travelled eastward toward Sandwich picking up a substantial number of followers along the coastal regions where the Godwinsons were most popular. They were described as a 'streaming, raiding army' as they pulled into Sandwich. A slight step down from the 'glittering sky and the ship-covered sea', but a wondrous sight none-the-less, their fleet having increased in size since crossing the Kentish sea.³⁷

Godwin moved east, though not before seizing more ships and hostages in Sandwich. Some of the ships he brought with him, went the opposite way, sailing around Sheppey and doing great harm, burning the royal estate of Milton Regis.³⁷ It is possible that some of the men manning the newly recruited ships were wholly disgruntled with Edward's mishandling of the Dover crisis and that by burning the royal estate of Milton they were venting some resentment.³⁸ However, at this stage of the campaign, it would not seem pertinent for the rebels to burn the king's properties, which would surely not win him over.

Godwin brought his fleet into the mouth of the Thames.³⁹ The air rang with exhortations from the men who had gathered to enter into the river.⁴⁰ According to *Vita*, it was with great joy the Godwinsons looked upon one another. The sea, was covered in ships, and the sky glittered with the press of weapons. Once in Southwark on 14 September, he came to a settlement with the people there, and we are told that they wanted for him to be restored, and having arranged his passage through the bridge, the flotilla sailed along the Southbank.⁴¹

By this time, Edward, in his palace at Westminster, was concerned that the threat of Godwin's presence was imminent.[42] His cousin Duke William may have been unable to assist or send men to aid him. After William's visit to England in the previous autumn, his ally, Henry of France, switched sides, going over to his enemy, Geoffrey Martel, who was challenging William for control of Maine. The French king and Geoffrey Martel made common cause against William and some of the Norman nobles began to contest William's increasing power. Henry's change of loyalty was probably due to his resentment towards his protegee's growing power in Normandy, threatening the king's dominance over the Duchy of Normandy.[43] William was not to completely consolidate his power in Normandy until 1060. As for Count Eustace, his power may have become limited with Godwin's ally, the Count of Flanders, exerting himself over Boulogne thus making it difficult for Eustace to do anything to help his brother-in-law.

When King Edward realised Godwin was advancing into London, he made moves to stop them from entering the city and called for urgent reinforcements.[44] He sent for his earls including Siward and Leofric, who came with fifty ships against the Godwinsons.[45] But they were too late. Godwin had passed through Southwark unopposed and veered their fleet to encircle the king's ships. The king was furious with the hostile and unlicensed entry that the exiles had made into the kingdom.[46] But, with such joy and applause, the whole of London came out to protect and show their support for the earl in his return.[47]

The king had his land army with him, most likely led by Esegar, (also known as Ansgar) the grandson of Tovi the Proud, and son of the disinherited Æthelstan. He was the port-reeve of London and was later to become sheriff of Middlesex. According to the *D* Chronicle, the earl's army marshalled themselves along the bank on the south side. With the king's warriors arrayed on the opposite bank, there was a sense of unease and an unwillingness to fight each other, for they each felt that there was 'little else of value but good English men on either side'.[48] The consensus was that they did not want to lay open the country to those foreigners who might look upon England as easy prey should there be civil war.

The time had come for Godwin to put his case before the king. He sent for permission to go to him and purge himself of all the crimes he and his sons had been accused of, but the king, still furious at Godwin's forced entry into the country, stalled. It seemed to be in his nature to keep people in limbo, though some might say he was weighing up all the options and things to consider. No doubt his friend the archbishop and his faction was there to advise, urge, and continue to remind the king of Godwin's part in his brother's murder.

Some on the earl's side were not as patient as Godwin and as the *Vita* and the *E* chronicle informs us, they urge him to make an attack, even on the king himself![49] It may have been the angry men of Kent, still aggrieved over the incident with Eustace. The *Vita* reports that 'the earl, so loyal and devoted to God, drew back in horror from these words and purpose'. The author has him say, 'May I have God in my heart today as witness to its loyalty – that I would rather die than have done, or do, or, while I am alive, allow to be done, anything unseemly or unrighteous against my lord, the king.'"[50]

The dramatic theme continued with Godwin throwing himself at the king's feet begging to be granted permission to purge himself of the charges levelled at him. The *Vita* suggests that the king was filled with mercy at Godwin's sincerity, but Godwin was far more superior in arms, and the king was wary that he had now been deserted by the archbishop who, fearing the earl's retribution, had run for his life.

Here the *Vita* reports that the king's mind was in tumult, and was at boiling point, but 'having heard the prayers of the supplicants', he was now calm. The author steers the reader away from the king's predicament of abandonment and advises that the king was now so overcome with emotion, that he walked with Godwin into his palace and planted the kiss of peace on his cheek, just as the *witan* advised him to. Thus, Godwin and all his sons – except Swegn – are resumed to favour. With 'royal pomp', the queen was summoned from Wilton back into the king's bed-chamber. 'And so, after this great evil had been checked without bloodshed by the wisdom of the earl, there was deep joy both at court and in the whole country.'[51]

That there was 'no bloodshed', has to be ignored. There had been bloodshed aplenty during that summer of 1052. The Godwinsons had stormed into England like an unrelenting tornado; sometimes force and bloodshed was what was needed, as at Portlock, and at other times they won favour with the people, as in Sussex and Kent. The *Vita*, as we have seen, makes their accomplishments sound like Caesar's return to Rome. The *ASC,* however, is more reserved in their reporting.[52] The *D* chronicle, much the same as the *C*, states that when the land armies lined up on either side of the banks, Godwin and Harold landed on the shore and 'wise men sent between them and a great council was called and the king granted Godwin his earldom, and his sons all they had owned before. Even the properties of Godwin's wife, Gytha, and their daughter, the queen, were returned and complete friendship between the family and the king was confirmed.[53] The king also promised complete law for all the people and the French men who had 'earlier promoted illegality and passed unjust judgements and counselled bad counsel in this country, except for as many as they decided the king liked to have about him, who were faithful to him and his people'. John of Worcester, names those who the king was allowed to keep as Richard FitzScrob, and his father-in-law, Robert the Deacon, Alfred, the king's marshal, and Ansfrid *Ceocesfot*.[54] The criminals were notably, Archbishop Robert of Canterbury, Bishop William of London, and Bishop Ulf, who escaped with some difficulty with their knights.[55] Bishop William was recalled, according to John of Worcester, for he was considered a harmless, good-natured man. John of Worcester also mentions that Osbern Pentecost, his companion Hugh, and their Norman retainers, fled from their castles and were given permission by Leofric to pass through Mercia and into the north until they reached Scotland where they were received by King Macbeth.

Chronicle *E* adds drama to the flight of the Franco-Normans, by reporting that when Archbishop Robert realised he was to be outlawed, fearing Godwin's wrath, he jumped on his horse and rode with bishops Ulf and William and their retainers to London's East Gate where they fought their way out, killing many of the young guards there, making their way to Essex.[56] At Eadulf's Ness they embarked on an unsteady ship. Robert was said to have abandoned his pallium – the stole that the pope presents to bishops to signify their position in the church – probably in the rush to get away.[57] *F* appears to be the only chronicle that mentions Stigand succeeds to the archbishopric in Canterbury in that year.

In the Aftermath of Glory

The *Vita* gives the impression that the king was easily defeated by the humbling of Godwin whose inflated virtues are loudly extolled throughout the book. On behalf of the queen, the author exposes Archbishop Robert as the evil-doer, with the innocent king under his spell, his dignity intact. The blame for the whole debacle is placed squarely on Robert's shoulders, 'the evil checked' so that harmony could once more reign in the kingdom.[58]

But how much of this should be accepted as gospel? At first, the king is 'furious' and full of rancour at the boldness of Godwin, acutely aware that the earl had a superior force behind him. Suddenly, though, he is overwhelmed at Godwin's plea for mercy. The author appears to be determined to implant two themes in the reader's mind: Godwin's ability to command support, and the idea that Edward was moved by love for the Godwinsons which he had previously possessed but that had been poisoned by the Norman clerics. But this is, of course, a hagiography, written on behalf of the queen whose love for her father and pride for her husband is the overarching feature of the book.

The more likely explanation for the Godwinson's reinstatement was that Edward, outmanoeuvred by Godwin, had no choice but to accept them back into the fold. However, despite his rancour at having to bend to Godwin, it is possible Edward had seen that the grass was not as green without him after all. Godwin and his sons had proved to be far more competent than their replacements. Swegn had built an effective workable relationship with the Welsh king in the north, and if he had been allowed to continue, might have gone on to create a secure and stable administration along the marches. Harold had been effective in building relations in East Anglia on the king's behalf, proving loyal and honourable. Godwin had always kept his jurisdiction well administered, and all the sons were proven capable sea-commanders, unlike Odda and Ralph. Edward may have found it galling having his hand forced, but by pardoning the Godwinsons with grace and humility, aesthetically, he remained kingly, dignified, and in control.[59]

The loss of the archbishop and his other Norman friends was likely to have caused Edward bitterness, though perhaps the return of Bishop William compensated a little for losing his long-time friend, Robert. Equally, having to deal with Leofric and Alfgar's resentments caused by the Godwinsons' restoration, can only have added to his stress. We do not know what Leofric thought about his son's earldom being stripped from him but it had always been in Leofric's nature to keep a dignified reserve. Alfgar was made to hand back his earldom to Harold and did so with no recorded trouble, which was unusual given what we see later of his character. Perhaps he had his eyes on Mercia or Northumbria, considering the ages of his father and Earl Siward, it would not be long before those lands would be up for grabs. The Mercian and Northumbrian earldoms would bring more prestige than East Anglia. This may have been the tact Edward used when having to confront a disappointed Alfgar. Earl Odda was compensated with an earldom further north that took in the lands of Worcestershire and possibly Gloucestershire.[60] He was to continue to be active in the area until 1056 when he passed away in his manor of Deerhurst.[61] It might be that he had been better suited to an ecclesiastical life, for his last wishes were to be professed as a monk, a request which Bishop Ealdred carried out. Finally, Ralph de Mantes was kept on in his earldom of Herefordshire to continue his mission to train the local militia in the Continental style cavalry warfare. We will see more of Ralph later.

There was also the question of the hostages mentioned only by the *E* chronicle, stating that it had been agreed between the king and Godwin that hostages should be handed over.[62] The only other chronicle to talk of hostages is John of Worcester, who mentions the exchange of them in 1051 before their exile, but not 1052.[63] It was common in medieval times to hand over members of family to a lord as surety for the good behaviour of the hostage giver, however it is not likely that Edward, as the 'wronged' party, and the man in power, would be required to do so in turn. In 1051, as the accused, it was reasonable to expect that Godwin hand over his relatives to Edward. In 1052, Godwin had not come as the master, but to lay himself before the king as his servant, clearly a statement that the king had been the stronger of the two, and had not been obliged to hand over hostages.

The issue of the those held by the king as surety is somewhat muddled in the chronicles, but going back to 1051, at Gloucester, it appears that Godwin handed over his son and grandson, named respectively as Wulfnoth and Hakon. Later, in Southwark, when he and Harold are summoned, it could have been thought reasonable for Godwin to request hostages from the king for surety of his and his family's safety. The king, however, did not think it was reasonable and refused. In September, 1052, the king already held the Godwinson boys from the year before, and Wulfnoth and Hakon are not documented having gone into exile with the rest of the family.

The last loose end to finish this episode in Harold's life, is to explore what happened to his brother Swegn. Godwin and Gytha, having achieved their goal of returning home and back to all that they owned previously, must have been looking forward to having Swegn home too. Having been reinstated with the help of Ealdred, he had gone back to his earldom with Edward's permission, likely on probation. It would not take much for Swegn to be banished again, just one step out of line, and he would be done for. What exactly he did is not known, he may not have done anything, however it could have had something to do with him falling foul of the French in Herefordshire. Whatever the case, it was clear Edward was going to use the conflict with Godwin as reason enough to outlaw him again.

When the time came for the Godwins to flee, Swegn declined to go to Ireland, and instead left his ship for Harold and Leofwin, and went with his father to Flanders. Having had time to reflect on his behaviour and his grave crimes, the only way forward was to abandon himself to God's mercy, whatever that might be. It appears he may have already decided to leave for Jerusalem and left, barefoot not long after winter of 1051–1052. His decision to go on pilgrimage appears to be out of genuine repentance and John of Worcester states it was for the killing of his brother.[64] England, it seems was done with him for the time being. As one historian points out, Swegn's journey was not a comfortable one, and held many dangers.[65] Therefore, it was not a flippant decision. Men were known to have died on such pilgrimages: Duke Robert of Normandy and his friend, Drogo, count of the Vexin, who had been married to Goda, King Edward's sister were men that had both died, despite having a company of forty knights with them. Swegn was travelling through hazardous lands in the east of Europe and then once in Asia Minor, the Seljuk Turks engendered a fanatical hostility toward the presence of Christian pilgrims in the area.[66] Nonetheless, Swegn did make it to the Holy Sepulchre in Jerusalem where he prayed and confessed his sins, receiving absolution. On the way home, Swegn's life sadly ended after becoming ill, probably in Lycia, and not Constantinople as the C version tells us, on 29 September.[67] Malmesbury suggests he was murdered by Saracens after leaving Jerusalem.[68]

Information of his death did not reach England until the spring of 1053. It must have been distressing for Harold to see the devastating affect the news had on his parents. Swegn had left them with the hope that he was genuinely remorseful and that he would come back a changed man. We do not know how Harold felt about the brother who had caused nothing but pain in the last decade of his life. The thoughts of historical players are rarely recorded. But he may have come to peace with Swegn before he left for Ireland. Perhaps the ship had been Swegn's way of atoning and Harold accepted this. At least it would have been of some comfort to know that he had made it to the Holy Land and was absolved when he died. How Swegn spent his last moments can only be imagined, and it is easy to feel that this troubled young man had got his just desserts at last. Nonetheless, it was a sad end to what could have been a promising life, for a man who was his own worst enemy.

Part Three
EARL OF WESSEX

'A Noble earl who, all the time had loyally followed his lord's commands with words and deeds, and neglected nothing that met the need of the people's king.'

Anglo Saxon Chronicle

CHAPTER TWELVE

Conflict and Diplomacy

Death of Earl Godwin

The first real worry Harold had to contend with after settling back into his office of earl, was that his father became very unwell. It was hardly surprising at Godwin's age. He was, after all approaching 60 and his recent exile and return had been another very stressful time in his life. Only chronicle *C* mentions his illness, but he was to recover after a few weeks.

Godwin and Gytha also had to contend with the added stressor that their son, Wulfnoth, and their grandson, Hakon, were missing. Nothing is mentioned in the *ASC* about the lost Godwinson boys, forced to become hostages in 1051. It is not till later that they turn up in other sources. Their disappearance would have been the icing on the cake of doom for Godwin and what actions Harold or any of the family took to try to locate them remains a mystery.

The only other significant event of 1052 was the death of the king of Deheubarth's brother, Rhys, who had been plundering the English border far too often. At Edward's Christmas court the *witan* counselled that he should be captured and put to death.[1]

Harold must have been content to be back home with his Eadgifu and their children. By now three sons would have been born and at least one of his daughters. It is possible that whilst Harold was in exile, Eadgifu would have had to vacate their property in Waltham. The king may have chosen to pass on the estate to Alfgar and Eadgifu could have either come to some arrangement with her new landlord or moved back to her manor nearby in Nazeing. It was later in the new year of 1053 when Harold would face his first emotional challenge of the year, the death of his father. It happened at Winchester, 12 April, the second day of Easter. Sometime during dinner, Godwin collapsed, unable to speak, his body stricken with weakness.[2] He had suffered a stroke, and was carried by his sons into the king's personal chambers. He suffered greatly, but even so, Harold and his family were hopeful that their patriarch would pull through.

On 15 April, he passed away.[3]

The *Vita,* as we would expect, described the passing of Godwin in elaborate terms. He was the people's father and protector of the kingdom, and of course there was an outpouring of grief, tears, and 'great sighs'. In the monastery of the Old Minster in Winchester, Godwin was buried, where he had given many gifts and rents of land for his soul.[4] Harold, mentioned as the eldest, was promoted to the earldom of Wessex in his father's place. *Vita* dramatically reports, 'at this, the whole English host was able to breathe again, consoled for their loss'.[5]

Malmesbury, writing in the mid–to late twelfth century tells an absorbing story about Godwin's death. In it, Godwin proclaimed his own death by choking on bread. Malmesbury is notable for his disdain for the Godwinsons, and has the Normans allege that 'both himself (Godwin) and his sons acted with the greatest want of respect and fidelity to the king and his party; aiming at equal sovereignty with him; often ridiculing his simplicity; often hurling shafts of wit at him: that the Normans could not endure this, but endeavoured to weaken their power as much as possible...'.

The earl's death at dinner appeared as divine vengeance for his piratical ravages against the kingdom during his return from exile. And as it usually did when the king's brother was brought up, the atmosphere became morose. Godwin, frustrated, confronted the king, heatedly, stating, 'I perceive O king, that on every recollection of your brother, you regard me with angry countenance; but God forbid that I should swallow this morsel, If I am conscious of anything which might tend, either to his danger or your disadvantage.' With this, he choked on the piece that was in his mouth and died, slipping under the table, dragged out by Harold.[6]

As the story of Godwin's death was retold over the next two centuries, the more embellished it became. The morsel of bread being the instrument of divine retribution seems to be the consistent theme. One particular thirteenth-century narrative has it that Godwin and Edward were drinking wine together and Godwin remarked playfully to Edward, 'So brings one brother to the other, help, who was in danger', to which the king replied, 'So might mine if he had been living, had you, earl, permitted him to.' After invoking the lord's intervention that he should either die or live depending on his guilt or innocence, Godwin popped the morsel of bread into his mouth saying, 'May God grant that the proof be true', and before he could say another word, the earl of Wessex slumped down dead.[7]

It is hard to imagine Godwin's death happening in such a manner, but as we often see, the occurrence of such miracles were common concepts during the medieval era. Nonetheless, it is not impossible to believe that Edward and Godwin had somewhat of a love-hate relationship, and Edward kept a lid on his displeasure, heavily dosed with passive aggression. A smirk here, a snide remark there, it would have been enough to drive anyone to distraction. Was Godwin frustrated to the point that, unable to restrain himself longer, his anger finally detonated his blood pressure, and he dropped dead with a stroke. The king was charitable enough to have given the family use of his own apartments to nurse their father. He might have even felt guilty if he had in anyway provoked a situation whereby Godwin's health was compromised. No doubt there was tears and much sorrow from many as Godwin was interred in the cathedral.

But how had Harold's relationship with his father been? Did he feel aggrieved over the last years, watching his father fawning over his devil brother, Swegn? It is hard to imagine that he would not have been affected by such a dynamic in the family. As youngsters, Harold and his siblings would have had to endure Swegn's disruption of the household's peace as he complained about his parentage. Then later, when Swegn repeats the accusations, Harold must endure as his mother's reputation was sullied and his father cuckolded, their good name dragged through the mud. His brother's abject selfishness could not have imbued Harold with brotherly love. Seeing his father hurt, and his mother furious, must have incensed Harold and one wonders if there was any physical aggression between the two brothers. This might account for why Harold was quick to disassociate himself from Swegn, refusing to give back Swegn's property.

When Swegn was eventually accepted back into the fold, Harold appears to have been resigned to the turn of events, perhaps seething with annoyance.

When the family were about to go into exile, Swegn changed his mind and offered his Irish plan to Harold so he himself could go to Flanders with his father. Harold appears to have been only too happy to comply. Was this because he did not wish to travel with his father? Or Swegn? Harold might have wanted to avoid conflict with his father. Swegn's disgusting behaviour had cast a shadow over all of them, causing them to become pariahs. If Swegn had not gone rogue and kidnapped Abbess Eadgifu, and killed Beorn, then they would not have all been tarred with the same brush. Godwin had constantly begged the king's forgiveness for Swegn. The king had had enough. Perhaps now that Swegn was out of the way, Harold was willing to repair his relationship with his father, but then Godwin died and Harold's hopes along with him.

Of course, it is impossible to know for certain what Harold felt or thought, but we can explore the credible scenarios that manifest out of the factors at play within the family dynamic.

Earl of Wessex

It must have come as a shock when Harold realised he was to take up the mantle of earl of Wessex in Godwin's stead. This would push him into the political arena's spotlight as the premier earl, signing ahead of everyone but the king on the witness lists. In a couple of years, he would be at the height of his power, but for now, the trajectory would continue to be upward until he was elected king.[8]

It was not necessarily that high office such as earldoms were allocated by primogeniture, though those who had been brought up in the nobility seemed to be better placed for it, having had the best learning opportunities. Harold was Sussex born and bred, and would have inherited Godwin's familial lands, as well as those endowed with the post. The family owned over 1,200 hides in Sussex which amounted to a third of the shire.[9] It would seem expedient to appoint a man as lord, whose interests were already embedded within the earldom.[10] The estates that went with the job of Wessex would have added to his wealth, and he would keep many of the lands that were personally gifted to him in East Anglia by men who had sought his patronage. It seems he still kept Waltham which the king had transferred to him as part of the estates that were for his own personal use and seems to have been the home he was to share with Eadgifu and their children.[11] It is important to note that nothing of Godwin's will survives, but we know that while alive, lands were gifted to various ecclesiastical factions for his soul.

Harold settled into his new earldom a much wealthier man than before. His dominion ranged across the whole of the south of England from Land's End in Cornwall to Sussex and Kent and as far north as Devon, Hampshire, Surrey, and Middlesex. Not only was Harold in possession of lands in Wessex and East Anglia, by the time of his death in 1066, there was not a county where he did not own land. Domesday book recorded the assessment of lands at their value for tax. We are fortunate that author Ian Walker has studied the values of Harold's estates for us and tells us about the combined value of all his properties as calculated in Domesday folios. By 1065 at least, judging by what he was worth, Harold Godwinson was the most powerful man in England on the strength of his own personal wealth which was £2,846 and the value of his men's wealth was an addition of £836, making the total for tax purposes, £3,682.[12] This does not account for the revenues made from these lands. The amount was almost on a par with the king, whose tax value was £3,840. Walker also tells us that the whole of the Godwin family's tax value including the holdings their men held from them, was well over £6,000, double the king's worth. This was also much more than Leofric of Mercia's family, whose total figure was just over £2,493 and included £171 owned by their men. Just to give you an idea how hugely wealthy these figures are, the income a slave woman was given to live on per year was just three pennies.[13]

With Godwin dead, Harold was now the head of the family. He was responsible for the welfare of his brothers, sisters, and his mother. It is likely he kept Leofwin with him, continuing his brother's education in statecraft as well as martial training. His mother most likely spent much of her time between visiting her daughter at court and the home she had shared with her husband in Bosham, and probably took a step back from political life now that Godwin was no longer around. It is possible that Harold visited her at his childhood home from time to time when he spent time away from Waltham. He may not have worried about his mother too much as she still had her two younger daughters, Gunhild and Eadgifu to console her unless they were both being tutored at court in Edith's care or elsewhere finishing their education with nuns. Harold's brothers Gyrth and Tostig, about 18 to 23 years of age respectively, were no doubt the 'king's favourites' as the sons of Godwin were often referred to and might have served the king at court under the tutelage of important officials. With his family in positions that would smooth the way for their advancement, Harold could relax knowing his brothers were well taken care of, had land to support them, and could afford to build their own circle of followers in the way that æthelings in the past had done. As royal favourites, they were not unlike royalty themselves.

Where Harold's base was situated is difficult to tell, though it seems likely however East Sussex and Kent would have been familiar to him. There were familial lands at Compton in the west of Sussex near Chichester which have been identified as *Cumtune* reinstated to Godwin in Æthelstan's will. This land had been given by Godwin to Osbern to hold from him so it is possible that Osbern still held it until 1066, but under Gytha. Osbern was likely to have been the king's Norman chaplain to whom also belonged the church at Bosham. The estate of Bosham, where Harold was brought up would have held some emotional attachment for him and he may have wanted to visit as much as possible. A substantial estate of some 56 hides, paying tax for thirty-eight, it is noted as being owned by Earl Godwin in 1066. It is likely to have passed into Gytha's hands after her husband's death as it was customary for the wife to inherit a third of her husband's wealth and property.[14] The other Compton in the east of Sussex was held by Harold of the king as his overlord, so would have come with his comital lands which the king had allocated to him for his personal use as earl. Two of the estates he also owned were Crowhurst which lay roughly 3 miles in between Hastings and Caldbeck Hill, and Whatlington, 7 miles north of Hastings and about 2 miles northeast of where the actual battle took place in 1066. Both of these manors were ravaged and wasted at the time of the conquest. It was a tactic employed in medieval warfare in order to engage the enemy in combat. Whether or not Eadgifu and the children spent time in Wessex with him cannot be ascertained, but it was not improbable. However, both Harold and his Lady *Swannehæls* were to have a close association with Waltham throughout their lives together and in 1060 they celebrated the consecration of Harold's project, the Holy Cross Church in Waltham.

The Ravaging of Hereford

The next two years were to be quiet for Harold, as far as the chronicles were concerned. In 1053, the *C* version of the *ASC* recorded that Welshmen killed a number of Englishmen on patrol in Westbury. This was feasibly thought to be an attack in revenge for the death of Rhys ap Rhydderch the previous winter, therefore led by Gruffudd ap Rhydderch and not as thought by some, Gruffudd ap Llywelyn.[15] The raid seems to have gone unpunished and perhaps with Harold and Alfgar moving into their new earldoms, the Welsh had taken advantage of the power void whilst the transfer of earldoms took place.

In 1054, Siward, earl of Northumbria, invaded Scotland in an attempt to put down the Scottish King Macbeth in support of Malcolm Canmore. During a hard-won battle in which the Anglo-Danish army had the field of slaughter, Siward's son, Osbeorn and his nephew, also Siward, both lost their lives. The following year, the old earl died in York and was buried in the minster he had built himself but which is now lost, called Galmaho.[16]

With the vacancy open in Northumbria, it was time to choose a new earl. There were now two possible candidates: Tostig Godwinson and Alfgar of Mercia, the current earl of East Anglia who had stepped into Harold's shoes upon his appointment to Wessex. The *C* version of the *ASC* reports that not long after the death of Siward, a council was called on 19 March, 1055, which resulted in Tostig being advanced to the position of earl in Northumbria and Alfgar being exiled for treason. The chronicles do not tell us much about Alfgar's situation other than he was exiled even though he wasn't responsible for any wrong-doing. Like Harold before him, he went to Ireland, and 'got himself a fleet' of eighteen ships. He then went to Gruffudd ap Llywelyn, king of Gwynedd and Powys, who received him under safe conduct. There, they plotted to scratch each other's backs and designed the invasions of the Deheubarth and Hereford. Chronicle *D* mentions Alfgar's outlawing and also states that it wasn't his fault. The *E* version is less sympathetic, reporting that he was outlawed for some treasonable offence, traitor to the king and all the people of the land. He was said to have admitted this before all the men gathered at court, 'although the words shot out against his will'.[17]

That these two episodes happened in close proximity to each other, they appear to be connected. The sources do not tell us if Alfgar had been an applicant for the earldom, though it seems likely that he was. No doubt Harold and Edith had promoted their brother Tostig as the man for the job, convincing Edward to give their brother the earldom. It seems he did not need much convincing. Tostig now in his mid-twenties, was given a substantial post over a wide area of land that would set him up nicely among the noble elite. In matters of statesmanship, it is possible he had been given a much smaller area to handle prior to this opening, however, for a tough jurisdiction such as Northumbria to be given to a relative newcomer over the experienced Alfgar, was another slight against the Mercians. It was not surprising Alfgar was unable to contain his rage. He may have felt he was the superior earl, not just in age but also in experience. He also had a son, Burghred, who was old enough to go on a mission to Rome in 1061, and a daughter who in a few years would be married to Gruffudd of Wales. Alfgar had probably earned his spurs during the Mercian family's conflicts with the Welsh, and had worked hard, patiently waiting for the role of a senior earl to come along. Now he had disgraced himself before all the court, his prospects and life in tatters.

Alfgar made his way to Ireland where he enlisted eighteen ship loads of Hiberno-Norse warriors,[18] and then brought them to Gruffudd ap Llywelyn's stronghold in Wales.[19] It seems incongruous that Alfgar would seek support from the man who had killed his Uncle Edwin at Battle of Rhyd-y-groes in 1039.[20] The Mercians had always been the natural enemy of the Welsh, though it was not unknown for alliances to be formed if it would benefit either race, as we saw with the short-lived alliance between Gruffudd and Swegn Godwinson. The *C* chronicle tells us that Gruffudd and Alfgar joined their forces to create 'a great army' and Earl Ralph, in turn also gathered a great army against them at Hereford market town and sought them out there.[21] But before a spear could be thrown, the English took flight because they were on horse'. John of Worcester is more specific, informing us that the battle took place 2 miles outside of Hereford, also giving us the date of 24 October (1055).[22] He also states that Earl Ralph had ordered them to fight on horse 'contrary to their custom'. But for some reason the earl, with his Frenchmen and Normans, left the field of battle, and seeing this the English also fled with the whole of the enemy in pursuit of them, cutting them down as they fled and slaughtering them as they went.[23]

Having gained victory over the English, Gruffudd and Alfgar then broke into the poorly fortified town and razed it to the ground, burning houses and buildings. Even the church and monastery did not get off scot-free. Having stripped the church of its holy relics, vestments and robes, its gold and silver ornaments, they killed seven canons, those who had defended the doors, and burned the church to the ground. Laden with spoils and booty, the invaders made off with captives from the burgh.[24] It seemed that Ralph had paid particular attention to getting his English forces to fight on horseback whilst forgetting to ensure the defences of the burgh were sound.

As a result of this military debacle, the English were slaughtered with the loss of between 400 and 500 men. The idea that the coalition forces and Ralph's were both 'great armies' suggests they must have been evenly matched. Eighteen ships plus Alfgar's own retainers would suggest a figure of around 1,000 fighting men, and combined with Gruffudd's who could, according to Malcolm and Sean Davies, command a levy of around 2,500 warriors would propose a total of around 3,500. This may have overwhelmed the local militia available to Ralph, whose numbers were likely to have been smaller and would account for the term 'massacre' reported by the *ASC*.[25] John of Worcester is particularly scathing about Ralph de Mantes. He called him 'the cowardly son of King Edward's sister'.[26] The Welsh source *Brut y Tywysogion* (Chronicle of the Princes), contrasts with the English sources and describes the battle as a hard won, bitter fight.[27]

When the court heard the news of Ralph's disastrous performance the king called out the *fyrd*, and assembled them at Gloucester, commanding Earl Harold to lead them in pursuit of Gruffudd and Alfgar. It is likely that Edward chose Harold to deal with the problem instead of Earl Leofric, the warlord whose jurisdiction was closer to Wales, due to the familial conflict of interest Leofric faced. The following year, however, Leofric would accompany Harold and Bishop Ealdred, to attend a peace treaty with Gruffudd.

This was Harold's first campaign as leading commander of the English *fyrd*, drawn, according to John of Worcester, from all of England, as opposed to the *C* version of the *ASC*, which reports that it was levied from all neighbouring England, which is the more realistic suggestion.[28]

Harold is described by John of Worcester as brave, zealous and 'unwearied in his pursuit of Gruffudd and Alfgar, boldly crossing the Welsh border, camps beyond the Straddle (the English and Wales Border)'.[29] The combined forces of Wales and the Hiberno-Norse did not wait around for the English to arrive but fled into the hills of south Wales. Already, Harold's reputation as a 'daring warrior' has the combined Welsh, Hiberno-Norse and Mercian armies unwilling to face him, though perhaps a scout's report of the size of Harold's host was what made them run. Walker describes Earl Harold as proceeding cautiously, not advancing too deeply into Wales beyond the Golden Valley, suggesting that Harold was being mindful of Gruffudd's past successes with ambushes, and the fact they did not have the backing of a Mercian army.[30] In their book, *The Last King of Wales Gruffudd ap Llewelyn*, Davies and Davies describe a difficult terrain in the valley: poorly maintained roads, muddy tracks bogged down in marshland, fast flowing streams and rivers, and many other hazardous perils.[31] One can imagine that a large army, hauling heavy carts laden with war gear would have had a severely uncomfortable, wearisome journey over mountainous undulating inclines, steep valleys, thickly forested with trees.[32] According to John of Worcester, Harold decided to leave the bulk of the *fyrd* in the Wye valley to resist any enemy attack, whilst he and a contingent of his men journeyed back into England to take a look at the damage done to Hereford.

What Harold's reaction to the carnage of Hereford was we do not know. Harold was no stranger to raiding after his campaigns in the south west country when he returned from exile in Ireland. There was not likely an earl or a staller or another important office holder that had not borne witness to atrocities or taken part in raids on towns and homesteads at some point in their career. One would like to think that the leading earls would not have taken kindly to their men raping and murdering innocents, and would punish perpetrators wherever they could. Such atrocities would not go down well with the populace whose homes were constantly being razed to the ground in times of conflict. They would have looked to their overlords to protect them, but this didn't stop them from being caught up in the customary strategies these men employed against each other. And it was not just peasants who suffered. Archbishop Wulfstan II, of York admonishes the thegns of England in his homily, *Sermo Lupi ad Anglos* (The Sermon of the Wolf to the English) in 1014, for standing by and allowing Scandinavian raiders to rape their wives and daughters.[33] In 1055, the raiders were no longer just invading Danes, but a mix of mercenaries from Ireland and Welsh warriors led by King Gruffudd of Wales, organised by an English traitor committing atrocities against his fellow countrymen.

The description provided us by John of Worcester of the damage done in Hereford is not as colourful as that described half a century earlier in Canterbury. This time the scribe was more concerned about the church being burned down, the loss of the canons who bravely did their best to defend it, and the fact that a few saints' relics were taken. Of the town-folk, he merely mentions that some were killed and some taken as captives. Considering the town was burned to the ground, the horrific visuals and the olfactory sensations of charred flesh and mutilated, decaying bodies would have been distressing to even the most hardened of warriors.

Harold responded by instructing builders to strengthen the town's defences with gates and bars, inserting a wide, deep trench around the outside of the walls, some of which can still be vaguely seen today. While this was being done, he recalled the still inactive army back from their encampment on the Welsh side of the border and arranged to meet with Alfgar and King Gruffudd at Billingsley, where Harold was said to have owned a manor, and where it was possible the treaty was held.[34]

It was thought that the reason for Alfgar's treason was connected to an alliance he had been making with the Welsh king,[35] however there was no evidence for any link between the two men until 1055. Even so, it is not unreasonable to believe that Earl Alfgar had been preparing himself for succeeding his elderly father in Mercia. Forming an understanding with the Welsh king would provide him with a powerful ally who could act as a buffer zone against the growing influence of the Godwinsons. Equally, for Gruffudd, a friendly alliance on his border to help him protect his conquests within Wales, would be preferable to the hostile Earl Ralph.[36] Although we cannot be sure that Alfgar's treason was due to an association with Gruffudd, the circumstances in which Alfgar and Gruffudd came together following his outburst at court, certainly points to a rational supposition.

For Gruffudd, this was to be the start of an operation to expand his territories, and it had been time to rid himself of the one stumbling block that obstructed his desire for supremacy in Wales, Gruffudd ap Rhydderch.[37] He had also been looking to the eastern lowlands, beyond the Welsh border to a territory disputed over for centuries, where, according to Davies and Davies, among the inhabitants, were those who still spoke Welsh and considered themselves descendants of the Britons, with the same customs and laws.[38] This was the *Ergyng*, known in old English as *Ircingafelda*. The lands are now known as Archenfield, west of Hereford and south of the River Wye. English sources neglect to mention that prior to the coalition's incursion into Hereford, Gruffudd ap Llywelyn defeated and slew Gruffudd ap Rhydderch, resulting in achieving his ascendency to the throne of all Wales. Though there is nothing recorded in the English sources to evidence Alfgar's participation in ap Llywelyn's campaign to eradicate ap Rhydderch, it is likely that the extra forces were one of the reasons ap Llywelyn had the strength to overcome his rival in the south.[39]

He travelled overland from his northern stronghold to the location assigned as the meeting place with Alfgar and his ships and their crews. The Davies' put the rendezvous place at somewhere near the mouth of the River Wye.[40] The lower part of the river lay in ap Rhydderch's eastern territory and was the gateway to Hereford.[41] Once the southern Rhydderch was dealt with and his forces and lands in the hands of ap Llywelyn, the former's death negated Llywelyn having to avoid Ralph's castles in the north.[42] One Welsh chronicle glorifies Gruffudd's success:

> Against him rose up the Saxons, and with them a mighty host with Earl Ralph as their leader, and they drew up their army and prepared for battle. And Gruffudd, fearless and with a well-ordered army, fell upon

them; and after bitter fierce fighting the Saxons, unable to withstand the onslaught of the Britons, turned to flight after a great slaughter of them. And Gruffudd pursued them to within the walls of Hereford, and there massacred and them, destroyed the walls and burned the town. And with vast spoil he returned home imminently worthy.[43]

Of the two *ASC* chronicles that mention the attack on Hereford, only *C* mentions Gruffudd ap Llywelyn by name and only hints at his participation in the raid by referring to the Welsh. The other chronicle to mention the event, *D*, does not refer to Gruffudd at all but refers to Alfgar turning to the Welsh for aid. The Welsh point of view places Gruffudd as the leader of the campaign and we must remember that after the death of Gruffudd ap Rhydderch he took the title King of all Wales.[44]

The meeting that Harold held at Billingsley saw Alfgar reinstated as earl in East Anglia and returned to all that he had before he was exiled. Alfgar's Hiberno-Norse mercenaries sailed out of the Wye into the Severn estuary and travelled along the Welsh coast to the port of Chester to await payment.[45] Similarities between Alfgar and Swegn Godwinson are glaringly obvious. It is quite shocking that one could kidnap an abbess, commit murder, and the other fire a whole town and its church to its foundations killing several priests and be politically reinstated.

We are not advised of what the king awarded to Gruffudd but it is likely that for the time being, he accepted the concession of *Ergyng*. According to Domesday, the land was recorded to have been wasted by Gruffudd himself, and was still in that state by the time of the survey in 1086.[46] The irony is that these were the lands that the Welsh king desired, and had to cross to reach Hereford, putting them to waste before destroying Hereford. As part of the treaty, the church of Hereford ceded *Ergyng* to Glamorgan, suggesting that the area had once been in Welsh hands before it fell into the hands of the Anglo-Saxons. I imagine that Harold may not have been overly upset about losing a piece of ground that was 'waste'.

The Battle of Glasbury

Not long after the 'massacre' which was how the *C* manuscript described the battle that took place in Hereford on that October day in 1055, the Welsh Bishop Tremerig died. He had been Bishop Æthelstan's suffran after he had become unwell.[47] Tremerig might have perished of the wounds he sustained in defending the doors of the church. We learn from John of Worcester that Bishop Æthelstan had been blind for thirteen years.[48] Consecrated around 1013, he was a part of daily life in Hereford for many years, and was a good age when he experienced the ravaging of Hereford. He commissioned the church dedicated to St. Mary and St. Æthelberht to be reconstructed. It would now have to be rebuilt again, but the loss of St. Æthelberht's relics and those of the other saints were irreplaceable. By February of 1056, when Bishop Æthelstan joined his deputy in death, at least part of the church was in an appropriate state of repair for his body to be carried from his place of passing in the episcopal manor of Bosbury and be buried there.[49]

Edward had commissioned Harold to see to the continued repair and reorganisation of the defences of Hereford in order to bolster the security along the Anglo-Welsh border. He was likely to have been in the area at least until the middle of spring when he appointed his own chaplain, Leofgar, as the new bishop of Hereford. It is the *C* and *D* versions of the chronicle and John of Worcester who we turn to for the events of 1056. Leofgar appears to have been chosen by Harold for his warlike nature having probably served among his huscarls for a time. This new bishop was said to have worn his moustache during his priesthood, which was against canon law.[50]

Leofgar, in position for under twelve weeks, decided to take it upon himself to reverse the gains that the Welsh had made the year before. The sources do not precede this with a rationale for Leofgar's decision, although Kelly DeVries states that Gruffudd had made a short 'but bloody raid into Hereford' shortly after the ratification of the agreement made at Billingsley.[51] The new bishop may have been passionately affected by the terrible tales of the invasion he had heard from his ecclesiastic brethren and the stories relayed by the town's survivors. His anger may have also been exacerbated by more Welsh raids, though there are none recorded and DeVries' statement about Gruffudd's bloody raid is hard to verify.

The *ASC* is very poetic about the new bishop giving up his spiritual tools, chrism and cross, to take up spear and sword to go against Gruffudd, leading an army of priests as well as men of the local *fyrd* under Sheriff Ælfnoth.[52] Bishop Leofgar's attempt at restoring Hereford's losses ended in disaster. For the second year running, an English army is slaughtered by a slick Welsh, fighting force, killing Leofgar, all his priests and the sheriff along with him, as well as the usual 'many good men'. Any survivors were said to have fled away. The date according to John of Worcester, was 16 June 1056 and the place was thought to be somewhere in the vicinity of Glasbury-on-Wye. It was believed to have been an important religious centre for a line of Welsh bishops called *Clas Cynidr*.[53] According to the Davies and Davies', a list of bishops' names found in a manuscript in France mentions that the final bishop, Tryferyn, left for Hereford. The authors believe that this was Bishop Tremerig who died just weeks after Gruffudd's attack on the town.[54]

Once again, an army was called out, led by Harold. It must have also included forces from Mercia, because this time, he is accompanied by Earl Leofric, and with them also was Bishop Ealdred who had been handed emergency care of Hereford.[55] In a tribute to the tough terrain, the *C* chronicle states,

> It is difficult to describe the hardship, and all the travelling and the campaigning, and that labour and loss of men, and also horses, which all the raiding army of the English suffered, until Earl Leofric and Earl Harold and Bishop Ealdred arrived and made reconciliation between them there, so that Gruffudd swore oaths that he would be a loyal and undeceiving under-king to King Edward.[56]

Unfortunately, the sources do not tell us what concessions were made in return for Gruffudd bending the knee to King Edward. We do not see Gruffudd attending the king at any of his seasonal courtly meetings with his nobles, and nor do we see him having to provide military service in anyway.[57] *Domesday* states that King Edward gifted to 'Griffin' all the land beyond the River Dee, which shows that the area between Dee and the Clwyd was in his possession at the height of his power.[58] It is not unlikely that the gift was made during the treaty that followed the Battle of Glasbury. Perhaps Gruffudd had bargained for this after Hereford but had not achieved it. It is possible he engineered the confrontation with Leofgar, goading the English by raiding along the border. If this was the case, he had cunningly dodged any retribution from Edward and had in fact succeeded in gaining more conquests with little loss on his side.

    Harold's willingness to avoid conflict may have evolved when he was faced with fighting Englishmen in the west country on his return from exile. No doubt the devastation of Hereford was not something he wanted to repeat in a hurry. It may have been why he preferred to use diplomacy over conflict. Loss of life was not only bad for morale, it was bad for the economy and the security of the land, and Harold would go on to play the diplomat in this way until the last years of his life.

CHAPTER THIRTEEN

A Lost Prince and The Invasion That was too Tedious too Tell

Search for an Heir

In August of 1056, the king's cousin, Earl Odda passed away and had been ordained a monk before he died as he had wished.[1] It is possible that his lands were encompassed within Harold's authority in Wessex as Ralph de Mantes' lands in Hereford were.[2] Ralph died in 1057, the cause unknown, however he does not appear in the records beyond his failure at Hereford. It is thought by some historians that he was removed of his responsibilities in Hereford after his poor showing in 1055 and compensated with lands in the West Midlands.[2] It is possible he became ill following his scandalous retreat from the battlefield, leaving his men to face the overwhelming troops of Alfgar and Gruffudd's coalition. For this action, he was to earn the sobriquet of Ralph the Timid.[3] How he survived the rout is not recorded. Bishop Ealdred of Worcester was now entrusted with the bishopric of Hereford.[4] Though a cleric, Ealdred had already had experience in dealing with military matters as he had done when previously in Hereford whilst Ralph was elsewhere employed. He would be useful to Harold to bolster support down in that troublesome region. Alfgar was back in his East Anglian region and does not appear to have played a part in Gruffudd's recent rebellion, though he may have supported him at the peace treaty.

In the autumn of 1056, Harold found himself abroad on a quest to locate and bring home the lost prince, Edward the Exile, son of Edmund Ironside. The news of his existence may have come before this, possibly in the autumn of 1051, when Edward had been thinking about the succession and coming to terms with the fact that it was unlikely he would ever produce a child with Edith who had been banished at that time. When they were reunited, there may have been a glimmer of hope that the royal couple would provide the kingdom with an heir, but by 1054, it was looking very likely a back-up plan was needed. Edward sent Bishop Ealdred to Europe on a fact-finding mission to discover the whereabouts of his brother Edmund's son, known as Edward the Exile.[5] Ealdred's assignment was made unsafe by the war between Emperor Henry and Hungary. Unable to travel east, the bishop returned back to England, his mission unsuccessful.

So we can understand the rationale behind the search for the exiled ætheling, we need to go back to the dark days of Cnut's conquest. Edmund's marriage to Ealdgyth, widow of the murdered Sigeferth, had produced two sons, Edward and Edmund. Born in such a short space of time, they might have been twins. King Edmund's death in November 1016 meant that his sons were a future threat to Cnut and any of his heirs, therefore he needed to dispose of them. He ordered they be removed from England to Sweden with a request that King Olaf put them to death. But Olaf was unwilling to carry out the infanticide of two small children. At some other point in their lives, the boys, once again became the focus of a threat from Cnut, and were transferred to Kiev where they were nurtured by the Grand Prince Iaroslav, harbourer of exiled royals.[6] There the English brothers met other such banished siblings, such as Andrew and Levente of Hungary, also sheltered by the grand prince. Edmund's sons were given a warrior's upbringing and were with Andrew when he fought for the crown of his homeland.[7] Edward had been living at the court of Andrew for approximately the last ten years of his life before he was invited home by his Uncle Edward, king of England. It is worthy of note that when Cnut's heirs died it was to Æthelræd's son, Edward, that England looked to for the succession, not those with the blood of Ironside. Convenience overruled any thought of the sons of Ironside then, and Edward was chosen.

October 1056 was to see the death of Emperor Henry III, making travel to that area easier and shortly after, in November, Harold was in St. Omer. We know this only because a *Haroldi Ducis* was among the witnesses of a diploma issued by Count Baldwin V of Flanders.[8] The chronicles do not give any inklings as to who it was Edward sent to lead the delegation to bring home the Exile, however, circumstantial evidence places Harold abroad at the right time.

Harold's decision to go straight to Baldwin in Flanders appears like a natural choice for the Godwinsons. The count and his father before him had always been helpful to the family. Baldwin's connections would certainly help Harold meet the right people to get him access to the Hungarian court. The earl did not confine himself to St. Omer whilst waiting for news of the Exile. He was able to indulge himself in the sophistication of the vast array of towns and cities, and many of the relics that he provided Waltham with are listed originating from various ecclesiastical establishments on the Continent.[9] According to the *Vita*, the queen's brother had made it his business to study the 'princes of Gaul'. With skill and 'natural cunning', he watched them intently, observing what he could about business management and statesmanship. It seems that Harold also learned how to recognise the deceptions used by these crafty foreign lords, and how to avoid any proposals made toward him in bad faith.[10]

The author of the *Vita* implies that Harold's reputation as an affable and intelligent man was well-known throughout the Continent, suggesting that many were eager to meet and entertain him. Remarkably, the *Vita's* author does not make any comment about the Exile and any possible mission to find him. According to Ian Walker, Harold takes advantage of the opportunity to visit Cologne as part of Count Baldwin's entourage as they travel to Germany to discuss the new accord with the widow of the Holy Roman Emperor and is able to network with a number of important officials.[11] In Cologne he might have met with Agnes of Poitiers, the old emperor's widow, acting as regent for her infant son, Henry IV. This powerful woman led the negotiation of the peace treaty with Baldwin of Flanders.[12] During the visit, Harold might have employed the charm that made him so popular, gaining her support in the search for Ironside's son. It was in Regensburg where the imperial party were to spend Christmas, Walker suggested that Harold was able to discuss his desire to meet with Prince Edward with important members of the cabal. He may even have been able to open negotiations with the ætheling himself.[13]

The *Vita* informs us that Harold visited Rome,[14] and may have accompanied Pope Victor, from Regensburg after the Christmas period.[15] The Hungarian king, Andrew I, would no doubt be eager to inform his friend, Edward The Exile, that an English earl had been enquiring about him. Any form of negotiations would take time, with all the travelling and stopovers. It seems reasonable that Harold thought a visit to Rome an efficient way to spend his time whilst waiting for a response from the Hungarian court. *Vita* does not give the date or the context for his visit to Rome, but describes him having worshipped there 'with fitting bounty the thresholds of the saints, by God's grace he came home, passing with watchful mockery through all ambushes, as was his way'.[16]

Such a line cannot be glossed over without comment, and one cannot help but detect sarcasm embedded in the words 'watchful mockery' from the author of the *Vita*. This may have been in relation to the experience of Tostig during his sojourn to Rome, for *Vita* discusses in the following passage the fate of Tostig's party, hinting that the queen's perception of Harold was that he was the luckier brother of the two, but not the best, a veiled theme throughout the narrative.[17]

King Edmund's son finally reached English shores in April 1057, when it was thought Harold accompanied him back from the Continent. Edward Exile's brother, Edmund, had died some years previously, leaving just one of the sons of Ironside alive. This newly found ætheling may have been accompanied by his wife, Agatha, and their children, Margaret, Christina, and Edgar, however it is thought by some that Bishop Ealdred may have brought them back in 1058 on his way back from his endeavour to Jerusalem.[18]

It is not known the exact age of the two daughters but they were likely to have been older than Edgar.[19] The boy was somewhere between 3 and 5 years old in 1057, if we accept he was too young to take up the crown of England in 1066. The family were certainly not from the lower echelons of Hungarian society when they travelled to England, bringing much gold, silver and treasure with them. Agatha was said by some to have been a German princess.[20] Others believe she was the daughter of Iaroslav of Kiev who was known to have married his daughters to exiled princes, some of whom went on to regain their kingdoms, such as Andrew of Hungary, and Harald Hardrada.[21]

Having found the lost ætheling Harold had improved the kingdom's prospects of a smooth ascendancy to the throne. If King Edward was to die the next day, his nephew, a full-grown man, proved in battle, and already tutored in the arts of statesmanship, would be there to take the reins.[22] The problem with this was, nobody was expecting Edward Exile to die after only three days of stepping on England's soil. The date was 19 April, 1057.[23]

The words of the *D* chronicle hints that the Exile's death was viewed as a catastrophe for England.

> The ætheling Edward came to England; he was the son of King Edward's brother, King Edmund (who) was called Ironside for his bravery. King Cnut had sent this ætheling away to Hungary to betray, but he there grew to be a great man, as God granted him and became him well, so that he won the emperor's relative for his wife, and by her bred a fine family; she was called Agatha. We do not know for what cause it was arranged that he did not see his relative King Edward's (face). Alas! That was a cruel fate and harmful to all this nation, that he so quickly ended his life after he came to England, to the misfortune of this wretched nation.[24]

Frustratingly, *E* adds little more to the narrative, reporting only that soon after he departed, and that he was buried in St. Paul's Minster in London.[25] Licence suggests that the *D* version speaks for Edward, who must have been in despair at losing his nephew.[26] After all the years of planning, the months of searching, God suddenly played a deadly hand of fate, denying England a secure succession. Even nine years before the death of King Edward, those in power were concerned with obtaining an heir with the blood of Cerdic. This was a policy that the English were keen to pursue, and perhaps one that those who found the idea of a return to the Danish dynasty abhorrent, were eager to prevent.

John of Worcester clearly states that King Edward had wanted his nephew to succeed him and notes that he died soon after arriving in England.[27] The chronicler then goes on to focus on the death of Earl Leofric and Alfgar's succession to the earldom of Mercia. Frank Barlow advises that the scribe of *D* chronicle hints that the ætheling was kept away from the king purposely, but does not suggest that there was any foul play.[28] Some may have believed that there was something underhand about the sudden death of the Exile. There could have been many reasons for this, one of them being that he fell ill and was too sick to travel and may have needed time to recover before continuing the journey to meet with the king. Harold may have taken him to one of his manors to rest after landing on English shores; he had the use of a manor in Southwark that had belonged to his father. Both the *C* and *D* chronicles do not indicate anything suspicious and nor does John of Worcester. There is not a shred of evidence, circumstantial or otherwise that Harold was involved in the death of Edward the Exile. Not even the Norman propaganda machine made use of the ætheling's mysterious demise to lay the blame on Harold. He had no motive either. Neither the Exile nor his children were a threat to him or his own family who were well set for office if they weren't already. Additionally, as historian Emma Mason concludes, the delegations of Harold and Ealdred had gone to a lot of trouble to bring him back to England, safe and alive, and indebted to them, as Edward had been to Godwin for his support.[29] Furthermore, there is no suggestion at this time that Harold had his eyes on the throne. No attempt seems to have been made at ending the life of the Exile's son, Edgar, who was to become Edward's adopted son, and the only male relative of Edward's to be known as ætheling.

Despite the tragedy of Edward the Exile's death, the situation was not dire. The country still had an heir in the boy Edgar.[30] That he was only a small child would only be an issue if Edward was to die in the next few years, but Edward was to go on to live healthily for another eight and a half years, time enough to groom Edgar in the skills of kingship.

Though nothing can be found of Agatha's fate, the children of Edward Exile were made wards of the king and queen.[31] It is uncertain if their mother ever came with them to England. Ealdred was to have journeyed to Jerusalem in 1058 via Hungary, which was an uncommon route for men travelling to the Middle East from northern Europe, and one that no English bishop had ever taken.[32] It is possible the Exile's family stayed behind in Hungary waiting for news of how Prince Edward had been received in England. He might have stopped there to bring the sad news to the family and to persuade Agatha to bring her children to England to fulfil their father's legacy. Having completed his journey to the Holy Sepulchre, offering up a gold chalice, Ealdred may have then returned to Hungary to collect the family on the return journey and bring them with him.[33] The idea is discussed by Mason in her book *The House of Godwine*,

The ruins of Waltham Abbey where it is possible Harold's collegiate was situated. (Author's own picture edited by REGB Films)

Conisborough Castle built upon land that was Harold's. (REGB Films)

The River Wharfe at Tadcaster where Harold may have ordered his ships to be moored on the way to York. (REGB Films)

Above left: East Gate through which Harold and his troops passed through on their way to Stamford Bridge. (REGB Films)

Above right: Memorial stone at the Battle Flats where the battle was fought at Stamford Bridge. (REGB Films)

The exterior position of the orignal placement of Harold's tomb. (Author's own picture edited by REGB Films)

Above left: Harold's statue on the outside of the North-East Transept in Waltham. (Author's own picture edited by REGB Films)

Above right: Interior of The Holy Trinity Church at Bosham showing the Saxon Chancel where the coffins said to be of Harold and Cnut's daughter were found. (Author's own picture edited by REGB Films)

Harold's high window can still be seen inside the abbey. (Author's own picture edited by REGB Films)

The gated entrance into the old Augustinian ruins where the collegiate may have been. (REGB Films)

Above left: Memorial to Cnut's daughter commissioned by the children of the village in 1906. (Author's own picture edited by REGB Films)

Above right: Holy Trinity Church in Bosham, the view of the Saxon Tower. (Author's own picture edited by REGB Films)

The old manor house was situated over the church (Holy Trinity) wall and may have been the site of the Godwinson's home. (Author's own picture edited by REGB Films)

The millrace where the daughter of Cnut was said to have drowned. (Author's own picture edited by REGB Films)

Above: Compton/*Cumtune*, lands owned by Godwin and Wulfnoth. (Author's own picture edited by REGB Films)

Left: St. Michaels, Bishop Stortford, where some believe that Harold and members of his family may be buried. (Author's own picture edited by REGB Films)

Ermine Sreet bypassing Gainsborough, where Harold was thought to have marched to York. (Author's own picture edited by REGB Films)

Bosham Holy Trinity Church. (Author's own picture edited by REGB Films)

Above: Pevensey Castle, landing place of the Normans where inside the walls are the remains of the Roman fort of Anderida. (REGB Films)

Below left: An ancient yew tree, at least 1000 years old situated in the grounds of the church of St. George in Crowhurst, Sussex, where Harold held an estate. (Author's own picture edited by REGB Films)

Below right: Ruin of the old manor house in Crowhurst that may have been built over the original that belonged to Harold. (Author's own picture edited by REGB Films)

Above: St. George's church in Crowhurst.

Right: Diagram of the Battle of Hastings. (Paula Lofting)

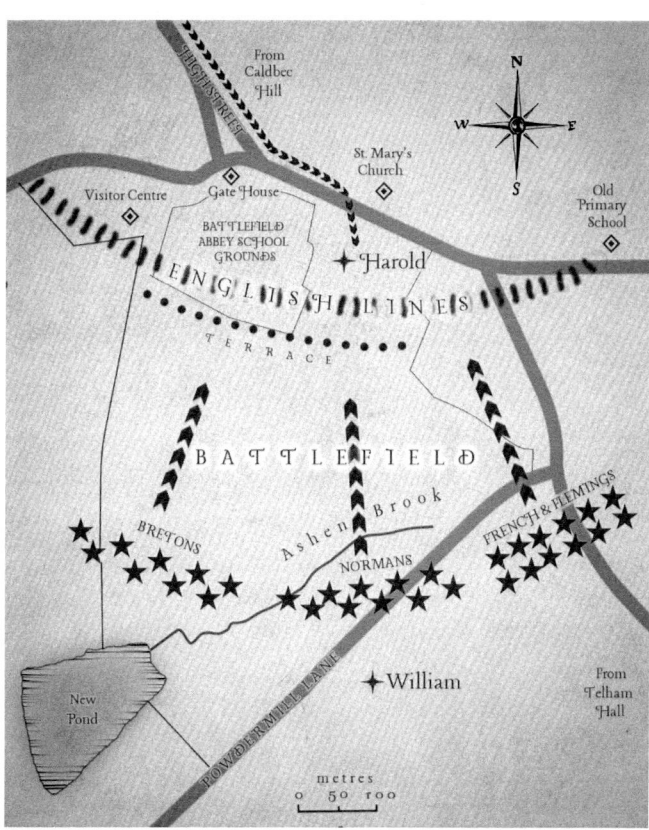

Left: Harold's huscarls marshalled for battle on the ridge. (Matt Bunker)

Below: Scene 57 Harold's death on the Bayeux Tapestry. In the (Public Domain)

Right: The Wanderer, first page of the Anglo-Saxon poem. (Public Domain)

Below left: Harold and Eadgifu/ Edith portrayed by Mitchell Lawrence and Jessica Bean. (REGB Films)

Below right: Eadgifu Swanneck portrayed by Jessica Bean. (REGB Films)

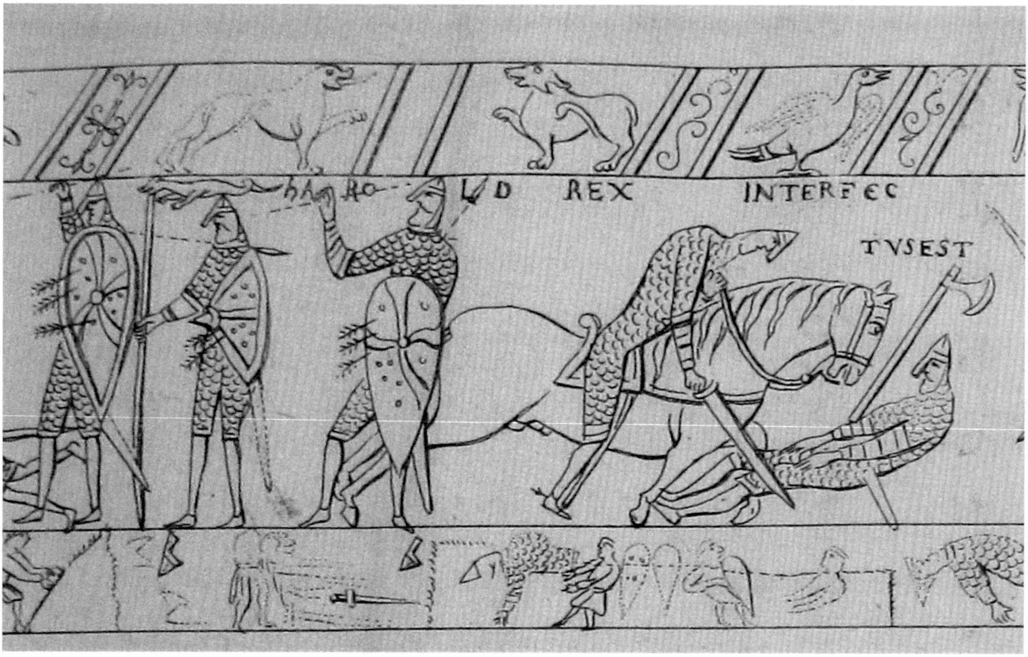

18th Century sketch of Harold's death scene. (Public Domain)

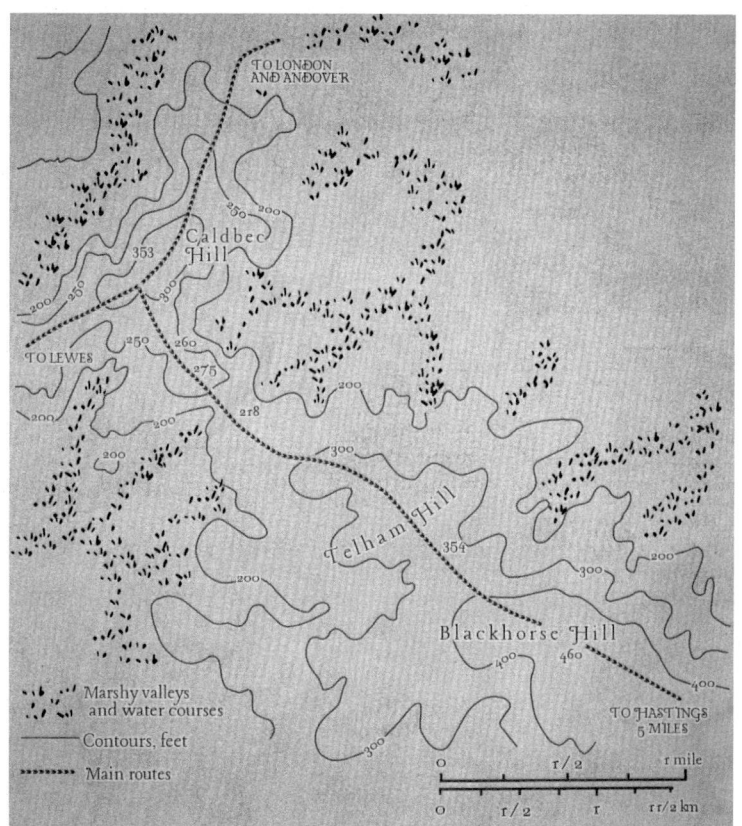

Topography of the Battle of Hastings. (Paula Lofting)

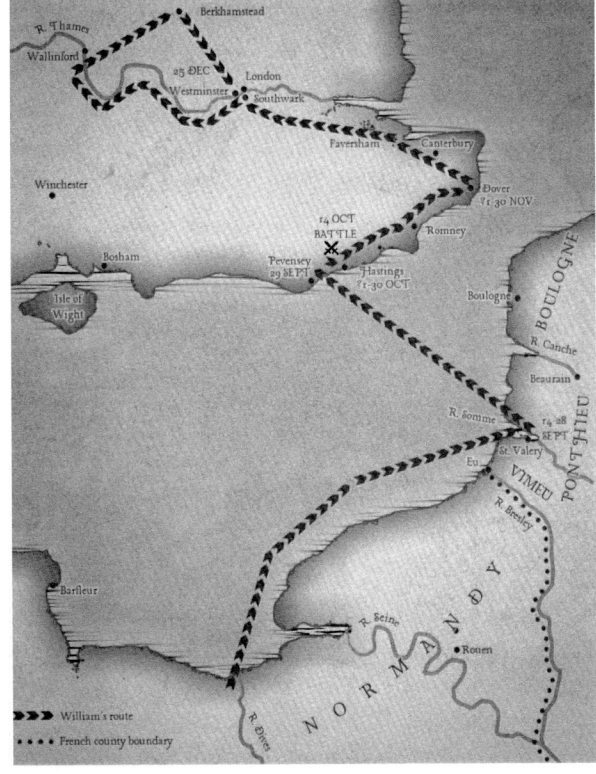

Above: Open coffin believed to be Harold's at Bosham Church. (Bosham Church)

Right: Map of William's crossing from Normandy to Pevensey. (Paula Lofting)

Pnls 2 and 3 of the Bayeux Tapestry, Harold and his men riding to Bosham. (Public Domain)

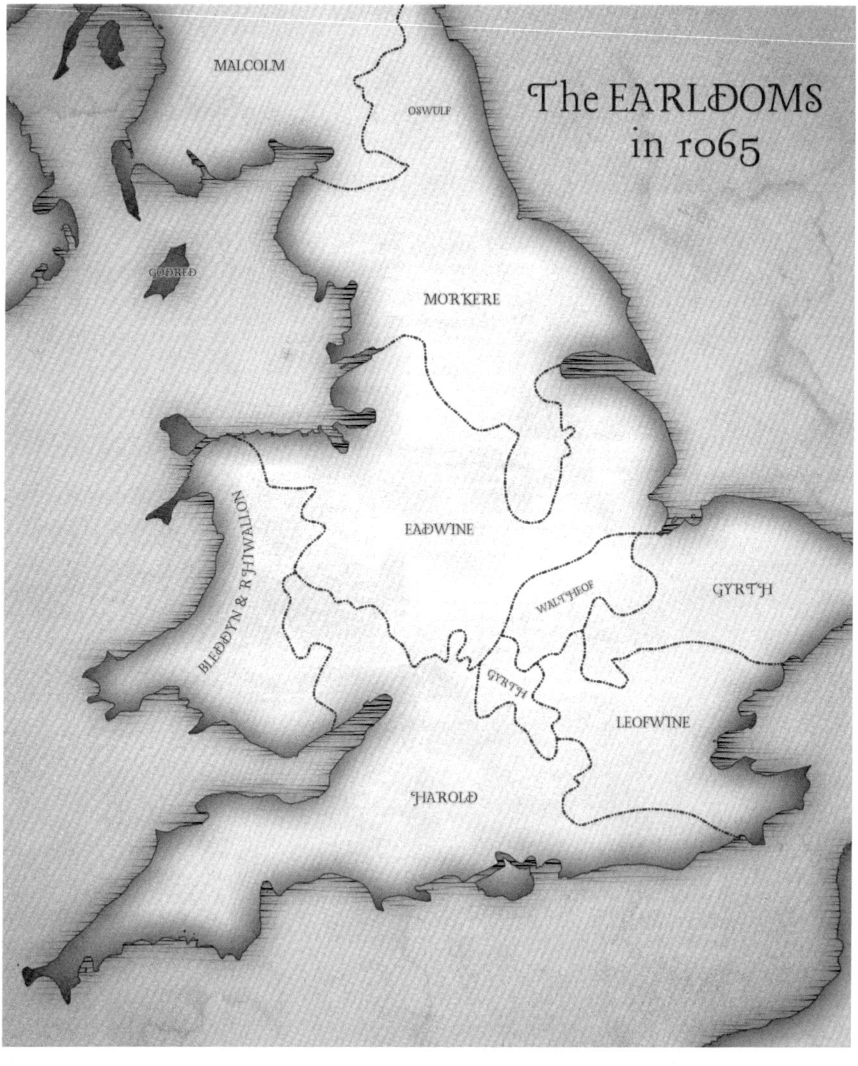

English Earldoms of 1065. (Paula Lofting)

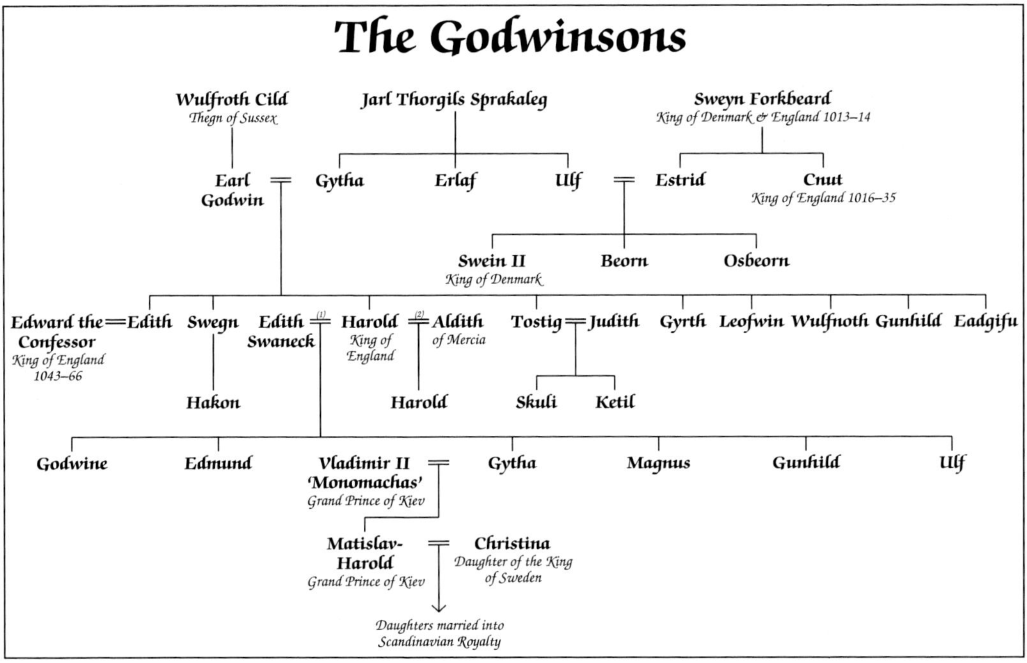

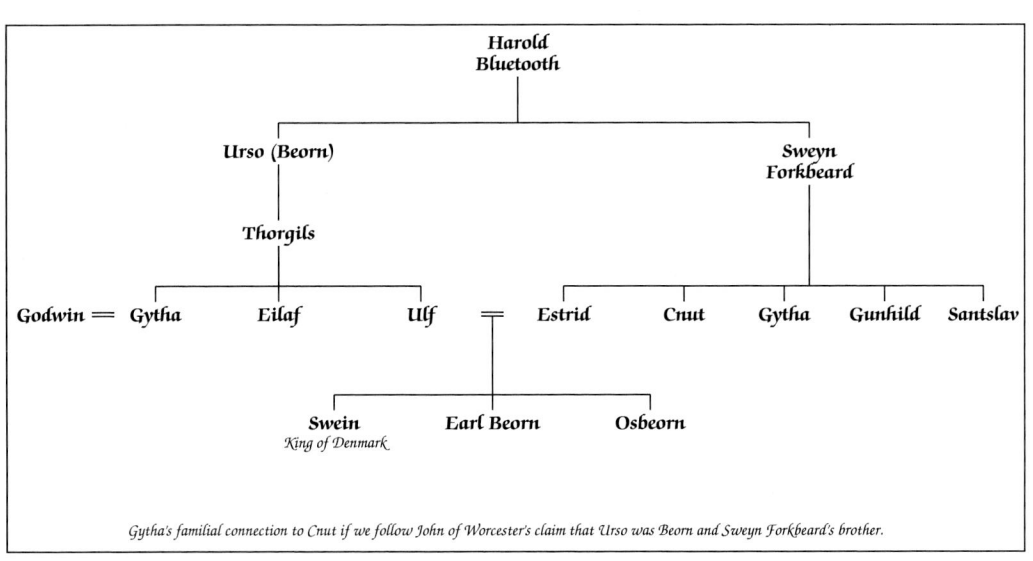

Family Tree of The Godwinsons. (Paula Lofting)

Family Tree of Harald Bluetooth. (Paula Lofting)

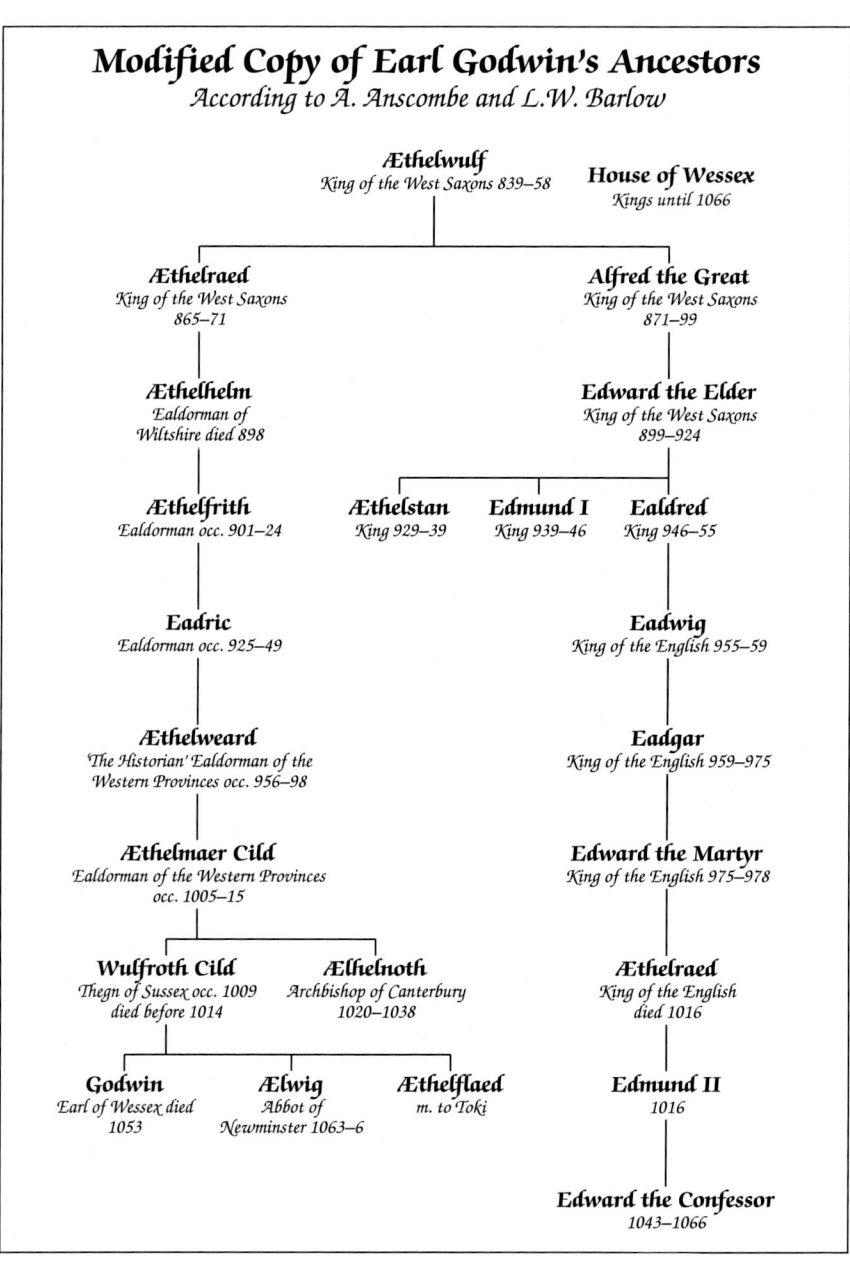

Family Tree of Earl Godwinsons Ancestors. (Paula Lofting)

and is arguably plausible and accounts for why Ealdred chose to go out of his way on his trip.

The children were reared in Edward and Edith's household. Christina was in her late thirties when she became abbess of Romsey Abbey in 1086. Margaret was to marry Malcolm III of Scotland after the Conquest. Edgar, we know is referred to as ætheling in all the sources.[34] *ASC D* records, the people would have him as king as his 'natural right'.[35]

Death of the Earls

Not only did England suffer the loss of its lost prince, but the year of 1057 also saw the deaths of earls Ralph and Leofric. Still referred to as earl, Ralph lost jurisdiction of Hereford to Harold who, with the assistance of Bishop Ealdred looked after its welfare from 1056 onwards. Not much is said about Ralph's passing on 21 December, apart from his burial place in Peterborough, but he left a wife, Gytha, who possibly may have been Osgod Clapa's daughter and widow of Tovi the Proud. Ralph and Gytha had a son, Harold, believed to be named after Harold Godwinson and thought to have been his Godson.

Earl Leofric passed on the 30 October, better loved by the chroniclers than Ralph. The *D* chronicle of Worcester praises Leofric: 'He was very wise, before God and before the world, in what availed all this nation. He lies at Coventry, and his son, Alfgar, succeeded to his authority.' John of Worcester gives his date of death as the 31 August, perhaps in confusion with Odda's death the year before. He and his wife, Lady Godgifu (Godiva) whom legend has it rode naked through the streets of Coventry, are lauded by the Worcestershire scribe. Ralph, had already been given a sharp dressing down by John for his dismal carry on in Hereford, and was afforded barely two lines in John of Worcester's obituary. It is also recalled by the *D* manuscript that Æthelric, monk of Canterbury, rose to the see of Selsey following the death of Bishop Heca.[36] He was thought to have been the relative of Godwin whom Edward turned down in favour of Robert Champart for the archbishopric. Another notable death mentioned was that of Pope Victor, whom Harold may have got to know well on his sojourn to Rome earlier that year.

With Leofric dead and buried in Coventry, Alfgar established himself in his father's seat of governance and set about planning his next move. Harold's brother Gyrth was promoted to the earldom that had been Alfgar's. *Vita,* when discussing the appointments of Tostig and Harold, tells us that younger brother Gyrth, although very young, the king gave him a shire at the extremity of East Anglia, most likely Norfolk, and promised that he would 'increase this when he was older and had thrown off his boyhood years', which he did in the year 1057 when Alfgar moved to Mercia.[37] It was not surprising to learn that the even younger Godwinson brother, Leofwin, was to receive an office of his own, succeeding to the lands left by the deceased Ralph in early 1058.[38]

Alfgar must have been frustrated to see his rival's family so favoured. He had three sons, one of whom, Burghred, was also ready for an earldom, but with the queen and Harold advocating for their brothers with the king, what chance did any of Alfgar's boys have? The Mercian earl once more needed an ally close to his borders. Luckily, King Gruffudd ap Llywelyn was in the market for a wife and a rekindling of his and Alfgar's alliance would benefit them both. A marriage between Alfgar's young daughter, Aldith, was just the thing to seal a bargain between them.

A marriage alliance may have already been discussed when the pair were in cahoots in 1055, but Aldith may not have been of age until 1058. She would have had to have been at least 12 to have been of marriageable age, and 15 at the eldest. A marriage such as this would have needed to have been approved by the king, but appears not to have been, and knowing that there would be opposition in every corner of England for the match, Alfgar made the arrangement secretly. Aldith's marriage to Gruffudd might well have influenced the decision to eject him from England once again.

Alfgar in Exile

The *D* version starts the year 1058 with, 'Here Alfgar was expelled, but he soon came back, again with violence, through the help of Gruffudd. And here came a raiding ship-army from Norway.' The scribe adds in shame, that 'it was too tedious to tell how it all happened'.[39] John of Worcester tells us with less detail that usual, 'Algar, earl of Mercia, was outlawed by king Edward for the second time, but, supported by Gruffydd, king of Wales, and aided by a Norwegian fleet, which unexpectedly came to his relief, he speedily recovered his earldom by force of arms.'[40]

There is no doubt that the events of summer, 1058, are mystifying. From the little that is mentioned, what occurred that year appears to be as equally dramatic as 1055, yet the sources are sorely lacking in detail. The Welsh chronicle does not even mention Alfgar.[41] They focus on the activities of Gruffudd and the Norwegians. 'Magnus, son of Harald, King of Germany (sic) came to England, and he ravaged the kingdoms of the Saxons, with Gruffudd, king of the Britons, as a leader and a help to him.'[42]

Nor do any of the sources say much more, though one Irish source refers to the boy, Magnus, son of King Harald of Norway, as arriving with forces from the Hebrides, Orkneys, and Dublin, 'to seize the English kingdom, but to this, God would not consent'.[43] It is possible that Magnus may have been acting on behalf of his father, who was busy raiding the coast of Denmark which he had been relentlessly doing on a yearly basis since the death of his predecessor and nephew, Magnus of Norway. Both father and son may have known about the *Göta älv* treaty between Harthacnut and the Norwegian King Magnus, in 1039 that whoever remained alive after the other's death would inherit their kingdom, and hoped to make use of the premise. Harald may have seen this as a chance to expand his Scandinavian territories to include England. However, it was more likely to have been opportunist moment for Magnus rather than a serious bid, and one that could be easily satisfied with the receipt of sufficient booty to fund future conquests. John of Worcester's suggestion that Magnus and his fleet 'came unexpectedly to his (Alfgar's) relief' may refer to an initial wariness on Magnus' part to join with him, but changed his mind at the last minute. As a prince of Norway, Magnus, would have arrived with a large, impressive fleet. This combined with the forces of Alfgar and Gruffudd would have been a formidable army, though according to the sources, Gruffudd appears to have been the dominant leader.[44] Magnus was 13 at the time, and Alfgar was earl, compared to Gruffudd's king.

Evidence for Alfgar's second expulsion in three years, points to his daughter's marriage to Gruffudd, suggesting Alfgar was eager to firm up his troublesome rapprochement with Gruffudd at this time. In fairness to the earl, it was a sensible thing for someone in his position to do, considering that he faced being surrounded by potentially hostile Godwinsons. With the Norwegians hanging around on the Isle of Man and in the western isles of Scotland, there may have been intel from Edward's spies that Gruffudd was negotiating with them. To the English court, it would have appeared that by marrying his daughter to Gruffudd, Alfgar was hoping to assert himself into their schemes, and by getting himself exiled, Alfgar now had an excuse to show Edward and Harold, that he was now a power to be reckoned with.

The incursion of the allied forces seems to have reduced from a mountain-sized problem, into a mole hill fairly quickly. In a repeat of 1055, Alfgar was restored to his earldom once more and young Magnus was sent away without an English kingdom, but with plenty of silver and a bounty of spoils grabbed from raiding the western coast. With Alfgar supported by Mercia, it could have been a full-scale civil war which the English, when it came down to it, had no stomach for.

The *D* entry for that year exudes embarrassment at letting Gruffudd and Magnus profit from booty taken from English lands.[45] Gruffudd's borders were now secure with his father-in-law back in the game, and his new friendship with the Norwegians would surely put him in a stronger position on the wider stage. Memories must have been stirred in those old enough to remember the Norse raids in the days of Æthelræd's reign when terror held sway over the lives of the English people, and must have sat uncomfortably with the *witan*.

The various narrations of 1058 give us no indication of Harold's involvement in tackling the invasion, nor do the sources anywhere speak of him having a role in any of the negotiations, though nothing is mentioned of negotiations at all. Tom Licence suggests that he was not even in the country when it happened, and places Harold in Rome in 1058 rather than in 1057.[46] According to Licence, Harold's journey to Rome occurred not in 1056/1057 when he was in St. Omer, but in 1058 and that it was he who brought back the pallium for Bishop Stigand, recorded in the ASC as an 'agent' of Pope Benedict.'[47]

This theory has some plausibility in answering the question of where Harold was during the crisis of 1058. However, with Alfgar at large again, and his relationship with Gruffudd renewed, it seems unlikely that Edward would allow Harold to leave the country at such a time with Ealdred in Rome, leaving Hereford without both of them.[47] Gyrth and Leofwin were new to their roles, and had not the experience in dealing with conflict as their older brother had. Each of the three *ASC* chronicles gives the impression that the pallium was sent to Stigand, delivered personally by a papal legate. None of them mention Harold being the agent.[48]

Tostig was also likely to have been absent during the crisis. Malcolm Canmore had finally rid Scotland of his rival Macbeth who he caught and executed on 15 August 1057. The new Scottish king began harassing Tostig with raids on his borders which Tostig was said to have 'worn down as much by cunning schemes as by martial courage and military campaigns'.[49] As a result of Tostig's strategy, we are told that the Scots and their king soon stop their harmful activities, for they 'preferred to serve him (Tostig) and King Edward than to continue fighting'.

With or without his two most experienced earls to support him against the rebellious Alfgar, the king dealt with the 'tedious' matter by paying the invaders off, and suggests that Magnus' intentions had not necessarily been to conquer, but to test the water and increase his wealth. The question of Stigand's pallium can be explained in multiple ways but it seems unnecessary to labour the point when there was more at stake than a bishop's stole. It is not inconceivable that there would still be time, for Harold to have left for Rome, after the emergency that summer was averted.

If Harold *had* been there during the crisis of 1058, and it seems likely he was, with Mercia against the king's faction and Tostig wrestling with Malcolm in Scotland, he would also have felt the pressure of having to avoid a bloody engagement and felt that the only solution to such a difficult decision would be to give in and negotiate a peace that whilst shameful, would avoid war.

No doubt Harold and Alfgar were unlikely to have been best friends after the horrors of Hereford, and this last debacle. Protocol would have enforced at least a pretence of decorum when around one another, and in the king's presence. But the real figurehead of Harold's antipathy, was never Alfgar. Harold may even have empathised with him, having run the gauntlet of expulsion himself. No, the man most likely to invade his nightmares at night was Gruffudd ap Llywelyn.

CHAPTER FOURTEEN

Fire and Sword

The Consecration of Waltham

> And so, with the kingdom made safe on all sides by these princes, the kindliest King Edward passes his life in security and peace and spent much of his time in the woods and the glades in the pleasures of hunting. After divine service which he gladly and devoutly attended every day, he took much pleasure in hawks and birds of that kind, brought before him, and really delighted in the baying and scrambling of the hounds.[1]

The year 1059 must have been a peaceful year for Harold and the king, for the chronicles are concerned mostly with ecclesiastic affairs abroad, including another new pope, Nicholas, bishop of Florence.[2] As we hear from *Vita*, the king was able to enjoy secular delights whilst still maintaining his devotion to all things Godly. His great project, the church of Westminster, was nearing completion. Harold, too, was still overseeing his own ecclesiastical dedication at his manor of Waltham. The construction of the church of the Holy Cross was almost finished. The earl of Wessex was now in his mid-thirties and like the king also enjoyed hunting and hawking. He was known, as aforementioned, to own many books on the subject. The year also saw the king of Scots attend Edward's court in Gloucester, sealing peace with England and giving hostages.[3]

Not recorded in the *ASC* or John of Worcester is the eight days of feasting to celebrate the consecration of Harold's church of the Holy Cross on 3 May 1060. *The Waltham Chronicle* refers to Harold as 'beloved' attesting that even in the late twelfth century, respect for him and his legacy still existed in the constitution of his holy establishment.[4] Harold adorned the interior of the church with many gifts which we know are listed in the records as being purchased or gifted to him from churches on the Continent.[5] The *Waltham Chronicle* assures us that this was a brand-new church, not constructed over the old one, but on new foundations, using 'bronze and gold inlay everywhere'. Once the construction was finished, the earl eagerly arranged for its dedication, inviting his sister the queen, the king, and Archbishop Cynesige of York. Also attending were eleven bishops, and eleven abbots and the four earls, which surprisingly included Alfgar, indicating some kind of peace had been made between them.[6] The chronicle hints that some attendees disliked him out of 'envy or personal malice, because he had no equal in the land'. One of these might have been the recalcitrant Alfgar. With four Godwinson brothers as earls, and just Alfgar, who was not a Godwin, the extent of this rather large dominant family was clear. Also listed as attendees were the leading magnates, as well as thegns, and king's servants.[7]

We hear that these men were invited with 'careful discretion' and note that neither Stigand or Ealdred were listed. Harold may have chosen not to invite Stigand for the reason that Pope Benedict who issued him with the pallium, had been overthrown in favour of Pope Nicholas II by a rival faction and become an 'anti-pope'. Everything Benedict had done, had been overturned a year later due to a reformation in the election of popes. It is not clear why Ealdred was not on the list, but Harold may have thought it wise to distance his church from him because he held both Hereford and Worcester in plurality. By the end of the year, Ealdred would become archbishop of York when the death of Cynesige created a vacancy.

The celebrations at Waltham went on for eight days. The abundant food and drink were not limited to the invited guests. The author of the chronicle claimed he heard from those whose fathers were present at the festivities, that great bowls of wine and mead were placed at crossroads for travellers to take their fill.[8] On the first day of the celebrations, Harold began by displaying all the holy relics he had acquired before all the guests; the collegiate canons, and the dean too were also summoned to witness. Harold stood, commanding in his appearance, before his guests, and surpassing in eloquence, spoke these words:

> Since from the time of man's original blindness 'a sacred hunger for gold' has descended upon the sons of disobedience from generation from generation up to this present time, I fear that, if these precious relics…may through the prevailing madness of wicked men, be stolen from the church…and put to the use of sinners. Yet these are things acquired by my own considerable toil and effort…Therefore, if it meet with your approval, my lord king, and that of your chief men, let them be buried in the ground, (in reliquaries) sealed with clay, to lie hidden in a secret place, concealed from all mankind…[9]

Later, we are told that the king confirms the relics that Harold has assigned to the church in a charter written in letters of gold. Edward then granted the lands of Hitchin to the church and in addition, Lambeth.[10] King Edward ratifies his confirmation with a warning that if any of his successors take anything from these lands, or allow it to be taken without restoration of the items, they should by God's law lose their kingdom and their crown. This was also unanimously agreed with by all the clerics present. Archbishop Cynesige gives a speech of his own, including an everlasting curse of excommunication and condemnation should anyone offend against the gifts given by the king and the earl.[11]

Tostig in Rome

In 1061, whilst Harold was conducting the business of peacefully administering his earldom and enjoying the lordship of the manor of Waltham, the widely itinerant Ealdred, now archbishop of York, travelled again, this time to Rome to plead with Pope Nicholas some business of the king's and to 'obtain the use of the pallium'.[12] He was accompanied by a party of companions consisting of Tostig, earl of Northumbria, the earl's wife, Judith, and Tostig's younger brother Gyrth. Also, in the party was a military guard, possibly led by Northumbrian noble, Gospatric, the grandson of Æthelræd's daughter, Ælfgifu and Edward's great nephew. Bishops Giso and Walter had succeeded to the sees of Somerset and Hereford respectively.[13] They may have arrived with Tostig's party, or they could have travelled separately. Tostig may have decided to combine a trip to Rome to convey the pope's tax of the third pence which England paid annually,[14] whilst supporting his new archbishop, Ealdred, who was proposing to revive the old custom of holding Worcester and York in plurality.[15] According to *Vita,* Ealdred was subjected to a somewhat hostile examination of the manner in which he had acquired sacred orders. Ealdred freely admitted to having obtained the bishopric of his 'first ordination to another, contrary to canon law' —in other words in plurality.[16] Ealdred gave the inquiry the information without hesitation and in all innocence was duly mortified by the mistake he had committed. Despite his integrity, not only did he fail to obtain the pallium but was also struck from the clergy! Tostig, who had been seated in a place of honour next to Pope Nicholas himself, lost his temper on Ealdred's behalf and threatened to stop the future payments of the 3 pence.[17] His threats, however, were not heeded.

Both Giso and Walter were successfully confirmed in their bishoprics by the pope.[18] The fact they were Lotharingian may have gone in their favour. Tostig's party, however, left Rome together somewhat dejected at their experience, though it was about to get worse. Not long after the group exited the gates of Rome they were attacked by bandits led by a Tuscan nobleman, Count Gerard of Galeria, an enemy of the pope.[19] They were robbed of practically all their belongings, some were even left naked.[20] Luckily, Tostig had despatched Judith home at the first sign of trouble in Rome, with an escort of most of his men and she was later to arrive home safely unaware of what had happened to her husband. It seems the bandits were looking for Earl Tostig whom they knew to be a very wealthy man, but thanks to the quick-thinking of Gospatric, riding in the vanguard of the entourage, the earl was able to escape.[21] The outraged party returned to Rome to complain to the pope and his authorities. This time they were met with sympathy by Pope Nicholas, and Ealdred was reinstated and presented with the pallium, whilst Tostig was placated with gifts and sweet words.[22]

Tostig and company were not the only ones to visit Rome and the pope that year, for Alfgar's son, Burghred, was said to have accompanied Bishop Wulfwig, charged with appealing to the pope for papal protection for the endowment of a church in Stow. It appears that on their way back, Burghred took ill and died in Reims. The community there must have looked after him, for his body was taken for burial in the basilica of the abbey of Saint-Rémi. Upon hearing of their son's death, his grieving parents gave the abbey an estate in Staffordshire, together with a beautifully illustrated gospel book, for the sake of their son's soul.[23]

Perhaps one of the first things Ealdred made sure of when he arrived home in the autumn of 1061, was to relinquish his see of Worcester, recommending that his deputy, the saintly cleric Wulfstan, be elevated to the bishopric. Having held various posts at Worcester Abbey, Wulfstan was certainly well qualified.[24] By the end of that year, Pope Nicholas was dead, and a new bishop was chosen as pope, Alexander of Lucca.[25]

Tostig was sure to report to the king on his return, where he was likely told of the raid on his lands by his 'friend' Malcolm, who had broken his oath.[26] According to *Vita,* Tostig resolved the issue of Malcolm without having to take military action and restored good relations once more.[27]

Sometime during the year of 1062, Alfgar was to follow his son in death. None of the sources mention his passing, which is baffling, considering every other notable earl's demise was recorded in that decade. His death, however, was likely to have been the spark that ignited Harold's next actions – the destruction of King Gruffudd ap Llywelyn.

The Time of Reckoning

With Alfgar gone, the king was now able to take affirmative action against the oath-breaker, King Gruffudd. The friendship with his father-in-law had previously made Gruffudd difficult to deal with, though it is likely that his association with Alfgar kept him in check. With Alfgar's demise, Gruffudd may have felt free to raid over the border, especially as he was running low on lands to gift to those he wished to keep loyal. *Vita* states that Gruffudd, 'discontented with his western bounds, carried wrongful war across the Severn'.[28]

In the midwinter (January) of 1063, Earl Harold was celebrating at Gloucester with the king. When the celebrations were over and it was time to get back to business, a court decision was made to put paid to Gruffudd's raiding.[29] In what appeared to have been something that had been on the cards for some time, Harold formed a small troop of elite mounted warriors to act as an assassination squad, and they rode rapidly on Edward's orders to the Welsh king's palace of Rhuddlan.[30] Davies and Davies however, provides us with a rationale for making the attack on Gruffudd at that time, for according to the Welsh lawbooks, after Christmas, the king's military household, led by the captain of the guard, (*penteulu*[31]) would make a tour of their lord's townships, before returning to their king's side where they would not leave him for the entire year. This suggests that Harold and Edward had planned the strategic move to coincide with the tour, to make use of the absence of Gruffudd's guards. Fortunately for Gruffudd, Harold's plan at catching him unawares was thwarted. The wily Gruffudd was pre-warned and, preferring not to fight unprepared without his *teulu* (warrior family), escaped with his attendants aboard one of his ships.[32]

Frustrated, Harold ordered that the palace and his whole fleet should be burned.[33] There was no opposition from Alfgar's sons, Edwin and Morcar, nor was there any indication of concern for their sister, Aldith, Gruffudd's wife. However, if this lightning raid into Wales came soon after hearing of their father's death, it is unlikely there would have been any time to consider it.[34]

Some sources suggest that Gruffudd went to Ireland to drum up some support as his father-in-law was inclined to do. Later historians, such as Frank Barlow, think this unlikely due to Harold's connection with Diarmait and the fact that Gruffudd's enemy, Cynan ab Iago, whose father's throne Gruffudd had seized in 1039, was established there.[35] Having failed to catch the Welsh king, the earl of Wessex and his troops marched home. But Harold was not done with Gruffudd, and toward the end of May of that same year, Harold and Tostig mounted a devastating two-pronged attack on Wales. Gruffudd meanwhile, returned from Ireland, or his hiding place, wherever that may have been, and energetically prepared for the invasion he knew was coming.

Tostig, free from the threat of Malcolm, was now able to exact revenge on Gruffudd for his part in the ravaging of the coast of West Northumbria in 1058 in cahoots with Alfgar and Magnus.[36] Tostig's forces entered Wales from the north[37] and Harold, using his naval skills once more, sailed out from Bristol with a fleet around Pembrokeshire and moored at Cardigan Bay. From there he went into the heart of Wales. His brother met him somewhere inland or perhaps somewhere near the coast. Uniting their forces, they swiftly laid waste to the country, a strategy that would draw Gruffudd's forces into skirmishes, where he would defeat them.[38] Harold and Tostig struck terrible fear into the foe with fire and sword. The Welsh, lightly armed for battle, were unable to meet their enemy on equal terms.[39] Harold pursued them into the 'fastness of Snowdonia' to beat them at their own game, wearing them down until they were jaded enough to reconsider their positions.[40]

Throughout his life, Gruffudd had rewarded riches and lands to those he would keep loyal to him. Now he was aging; new conquests were no longer forthcoming. He had exhausted the supply of bribes he could give and the death of his father-in-law, Alfgar, was to presage his downfall.[41] Eventually the Welsh in the south deserted their king in the belief that their energies would be best placed elsewhere. There is some evidence that even some of Gruffudd's Gwynedd men were among the rebels, but may not have been from among his inner circle.[42] It is possible that men in the south saw Harold's invasion as advantageous. Davies and Davies cite Tudor historian David Powel as claiming that the earl of Wessex entered south Wales by procuring the nobles of the south to his cause.[43] This would have been likely to have included Caradog, son of the king of the Deheubarth, whom Gruffudd ap Llywelyn slaughtered in 1055. No doubt he would not have had too many issues recruiting men to him, just as Harold found Caradog easily persuaded, using the Welsh penchant for feuding amongst each other to his gain.[44] Caradog was not the only one keen to put a dagger through Gruffudd's heart, there were a few others among the nobles, especially in the south of Wales.[45]

Gruffudd's half-brothers, Bleddyn and Rhiwallon, were likely to have been part of his inner circle, but they eventually capitulated to Harold, either before or after his own men had him killed. *D* chronicle says that King Gruffudd's men killed him on the 5 August (1063) 'because of the struggle he had been waging with King Harold'. They sent him his head and the beautiful prow that adorned his ship. Harold then brought it to King Edward, and upon oaths of fealty sworn to him by the brothers, agreeing to pay tribute to him, the king gave them the whole of Wales.[46] *E* reports succinctly that Harold, with his brother Tostig, invaded and conquered the land of Wales. The people submitted and gave hostages, then killed their king, Gruffudd, and brought Harold his head, and he set another king for it.[47] John of Worcester confirms the *ASC*.[48]

The idea that Gruffudd's own *teulu* murdered him goes totally against the customs and laws that governed the duties a lord's household owed him. According to Welsh literature and such songs that the bards would have sung in court in the day, a household who abandoned their lord in his time of great need risked eternal ignominy.[49] This does not mean that the Welsh king did not meet his death at the hands of his *teulu*, but does suggest that this would have been done at great risk to their reputation, making them pariahs in the eyes of society. And so it is worth exploring further, and more answers lie in *The Annals of Ulster* and *The Annals of Loch Cé*. The Irish annals declare that Gruffudd was slain by a son of Iago ab Idwal, whose throne Gruffudd had seized in 1039.[50] This would be the aforementioned Cynan, who had been given refuge by Diarmaid mac Máel na mBó.[51] In the chaos of Gruffudd's rejection by his own people, Davies and Davies suggest that Cynan saw the opportunity to return to Wales and claim kingship of Gwynedd. Whether or not Cynan was unable to convince the local populace to support him is not clear, however, upon Gruffudd's death as we have already mentioned, it was Rhiwallon and Bleddyn who benefited from their brother's death. Cynan's son, Gruffudd, was to continue his father's mission at establishing himself in Gwynedd in the future with the backing of Hiberno-Norse mercenaries.[52]

The remarkable Welsh king, Gruffudd ap Llywelyn met his death on 5 August. He was the first to have ruled the whole of Wales, which he did for eight years, and the northern kingdoms of Gwynedd and Powys for twenty-four. It was an ignominious death for this great warrior, who had fought and killed his way to the kingship, his head removed along with the embellished figurehead of his ship and given to the king of England. No doubt, Edward gratefully received the grisly spectacle and the people of Hereford and Shropshire rejoiced.

Gruffudd had two sons, Maredudd and Idwal. Gruffudd's other son, Owain, was killed in battle in 1059. Perhaps his other sons were still minors and so were overlooked by Edward and Harold, though they were old enough to participate in military operations in 1069.[53] Walter Map says of Gruffudd, that he denied killing anyone, but that he would only 'blunt the horns of Wales so that they may not hurt their mother'. He had made many enemies in his long reign. Eventually, although fighting to the bitter end, hiding in dykes and leaping out of them to ambush the enemy, Gruffudd was captured and killed by his own people, putting an end to the war which had gone on for three months.

Some have criticised Harold's destructive campaign in Wales as heavy-handed, claiming that the English earl was to blame for the inability of the Welsh to withstand the Normans later.[54] Gerald of Wales and John of Salisbury, are two twelfth century writers with similar opinions. Gerald of Wales writes:

> Then last but fully the greatest, Harold came, who on foot with his lightly clad infantry crossed through and around all of Wales, living off the land so strongly that he left not one that pisseth against the wall anywhere. In commemoration of his conquest, and to his perpetual memory, according to ancient tradition, he erected inscribed stones in many places in Wales where he had won victories. On these stones you will discover many having the following insignia sculpted: Harold was the victor here.[55]

Interestingly, none of these stones have ever been found.

John of Salisbury reports that Harold, 'devastated everything along the way to Snowdon and he captured their heads to the king who had sent him. And killing every male he could find, all the way to pitiful little children, he pacified the province with the edge of a sword.'[56] It was also said that so many Welshmen were killed, King Edward allowed Welsh women to marry Englishmen to compensate.

Neither of the claims that these two chroniclers make are corroborated in such detail by any earlier sources. It is difficult to understand how Harold could successfully negotiate treaties with the Welsh after inflicting such harsh punishment on them. Whether or not these claims are hyperbolic, it was no doubt no more or less what the Welsh had done in Hereford and the marcher lands for years some of Harold's soldiers may have been burning with a lust for vengeance. This was the darker side of campaigning, it was always the innocent who suffered the most.

It is difficult to know what else a medieval warlord could have done under the circumstances. For years the people who lived along the Welsh border lands had endured raids over the borders, the obliteration of their lands, kidnapping and rape, and the enslavement of men, women, and children. We should also not forget the enticement of Vikings to aid them. And the English bore this with restraint and the Welsh without punishment. John of Worcester reports that the Welsh king often made frequent destructive raids over the borders within England,[57] and *Vita* also follows in the same vein.[58] Davies and Davies, acknowledging the declarations of the former sources, dismissed this as propaganda from a winning side, though credibly points out that it was in Harold's interest to ensure that he destroyed the alliance between Mercia and Wales once and for all, leaving Alfgar's successor, the young Edwin, malleable to his influence and paving his way to the throne.[59] This was a thing that Alfgar would never have borne willingly.

In their book about Gruffudd, the brothers Davies mention an incident accounted in the *Life of St. Gwynllyw* involving Harold and the saint's church on Stow Hill. This was said to be motivated by unfair tolls and the ill treatment of English merchants sailing on the River Usk and the confiscation of their anchor which was taken to the saint's church in Stow. On hearing of this, Harold was said to have assembled a formidable army to take vengeance, which considering the peaceful way he dealt with worse encroachments by the Welsh, seems rather disingenuous. The story goes that Harold laid waste to Glamorgan, causing the people to flee, leaving their valuables hidden in the church. Like 'wolves most greedy for rapine', the English seized everything they could get their hands on. Later Harold repented and returned the plunder to the church.[60] This account could be conflating two separate incidents, the attack on Wales in 1063, and another incident later in 1065, which may have involved the stolen anchor.[61]

The *Life of St. Gwynllyw* was written in the late eleventh century, possibly within living memory of its composers, and there is no reason to doubt its veracity although dating the incident proves difficult. However, the account should be handled with care.[62] The inclusion of outlandish miracles and divine interventions including cheeses that bled when they were cut into, should naturally be discarded, leaving what might be a plausible account of what may have happened at the church.

The Welsh chronicle does not record details of the English invasion of Wales, focusing on the manner of Gruffudd's death:[63] Gruffudd ap Llywelyn was slain, after innumerable victories and the taking of spoils, gold and silver treasures, and precious purple raiment, through the treachery of his own men, after his fame and glory had increased, and after he had been unconquered, but was now left in the waste valleys. And after he had been head and shield, and defender to the Britons.[64]

It has been intimated that it was Harold who broke the oath of peace made between Gruffudd and Edward in 1056, by violently invading Wales.[65] However, Harold was present to broker the terms for at least two of the treaties that had been made, first in 1055 and again in 1056. He may also have been involved in the treaty of 1058 after Gruffudd had orchestrated a full-scale invasion that saw raiding around the west coast of Tostig's territory. Again, there was no reprisal against Gruffudd. There is no evidence that Harold betrayed any of those treaties. Gruffudd's involvement in the invasion of 1058 with Alfgar and Magnus, reveals it was Gruffudd who broke the terms of the accord of 1056. It is unlikely that Harold would have sanctioned an invasion Wales without prior provocation, as we see in John of Worcester's entry for that year. And even if Gruffudd had been quiet on the borders, Gruffudd's track record at keeping oaths proved him less than trustworthy and probably even more so without Alfgar to contain him.[66] Edward and Harold had no choice but to put an end to the savage and damaging incursions once and for all. It was what any strong medieval king would have done. Most warlords would have treated their enemy with far less restraint in the face of such hostility as Harold had done over the years. Offa for example was often at war with Wales.[67] Edward the 1st responded forcefully to conflicts with the Welsh by brutally conquering them. He built a series of castles, and imposed English rule and settlement there in the late thirteenth century. He was later to do the same to Scotland.[68]

King Gruffudd ap Llywelyn of Wales was undoubtedly a remarkable leader, an effective, strong ruler; defender of his people. Despite his successes, he ruthlessly fought his way through his enemies, and by doing so gained himself many more. It is unlikely he would have lasted into the 1060s, had it not been for his wily avoidance of assassination, and Harold's restraint. Davies and Davies makes this interesting statement:

> The tone taken by English and continental sources in dealing with Welsh nobles was to become increasingly patronising in the course of the twelfth and thirteenth centuries, a reflection of growing imperial outlooks and of a very real reduction in the power of Welsh leaders. The attitude stands in stark contrast to the neutral tone taken by Anglo Saxon sources in their dealings with Wales and ties in with the growing idea that cultures on the edge of mainstream Europe were 'barbaric'.[69]

The English invasion and defeat of Gruffudd opened up opportunities for his enemies – the old royal houses – to reform. Harold's decisive subjugation of the Welsh solved the problem of Welsh incursions for some years to come. Gerald of Wales states that the Normans had no trouble with the Welsh once they had taken England, and initially this might have been so, but gradually things for the Welsh became tougher when the Normans asserted themselves more fully in their expansions in the West. Had Hastings had a different outcome, a victory for Harold would have been better, not only for England, but for Wales too.

CHAPTER FIFTEEN
William and the Crown

William of Normandy

It's only right that we should explore the background of Harold's future opponent, Duke William of Normandy, even if only briefly. Born in either 1027 or 1028 in Falaise, William was the only illegitimate son of Duke Robert, and Herleve, thought to be a daughter of a tanner, and, or, an embalmer.[1] Her name and father's occupation are given in Orderic's interpolation of William de Jumièges account of *Gesta Normarum Ducum*. Orderic was the first chronicler to name her, and it was he who also gave her father's name as Fulbert.[2] Sometime after William was born, his mother was married to the *vicomte* of Conteville, Herluin. It was to this man she gave birth to William's half-brothers, Odo and Robert. Both distinguished themselves among his supporters at the Battle of Hastings. Herleve's affair with Robert is shrouded in myth and legend, though it is clear it advanced her family into the service of the duke. Fulbert was given an office at court and her brothers, Osbern and Walter witnessed charters. Therefore, it is doubtful that they came from the lowest of the peasant community as has been previously thought.

Robert did not always enjoy good relations with his own relatives. Conflict between Robert and his brother, and predecessor, Richard, divided the nobles of Normandy over the succession. Robert rebelled against his brother's rule, and some thought that he had caused his brother's death. Though he had the most to gain, it could not be proved.[3]

According to Douglas, William was brought up among his mother's family in their home of Falaise. He was known mostly as William the Bastard among his contemporaries, but later he was to become known as the Conqueror, at a time when none would dare to call him bastard to his face.[4] When William was 7 years old, Robert made him his heir, just before leaving on pilgrimage to Jerusalem. It is difficult to fathom why the duke made this decision when his magnates expressed their outrage at such an undertaking at that time of recent instability. Robert did not listen and departed for the Holy Land never to return. Drogo de Mantes was his friend and companion, and was the husband of King Edward's sister, Goda. Together they died of mortal sickness, during the pilgrimage. It was under this cloud that William, illegitimate, and of humble origins on his mother's side, began his reign as duke.

Not everyone was keen. As well as being born a bastard, he had another disadvantage. He was only a child. This gave William's enemies the ammunition to try to have him deposed.[5] After William's main supporter, the powerful Archbishop Robert died, the Duchy of Normandy descended into chaos. One of his mother's brothers, Walter, who held a position in the duke's household, became a steadfast supporter of his nephew and he and William had some lucky hair-raising escapes from would-be assassins. It was said that Walter was often forced to hide William in the peasant homes of his mother's people.[6]

Though young William had many supporters, one being King Henry of France, many of William's guardians were killed protecting him and one, Osbern the Steward, was killed after a scuffle in William's own bed chamber.[7] The minority of the young duke was a tumultuous time. Almost all of those who had been supporting William at the time of his accession died violently.[8] It was a dangerous time for William and for anyone close to him. In 1040, Count Alan of Brittany, William's chief tutor, died suddenly. His replacement, Count Gilbert, died soon after whilst out riding.[9] The next few years saw the rise of various branches of the ducal family. Brothers Maughan and William rose to the archbishopric of Rouen and the *comte* of Arques.[10] These were the sons of William's grandfather Richard II. Maughan, who had taken over from William's beloved uncle Robert, was to dominate the political landscape in the 1040s. In return for receiving the honour of Arques, William was to discharge loyal service to his great nephew.[11] Other members of William's family rising to positions of importance were the son of Archbishop Robert, Ralph de Gace, said to have been the murderer of Count Gilbert; and Guy of Burgundy, grandson of Richard II received both Vernon and Count Gilbert's castle of Brionne.[12]

Astonishingly, William survived those turbulent years. The traumatic events in which his guardians were killed must have affected him psychologically, shaping him into the ruthless man he became. Understandably, trust must have been an issue for him. In 1046, an attempt to overthrow William when he was only 19, was thwarted. Having escaped the western barons plot to kill him, he sought refuge with the king of France. The following year, William defeated the rebels with the aid of King Henry at Battle of Val-ès-Dunes.[13] The battle was won, says William's biographer, Poitiers, because of William's efforts stating, 'hurling himself upon his enemies, he terrified them with slaughter'.

William could now return to his duchy and assume power again. This brought about the Truce of God, a proclamation that would limit warfare throughout his duchy by restricting days when fighting would be allowed.[14] Val-ès-Dunes was a pivotal point for William in gaining control of his realm; however, there was still a long road ahead before he would gain full control over his nobles and duchy. It has been said that during his minority, he was supported by his cousins Roger de Beaumont, William FitzOsbern, and Roger de Montgomery. All remained close to the duke, and were not among those who had rebelled against him.[15] William Fitz Osbern and Roger de Montgomery were rewarded for their loyalty with lands in England, whilst Roger Beaumont, too old to accompany William to England for the invasion, supported the mission financially. Roger's eldest son fought bravely at Hastings, and both his sons were gifted generously with lands.

Conflicts continued to occur in the period between 1047–1060. It was around 1052, that William's protector the king of France, turned on him and joined another of the Norman rebels' attempts to overthrow him.[16] The duke, however, was resilient, and repelled all the incursions. The hostilities between his internal enemies persisted until 1060, by which time William had more or less consolidated his position in Normandy, and had been married to Matilda of Flanders for at least a decade with a brood of sons and daughters. It was time for this battle-hardened warlord to settle into a period of peace and draw his thoughts to an event that happened nine years ago, when it was said that King Edward of England promised him the throne.

Harold in Normandy

Harold seems to have never met Duke William prior to his embarkation to Normandy in the autumn of 1064. It is difficult to imagine that if Harold had known of William's manipulative and wily character he would not have gone ahead with his trip to Normandy. The political state of England at that time is difficult to fathom, for the only chronicle that includes the year 1064, is the *E* version, who records what happened in 1065 erroneously as in 1064. Perhaps it was a year that the English wished to forget. The earliest sources we have for his going are Norman sources. The only English version is an early twelfth century source.

Why Harold chose to go to Normandy at this time is baffling to some historians. Many differing opinions about his intentions have been transmitted through time. At this point, Harold had no effective rival. England was now run by the Godwinsons, and the only non-Godwinson was Edwin, the teenage son of Alfgar, at the helm of Mercia. Edward seems to have gone into semi-retirement, leaving most of his kingly duties to Harold to indulge in his love of leisurely pursuits, and more questionably, prayer. By this time, Harold was known as *dux Anglorum,* duke of the English, similar to that of his father. *Vita* had used the term *baiulus* when referring to Godwin.[17] Later writers such as John of Worcester, were of the opinion that he was acting as *sub regulus*,[18] suggesting he was recognised as vice-regent, second only to the king.[19] Peter Rex suggests that some historians saw him as a Hugh Capet figure. Under the French King Louis V in the late tenth century, Hugh had been installed as 'Mayor of the Palace', *major palatii*, which was a Merovingian term for someone tasked with the head duties of a royal administrator. When King Louis died in 986, Capet was elected to the throne, starting the Capetian dynasty, despite there being a hereditary heir, Louis' uncle, Charles, Duke of Lower Lorraine. Rex states, that Harold was acting in an equivalent role.[20] Wace, the author of the *Roman de Rou*, acknowledges Harold as holding the seneschal of England, and that he 'had great influence, and was in truth the most powerful man in all the land'.[21]

During his years as Earl of Wessex, Harold had acted as the king's representative, leading negotiations and ensuring the security and safety of the kingdom, especially along the borders of Wales. In the 1050s, he was restrained in his dealings with the Welsh, being acutely aware of the problems that Alfgar and Gruffudd combined could bring if inflamed, but by 1062, with Alfgar dead and Gruffudd threatening the peace treaty of 1056 once more, it was time to act more effectively, and bring about peace in the long-term. This meant that by 1064, the king could afford to send Harold abroad if he so desired.

As previously mentioned, we have no contemporary English explanations of the visit, not even from the *Vita*. Consequently, we have to be dependent on the Norman chroniclers such as William de Jumièges, and Poitiers, who wrote post Battle of Hastings but within the eleventh century. Guy of Amiens' *Carmen* is the earliest account we have of the Battle of Hastings, and tells the story of the invasion and its aftermath. We cannot rely on it as a source for Harold's time in Normandy. Jumièges' work appears to be written to compliment *Carmen* and to justify the invasion and William's legitimacy of the throne using propaganda. Poitiers elaborates more propaganda and makes absurd claims about the duke's right to the throne. Lastly, we have the Bayeux Tapestry, which was designed and created by English hands, though for whom it is not certain. Some of the various candidates are Odo of Bayeux, the Conqueror's half-brother; Queen Matilda, William of Normandy's wife; and Eustace of Boulogne. It gives us a uniquely visual reference for the battle, though that in itself is problematic, for it is ambiguous and should be treated cautiously.

William de Jumièges, writing in about 1070, takes up the story, not where he previously left off in 1060, but describes events that have been attributed to 1064 and Harold's visit to Normandy. It was, he advises, a planned mission in which King Edward is suddenly imbued with urgency after more than a decade, to affirm his promise to the duke originally made by the Archbishop Robert in 1051.[22] According to Jumièges, Harold fell into the hands of Guy de Ponthieu after bad weather blew his ship off course.[23] He was freed by the intervention of Duke William. It is a straightforward tale and has Harold being sent back to Edward to report on how it all went after he had sworn the oaths, and performed fealty, in which he became William's vassal. When Edward died in January 1066, Harold violated his oath by irreverently seizing the throne and ignoring William's pleas to remember his promise. We are told that following this, the duke constructed a fleet and invaded England with a substantial force, defeating Harold at Hastings, and taking the throne that was his right. The story that Edward had offered the duke the crown is not mentioned in any sources, either English or Norman, and neither Poitiers or Jumièges mention the visit that was recorded in the *D* chronicle of the *ASC*, which, if we trust John of Worcester in his Chronicon ex Chronicis, *Chronicon ex Chronicis*, and the *Roman de Rou*, Norman apologists certainly would have used it to their advantage. It was only after the conquest, when William needed to justify the invasion, that the claim emerges.

William of Poitiers adds far more detail to his revision of the *Normanorum*. In his *Gesta Willelmi ducis Normannorum et regis Anglorum*. Drawing on Jumièges' earlier account, he embellishes, starting with the claim that Edward the Confessor, concerned that the 'perfidious' English would not accept his choice of heir, sends Harold to reinforce the oath he had made earlier, establishing him as successor with a 'stronger pledge than ever before'.[24] The idea that Edward could just gift the throne without the approval of the English *witan* is utterly disingenuous. Such decisions were not made by the king alone. The king was welcome to nominate his heir but ultimately the final say was the remit of his counsel and not his to assert.[25] Poitiers' claims that Edward chose Harold to protect the earlier decision made by Edward, suggests that the Normans were acknowledging that Harold's importance went beyond the premiership of *dux Anglorum*. Harold, they knew, was a very powerful man, and one that Edward trusted implicitly.

Poitiers agrees with Jumièges that Harold was detained by Guy of Ponthieu. He continues his elaboration of the former's account, emphasising the magnanimity of the duke's actions in which he demands the English earl's release, a clever ruse to highlight the duke's benevolent nature. Poitiers' narration of the 'Gauls' penchant for incarcerating shipwrecked nobles, torturing and leaving them to die in dungeons, accentuated the danger Harold had been rescued from. Harold had possibly already met Guy in the presence of Count Baldwin in 1056 and they may have been on good terms.[26] According to the images on the Bayeux Tapestry, a confused and shipwrecked

Harold lands on Ponthieu's shores. Believing that the escort arriving from Count Guy's castle was there to arrest him, he drew his *seax* to defend himself, though he seems to have misread the situation.[27] He was apprehended, this is true, but Count Guy treats him honourably and he is not shackled, nor is he thrown into any dismal dungeon as the Norman sources claim. Upon hearing that Harold, on his way to visit him, had been taken prisoner, William warned Guy sternly, and the earl was released into his custody. In order to gain his compliance, William had to bribe him with gifts and lands.

Having been settled in Rouen and treated with respect and hospitality, Harold was taken to Bonneville-sur-Touques where it was arranged that he should freely swear an oath that he would be William's vassal. It is absurd to think that the duke was able to extract such an obligation from Harold when an earl was the English equivalent to a duke. Furthermore, Harold was stylised officially as *dux Anglorum,* Duke of the English, second only to King Edward and recognised as such by Poitiers.[28] The oath meant that he would return to Edward's court as William's man, acting on his behalf, using his wealth and influence to ensure the smooth transfer of the crown onto the duke's head. This is surely not something that a man of Harold's status would have done without coercion, and quite possibly in fear of his life. Poitiers adds clout to William's claim by stating that there were many good honourable witnesses to the oath ceremony, but conveniently he declined to name.[29] If anything, a recorded list of 'honest and truthful' men would have supported his claim.[30]

Ludicrously, we are expected to believe that Harold, in order to gain his freedom, willingly agreed that on his return to England, he would garrison the stronghold of Dover with Norman soldiers paid for out of his own pocket, and promote William's interests at Edward's court.[31] His reward? William promised he would 'confirm him in all his lands and dignities'. Harold would not have agreed to undertake this imposition on his purse and standing, at least not without being under duress. And an oath given under such circumstances was known to have been invalid under canon law.[32] Rex argues that by stressing the danger that Harold was in, William is shown to be something of a hero when he rescues the poor English earl from such terrible danger. Thus, Harold is set up to be indebted to William for his life.[33]

Harold, however, makes no attempt to garrison any Normans at Dover, nor does William send a contingent for him to use. Poitiers may have drawn upon earlier tales of an attempt by Eustace to occupy Dover in 1051.[34]

Some historians seemed to prefer the tale that William de Jumièges offers.[35] It is a simpler, more straightforward account without the exaggerations and propaganda we are subjected to by Poitiers, desperate to impress upon the reader that William was wholly justified in his invasion of England. However, there are plenty who enjoy the extra detail Poitiers puts forward. It certainly makes for an interesting read. The idea that Archbishop Robert was the conveyor of Edward's pledge to William, seems more convenient, although unlike Poitiers, who mentions that Champart brought the hostages with him, Jumièges does not, and gives no date.[36] It has been mentioned that the boys were taken to Normandy when Robert travelled to Rome to fetch his pallium, either on the way there, or on the way back in 1051, before the Godwins were exiled. On the other hand, some believe it to have happened in 1052 when the archbishop and his friends broke out of London and left for Normandy in order to escape Earl Godwin's wrath. The problem with this, as mentioned earlier, is that no sources report Archbishop Robert passing on any message from Edward to William, prior to his victory over the

English in 1066. We know that the boys were in Normandy because they are mentioned in the later sources. Circumstantially, it is likely that they travelled with Champart somewhere either in 1051, or '52. If there was a message from King Edward, why was it not documented, either by the English, or Norman sources?

As mentioned previously, historians have differing views on the purpose of Harold's visit to Normandy. Malmesbury's fishing tale that went wrong seems ridiculous and unlikely. It is hardly something an Anglo-Saxon elite such as Harold would do. Hunting, perhaps, but not fishing. Henry of Huntingdon suggests Harold was on his way to Flanders. There is no evidence to back up either of these later theories. As said earlier, the Bayeux Tapestry gives us a visual insight into the story of Harold's arrival and time spent in Normandy before he travels back to England. But this, too, can be problematic, as Rex points out, it is evasive of any detail to explain what the images actually represent. However, it is only when we read the Norman accounts that it is possible to make sense of the scenes. It is worth pointing out that the Bayeux Tapestry is incomplete, and it has some anomalies, one being that it has Harold swear the oath at Bayeux instead of Bonneville-sur-Torques.[37] It starts with Harold supposedly receiving his instructions from Edward to leave for Normandy, and ends with the Battle of Hastings, though it is believed that the original conclusion is missing.

Poitiers adds to the inconsistency of the pledge given to William, by stating that it was done with the approval and consent of Earl Godwin, Earl Siward, and Earl Leofric. He also mentions 'Archbishop' Stigand, too, was there, representing the church.[38] It is doubtful that Earl Godwin would have agreed to this considering he was still hopeful of having a grandson on the throne at this time. Moreover, it is unlikely that any of these earls would have agreed to William as the heir to Edward's throne. Regardless, if the statement was true, the pact must have taken place before Godwin's exile in 1051. As Godwin came back from Normandy through the front door in the autumn of 1052, Champart was on his way out the back door and on his way to Normandy.[39] Furthermore, Stigand was bishop of Winchester, not archbishop of Canterbury until after Champart was gone, sometime after the autumn of 1052.[40] Again, there is nothing in the English chronicles that corroborate this claim that these men gave their approval. Something so important as the succession would have been documented, just as Edward's brother was said to have made him joint ruler with him in 1041. To cast even more doubt over the statement, why would Edward make William his successor and then send his subjects all over Europe to bring home the Exile, his brother's son? None of it makes sense.

Significantly, Jumièges and Poitiers do not give dates for any of the events they mention. Were they being deliberately vague in order to avoid being caught out?

The Hostages

At this point, we should talk about the hostages. As we have seen previously, the boys were handed over to Edward to ensure Godwin and Swegn behaved honourably. The children were likely to have been residing in the queen's apartments at the time. When the Godwinsons fled into exile, they believed that their children would be safe in the hands of their daughter. The exact circumstances of their disappearance lie not in the history books, so we do not know how they came to be spirited away, however it appears that upon the Godwinsons' return they were gone, and so was Archbishop Robert. The *Carmen* does not mention hostages, however, Poitiers does. It was one of the few things that Poitiers spoke about that is corroborated by other independent sources. Eadmer, writing in the early twelfth century, mentions the hostages by name, Wulfnoth and Hakon, who were probably aged respectively 12 and 5 at the time of their disappearance, and that they had been despatched to Duke William after Godwin's return from exile.[41] Guy of Amiens was either unaware of any hostages, or did not believe they were important. On the hostages, Poitiers was correct, and that the archbishop brought the boys with him to Normandy, though neglects to name the date.

It does not seem possible for the archbishop to have taken the children in 1051 during his trip to Rome. The situation with Eustace had not yet occurred when Robert travelled to fetch his pallium which probably took place in the summer of that year. There appears to have been no reason to send the boys to William's court at that time. Thus, it would be more realistic to assume that Robert took them with him when Godwin was reinstated.[42]

The other question we must discuss, is why Robert Champart burdened himself with the hostages when he fled? Robert and his companions, bishops William and Ulf, appear in the Anglo-Saxon chronicles to have been fleeing for their lives.[43]

The new, independent Edward may have at times been irritated by Robert, but when it came to it, he was not going to allow Godwin to get his hands on his archbishop. He had wanted rid of the Godwinsons but they had the backing of much of England. Edward had no recourse other than to accept defeat. All he could do for Robert was give him safe passage to leave. He may even have suggested he take the boys with him as collateral. Champart had been in such a state that he even forgot his pallium as he grabbed whatever he could and made haste on horseback to the coast. The chronicle does not mention that the hostages were with him, however, it does tell us that the archbishop and his bodyguard, burst out of London's East Gate, killing the men manning it, suggesting they were in fear for their lives. Was Godwin baying for Champart's blood? And because of this, had Champart kidnapped, or took the boys with Edward's permission, to use as leverage to gain safe passage out of the country? Edward's hands were tied. Godwin, supported by the *witan*, saw to it that not only Robert, but other certain Frenchmen were also outlawed.

The exile of the archbishop need not have been permanent. Bishop William, after all, was found not guilty of any wrongdoing and returned to his episcopal see in England.[44] Edward's plan may have always been to use the hostages to force Godwin to allow Robert to come back. And was Edward's mindset about the succession different at the time? Was he open to the idea of William as his heir? If he had been, he would soon change his mind. The shock of having been thwarted by Godwin, the loss of his confidante, may have made him feel particularly vengeful, knowing that it would hurt Godwin to send his son and grandson away. There are many possible scenarios, however due to such little attention to detail given by the monks who wrote the chronicles, we can only conject and piece together a plausible narrative based on what evidence we have for the king's involvement in Robert's machinations. It is also conceivable that Edward new nothing of these plans and that Robert acted independently. Prior to Godwin's exile, it did not appear that Robert was encouraging Edward to make William his heir, but after Godwin's return, the exiled archbishop may have realised that the only way back, was to promote William as Edward's heir in Normandy.

Back in Normandy, Robert would have heard the news that he had been replaced by Stigand as archbishop of Canterbury. His friend, the king of England, had abandoned him. Champart never seems to have resolved his issues with England, and perhaps once back in Normandy, was unable to move forward his plans for the succession since William was preoccupied with the conflicts with Martel and King Henry who was now the duke's enemy. Leaving the English hostages at the Abbey of Jumièges where he had previously been an abbot, Robert travelled to Rome to complain about his treatment in England. This was to negatively influence the reputation of the English church with future popes.[45] We do not know if Robert ever spoke personally with William, for he was dead by 1055.

If Edward, in a moment of anger, ever thought he might consider William as heir and was stupid enough to voice it, he no doubt regretted it, and certainly changed his mind, for Robert remained in Normandy, never setting foot back in England again. Two years after the return of Godwin, Edward was to commission the search for a successor, and feelers were sent out to find the man they called the 'Exile' in Hungary. Perhaps by doing so, Edward hoped that all parties concerned, would forget he had ever thought about William, even if it was just for a fleeting moment. As for the hostages, we do not know why they were left to languish in Normandy for so long, or what the Godwinsons did to try to get them back before Harold went to Normandy. Whatever the case, it is a sad story that we shall never fully know the truth of.

CHAPTER SIXTEEN
Threads to the Past

The Tapestry

There is one source that we have yet to explore more fully: *Historia Novorum in Anglia* (*A History of Recent Events in England*). Written by English historian, Eadmer, it is often shamefully disregarded by historians. Eadmer's work, in contradiction to Norman sources, deserves to be given more credibility than it often receives providing a convincing explanation as to why Harold travelled to Normandy, and ended up hostage to Duke William.[1] Born shortly before the Norman Conquest, Eadmer was sent to Canterbury to become a monk by his impoverished parents shortly after 1066. In 1093, Eadmer was appointed by the pope as the director of the well-respected, Burgundian cleric, Anselm, in his position as the new archbishop of Canterbury. Among Eadmer's extensive number of writings, the one we are most concerned with is the *Historia Novorum,* written between 1095 and 1123. Scholars agree, it is one of the most valued writings of its kind.[2] Starting with events in 1066, Eadmer gives us an account of Harold's trip to Normandy. He follows the same line as Poitiers, stating that Godwin was made to hand over a son and grandson to ensure honourable conduct during the crisis of 1051–1052.[3] However, Eadmer adds that the boys were later transferred to Normandy with Archbishop Robert for 'safe-keeping', without Godwin's consent.[4]

The Bayeux Tapestry, essentially an embroidery, 70 metres long and roughly a half metre wide, was an enormous undertaking for its time.[5] Possibly the original was much longer, for the final scenes appear to have been lost on its journey over time to its last resting place, Bayeux, in northern France.[6] Created on behalf of persons unknown, it is believed to have been sewn by English embroiderers, famous for their skills. The events that led up to the Conquest of England and the Battle of Hastings are set out chronologically in panels. Some of the various candidates said to have commissioned it are Odo of Bayeux, the Conqueror's brother; Queen Matilda, his wife, and Eustace of Boulogne. It gives us a uniquely visual reference for the battle, though that in itself is problematic and has to be treated cautiously, like the propaganda of Jumièges and Poitiers. However, due to the ambiguity of the images and the text on the Bayeux Tapestry, it can be viewed as both complimentary to William as well as sympathetic toward the English. The lack of meaning within the tapestry is frustrating to modern historians, for it has been lost over time.[7] Later chroniclers, such as John of Worcester, Hungtingdon, Malmesbury, Orderic, and even Wace followed Eadmer's example of empathy toward the English, whilst still justifying the Conquest as bringing about ecclesiastic reform – which to the religious community, was the most important concern at the time.[8]

A good place to start would be the beginning scene in which we see the king in all his finery, sceptre in hand, sitting on his throne with his favourite hound beside him, talking to two men, both of whom could be Harold. The smaller version of Harold stands in front of his companion and he and Edward touch fingers. It is hard to fathom why there are two versions of the earl. The one standing behind the smaller Harold looks a far more formidable version. Perhaps the artist was trying to create the image that Harold was an important man but that he was second only to the king. In his work, *Historia Novarum in Anglia,* the chronicler, Eadmer, tells us what Edward said when Harold advised him he wanted to go to Normandy to free his brother and nephew. Contradicting Jumièges and Poitiers, Eadmer has Edward say these words:

> I will have no part in this; but as I do not wish to give the impression of hindering you, I give you permission to go where you will, and to see what you can do. But I have a presentiment that you will only succeed on bringing misfortune on the Kingdom and discredit upon yourself. For I know that the duke is not so simple to be inclined to give them up unless he foresees that in doing so he will secure some great advantage to himself.[9]

Eadmer advises the reader that Harold trusted his own judgement rather than Edward's and naively undertook the journey to Normandy, loaded with the most trustworthy of his men, and a 'lordly provision' of gold and silver and costly clothing.

The sequence of events according to the Bayeux Tapestry, is as follows: Harold rides with his men to Bosham, bringing hawks and dogs. In the next panel, they enter the church through the archway and after praying, spend the evening feasting in the manor. The next morning, they leave for Normandy. As they wade into the water, Harold and a companion hitch up their tunics, revealing bare legs, carrying hunting animals with them as they board the longboat.

Eadmer's narrative of what happened next is probably more detailed than any other. The group of around fifteen men sailed out from Bosham and were soon hit by a storm. The terrified travellers were tossed about by tall waves until they were driven into the River Maye in Ponthieu, home to Guy, count of that territory, and well off their course.[10] Bayeux Tapestry, giving no indication of a storm, shows them landing on the shore of Ponthieu. Eadmer follows de Jumièges and Poitiers, reporting that Harold and his men were taken to Beaurain and imprisoned with his men. Guy must have thought all his dreams had come at once. There he was, going about his business, and who should roll up on his shore? The famous English Earl Harold of Wessex. It would have been rude to have not offered him the hospitality of his castle, even if it was a dungeon. It was common knowledge from the time of Charlemagne, the count was entitled to hold anyone driven onto his shores prisoner, along with any of his property. William of Poitiers also knew this when he referred to 'certain Gallics' and their unseemly habits of capturing stray nobles and ransoming them.[11]

In the next tapestry scene, Guy and Harold talk. Eadmer tells us that Harold manages to bribe 'one of the common people' with a promise of reward if he will take a message to the duke.[12] Upon receipt, William demands that Guy release Harold and his men immediately and send them to him. Guy refused and William beefs up his request by threatening Guy with force. This had the desired effect, however, the wily, piratical count, confiscated all Harold's valuables and thus 'he came this way to William' and was received honourably.[13]

What happened next in Eadmer follows the Norman sources but with the exception that the Eadmer has William acknowledge that Harold has arrived in Normandy with the intention of negotiating the release of his kin, Wulfnoth and Hakon. William, assured Harold that his mission would be accomplished, but for a price. William then employed manipulation and extortion to pressure Harold to agree. The duke made it very clear that if Harold refused to do William's bidding, it would be his own fault if the desired outcome was not achieved.[14] Over the next few days, we see how William used Harold's presence at his court to insidiously bind him to his cause, cautiously revealing the contents of his plan for England to Harold.[15] William spoke to Harold of a ludicrous story that supposedly occurred many years ago, relating that when he and Edward 'were boys together', his cousin promised that when he was king he would make William his heir, an assertion Eadmer likely drew from Poitiers, and later repeated in Wace.[16] Eadmer makes no mention of the roles the Archbishop Robert played in the alleged offer of the throne; nor was there anything about the archbishop's conveyance of a message from Edward to William about the succession.

Eadmer has William make this statement to Harold:

> If you on your side undertake to support me in this project and further promise that you will make a stronghold at Dover with a well of water for my use and that you will at a time agreed by us send your sister to me so that I may give her in marriage to one of my nobles and that you will take my daughter to be your wife, then I will let you have your nephew, now and at once, and your brother safe and sound when I come to England to be King. And if I am with your support established there as King, I promise that everything you ask of me that can reasonably be granted, you shall have.[17]

Seems reasonable, right? The problem for Harold was that he was *sub regulus,* and as such, in a far better position to call the shots. Futhermore, he had no obligation to follow orders given to him by a duke of Normandy. He must have tried to explain this to William, but the arrogant duke was not having any of it. Acutely aware that he had fallen into a trap; Harold knew he was in danger. He may have learned of the deaths of Walter, Count of Mantes and his wife Biota, poisoned whilst enjoying William's hospitality.[18] Walter, older brother of Edward's nephew, Ralph de Mantes, was a possible contender for the English throne. His suspicious death may have been what King Edward had in mind when he gave his warning to Harold that he would be asking for trouble by going to Normandy. This could have been the moment when Harold realised he should have listened to Edward's cautionary lecture. By now, Harold must have gleaned that his status in Normandy as a free man could easily transform, and he would never be released until he agreed to William's plan. Whichever way he turned, the lives of his brother and nephew and those of his men, were in danger. He had no choice but to agree to the duke's demands.[19] How could he have been so naïve?

He was an educated man, and must have known something of church law in respect to pledges. As mentioned earlier, an oath made under duress, could be rescinded at a later date. It was his only way to get himself, his crew, and at least one of the hostages, home.

But William was as clever as Harold was educated, and not as trusting. He was not letting him off so easily. Eadmer tells us that in order to bolster his case, William called for holy relics to be brought and Harold was made to swear, both hands touching them, that he would carry out all that William desired him to.

The Bayeux Tapestry fills out the story with more detail. We see that after William and Harold have discussed his purpose for coming to Normandy, he takes Harold and his men with him on a campaign against Count Conan of Brittany. The tapestry depicts William arming Harold after his victory in Brittany. Eadmer omits the Breton campaign completely. William of Poitiers states that Harold and his men were kitted out with the best horses and armour and then takes them on the campaign to Brittany.[20] It is likely that William would have wanted to make Harold his vassal before the campaign so he could parade him around as his liegeman for the whole world to get wind of.

The scene in the tapestry shows the two men standing before each other, Harold is clutching a banner in his hand, his eyes look downward as though he finds it hard to look William in the eye. The duke is depicted with his hand touching the side of Harold's helmet and he appears to have pinned something on the earl's torso. Above the scene, the text says in Latin, 'Here William arms Harold.'[21] Harold would have been taken aback, but what could he do? William had already explained what was expected of him and that if he ever wanted to see his kinsmen again this is what he had to swear to. And as Eadmer suggests, Harold had been caught in a web of deceit.

The trouble in Brittany was an opportunity for William to show off his new brother-in-arms, the duke of England, no less. Harold's presence on the campaign would add more substance to William's claim that Harold had come to declare his fealty to him.[22] Harold, in a dramatic exhibition of courage and strength, pulled two men out of quicksand along the banks of the River Couesnon as they rode deep into enemy territory. The tapestry shows Harold dragging a Norman in one hand and in the other, a shield. The man hanging around his neck appears to be English. This event is only ever mentioned in the tapestry, but it is so specific that one has to wonder why it was not talked about elsewhere.[23] The outcome of William's supposed victory in Brittany is confusing for it is only the Bayeux Tapestry that gives William a victory and capture of Conan by fire at Dinant. Elsewhere, the campaign is inconclusive.[24] Whatever the case, two years later in December 1066, Conan met his end.

The panel shows the arming of Harold after the end of the campaign. This is contrary to Poitiers who seems to have better placed it before the campaign. The tapestry then shows William coming into Bayeux. The duke is sitting firmly on his throne, his sword held ceremoniously. Two Normans stand behind him, one is pointing at Harold, as he is made to swear an oath whilst lightly touching two portable jewelled reliquaries containing holy relics. The other Norman has a finger at his mouth in the manner of someone calling for silence. Beside Harold and the relic boxes, stand another two Normans with spears at rest. These armed men offer us a glimpse of the threat that Harold was under.[25] 'Swear by God Almighty on these holy relics that you will carry out everything that I have asked of you', *or never leave…*

In the arming scene, for the Normans, on show was their duke's magnanimity to the English nobleman. From Harold's point of view, this was the worst thing that could have happened. William had pressed him into his service at a time when Harold could hardly have had his wits about him. It is preposterous that Harold could be made the duke's vassal. William was not even Harold's equal. He did not have jurisdiction over a whole kingdom. If either of these men could make the other a vassal, it was not William. But what could Harold do? He could refuse and try to fight his way out of Normandy with his small band of men, but this would only get them all killed. The earl had to go along with it. If he backed out of it now, there would be no chance of anyone getting home alive. At least he had secured one of the hostages. He would be free, but the future, fraught with consequences – would just have to be dealt with later.

Whilst Harold was swearing William's oath, Harold's men could be seen waiting for him in their boat, apparently laden with gifts.[26] On his approach, their earl's expression told them everything they wanted to know. The oath swearing on holy relics had made the matter a whole lot worse. William had played a deceitful game, making certain that if Harold reneged on his promise, he would perjure himself.

The journey home must have been a relief, but the words, 'I told you so,' surely echoed forebodingly before he even set foot on home soil.

The Veracity of Eadmer

According to Eadmer, Harold's first stop once he was home, seems to have been to seek audience with King Edward, who, as expected, said 'I told you that I knew William and that your going might bring untold calamity on this kingdom?'[27]

Eadmer's work contrasts wholly with the Norman sources written much closer to events. Writing approximately forty years after the event puts him at a disadvantage and he appears to be the only source that tells us that it was Harold himself who organised the trip to Normandy and for what purpose. He was also the only Englishman writing on the history of the Conquest at this time, and was sympathetic to the English. Writing sometime after the death of William made it safer for him to propose that Harold's sole purpose of going to Normandy was to retrieve the hostages. Despite Edward's warning, he went anyway. However, the warning was not meant to be taken verbatim, but allows the author to use rhetoric via the mouths of his protagonists in order to paint a picture of what occurred in addendum. In other words, this is how it likely went.

But where did Eadmer get his information from?

We know that he entered Christ's Church in Canterbury, as a child in the latter half of the 1060s. Canterbury was an institution that had always been considerate toward the Godwinsons.[28] Born a few years before the Conquest in 1066, Eadmer considered himself an Englishman and like his contemporary, Orderic, showed empathy for the plight of the English following the invasion. Growing up post-Conquest he easily adapted to the changes that Stigand's successor, the Italian, Lanfranc, made to the English church. Eadmer also witnessed the decline in English prelates, and their contempt for English customs. Suffering the insults in silence, he accepted the imposed new discipline without complaint. At 19, he was introduced to Anselm whose visit to Canterbury saw the two men form a bond. It was not until some fourteen years later when Anselm ascended to the archbishopric of Canterbury in 1093, that he and Eadmer would rekindle their friendship that would last the rest of Anselm's life.[29] Eadmer spent his time forever at the side of his beloved archbishop, becoming his historian. They went everywhere together, often to court, and abroad, twice to

Rome, making notes of any significant events so Eadmer could cover them in the *Vita Anselmi* which he did in vivid detail.[30]

Through Canterbury, Eadmer was familiar with a man thought to be Godwin's relation, Æthelric, the monk of Canterbury who had lost the archbishopric election to Champart, in 1050. It is unlikely that Eadmer ever met Æthelric in person, however it was an associate of Æthelric's, a cleric called Æthelred, that Eadmer claimed he had consulted when writing the life of Dunstan.[31] Æthelric had been promoted to the bishopric of Selsey in 1058, on the Sussex coast, and it may have been to him Harold went first to see as he landed in Bosham, and not Edward, as shown in the Bayeux Tapestry. Bishop Æthelric would have been in a position to allay Harold's fears about the oath and discuss with Harold the possibility of renouncing it under canon law. After all, he had been in fear of his life, and for those he was responsible.[32] If Edward had warned him against going to Normandy, the tapestry's artist's impression of Harold going before Edward on his return to beseech his forgiveness, is one of humble devastation.[33] He is shown hunched over, riddled with guilt that he trusted his own judgement before his king's. Is it possible that Harold, buoyed by his successes in Wales, had been filled with overconfidence – even arrogance, perhaps? On his return home from Normandy, Harold would likely have sought spiritual guidance, and perhaps after some reassurance, was able to meet with his king. The theory is not implausible, though we cannot be certain of it. Nonetheless, when Eadmer was discussing the famous Archbishop Dunstan with Æthelred, the pair may have touched on the subject of Harold Godwinson's trip to Normandy that Æthelred had heard from Æthelric.[34] This makes the concept that Harold told Æthelric, Æthelred who then passed it on to Eadmer more credible.

As mentioned previously, Eadmer's theory on why Harold went to Normandy has often been disregarded, even to the point of being referred to as ridiculous. One historian claims that Harold did not give a fig for any of his brothers, or the rest of his family so Eadmer's 'daft' theory was rather unlikely.[35] This statement cannot be taken seriously, there is no evidence that Harold viewed his family with disdain. On the contrary, there cannot be any doubt that he helped to promote all three of his younger brothers into their positions as earls. Harold's discord with Tostig, as we shall see, came much later, but until 1064 there had not been any reason to doubt their unity as brothers when circumstance warranted. Their Welsh invasion is evidence of this.

The Bayeux Tapestry at first glance, seems to represent what must have been mainstream news post-Conquest. It clearly tells the Norman point of view that Harold was sent by Edward to confer the succession on William. But if we look closely, we can also see the story that Eadmer tells. Whichever way you look at it, it is there. In the beginning we can see that Harold is discussing something with the king. The Normans would have us believe that Harold is being given orders to visit Duke William with the promise from Edward he was to be his heir. This can also be interpreted as Harold asking permission to visit Normandy for the sake of his brother and nephew. The same can be said about Harold's return. Edward is happily hearing the news that William has gratefully accepted the king's wishes. The English version is clear also, that instead of happily hearing the news that William was preparing for his ascension to the throne, he is admonishing Harold. 'I told you about him, did I not?' And so it continues throughout the tapestry, despite the variables and nuances of the sources.

Historian Andrew Bridgeford says of the tapestry that the Normans, eyeing it at gatherings and feasts, could walk around it and be in no doubt it met their expectations of what happened in 1066.[36] The English, who knew a different story, if there were any of them permitted to see this work, could also relate to what they saw.

The assumption we must come to is that the tapestry tells the story of how Harold came to Normandy and agreed an alliance with William that would set him on the throne. But, woven within the threads of the woollen images, another interpretation is clandestinely hidden. Bridgeford concludes that it is the English viewpoint that the monks of Canterbury had known all along.[37]

Eadmer's empathy toward his fellow Englishmen and his sympathetic view of Harold in his *Historia*, might be seen to discredit his work, however he demonstrates far less bias than the Norman sources whose agenda is to justify William's actions. Eadmer at least appears to genuinely wish to write an impartial account about the events of the Conquest. He describes William's victory as truly a miracle by the grace of God, unwilling to allow Harold's perjury to go unpunished.[38] Eadmer speaks empathetically toward Harold's plight, without coming across as pro-Godwin. Eadmer's retelling of Harold's expedition to Normandy, is uniquely different, allowing the reader to experience the tale through Harold's viewpoint. It is emotive and evokes questions of ourselves as we feel Harold's tensions, just as he must have relayed it to Æthelric. What would we have done if we had been in his position?

CHAPTER SEVENTEEN

Tostig

1065

In this year, before Lammas, 1 August, Harold ordered the construction of a hunting lodge on the estate of Portskewett, now in Wales. Barlow suggests the estate was built on a strategic point along the Wye opposite Tyddenham and southwest of Chepstow. It was used to provide the merchants who used the river with a safe base from which to conduct their business.[1] The *ASC* suggests that it had been won from the Welsh, perhaps during the war of 1063. Harold also hoped to host King Edward there in the coming autumn, for the hunting season which Edward loved so much. In what the *C* version of the chronicle calls 'a massacre', Caradog and a band of his men, attacked and slaughtered the workmen preparing it for Harold's use, and rode away with all the provisions that had been readied for the king's stay. The *D* version gives the date as St. Bartholomew's Day, 24 August, and remarks that 'We do not know who first advised this folly.'[2] Soon after, on 3 October, word hit the court that there was trouble in the North. Tostig was hunting with the king in Britford. Had the brothers entered into a tug of war for Edward's attention?[3] *Vita* tells us that at this time, Tostig was at court, seeing to some palace business that had been 'put on him' by the king. *Vita* also adds that he had been 'detained by his love of the king'. The *Vita* goes on to explain that a party of noble miscreants he once had punished with the 'heavy yoke of his rule, conspired against him'.[4]

The 'noble miscreants' turned out to be a large number of unhappy Yorkshire and Northumbrian thegns, enraged by various grievances including the murder of three of their friends. The men descended on the earl's residence in York, intent on ousting Tostig or worse.[5] The charges laid against him are listed in the *ASC*. They consist of acting unlawfully robbing churches, men of their lands and property, and in some cases their lives. John of Worcester specifies the ills as follows: the treacherous murder of thegns Ulf, son of Dolfin, and Gamel, son of Orm, and a great tax that was unlawfully laid upon the whole of Northumbria. Ann Williams identifies Gamel's father as Orm Gamelson, who was married to Æthelthryth, daughter of Earl Ealdred (d. 1038) of Bamburgh, linking them to one of the feuding families of Northumbria.[6] In 1063, Tostig had invited these men to a peace treaty held in his own chamber to discuss their complaints. Perhaps a disagreement ensued and weapons were drawn. The two men ended up dead. A year later on the fourth day of Christmas, Queen Edith had a thegn, Gospatric, executed on Tostig's behalf.[7]

There were three Gospatrics known to be connected by blood to the House of Bamburgh. The slain Gospatric was the youngest son of Uhtræd the Bold (d. 1016) and his second wife Sige, daughter of Styr. She had married into the House of Bamburgh on the proviso that her new husband would avenge her father's slayer, a man called

Thurbrand (d.1024). Before Uhtræd could do so, Thurbrand killed Uhtræd, on the orders of the traitorous Eadric Streona. Following Uhtræd's death, his eldest son, Ealdred, son of his first wife, Ecgfrith, stepped into his father's shoes as earl of Bernicia, and avenged Uhtræd by slaying Thurbrand. If you are not sufficiently confused yet, there is more: Ealdred, in turn, was killed in 1038 by Thurbrand's son Carl, leaving Ealdred's younger half-brother, Eadwulf, whose mother was Sige, to rule Bernicia. Prior to this in 1031, King Cnut had appointed his retainer, the nobleman Siward, as Earl of York. By 1041 Siward had done away with Eadwulf, so that the whole of Northumbria and Bernicia came under his control. The families of the north certainly knew how to throw a good bloodfeud![8]

Siward, however, didn't want to stop at Northumbria and Bernicia, and within ten years had managed to expand his dominion to include the province of Cumbria, driving out the Scots who had ruled there since 1018. But there was still one last son of Uhtræd to deal with, a man whose name was Gospatric (d. 1064) birthed by Uhtræd's second wife, Sige. Instead of killing him, Siward decided to make peace with him, offering him the lordship of newly conquered Cumbria to compensate for the loss of his ancestral lands in Bernicia.[9] Siward may have considered it expedient to make Gospatric his oathsworn man.

Siward's conquest of Cumbria over the Scots, at that time ruled by King Macbeth, is evidenced in a writ probably created just after 1041, when coming to terms with Gospatric had been necessary. In the document, Gospatric, acting as Siward's representative, settled the gifts and privileges of certain landowners in Cumbria, with the agreement of Earl Siward. This confirmation guaranteed the rights of Cumbrian men under the old Scottish rule, within Siward's Northumbrian regime.[10]

As we have discussed before, Tostig was appointed to Northumbria in 1055 following the death of Siward, much to the annoyance of Alfgar, earl of East Anglia. The appointment had been the catalyst that caused Alfgar's ravaging of Hereford. Tostig's selection had been to the exclusion of Siward's young son, Waltheof, who was thought to be too young for the post in 1055. What the Northumbrians thought of Tostig when he succeeded to the post, is not recorded, however, it is likely they would have preferred one of their own to a southerner. Nonetheless, they seem to have worn the insufferable actions of this Godwinson peacefully for some years until Tostig overstepped his boundaries and executed the aforementioned thegns. But there was much more to the agitators' reasons for their anger, than the deaths of these few men.[11]

To understand the mood of the Northumbrians, we need to go back a few years to 1040 when Siward harboured the Scottish royal victims of Macbeth's defeat of King Duncan I. His son Malcolm, his two younger brothers, and his uncle Maldred, fled south to the court of Siward. In 1054, Edward gave his approval to Siward to invade Scotland, depose Macbeth and put 24-year-old Malcolm on the throne in the belief that this son of Duncan, reared among the English, would be a better man to deal with. Macbeth was defeated at the Battle of the Seven Sleepers,[12] but escaped and remained at large until 1057 when he was caught and executed by Malcolm who was finally crowned king, the third of that name.

We have already spoken about Tostig's dealings with Malcolm, and how he used his wit and guile to manage him, even bringing Malcolm south and presenting him to Edward.[13] It was about this time, Tostig and Malcolm entered into a pact of sworn brotherhood. If this was one of the 'cunning schemes' that *Vita* talks about, then it was about to go awry, for in 1061, Malcolm took the opportunity of Tostig's absence abroad in Rome, to invade the earldom of his 'sworn brother'. He 'savagely harried the earldom, irreverently violating St. Cuthbert's peace on the Island of Lindisfarne'.[14]

In his work, *The Norman Conquest of the North,* William E. Kapelle suggests that during the meeting Tostig had arranged between Malcolm and King Edward, the Scottish king audaciously requested that Edward relinquish Cumbria back to Scotland. Needless to say, Edward refused.[15] Kapelle goes as far as to state that it was during Tostig's sojourn in Rome, that the Scottish king organised a two-pronged attack on Tostig's earldom. English rule was expelled from Cumbria and a Scottish government installed by Malcolm. Evidence from the Domesday Book, marks Cumbrian lands in Amounderness as being wasted. Richard Fletcher in his book, *Bloodfeud: Murder and Revenge in Anglo-Saxon England* supports this theory, stating that 'Cumbria, laboriously brought under English rule by the campaigns of earls Eadwulf and Siward, was 'violently subjugated' by the Scots'.[16] *Vita,* however, makes no mention of the loss of Cumbria to the Scottish king, Malcolm, although it was definitely in his hands by 1070, where he launched his campaign against William of Normandy from. Other historians disagree stating that there is no clear evidence that the Scottish takeover happened at this time. Walker contends that lands marked by Domesday as waste, could easily have been caused by Magnus' invasion in 1058 or William's harrying of the north in 1069.[17]

Kapelle's hypothesis is convincing as is the theory expressed by Fletcher that Gospatric was expelled from Cumbria due to Tostig's negligence, causing him to complain to the royal court. It also raises the question of why Tostig did not retaliate against Malcolm. The loss of Cumbria should have warranted a full-scale invasion, but Tostig merely accepted Malcolm's takeover, and there is, though later, evidence from Gaimar that in 1062, he went to Scotland and made peace with him, after he had returned from Rome to find Cumbria no longer part of his earldom.[18] If Tostig had failed to protect his people by disregarding the security of his earldom, would not the loss of Cumbria be among the charges laid against Tostig listed by the chronicles? As it was not, we cannot be sure that it occurred at all, but the circumstantial evidence presented by Kapelle cannot be ignored. Rightly or wrongly, the queen would need a reason to justify Gospatric's execution, or was it simply to silence his claims that Tostig favoured the Scottish king over the people he was sworn to protect? Tostig may have been on poor terms with Gospatric from before he went to Rome, but relations with his people seemed to worsen after the earl's return in the autumn of 1061.

Interestingly, Gospatric's nephew, also called Gospatric (d. 1080) had been in Tostig's entourage in Italy.[19] This Gospatric was thought to be the son of the Scottish refugee Maldred, brother of the slaughtered King Duncan I, and the aforementioned uncle of Malcolm III. Maldred had married the daughter of Earl Uhtræd, Ealdgyth, by his third wife, Ælfgifu, daughter of King Æthelræd. Fletcher submits the interesting theory that the young Gospatric may have been a hostage for his uncle Gospatric's good behaviour though this seems unlikely as he had both English and Scottish royal blood and it is unsure what affiliation, if any, junior Gospatric had with his Uncle Gospatric. It has been suggested by Walker that young Gospatric's interests were being promoted by Tostig, as he was also nephew to King Edward, and that this may have caused friction between different branches of the House of Bamburgh.[20]

The men who marched on Tostig's headquarters in York were identified by as Glonieorn, son of Heardwulf, Dunstan, son of Æthelnoth, and a man called

Gamalbearn.[21] Their grievances against Tostig have already been mentioned, and it seemed that the slain men, were connected to the House of Bamburgh, either by blood or marriage.[22] The ringleaders were wealthy landowners, which Tostig's deputy, Copsige, to whom he delegated much of the business of running the earldom. These men were likely to have been resentful that a man of much lower status as Copsige, was lording it over them when Tostig was out of town, which he was most of the time. Copsige was also in charge of collecting the heavy fines being imposed on men for their misdeeds and one of the accusations was that Tostig was more interested on getting his hands on their wealth, than the love of justice, extracting large amounts of money from the families of such men so they could evade the worst of punishments; death.[23]

As we know, Tostig was not around to hear the charges laid against him. Whether the insurgents knew he was not there is not known. According to John of Worcester, Danish household guards, Amund and Ravenswart, known to have lands close by the rebels, were caught trying to escape and lynched.[24] The following day, more than 200 of Tostig's retainers were slaughtered in a pitched battle on the northside of the River Humber. They also broke open his treasury, and stole his money and weapons.

The strength and depth of their anger can be understood through Tostig's actions.[25] After ten years in office, he had become complacent. Raising taxes in line with the rest of England may have seemed fair and just, but he failed to consider that the northern earldom was a much poorer province than those of the south. Accusations that he stole from churches may have been unfair, but his men, it seemed, were only too happy to be heavy-handed in exacting justice disproportionately, and the accusation of corruption, too, was not a good look for Tostig and his administration. Previously, Edward had granted the Mercian boroughs of Northamptonshire and Huntingdonshire to Siward to augment his revenue to make up for the shortfall of less revenue-producing lands.[26] But this personal gift to the Danish earl did not help the landowners in Northumbria, to whom the rise in taxes were hard to cope with.

Taking charge of Tostig's base at York was not the end of it. These gritty insurgents insisted that Tostig had to go. They were done with him, and would have only Morcar, son of Alfgar, for their earl.

Northern Justice

What happened in Portskewett that summer was the least of Harold's issues. He was about to be reluctantly drawn into the feud between his brother, Tostig, and the men of Northumbria. Harold's role as peacemaker would end in friction between two or three parties, with Tostig accusing Harold of betraying him.

The well-planned rebellion looks to have taken place after careful negotiations with Edwin and Morcar. Both Mercian brothers cannot have been much older than 17 or 18. Burghred, as previously mentioned, was already dead, so the earldom of Mercia had fallen to Edwin after Alfgar's death, and now with Morcar, about to step into the shoes of a Godwinson, it must have felt like revenge to the brothers. Soon after the havoc wreaked on York, the Northumbrians and Yorkshiremen called for Morcar to join them and travel south to Tostig's province of Northampton. Along the way, they gathered the men of Nottingham,

Derbyshire, and Lincolnshire.[27] At Northampton they met with the Mercians and also a great deal of Welshmen aligned with Edwin.[28]

Once word reached Britford, Tostig demanded that Edward send Harold to restore peace with the rebels at Northampton.[29] The *D* chronicle is the easier of the *ASC* to follow. It records that they charged Harold with taking a message to the king, that they might have Morcar for their earl. Harold returned to the king, bringing messengers from among the rebels with him to validate the request. The king acquiesced and sent Harold back to Northampton to convey his acceptance of their wish, also agreeing to renew the laws of Cnut there. Harold is said to have given his hand on it.[30] *C* is the only one that mentions that they met at Northampton *and* Oxford, on Saints Simon and Jude's Day, 28 October. It gives some idea of the role Harold played as peacemaker, explaining with a hint of regret that he wanted to 'work their reconciliation if he could, but he could not'. The scribe writing this entry differs from the *E* and *D* manuscripts, telling us of the outlawing of Tostig and 'all those with him who promoted injustice, because he robbed God first, and despoiled of life and land, all those he had power over'. It then adds that they took Morcar as their earl. Tostig and his wife, Judith, were forced to flee to the land of her brother, Count Baldwin, in Flanders, taking winter quarters at St. Omer.[31]

Having failed to negotiate Tostig's reinstatement Harold hurried back to the king with their reply. Meanwhile, to show the king they meant business, the northerners ravaged Tostig's lands in Northampton, burning houses and looting corn, seizing thousands of cattle and taking hundreds of men captive.[32] They were not going to take no for an answer! Sadly, John of Worcester is not as well detailed about the negotiations as he usually is and follows the *C* chronicle closely, but omits the mention of Morcar. He does, however, mention that on the 1 November, Earl Edwin assisted in driving out Tostig from England, suggesting there was some force involved.[33]

We have a more detailed image of what happened in the *Vita*, which goes well above and beyond the descriptions from the other sources. *Vita* appears to blame Alfgar's sons for the rebellion, accusing them of longstanding 'ill-will' and refers to them as 'boys of royal stock', though there is no connection to any ancient Mercian royal bloodline, just the nobility of Hwicce. Alfgar's father, Leofric, seems to have kept a distance from his son's feud with the king and the Godwinsons, but his own sons might have understandably had a different outlook.[34] *Vita's* author also notes that the rebels ordered the deaths of anyone that had been 'put down as a personal enemy', by 'open force or in ambush'. Many were slaughtered in the streets of York and Lincoln, in woods, water, and on roads trying to escape. Anyone recognised as a friend or member of Tostig's administration were instantly dragged to their deaths without a trial.[35]

The *Vita* is, of course bias toward Tostig, and compared his rule with that of Siward's, claiming that the Dane had also been greatly feared for his severe justice. Tostig, however, is portrayed as a lover of peace, reducing the crime rate with his vigorous justice, so that any man could travel alone without being attacked'.[36] The *Vita* agrees with the *C* manuscript, stating that the rebels arrived in Oxford in hostile array. The author tells us that the king in his wisdom, sought to appease the feral mob by sending messengers begging them to desist the madness, and that if they could prove their case, they would receive justice. The rebels rejected the king's promise of peace and issued a bold statement demanding the dismissal of Tostig from the kingdom, or he (the king) would also be treated as enemy of the people.

Seeing the negotiations were going badly, Edward retreated from Oxford to his royal demesne in Britford, to seek counsel from his advisors. In an effort to play down Tostig's cruel streak, *Vita* refers to him as 'that glorious earl', who was wrongfully charged with punishing disturbers of peace, more for the desire of confiscating their property, than for love of justice.[37] Tostig publicly accused Harold of stirring the northerners up and *Vita* reports that 'some' suggested that Harold had instigated the rebellion with 'artful persuasion'. This appeared to shock the anonymous author, who denied that he would believe such a thing of Earl Harold, but when the earl cleared himself with vows, he was accused of being 'rather too generous with oaths'.[38]

Unlike the *ASC,* Edith's hagiographer shows us a less pliant Edward. The chronicles give the impression that Edward happily gives into the rebels and agrees to their demands, like the father who cannot control his unruly children. After unsuccessfully using diplomacy and negotiation to persuade the rebels to comply, a furious Edward announces a royal edict to crush the rebellion.[39] *Vita* blames the reluctance to invoke a civil war by the nobles in the south on a bad turn in the weather. It was out of season for campaigning. The author also touches on the aversion of the English to engage in civil war, with some seeking to 'calm the raging spirit of the king', urging against mounting an attack on the northerners.[40] Edward, however, was not for turning, and seeing this, the men who should have obeyed him, deserted him. Edward was forced to capitulate, to the determination of the Northumbrians, agreeing to restore the laws of Cnut upon them and accepting their choice of Morcar as their earl.[41] Sometime during his rule, Tostig had imposed West Saxon law on the administrative area of the Danelaw, created by Cnut, which some northerners had been eager to point out. It would have probably served Tostig better to have been mindful that there was a reason that the north and south were taxed according to their wealth and that the north was not as rich as their southern counterparts.[42]

It may be worth pausing at this moment to examine the possible choices of candidates for Tostig's position, starting with Waltheof, son of the previous earl, Siward. It is interesting that the northern rebels had not risen up in favour of him. Some may have thought him still too young to take charge of the earldom, though King Edward, or possibly Harold, had not thought so, and sometime in 1065 or later in 1066, the young Waltheof was allocated Tostig's lands of Northamptonshire and Huntingdonshire. Such an appointment would not in any way have matched the difficulties the inexperienced teen might have had under the belligerent Northumbrians and Yorkshiremen. Paul Hill, in his work, *The Road to Hastings,* argues that it was Harold, rather than Edward, who later appointed Waltheof to Tostig's lands.[43] The claim is plausible, as Hill points out, Harold, as king, would later need to impress upon the northerners that he would not support Tostig's return. Waltheof's appointment in the East Midlands was evidence of that.

Looking at the situation from a historian's point of view, Waltheof would seem the most likely choice for the northern thegns. He was the son, not only of the previous earl, but also had connections to the house of Bamburgh through his mother, Ælfflæd, daughter of Earl Ealdred, son of Uhtræd the Bold. The issue with his age may also be inaccurate, for Morcar, was also a teen and inexperienced. Another contender with Uhtræd the Bold's lineage, was Gospatric, son of Maldred. The young nobleman who had accompanied Tostig to Rome in 1061, had also been overlooked, conceivably on the grounds that he was a member of Tostig's circle. He seems to have escaped the cull of Tostig's men, however, and was later to become earl of Northumbria under William of

Normandy's rule. One more candidate was Oswulf, son of Eadwulf. Morcar's first act was to put him in charge of Bernicia, restoring the House of Bamburgh its rightful ruler. Blood related to the earlier dynasty of rulers of Northumbria, he had a hereditary right to be earl of Northumbria. With these nobles in the running for the job, the question of why the men of the north were so desperate to select Morcar as their earl, cannot have been due to his experience or abilities.

It has been thought that the rebellion was triggered by the northerner's dislike of the south. Some historians opted to believe that the region, was populated with Anglo-Danes who were not happy about being ruled over by an earl imposing southern laws on them. But the only person who, at the time of his appointment in 1055, openly demonstrated unhappiness at Tostig's installation in York, was fellow Englishman, Alfgar. Tostig started out as a prudent administrator, appointing a deputy, Copsige, installing a new bishop of Durham, Æthelwine, both supporting him well in his position as earl. He certainly had the approval of the clerics of the *Durham Liber Vitae*, a brotherhood who entered into a spiritual confraternity with a church or monastery.[44] The earl's name was also incorporated in the inscription on a sundial of St. Gregory's Church in Kirkdale, commissioned by Orm Gamalson. It was not until some six years into Tostig's leadership that the decline began, perhaps starting with the earl's fawning over King Malcolm. Some of Tostig's personal attributes thought to be abhorrent to the northerners can be debunked. Tostig, an Anglo-Dane himself, was brought up with both English and Danish customs, and was no doubt bi-lingual.[45] He had, however, no connections with the north, though nor had Siward. The animosity toward Tostig must have run deep, borne out of years of harsh rule. Those who backed Tostig probably saw it as unfair, but it seems that the appointment of a very young Morcar, whose connections to the north came through his mother Ælfgifu,[46] was politically arranged. It was a punitive act against a tyrannical overlord, designed to hurt the Godwinsons as a whole.

On the face of it, the cause of the uprising seems to have been that Tostig had unwittingly embroiled himself in the feud between the families of Bamburgh and Thurbrand, and in his harsh efforts at law and order, he allowed corruption to infiltrate his administrators. Furthermore, his lack of consideration for his own people, and favouritism of the Scottish king, Malcolm, led to his downfall.[47]

Part Four
KING

'here also Harold became consecrated as king and
experience little quiet in it whilst he ruled it'
          The Anglo-Saxon Chronicle

CHAPTER EIGHTEEN
The Old King Dies

Tostig in Exile

The lack of support for Tostig and the military's refusal to go to war with the north, brought a deep depression upon the king. That Tostig was Edward's favourite has been accepted by many historians, and his loss clearly affected Edward's health and well-being.[1] According to *Vita*, 'from that day until the day of his death he bore a sickness of the mind'.[2] The king's grief is dramatically expounded in the *Vita*, as he complains to God, demanding a terrible vengeance to those who disobeyed him (Edward). The queen was confounded by the quarrel between her brothers, and at a loss without the support of her husband, gravely ill, bearing a 'sickness of the mind'.[3] She had always given excellent advice to her brothers, navigating their foibles with the expertise of a beloved sister who knew them well. It was not her fault that they would not listen. Why, for goodness sake did they never talk to her about their plans?[4] If they had, could she not have then averted the crisis?

Though not reported in the sources, we can presume that the remaining brothers, took Harold's side, and that whatever reconciliation was endeavoured, it was not successful. Gyrth, closer to Tostig, and Leofwin, closer to Harold, may have tried to mediate. Gyrth and Tostig had been together in Flanders during their exile, and in Rome, a decade after Flanders. But there are no references to Gyrth supporting Tostig on his enterprise with Harald Hardrada. The missing chapters in the queen's book might have given us a glimmer of the younger brother's characters, but we have no way of knowing for certain. In any case whatever role Gyrth may have played that crisis of autumn, similarly, Leofwin and Harold's time spent in Ireland probably had done the same for them as it had for their brothers. It was, however, as we shall see shortly, to have been Gyrth that offered to lead the troops at Hastings against William so that Harold should not perjure himself.[5]

The situation must have distressed the other female members of the Godwin family. We know the brothers' mother, Gytha, was distraught when Tostig took leave of his 'sorrowing mother', but it was Edith, however, who suffered greatly the loss of Tostig, weeping inconsolably as a mourning sister.[6]

Any concerned members of Tostig's family need not have been worried about his physical welfare, for he, his wife, and their sons, Skuli and Ketil, were welcomed by Judith's brother, Baldwin, Count of Flanders, and even given an estate and revenue in St. Omer. Baldwin, generously as he always was toward the politically exiled English, made his brother-in-law his deputy commander and instructed the knights attached to the town to submit to him. There Tostig stayed through the winter, nurturing his resentments and thoughts of vengeance.[7] Yet the new life offered to him in Flanders, did not make up for what he had lost. In the following year, he would make plans to take back what had been unlawfully taken from him, just as his father and brother had fourteen years before.

Harold's Intentions

It has been mentioned that Harold had designs on the crown long before 1065, and that the northern rebellion manifested as an opportunity for him to rid himself of Tostig, leaving him a clear run to the throne.[8] The assertion is certainly plausible, though on the other hand, Tostig's exile and the appointments of the sons of Alfgar in the whole of the north, made the balance of power more of a level playing field. Either way, there were two possible directions to proceed: civil war, or Tostig's exile; both of which would have been detrimental. Bearing in mind Harold's track-record, his preferred option was to avoid the former. When his father died, he found himself slipping naturally into primary position, starting with 1055 when he picked up the mess Ralph de Mantes had made of Hereford. It is not beyond imagination to assume at some point that he had been thinking about what would happen should Edward pass before Ætheling Edgar was old enough to lead the kingdom. There is no contemporary evidence that there had been any division between the oldest Godwinsons, certainly not in the years leading up to 1063, apart from the wrestling match that went wrong written in later sources!

When it was clear Edward's health was indeed failing, Harold may have confided in those he trusted. In his position as *subregulus*, it would have been appropriate for him to seek counsel over the issue of the succession. Barlow has Edgar at age 14 at this time, but he could have been even younger.[9] The history of the previous century has some powerful examples of how underaged kings had caused chaos and division. The reign of the ætheling's great uncle, Edward the Martyr, had been short-lived and contentious, split between those who supported Edward and those who backed Æthelred. Going back further, the double reign of brothers, Eadwig (r. 955 – 959) and Edgar, (r. 959 –975) was also beset by problems, with Eadwig dying at an early age, just as his nephew, Edward the Martyr, would a couple of decades later, in mysterious circumstances.

King Edward the Confessor had still been robust enough to go hunting in 1065. At that time, it may have seemed unlikely that he would die within the next couple of years. If Harold and the highest officers in government were future looking and reconsidering Edgar's suitability due to his youth, would it not be a sensible decision to consider the next possible suitable candidate? And who should that be if not Harold? After all, he was able to call on a large swathe of retainers to support him. His successful incursions into Wales had given him the wherewithal to be a competent military strategist, which was what England needed at that time. He was a capable statesman, diplomat, and had pacified a dangerous uprising in the north. Edgar was too young, too inexperienced, had no lands or power to take on the responsibility for the defence of all the kingdom, especially under direct military threat from Normandy.[10] Harold could have seized power by supporting Edgar as his regent, but there would still be the risk of rival dissenting voices influencing Edgar against him.[11]

There were still those who were old enough to remember the division caused by the friction between King Æthelred and his sons in the earlier part of the century. The interference of Eadric Streona, who supported the younger half-brother of Edmund

(Edward the Confessor) rather than Edmund himself making it difficult for the ætheling to organise an effective resistance against the Danes. This what eventually destroyed any chances England had of clawing back power. Young æthelings often posed a threat to the stability of the kingdom, and of course they also grew up, which was why Cnut ensured that he got rid of the sons of Ironside, one such who was Edgar's father. It is understandable why, from the viewpoint of the *witan,* they would choose Harold if they desired a strong leader and a secure country

There is a strong argument that there was no desire among the English to support a Norman, or a boy on the throne. We only have to look back at the events of the early 1050s to see how most of the Normans fared after the return of the Godwins.[12] The only official ætheling in 1066 was Edgar. In 1060, the English nobility, including Harold, swore to accept him as the heir to the Confessor's throne. The event was recorded by Hariulf of St. Riquier, in the *New Minster Liber Vitae.* Edgar is entered as 'clito', meaning ætheling, alongside King Edward and Queen Edith.[13]

The title, Ætheling, was reserved only for the sons of a king, which is why Edward legally adopted Edgar and brought him up at court amongst the other wards Edith and Edward had in their care.[14] There is no evidence of Edward ever adopting William, if he had, as mentioned earlier, William would have ensured everyone knew about it. The issue was that there was no recent precedent for electing kings who were not of the blood royal, though as mentioned earlier, it was not unknown in Europe.[15] But the people involved knew only too well that these were unprecedented times, and called for unprecedented measures. Harold was not of the blood royal, but he was the man best suited to the job. Who better than the king's *subregulas,* the mayor of the palace, the duke of the English to lead them into and out of the storm to come.

The Death of Edward

There must have been a grim atmosphere around the court in the next coming weeks, with Tostig in exile, and the royal couple in mourning, and Harold persona non-gratis with anyone who was a friend of Tostig.[16] As the hallowing of the church of St. Peter of Westminster approached, the apathetic Edward perked up enough to attend the celebrations. Edward's health had been getting rather more serious. Today we know that depression can be a symptom of a post ischaemic attack, so it is possible that he had suffered a mild stroke after Tostig's exile, undoubtedly caused by stress of the events that led to Tostig's exile. Not only did he lose a boon companion, the trauma of realising he no longer had control over his kingdom, seems to have gravely added to his demise.

It was timely that Westminster was now complete, for Edward had intended to be buried there. A contemporary list of attendees reports that the two archbishops were present, eight bishops, eight abbots, and all the five earls and the usual nobles of the court.[17] Strangely, if the claim that William had been granted the heirdom, surely William or a representative from Normandy would have been at court, but none was noted.[18] The effort in attending to his duties and hosting feasts, meant that Edward was laid low again on Christmas Eve. He managed to disguise his condition with a cheerful smile, with only those close to him noticing him picking at his food, and the clammy, paleness of his demeanour.[19] Eventually, he was unable to tolerate his condition and he took to his bed, insisting that the consecration go ahead on the 28 December, and that his people should enjoy the occasion.[20]

Over the next few days, the king grew weaker, falling in and out of sleep, surrounded by those closest to him.[21] At some point the king woke, startled with terror. When he recovered, he told them a story of a dream about two monks from his youth in Normandy. They had come with a message from God to advise that those bishops, abbots, priests, and monks, who had reached high office, were not what they seemed to be but servants of the devil. The dream foretold that in a year and one day, from the date of his death, God would curse and deliver his kingdom to the enemy, 'devils come through all this land with fire and sword, and the havoc of war'.[22] He rambled on about a green tree, cut down the middle of its trunk, one part of it carried some way from its roots, would then be re-joined to its trunk in the future. And it would push leaves and bear fruit from its sap, and then, and only then, would there be a remission of the great ills brought on by the events of God's curse.[23]

As in much of the *Vita*, there are references to and passages similar to those of the bible. The story about the tree is reflective of the prophecy of Jesus, about to be crucified. The vision itself is thought to be based on Nechabadnezzar in Daniel 4.0. Used to highlight Edward's holiness, they are also a device for the anonymous author to disguise what he knew in hindsight. The deathbed scene in the *Vita* was written a few years after the Conquest when the political landscape had changed beyond recognition. There is much of Edward's career in the closing chapters, and that of Harold's, tinged with irony.

What is interesting is that the *Vita* gives insight into who shared the space around Edward's bed which is agreed by the Bayeux Tapestry. The author describes Queen Edith as sitting at the end of the royal bed with his feet in her lap. Earl Harold was also there, and a kinsman of Edward's, Robert FitzWymarc, the Staller, referred to by the *Vita*, as the king's steward and royal standard bearer.[24] Present also, was the premier archbishop, Stigand of Canterbury. The king's confused premonitions caused consternation among those who have insight into their own behaviours. However, Stigand uses levity to put them at ease as he murmurs to Earl Harold that the king 'was broken with age and disease and knew not what he had said'. Which of course seems a rightminded thing to say, but not if you were the eleventh-century scribe, writing the queen's propaganda.[25] Of course, Queen Edith, being the God-fearing sage that she was and commissioner of the book, had no problem understanding the hidden connotations behind the king's prophesising, which was perceptibly more than the religiously-minded among them could. The author adds a further monologue detailing the failings of the anonymous sinful clergy, which essentially meant that they were remiss in not heeding the king and queen's admonitions to change their corrupt ways, leading to their downfall.[26]

Eventually the narrative returns to what happened in the darkly lit king's private chamber. Edward addressed his wife, thanking her for the 'zealous solicitude' in which she had devoted her service, having stood by his side as 'a beloved daughter'. The king implored God to gift her eternal happiness, then turned to his second in command, with an outstretched hand, slightly touching Harold's, he says, 'I commend this woman and all the kingdom to your protection.'[27]

Exhorting his brother-in-law, Harold, to serve and honour his sister, he warns him not to despoil her of any of her properties she had held from her husband. *Vita* then advises the reader that the king also commends to Harold, his foreign courtiers, who had served him well, having left their native lands for love of him.[28] He requests that Harold take oaths of fealty from them, or if they preferred, send them home with safe conduct, complete of all that they had acquired in service of the king.

Having spoken his last, sometime in the late hours of 5 Jan, the king's 'holy' remains, were carried from Westminster Palace into his last resting place, the church that for years had been his wondrous project, his gift to God.

The Crowning

That following morning, Edward, bitterly mourned overnight, was entombed in Westminster. Harold, who held the position of *subregulas* was entrusted by the king with his kingdom and his wife, was elected by the *witan* to the 'dignity of kingship' and crowned the same day. Not by Stigand, but by Archbishop Ealdred of York, so John of Worcester tells us.[29] It is the only source we have that clearly states that it was Ealdred who performed the anointing. The coronation scene in the Bayeux Tapestry, names the cleric in the crowning scene as Stigand in the next panel.[30] The tapestry was likely to have been commissioned by a Franco/Norman faction, and it suited them to have Stigand consecrate Harold as king. Stigand's appointment to archbishop was seen as unlawful, making Harold's position on the throne also unlawful.[31] This, and the claim that Edward had offered the throne to William, are the foundations upon which the Normans argue that the duke had the right to invade.

Some historians believe it unlikely that Harold would have risked Stigand performing the ceremony. The archbishop had been without a pallium since Pope Benedict had been deposed by Pope Nicholas on the grounds of corruption. Ever since then, Stigand's office had not been recognised in Rome and his consecration was denied by Pope Nicholas and the deposition also extended by his successor, Pope Alexander. During that time, Stigand had not been used to sanctify any bishops in England, apart from those he had when he held the position legally. To dodge problems with Rome, Ealdred performed any consecrations that were needed. Harold had even taken care when consecrating his own church at Waltham, avoiding any issues by ensuring it was Cynesige of York that performed the ceremony.[32] Even Edward's church was consecrated by Ealdred using the Third English Ordo, composed by the archbishop himself in 1054, in Cologne.

It was not necessary for a king to have a coronation ceremony for them to act in their role as monarch, and it has been remarked upon that Harold acted with unholy haste to have his coronation performed on the same day King Edward was buried. It would seem fair, however, to believe that once he was anointed before God, it would be harder for William to depose him. Doubtless the Normans were keen to push the idea that it was Stigand who anointed him, discrediting Harold's coronation to avoid being accused of the most serious crime of regicide.

The *C, D,* chronicles of that year, mention in a poem that the king 'committed the kingdom to a distinguished man, Harold himself, a princely earl, who at all times loyally obeyed his superior in words and deeds, neglecting nothing of which the nation's king was in need'.[33] The *Waltham Chronicle,* written later in the latter part of the twelfth century, states that Earl Harold was elected king unanimously, 'for there was none in the land more knowledgeable, more vigorous in arms, wiser in the laws of the land or more highly regarded for his prowess of every kind'.[34]

But not everyone was as pleasant. The half-English, half-Norman scholar, William of Malmesbury reported that Harold 'seized the diadem' and 'extorted consent from the nobles, though the English say it was granted to him by the king'.[35] The early twelfth-century chronicler also implies that it was out of regard for Harold, rather than sound judgement, that Edward gave his inheritance to the man whose power, he had always been jealous of. Malmesbury also insinuates that had Harold acquired the crown lawfully, he would have 'governed it prudently and with courage' pointing to the service he had given the king and his fellow countrymen as proof of this. So, in other words, throughout his career, Harold was law abiding, loyal, efficient, and competent until he 'illegally' assumed the throne.[36] By Malmesbury's time, Harold was long gone, and there were few left alive that could speak for him. There was nothing illegal about Harold's ascendancy to the crown, and yet he was still being maligned many years after his death.

Henry of Huntingdon, thought to be the son of a clerk, wrote a history of the English people from the year 1000–1154, and was an English speaker, implying he was perhaps another mixed-race product of the Norman invasion. He wrote that after King Edward's death, the English wanted to elevate Edgar to the kingship, but Harold, 'relying on his forces and birth, usurped the throne from him'.[37] In the same passage, Huntingdon continues to defame the Godwin family by suggesting that William of Normandy was 'provoked in his mind' for three reasons: Godwin and his sons had dishonoured and murdered his kinsman, Alfred; they had Archbishop Robert, and Earl Odda, and all the Frenchmen exiled, and lastly, Harold had perjured himself by usurping the throne of England which should, by right, have belonged to William. Let us debunk this: firstly, the 'sons' of Godwin were not involved in the death of Alfred. Harold was at the time, only around 11 years old, and his brothers, much younger, if born at all. That Godwin murdered Alfred was never proven, and kings Harthacnut and Edward and had accepted his oath backed up by oath supporters that he was innocent of the murder. Furthermore, Alfred's mother, Emma, had exonerated Godwin of any involvement by accusing Harold Harefoot of being wholly responsible.

The fact that Alfred had shared the same fate of Harefoot's uncles, may suggest that his mother, Ælfgifu, had encouraged her son to take vengeance against the son of Æthelred for the blinding of her brothers. Secondly, Archbishop Robert fled from England of his own volition, essentially kidnapping the son and grandson of his enemy Earl Godwin. Earl Odda was never exiled, dying peacefully at his home in Deerhurst.[38] Thirdly, there is substantial evidence that Harold was granted the throne by the *witan* and nominated by the king. Even William of Poitiers agreed that Edward commended him his kingdom on his deathbed.

It is likely that whatever the English did to safeguard Harold's position as king, William's supporters would have discredited it one way or another. The hatchet job on Harold's reputation by the Norman press, lasted long after his death. It has been suggested that if Harold had taken power by promoting Edgar to the throne with himself as regent, then with Edgar on the throne, William would not have been able to challenge the English decision. If Harold had attempted to put forward the argument to William whilst in Normandy that England already had chosen Edgar to be their future king,

William would likely have disregarded it on the basis that Edgar was a child and unable to match him in all things kingly. Even when the English were said to have tried to elevate Edgar as king, William flouts his claim as inconsequential, and he had not even been crowned himself at that point. Therefore, it is reasonable to believe that putting Edgar on the throne would not have deterred William any more than it had in 1064.

Harold seems to have done everything he could to steer clear of any impediments to his ascendancy to the throne. He continued to use the officers that had been in service to Edward, safeguarding their positions and their loyalty to the crown. He ensured he had the backing of the *witan;* he chose the right archbishop to consecrate him and had Edward's deathbed commendation, and the oaths of his Normans.

CHAPTER NINETEEN

England's Chosen King

Edwin, Morcar, and Edgar

There has never been any evidence that there was ill-will between Harold and the sons of Alfgar, at least not of the type that had existed with Tostig during the rebellion of the north.[1] But Harold, like Tostig, had also been an enemy of their father's and they would not have trusted him easily, even though he had supported Morcar as the insurgents' choice for earl. Harold would need to make sure he had the young earls on his side, for they now controlled vast areas in the midlands, the Danelaw, Yorkshire and beyond. We know that Harold travelled to York sometime after his coronation and before Easter that year. For what purpose the sources do not divulge. The *ASC* merely states that he came from York to Westminster before Easter.[2] Perhaps the lack of detail had something to do with lazy clerics, perhaps it was already a well-known fact. The disinterest is frustrating. John of Worcester does not even mention the trip to York, however, we are told that in a short while following his coronation, the new king revoked unjust laws and replaced them with virtuous ones. We find that he established himself as protector of churches; showed himself to be humble, kind, and courteous to all men, except criminals, to whom he acted harshly. He gave powers to those with jurisdiction to arrest thieves, robbers, and disturbers of the peace. Then at great labour to himself, he set about reinforcing England's land and sea defences.[3] In an exemplary display of robust kingship, he accomplished all this from the time he was crowned until sometime in March of that same year. Then he travelled north.

The reason for the journey is not well explained in the *ASC*. William of Malmesbury, writing the *Life of Wulfstan (Vita Wulfstani)* explains that Harold rode north taking Bishop Wulfstan with him and that it was because the Northumbrians had not given their allegiance to Harold.[4] The record of attendees tells us that all five earls were present at court during Christmas when Edward passed away. Considering the Northerners dislike of the Godwinsons, it is not unreasonable that Edwin and Morcar would be worried on two accounts. One: that the men they had promised to rule over, may have expected the designated heir, Edgar, to be elected to the throne rather than Harold, preferring not to have their young earls in the pocket of a Godwinson not long after they had ousted one. And two: now he was in the exulted position of king, Harold might restore Tostig to his earldom.[5]

Edgar seems to have been missing from the chronicles during this period until he appears after Hastings in the *ASC* when Edgar, Morcar, and Archbishop Ealdred, proclaimed him king. So where did he go in the interim? It has been suggested that the new king expelled him from the realm after he was crowned, whilst others expected Harold to keep the young prince by his side, and not let him out of his sight.[6] Exiles often had a habit of bouncing back, as Harold knew well, having been one himself. However, Edgar's fate between Harold's coronation and the announcement of his own election, is worthy of exploration. The clue appears to be hidden in Harold's journey to York and return to London before Easter.

Malmesbury's story that the brothers had not sworn their allegiance to the new king is plausible. Malmesbury translated Wulfstan's original English biographer, Coleman, from the vernacular to Latin.[7] Edwin and Morcar, fearful that Harold would betray them by bringing Tostig back, may have wanted to draw Edgar to their side so they could have control over him. Did they convince Edgar he was in danger from Harold, and that he would be safer with them? The scenario may have seen the young schemers leaving the court shortly before or after Harold's coronation, taking Edgar with them. Harold had been busying himself with the needs of the realm, not noting the boy had slipped away. When Harold twigged that Edgar was missing, and the young earls also, he put two and two together. He had to act fast, but first he needed to see to the defence of the realm amongst other things. Then he travelled north, taking the well-respected Wulfstan with him, to help win the Northumbrians over.[8]

Knowing that Edwin and Morcar had the military power to support Edgar, must have raised Harold's anxieties. He would need to get to them before they started something that could only be finished with violence.[9] Harold did not need the added worry of a rival to the throne being at large. Nor would he risk the ætheling being the figurehead for an invasion by Tostig, Swein Estridson, or even Harald Hardrada. If Edgar had managed to evade Harold's watchful eye in a moment of complacency, then Harold knew he need not look anywhere else other than York.

It is unlikely Harold charged at them, sword blades blazing in the midday sun. There was no need to threaten them with execution for plotting sedition. That was not Harold's style. Harold was not interested in causing trouble with the north, not with the menace of Tostig and William hanging over him. He needed to win them over. A small bodyguard and the likes of Wulfstan as spiritual support was certainly enough.[10] It's likely he had the support of Archbishop Ealdred also. There, in the palace that was once his brother's in York, using a softly, softly approach, he negotiated with the young sons of his old enemy. Both sides put enmity away for the sake of the realm, and to seal the deal, Harold agreed to take their sister, Aldith, to wife.[11] Taking Wulfstan with him was the best thing he could have done, as the *Wulfstani* claims, 'Such was the respect the rough northerners had for Wulfstan's holiness', he was able to persuade them to Harold's cause and they readily submitted, 'suppressing their dislike of the soft southerners and mistrust of Tostig's brother'.[12] Thus, a crisis was averted. Edwin and Morcar were now in a better position as brothers-in-law to a king, and uncles to any potential royal princes. It was around this time that as part of a marriage contract made between the king and the Alfgarsons, Harold was endowed with some lands in Mercia.[13]

The English chronicles do not mention Aldith at this time, nor do they mention Harold returning from York with a wife. The Norman scribe, William de Jumièges, however, refers to him marrying her after he 'seized the kingdom'.[14] It is from Jumièges, that we are advised of Harold's second wife's identity, as he calls her the daughter of Earl Alfgar who had married the Welsh king, Gruffudd. Aldith must have had mixed feelings at the prospect of marriage with the man who engineered her first husband's death, but it would put her in a powerful position, enough for her to forget

Gruffudd, perhaps. From Jumièges, we get no detail of her, apart from the remark about her beauty. We do not know if she had her daughter by Gruffudd, Nest, with her at this time. The child would have been no older than 8 years old, and her mother somewhere in her mid-twenties. Nest would later wed Osbern, a Norman marcher lord.[15]

It is interesting to imagine if, on their way back to London, Harold and his new wife stopped at Harold's estate in Conisburgh for a few days honeymoon. It might have been there that the child they were to have together, a son called Harold, was conceived.[16] We do not know how well-matched they were, but they would not have long together and she may not have seen him again after their first nights together. It is doubtful that she was ever crowned, and there are no charters or diplomas witnessed by her as queen. It is odd that something so important as a marriage to a noble lady such as she was not documented anywhere and the reason for this omission remains unknown. However, events were spinning out of control and the impending invasion seems to have been all that Harold was able to focus on. He no doubt intended to put that right once the trials of the year were over.

As for Eadgifu, Harold's handfasted wife, just as Cnut had put aside Ælfgifu for Emma, Harold did the same with Eadgifu, though perhaps not completely. Their love, it seems, if the *Waltham Chronicle* is anything to go by, was to last till the end, when she was brought to the battleground to search for his body.

Portents

As we have seen, Harold took over the reins of government with gusto. Apart from the aforementioned activities, he also facilitated the initiation of a new coin, designed with his crowned head, bearded chin, and sceptre on one side, and his *PAX* motif on the other.[17] Whilst he still had time, he addressed a writ for the rights of Bishop Giso of Wells, to Bishop Æthelnoth of Glastonbury, witnessed by Tovi, Sheriff of Somerset, and all the other thegns that were there.[18] Of course, there were the usual new appointments to be made for the vacant bishoprics and abbacies. It might have been at this time that Waltheof was installed in his father's old counties that Tostig had not long vacated in the shires of Northampton and Huntingdon. Harold installed a man called Marleswein in Lincolnshire as staller. This important, royal position would strengthen Harold's power in the north, giving royal authority in local government and bolstering the local militia perhaps with huscarls under Marleswein's direct command. The other stallers that had served in Edward's command, FitzWymarc, Ralph, Esegar, Bondi, and Eadnoth also remained in situ. Harold would have known and worked with these men as their superior for many years, so their loyalty was unquestionable.[19] Some minor thegns, however, did lose their lands as Domesday shows us.[20]

That the English administration appeared to be running smoothly with no opposition and now, with the agreement of the north, tells of the confidence that these men had in Harold. For over ten years as earl, he had been running the country on Edward's behalf and had made the transition from earl to king with ease. His initial actions so soon after his coronation, showed his competency in organising a tight ship. No one can have doubted then, that the decision to crown Harold instead of Edgar had been wrong. It is hard to say if anything would have been done differently, had Edgar been elected.

Harold would still have been at the helm, making all the state decisions. He had worked tirelessly and loyally for king and country, for a great deal of his life. He deserved now to be rewarded with the kingship.

Harold and his bride had barely arrived home when the sky was lit up with the phenomenon of Halley's Comet. As John of Worcester reports that year in 1066: 'a comet was seen on the eighth of the calends of May, not only in England, but, as it is reported, all over the world: it shone with excessive brilliance for seven days'. The Bayeux Tapestry shows men outside Westminster Abbey, looking up in admiration, at what appears to be a shooting star. In the next panel, an enthroned Harold is leaning closely to a messenger, listening to some secret intel being explained to him. Underneath that image of king Harold are six unrigged boats, an indication the messenger is relaying information coming out of Normandy. In the next panel, a boat has arrived in Normandy, and a messenger conveyed news of Harold's enthronement to William. William then orders boats to be readied for the invasion of England.[21]

It was time for Harold to consider his military strategy.

CHAPTER TWENTY

The Papal Banner

Jumièges and Poitiers do not record Duke William's reaction to the news that King Edward was dead, and Harold had taken the throne, but Wace gives an animated account of how he received it.

Making ready his bow to go forth to the chase with his hunting companions, a messenger appeared to William, saluted him, drew him aside, and gave him the news that King Edward was dead, and Harold had taken the crown. The duke, enraged, fiddled with the ties of his cloak and left the hunt, speaking to no one, and no one dared to speak to him.[1] In his hall, he sat down on the end of a bench, still maudlin, shifting from one position to another, covering his face with his cloak, and resting his head against a pillar. He stayed like this for some time, and still there was no one who dared to ask him what was wrong. Instead, they asked his companions, 'What ails the duke? Why makes he such bad cheer?' Then his seneschal, William FitzOsbern, entered and said to them, 'Ye will hear news, but press not for it out of season; news will always spread some time or another, and he who gets it not fresh, has it old.'[2] Then the duke rose and FitzOsbern asked him why he concealed the news, when they will hear it anyway second hand. He advised the duke that concealment will do him no good. 'What you keep so close, is by this time known all over the city. Edward is dead and Harold has become king, and possesses the realm.' The duke being in such a state declared: 'I sorrow for Edward, and for his death, and for the wrong that Harold has done me. He has wronged me in taking the kingdom that was promised to me, as he himself had sworn.' Here, reports Wace, FitzOsbern, the bold of heart, replied:

> Sire, do not vex, bestir yourself for your redress; that you may be avenged on Harold, who hath been so disloyal to you. If your courage fail not, the land shall not abide with him. Call together all that you can call; cross the sea, and take the kingdom from him. A bold man should begin nothing unless he pursue it to the end; what he begins he should carry through, or abandon it without more ado.[3]

Earlier pro-Norman sources are not as explicit as Wace. Jumièges carries on the story from Harold's release by William, to his return home, laden with gifts, then to Edward's demise with very little detail. Following that, it is hit on immediately that Harold seized the throne, perjuring himself and breaking the oath made to William.[4] Poitiers refers to Harold as the mad Englishman, too eager to wait for a public election, grabbing the throne on the same day 'the best of men died' (Edward) and 'with the connivance of a few wicked men' took the throne. Poitiers, implies that Harold's crowning was impiously carried out by Stigand unlike John of Worcester who claims it was Ealdred.[5]

Such scenes are used to convey what was likely to have happened and likely to have been said, rather than what had occurred verbatim. Despite its problematic late date and obvious use of fiction, there are some very specific elements, such as the hunting story with its detail of the bow, that perhaps came from an orally preserved tradition. Jumièges may not have included William's tantrum as it may have shown the duke in a bad light.

Wace goes on to report that William, once cajoled out of his mute state, sent messengers to England demanding that Harold stand down from the throne and renounce the folly that caused him to break his oath. The king refused, and is accused of treacherously turning the English against the rightful heir, William.[6] William's great friend, William FitzOsbern, encouraged the despairing duke, spurring him into action; lifting him out of his depression.[7]

Wace represents Harold as harsh and has him refuse to do nothing for the duke. Nor would he take William's daughter to wife. None of the duke's daughters were very old at the time the claim was made.[8] In short, Harold was not playing ball, and William was injured by his wickedness, and refusal to give up the crown. Eventually William became defiant, and Harold replied that he was not scared by him.[9] Harold proved his fearlessness and all the Normans who gave their oaths to him by behest of Edward, were 'chased out of the country', whole families, children too.[10] Soon, all of Normandy was to hear of the nasty, tyrant, Harold, and the terrible treatment of their countrymen. The *Estoire de Seint Ædward le rei*, makes Harold's tyrannical proceedings a prime motive for William's expedition of the conquest.[11]

William gave up the war of words and called a counsel of bishops and his closest vassals. Many of William's allies were reluctant. An invasion was far too risky an enterprise and beyond their financial means.[12] Orderic adds that some were specifically concerned about the danger of the crossing itself, and the problems of raising a fleet. Harold, they also knew, had access to great resources, especially man-power.[13] But William's ambitions could not be quelled, and he eventually won them over with his dogged determination in a series of war councils travelling around the whole of the duchy of Normandy.[14]

Was there a Papal Banner?

The only contemporary source that mentions the pope's support for an invasion of England, was the *Gesta Guillelmi*, written by William of Poitiers. 'Seeking the approval of this pope, whom he (William) had informed of the matter in hand, the duke received a banner with his (Pope Alexander II) blessing… following which he may attack the enemy with greater confidence and safety.'[15] Orderic informs us that the duke arranged a mission to Rome led by Gilbert, archdeacon of Lisieux.[16] This is neglected by Poitiers, Guy d'Amiens, and William of Jumièges'. Both the latter two accounts are chronologically earlier and better placed to know if there was a papal banner given to William before the invasion. And yet neither mention the trip to Rome nor the receipt of a banner at all.[17]

There is no evidence of William's appeal to Alexander in any of the papacy's letters or records. Nor is there any indication that Harold was called to give his defence, which he surely would have been, as an anointed king.[18] Malmesbury states that Harold omitted to put his case before the pope because he knew his case was not just, and was worried that any party he sent to do so, would be obstructed on their journey by William's partisans.[19] Recent suggestions have been made that Harold made no counter claim because of Stigand's dubious position, disregarding the claim that John of Worcester made that it was Bishop Ealdred who consecrated Harold.[20] Poitiers brief mention of a papal banner suggests that William's cause easily carried the day.[21] Orderic, writing after Poitiers, indicated that William was seeking advice from the pope rather than approval.[22] Malmesbury, drawing on Poitiers, stated that Pope Alexander weighed the arguments up before determining that William's claim was righteous.[23]

William's main arguments were 1) his claim that Edward offered him the crown, which he made to him through Harold, and 2) the latter's violation of the oath sworn to him on holy relics.[24] Harold was also a perjurer, and had been consecrated unlawfully by an unsanctified bishop. Since Harold was neither there nor represented, he could not defend himself. Therefore, Alexander had not weighed up both sides of the argument. However, if Harold had been given the chance, it is likely he would have counter argued that he had been consecrated by Ealdred, not Stigand, and that the oath to William was coerced, and if believed, this would have made the oath void in the eyes of the church as was its law. Though much has been made of William's case to the pope, Harold does not appear to have been given the same consideration or opportunity to put forward his argument.

Despite there being a number of flags on the Bayeux Tapestry, it is odd to find that no such papal banner was identified in any of its panels. Attempts made to pinpoint it on the embroidered work, have proved fruitless.[25] If you wanted to show the world that your deeds had the support of the most elevated man in Christendom, then surely the banner would not have been omitted from the one piece of visual evidence that could have exploited it to the world. Poitiers, speaks of the banner just three times in his work, and only in laconic terms.[26] Dan Armstrong, in his thesis about the papal banner,[27] highlights the lack of information regarding papal support for William's intended invasion. The first reference to the banner has already been mentioned above, the second when William's men line up behind it to advance onto the field at Hastings.[28] Lastly, we are told that William sent Harold's own famous fighting man banner, gloriously woven in pure gold, as a gift to the pope, 'in return for the banner he had given him'.[29]

Poitiers lack of detail in the passages concerning the papal banner, needs to be considered. It was as if he wanted to gloss over the facts whilst simultaneously ensuring it received just the right amount of attention to prove its presence on the battlefield.

The banner's existence has largely been the consensus of modern historians,[30] however, some believe much of the Norman post-conquest sources have been fictionalised in order to justify to any doubters that William's invasion was lawful, and that Harold was a monstrous usurper.[31] Dan Armstrong points out in his thesis, *The Norman Conquest of England, the Papacy, and the Papal banner*, that historian, Catherine Morton argued plausibly against the banner, but has been largely ignored in the footnotes.[32] Her opinions rest on Poitiers being the only source that mentions it and that it undermined the Penitential Ordinance imposed upon the Normans for homicides committed during and after the Battle of Hastings.[33] Morton's ideas had little influence among her fellow historians, but despite this, Dan Armstrong, building upon Morton's original critique of Poitiers' papal sponsorship, has written an extensive thesis aimed at shifting the consensus that the banner was indisputable, to one that fully and convincingly challenges this argument. His theory differs significantly from

Morton's, and believes that her points should not have been as readily dismissed as they were. It seems that by taking Morton more seriously, we are able to understand Poitiers rationale for his claim that Pope Alexander supported the invasion.

Armstrong's thesis offers a different narrative that moves the date of William's receipt of the banner from 1066 to a more likely date of 1070, refuting the idea that Pope Alexander had approved William's request before the invasion.[34] He does this after some lengthy examination of various leads, and counter leads, and creates a new narrative of events that took place in the years between 1066 and 1070.

According to Poitiers, William put his case to his vassals and ecclesiastical VIPs, discussing his plans for England.[35] He then reached out to his neighbours, Flanders, Boulogne, and the various provinces of France. Knights flocked to William fully confident of the justice of his cause, enthusiastic for land, wealth and reward, lured by the duke's eagerness to repay those well who came to his aid.[36] Having been assured of help, both financially and militarily, William ordered the building of ships and preparations for the excursion began. Poitiers also suggests that William sent embassies to Denmark, Germany, and Rome.[37]

It was a smart move for William to send a delegation to Rome to bolster his claim. But the arguments of Gilbert de Lisieux used to win the papal curia over failed in the immediacy. This did not mean that Alexander did not want to support William. Armstrong explains that the pope wanted to hear both sides of the argument before deciding. After all, Alexander was having issues with Honorius the Antipope, elected by supporters of the Holy Roman Emperor, Henry IV, Alexander's enemy. Whatever side the pope refused to back might want to side with Honorius, so it is possible he wanted to take a neutral stance and sent the Norman delegation away intending to give his decision when he had completed his investigations. This, combined with the silence of the earlier sources regarding papal support, makes it improbable that Alexander sanctioned the invasion.[38] With this in mind, we should accept there was no papal support and no banner before William embarked on his expedition to conquer England. Alexander was known to prefer peace over war.[39] Armstrong's research informs us that Pope Alexander would have wanted to mediate and see what he could do to quell the bloodshed. But in this case, events moved faster than expected, and by the time the legate, Ermenfrid, arrived in Normandy sometime in 1067 to start preliminary discussions, the invasion was done and dusted. Alexander's hopes for a non-violent solution had been thwarted.[40]

Upon William's return to Normandy, proclaiming himself victor and king of England, he may not have been happy about the criticism levelled at him throughout the Continent, and from the papal curia. It may have been at this point that Ermenfrid, having worked on the Penitential Ordinance with the bishops of Normandy, returned to Rome with William's delegation, bringing gifts for Alexander from the duke to appease him. If anyone thinks that the Ordinance was designed to punish those who fought against the English at Hastings, they are completely mistaken. It was designed out of concern for the souls of the Norman/French army and sets out the level of penance for crimes committed on the battlefield. William won his crown with the blood of his own people as well as the English, and also committed regicide, a heinous wrongdoing in this time. His name, however, was not mentioned in the Ordinance, so it may be that he had arranged to purge himself by building the church on the spot where Harold was said to have been slaughtered. The Ordinance was, in manner of speaking, a ploy to make the invasion seem like it was a justifiable pious act against a tyrant.[41]

According to Armstrong, the papal curia may not have been as welcoming of the William's representatives. Some may have remembered Harold fondly from his visit there in 1056/1057, an honourable, pious man, collecting holy items with which to endow his church back in England. This would have made the decision to accept William's cause difficult for Alexander. However, William's actions were objectionable to some in the curia, the problem with Honorius still existed, and Alexander no longer needed too worry about which rival he should back, as Harold was dead.[42] Not wishing to lose an ally like William to Honorius, Pope Alexander gave way to William, excused his sins, and proclaimed his invasion of England as legitimate.[43]

The Second Coronation

Just like William's fight to consolidate his power in Normandy, his fight for England would not come easily. The struggle went on for several years before he was comfortably established. William was beset by several rebellions from 1067 onwards but between 1069–1070 the rebellions were prolific. William was putting out one conflagration after another, and his position in England was regarded as precarious, despite supposedly receiving the pope's acceptance post-conquest. Still desperate for approval from the beleaguered English, he turned again to the pope, requesting further affirmation. Alexander agreed. This time it came in the form of a papal delegation. According to Orderic, William was crowned in Winchester by two cardinals, and papal legate, Ermenfrid of Sion, sent by Pope Alexander, without the burning of buildings as happened in London at the first coronation.[44] We can surmise it was in the year 1070, as it was around this time that Stigand was deposed at Winchester during Easter, an event corroborated by John of Worcester.[45] *Vita Lanfranci*, (The Life of Lanfranc) also states that at this ceremony he was confirmed as king.[46] During this second coronation, the pope at last gave official approval with the gift of a banner, seen in the image of the ceremony of William, enthroned between the two papal legates, whilst holding a crude version of a papal standard.[47] The crowning ceremony at Winchester was the time for him to establish himself with God's approval and it fits that he should have acquired the banner, not in 1066 when Harold was still alive and the anointed king of England, but after he had been dead for some time and could not speak for himself.

But why did Poitiers choose to be economical with the truth? It seems that a banner granted in 1070 would have had far less impact than one granted in 1066, a legitimization of the proposed invasion that was due to occur that same year.[48] William's reputation in Europe had taken some stick, invading England and slaughtering her king was not a popular achievement among the Continentals. He needed some better publicity, and Poitiers was just the man to do it. Whether or not William commissioned Poitiers to resume his chronicle in the 1070s, we have no way of knowing, though some historians believe the archdeacon did so in order to win William's favour.[49] Finding earlier attempts to defend William's right to invade unsatisfactory, Poitiers, using Jumièges earlier work as a framework, took it upon himself, to rewrite, outrageously embellish, and fictionalise the story.[50] Thus, Poitiers made it appear without inviting too much questioning, that the Papal Banner was actually given in 1066 and was taken onto the battlefield at Hastings, to shut the nay-sayers up for good.

As expected with works of this kind, everything Poitiers says about William praises him, leaving the reader in no doubt that his purpose was to ensure that William came out of his investigation squeaky clean. Harold, however, is the murdering, perjuring, tyrant whom everyone, including the papacy, and Poitiers were glad to see the back of. It is interesting that as time progressed from the victory over the English at Hastings until William died and beyond, the stories became more and more blatantly imaginative with each chronicler, and Harold's reputation wholly demonised.[51] The Penitential Ordinance which Bates reports as being issued sometime in 1067, was distributed by the Norman bishop, Ermenfrid Sion backed by Pope Alexander, setting out the requirement of atonement to be performed by William's soldiers. William, as stated already, was not mentioned in the Ordinance. According to Garnett, even the eleventh-century Flemish chroniclers were scathing in their condemnation of the conquest, despite their fellow countrymen fighting on William's side.[52] Did they believe that they had been hoodwinked by William?

In any case, it seems that the new Norman king of England, sought help from the pope to restore his reputation. Poitiers assisted in this mission by creating a monster out of Harold so horrific, it made anything William did look holy. It was not until 1071 when the revolt of Hereward in Ely was put down could he relax, and concentrate on the new troubles in Normandy.

CHAPTER TWENTY-ONE

It Begins

Tostig's Plan

Harold had not only taken the throne, but was now in bed with the Alfgarsons, a double-edged sword for Tostig who had not only been betrayed by his brother, but with the brothers who had helped to engineer his exile. It is possible he had expected to hear from Harold. His brother's elevation to the throne now meant he had the power to restore him. But Harold was clear where his loyalties lay. For Tostig, it was the last straw.[1] Harold's point of view was understandably different, he could not have reinstated him even if he wanted to. As part of the Northumbrian deal made with Edward, Tostig's exile was permanent.[2] In view of this, nor was Harold able to offer him Wessex. Tostig's return with the agreement of the North was impossible. And with William preparing to contest his throne, Harold could not afford to provoke them.

Last we heard, Tostig had been welcomed with his family in St. Omer. His brother-in-law, Baldwin V, had appointed him as his castellan there. In 1066, the count, had been co-regent of France with Anne of Kiev to his nephew, Phillip I, and was not only William of Normandy's father-in-law, but his overlord too. Tostig's existence in St. Omer was a come-down for an English earl. The winter spent in Flanders gave him plenty of time to ruminate on his brother's betrayal and further cultivate bitterness toward his brother.[3] By the time news of Harold's marriage to Aldith reached him, Tostig's desire for vengeance must have sprung to an all-time high.

According to some, Tostig sought out William with a view to an alliance of some sort against Harold. Orderic is the only source that proposes there was a meeting between them. Baldwin may have used his connection through marriage to both parties, to suggest the idea to Tostig.[4] Orderic gives us the impression of a bold Tostig rebuking the duke for his 'inaction' against Harold. This might have been meant good naturedly, for he then follows this by promising to 'faithfully assist him to retrieve the crown, if he would cross to England with a Norman army.'. William, we are told, was grateful for Tostig's chiding, and persuaded to call his councillors to see what could be done about the issue.[5] Meanwhile, Tostig was to start the ball rolling in England by raiding the south coast.

Many variations on a theme exist as to what Tostig did next. It seems natural that Tostig would approach a member of his extended family to try out his chances elsewhere so as not to place all his eggs in one basket. It is doubtful, however, that William would ever have been serious about a coalition, though this did not stop Orderic believing that Tostig was given the duke's permission to sail to England and muster support for William. The duke, in the meantime, carried on with his preparations for the invasion, and according to Norman sources, they did not include Tostig Godwinson.

The Norwegian Kings' Sagas neglects Tostig's visit to Normandy, though the most detailed of their sources recall that he visited his cousin, King Swein, in Denmark.[6] Feeling sorry for Tostig, King Swein, we are told, offered him a jarldom in Denmark. The Danish king had no intention of joining Tostig for an invasion of England, at least not at this time. Perhaps Swein had more respect for Harold, whom he had grown up with. But something did not go well between them and whatever it was, the two men did not part on the best of terms. Forced by Swein's refusal to look elsewhere for help, Tostig next visited King Harald of Norway.[7]

Hardrada, or Harald Sigurdsson, was in his early fifties in 1066. At the age of 15, he had fought at his first battle in Stiklestad on behalf of his brother Olaf, and been seriously injured. He spent some years in Kiev and later took service as a young man with the famous Varangian guards of the eastern emperors from 1034 – to 1043. He won titles and wealth for his exemplary skills as a war commander which he used to fund his return to Norway in 1044. Hardrada convinced his nephew, Magnus, the then King of Norway, to let him have half the kingdom.[8] In 1047, after Magnus' death, the whole kingdom was his, and he continued to fight his counterpart, Swein Estridson, for Denmark, until Swein finally established himself as king. Known as the Thunderbolt of the North, Harald Sigurdsson had the reputation of a killer. In a poem he wrote about himself, he openly bragged having caused the deaths of thirteen of his enemies, admitting that he had no regret in the taking of life and remembered each and every one of his kills.[9]

Harald the Hard Ruler, Hardrada, welcomed Tostig, but not his scheme. Nonetheless, the former earl of Northumbria was not going to give up that easily. He offered the grizzly old Varangian what he had offered William, the loyalty of Tostig's own men, whom, he assured Hardrada, were waiting to welcome him back to his earldom. Tostig reminded him of the pact his predecessor, Magnus, had made with Harthacnut in 1039, suggesting to Harald as he had to William, he had been remiss in not claiming his inheritance. Some of Hardrada's Norwegians, however, were concerned. They had heard that the English huscarls were well trained, renowned for their bravery, and that one of Godwinson's men was worth two Norwegians. But Tostig was determined, and after debating with Harald into the night, the Norwegian king and his men were convinced. Suddenly the quiet retirement Hardrada had in mind did not seem so attractive.

Meanwhile, William was unaware what had happened to his English ally whose attempt at the initial raid in England had gone awry. This was due to William's own preparations taking so long.[10] In Orderic's version, Tostig convinced Hardrada to invade England with him, suggesting that the Norwegian king would keep half of England, and he, Tostig would hold the other half as his vassal.[11]

The *ASC,* in the entry for the year of 1066 reports that after the sighting of the 'haired star', Earl Tostig came 'from beyond the sea' into the Isle of Wight with a 'great fleet' and was given provisions and money by its residents.[12] Elsewhere, John of Worcester reports more forcefully that Tostig demanded tribute from the men who held land from him on the island. From there, Tostig raided villages along the Sussex coast, up to Sandwich in Kent. In London King Harold heard wind of Tostig's operations.[13] He had already been gathering a large ship and land army, because he knew that William of Normandy wanted to invade and take his kingdom.[14]

Hearing of Harold's advance to Sandwich, Tostig retreated by sailing north up the east coast, taking the boatmen already stationed there with him; some willingly, and some unwillingly, according to the *ASC*. Tostig and his ship army sailed into the Humber, raiding in the usual way. At Lindsey, some brave locals attempt resistance and are mercilessly crushed, their houses and property burned.[15] Both *E*, and *D*, chronicles state that Tostig had sixty ships when he went to the Humber, some of which were obviously pressed into his service at Sandwich.[16]

Edwin and Morcar acted swiftly in driving them out of the land. The attack was savage and not only did the boatmen from Sandwich, take the opportunity to flee, a later version says that most of Tostig's Flemish troops also fled.[17] The loss reduced Tostig's ships to a mere twelve cutters, and in this state, Tostig fled to his old chum, King Malcolm of Scotland, where he remained for the rest of the summer.[18] Gaimar reports that Tostig landed at *Wardstane*, harried there and afterwards went on to Thanet where they were joined by seventeen ships from Orkney, led by his old deputy in Northumbria, Copsige. Then having caused great damage in *Brunemue*, and elsewhere, they went into the Humber.[19]

Charles Jones in his book on the Battle of Fulford, presents an intriguing theory that by aligning himself with both William and Hardrada, Tostig was playing them off against one another in order to see who would be the last man standing.[20] Could it be possible that Tostig offered aid to both men, hoping that whosoever won, would be grateful enough to make him their *sub-regulus?* One thing to consider in this situation was what would he have done if Harold was the victor? Tostig may have believed that by causing as much chaos and mischief as he could, he was wrecking his brother's chances of fighting and winning two bloody battles that he knew were going to occur very close together. After all, *Vita* did not describe Tostig as 'cunning and impetuous' for nothing.

Undivided English forces would be more than a match for William. Equally for Hardrada, if the northern contingent was diverted away from any trouble in the south, then each of the invaders would only have to fight a dissected English army. Keeping the coastal regions safe was imperative, and would stretch Harold's forces, reducing the availability of the fyrd's main body. What appears to have been Tostig's plan all along was to provoke Harold into focusing on the south coast, leaving the north in the inexperienced hands of the young northern earls. It is not impossible that Gaimar was right about Tostig and Copsige meeting up in the summer. He and Tostig had been like crossed fingers throughout the earl's term in Northumbria. Copsige may have had trading connections with the jarls of Orkney, and gone there in the diaspora of Tostig's exile to enlist their help. Was Tostig's ultimate aim to see the defeat of all contenders, leaving the whole of England to himself? Had Tostig been formulating this plan before he had even set foot in the boat that took him to Flanders? What would be a better revenge against his brother, than he, Tostig Godwinson, would sit on the throne of England?

CHAPTER TWENTY-TWO

War in the North

Prelude

In the meantime, Harold had arrived in Sandwich to await the gathering of his fleet.[1] It may just so have happened that Tostig's deserted boatmen returned to Sandwich in time to greet their king and give him the low down on Tostig's plan to invade with Hardrada. Aware of their inexperience, it is possible that Harold sent messenger to the young earls to advise them that if Hardrada arrived, they should not engage him in battle, but to wait for reinforcements to arrive. But Harold now had the dilemma of chasing Tostig up the east coast, or taking the fleet to the Isle of Wight to watch for William, waiting for a compliant wind so he could cross the channel.[2] Harold chose to let Tostig go on his way and sailed to the Isle of Wight. Depending on which source you read, Tostig sailed to Scotland where he spent the summer waiting for his ally, Hardrada, to ready himself for the invasion. Harold and the *fyrd* stayed in his base along the south coast by the Isle of Wight until September, spreading his troops along the main coastal ports of Sussex and Kent. One scribe poignantly adds in hindsight to his entry of 1066, that what good Harold did to defend the realm, was all in vain.[3]

But the days dragged. There was no sign of the Normans, nor Hardrada. On 8 September, *The Nativity of St. Mary*, the provisions that kept the warriors of the *fyrd* fed, ran out. It was time to go home and for some, to bring in the harvest. The *ASC* says 'that no one could hold them (the fyrd) there any longer and they were permitted to go home'. Two different hosts had been held for four months on a rota system. Little did they know that as they rode back home, happy knowing they had got away without risking their lives in battle, things were about to go awry.

The Peterborough manuscript, *E*, is the only source to mention that there was an unofficial sea-skirmish off the south-coast between the English and Normans.[4] This may refer to William's failed embarkation sometime in the summer, where unfavourable winds blew them westwards along the Normandy shore.[5] The *C* chronicle has King Harold taking the inland route back to London, and the fleet sailed to meet him there along the coast. Many of the boatmen perished before they reached London's harbour, but the scribe is not specific about the cause of deaths. Were the two fleets, hit by the winds at the same time in the same place? Or was this not about the weather at all but a battle at sea?

The evidence of Domesday gives substance to the idea of a sea-battle before William landed at Pevensey. A man named Æthelric who owned land in Kelvedon, Essex, 'went away to a naval battle against King William'. He was said to have taken ill when he returned to London and left his estate to Westminster.[6] Frank Barlow mentions that

Harold had appointed Abbot Ælfwold of St. Benet as guardian of the shore along the Norfolk coast suggesting that his naval defences stretched further than just the south coast.[7] Both the English and the Norman fleets appear to have been afflicted by losses due to some calamity at sea. The Domesday mentions a sea battle against William, when no other such conflict is known.[8] There are grounds to believe that William had attempted to launch the invasion in early September, and that unfavourable winds may have been the reason why William ended up in St. Valery later in the month. This may have been when the skirmish occurred and the English fleet had driven William back to Normandy. His chances of invading that year were looking slim at that time. Harold may have hoped that William would not receive the same practical and financial support to launch another invasion the following year, and felt secure enough to think about matters of kingship. And then came Hardrada with a massive fleet of 300 ships and thousands of warriors, into the mouth of the Tyne.[9]

Earl Tostig joined him there with all that he could muster.[10] They sailed down the north-east coast and went into the Humber, perhaps to meet with Copsige and his seventeen ships loaded with Orkney men, and their earls, Paul and Erland, and sailed up the Ouse toward York. There are variations on a similar theme, which are as I have interpreted, leaving out the *E* Chronicle which suggests that, Harald, King of the Norwegians, met with Tostig in Scotland.[11] It appears more likely that the Norwegians sailed straight for England rather than Scotland. They were said by John of Worcester and Symeon to have moored their ships at Riccall, along the Ouse.[12]

Harold heard whilst in London, that Hardrada and Tostig have stormed their way to victory at Gate Fulford. As was usual for Harold, he acted immediately. Gathering his huscarls to him, he went northwards by day and night, mobilising his army from the shires as he went.[13] It could also have been at this point that word was sent to Edwin and Morcar they should not engage with Hardrada's army until Harold arrived with the fyrd. It may have been difficult for the young earls (*King Harald's Saga* included Earl Waltheof) to ignore the approaching army of Norwegians that threatened to overwhelm them. They may have felt that it was their duty to engage with them, or be overrun, and having summonsed their army from all over their earldoms, they possibly felt they had no option but to march out to fight them at Fulford Gate.[14]

Gate Fulford

The first battle of the three that were fought that year, was said to have been fought on the north bank of the River Ouse just outside York, on Wednesday 20 September.[15] It was Symeon and Gaimar who supplied the name of the place as Fulford. The name derived from it being the ford over the beck, a north English word for a stream, usually with a stony bed. It was referred to as *Gate Fuleford* in the Domesday, *fule* meaning dirty or foul and Morcar was owner of an estate there.[16] Gate was old Norse for street, so the road upon which the Battle of Gate Fulford was fought is where today, a housing estate was built about a decade ago. Despite 'fighting manfully in the first thrust of battle' and laying many of the enemy low,[17] the young earls' soldiers were defeated, drowning in the river as they turned to flee, leaving the battleground to the victorious enemy. The earls and their survivors escaped from the field, Morcar to his manor and Edwin and Waltheof into York.

Many historians are sceptical of using the Scandinavian sagas as evidence, but as said previously, we cannot dismiss them outright any more than we may dismiss later Anglo-Norman sources such as Orderic, Malmesbury, or Huntingdon. Like the aforementioned, they are not always reliable, but every source, even the earlier sources can be said to have their biases and problems. *King Harald's Saga* gives us far more detail than the earlier chronicles which is what makes them so entertaining and tempting to believe. But like other sources that are considered far more reliable, the details are more about what might have taken place, rather than what happened word for word.

Harald's Saga differs from the English sources and strangely, Tostig gets no mention at Fulford, as though he was never there at all. In it, Hardrada sails to Shetland and then on to the Orkneys, gathering a large force. He was joined by earls Paul and Erlend, the sons of Thorfinn the Mighty. From Orkney, he navigated down the south coast of Scotland and England, mooring at Cleveland. He went ashore as soon as he landed, plundering, and subjugating the whole area, receiving no resistance from the people. He then made for Scarborough and fought with the townsmen, hurling burning faggots down onto the town from a cliff, setting the whole place on fire, completely destroying it. The English had to die or submit, and according to the saga, this was how he 'subdued the country wherever he went.'. The sort of tourist that the locals would hate. When he thought he had done enough damage, Hardrada moved onto Holderness where he engaged the local militia and defeated them.[18]

His next tour-stop was to sail into the Humber and although the saga does not name the place as they do in the English sources, he was said to have dropped anchor close to the riverbank. Morcar and Waltheof were in York at this time with a huge army. Edwin is probably mistakenly left out of the saga. Hardrada lay in wait with his anchored ships when the earls' armies came down to meet him. He went ashore and marshalled his men, with one group flanked down the river and the other stretched toward a dyke filled with a swamp.[19] The English earls brought their men slowly southwards along the river in close formation. The earls, seeing that the Norwegians were thin near the dyke, advanced on it and the enemy's flank gave way. The English pursued them, Earl Morcar's banner in the vanguard. They must have thought that Hardrada's army would flee when they saw them coming, but the Norwegian king, whose famous *Land Waster* banner was down by the river with him, sounded the attack and urged his men forward. The Norwegian onslaught was so fierce that everything before the king's banner, went down like ten pins. The English army broke and the chaos that ensued saw fighters charging into the swamp, either sinking into its grip, or bolting upriver. The dead piled up so quickly that the Norwegian warriors could cross the river without getting their feet wet. Masses of English were killed there, including Morcar, which was recorded in error, as we know he survived the battle. Waltheof, the son of Siward the Strong, who cannot have been no more than 15 or 16 years old, got a mention in a poem in the *King Harold's Saga*:

> Waltheof's warriors
> All lay fallen
> In the swampy water,
> Gashed by weapons;
> And the hardy
> Men of Norway
> Could cross the marsh
> On a causeway of corpses.[20]

English sources are clear that Harald and Tostig's army advanced on York as soon as they landed at Riccall and the earls came out of York to bar their way into the city, drawing up their men on the eastern bank of the Ouse near the village of Gate Fulford, 2 miles south of York.[21] The next chapter of *Harald's Saga*, number eighty-six, is headed 'Stamford Bridge'. It starts with, 'Earl Tostig travelled north from Flanders to join King Harald as soon as he arrived in England, and so the earl took part in all these battles', as though the scribe had just remembered he'd left him out previously. He brought a large contingent of Englishmen, Tostig's friends and kinsmen, and added greatly to the strength of Harald's 300–500 plus ships of his own Norsemen. The chronology of the saga is a little confusing but it seems that after Fulford was won, Harald and Tostig assemble with their armies at Stamford Bridge.[22] The leading people of the town sent a message to Harald offering their surrender. The whereabouts of the young earls is not mentioned, but they may have been among them.

On Sunday, 24 September, Hardrada and Tostig went into the town and was given the allegiance of all the townspeople, and according to the saga, Tostig was able to name all the leading men in the town and hostages were demanded from the main families. Chronicle C adds that they agreed to hand over provisions, and John of Worcester numbers the hostages at 150, and adds that captives were given on both sides.[23] However, this would be unlikely, for the balance of power was with the victors so giving hostages was pointless. Nonetheless, Hardrada was delighted with such an easy win, and the people of York, probably out of necessity, agreed to support him to win the kingdom. An agreement was made for the two sides to meet again the following morning in York to appoint titles, officials, and to distribute estates.[24] However, the meeting place, according to the *D* chronicle was at Stamford Bridge, not York, where they had agreed to bring the promised supplies and hostages once they were rounded up from the whole of the shire.[25]

Stamford Bridge

The *C* chronicle states that King Harold Godwinson marshalled his fleet (*lið fylcade*) at Tadcaster on Sunday evening, and stayed overnight there.[26] This suggests that some of the king's troops may have travelled by ship via the River Ouse into the Wharfe. Harold learned that Hardrada and Earl Tostig, had gone beyond York to Stamford Bridge. It was there they had been promised a delivery of more hostages and provisions from all over the shire.[27] On Monday, they woke early and marched right through York and out again, perhaps stopping only to speak with the townsmen to learn of the whereabouts of the Viking horde and gather any fit troops to augment the battle host.

Harald's Saga reports that the English King Harold and his troops spent the night in York and not Tadcaster. It claims that they blocked all the roads and shut the gates so that news of his arrival would not reach the Norwegians.[28] There is some confusion in the saga as to where Harald left his ships, and seem to conflate Stamford Bridge with Riccall. In any case we are told that Hardrada divided his army into those who go with him and those who stay at their base, so that when they are confronted by Harold Godwinson's army, they have only two thirds of their army. Among the men left behind to guard the ships were the king's young son, Olaf, and the earls of Orkney, Paul and Erland, and the king's close companion, Eystein Orri, brother of Hardrada's concubine, Thora, and who was promised to wed the king of Norway's daughter Maria.[29]

The weather was exceptionally warm for the time of year, so as not to be unnecessarily burdened, the Norwegians left their armour behind at the ships, taking only their shields, helmets and weapons. Some brought bows and arrows and we are told that they were all feeling carefree after their magnificent triumph.[30] Imagine a happy band of hairy Vikings, skipping along in the sunshine without a worry in the world and they have no idea they are about to be busted by the king of England's army. Still in this convivial, merry condition, they approached the town only to be met by a great cloud of dust, raised by the hooves of thousands of horses' as they snaked over the crest of a hill. Hardrada halted his troops, you can never be too sure in a strange country who is about to confront you. As the gleam of handsome shields and white coats of mail came into view, he called up Tostig and asked him who was this army. Tostig advised that it might be a hostile force, but could also be his friends, coming to offer their fealty for their protection. At least that was what he hoped. Hardrada waited whilst the horde drew closer and the closer they came the greater the army grew, their glittering weapons sparkling like a field of broken ice.[31]

It dawned on Hardrada that this was a not a friendly army. If Tostig truly had so many friends, he thought, surely, he would not have been exiled. 'It must be the king himself,' Hardrada said, meaning Godwinson. Tostig suggested they should leg it back to their ships where they would be in a stronger position to defend themselves from Harold's cavalry. Hardrada instead, preferred to send three men on their fastest horses to fetch the others from their base to come to their aid. 'The English will have a very hard fight of it before we accept defeat.' The decision made, his banner, *Land Waster* was raised defiantly, and he drew up his battle formation, forming a wide, thin circle, facing outwards around Hardrada and his chosen bodyguards, their shields overlapping in front and above.[32] Tostig was also inside the circle of defence with his banner and company. The author of the saga based his account of the battle arrangements on the idea that Harold was making use of cavalry, riding up to the static defensive wall in small detachments, launching javelins and immediately wheeling away before the enemy in the front rows would be able to reach them with their spears. Hardrada's plan was to use archers, and his and Tostig's men would break out of the circle to sortie wherever the need was greatest.

Stamford Bridge is 7 miles east of York, and was 15 or so miles from their ships in Riccall. Why Hardrada chose it as the meeting place is not clear, however, Tostig would have known that all the roads in east Yorkshire met at the crossing of the Derwent making it a strategic position from which to dominate the county. But the *C* chronicle implies that the townsfolk had suggested they wait there for them to bring them the hostages they required from the rest of the county.[33] At this time the people of York may have known Harold was on his way and wanted them away from the shelter of the city so Harold could engage them out in the open, where they would be unprepared. And unprepared they were.

According to the saga, King Harold arrived with a vast army of cavalry and infantry. The English chronicles are not detailed in what his army consisted of, nor do we know what strategies he employed. We have only the saga to turn to which was written in the early 1200s by Snorri Sturlusson, and its reliability is often cast as doubtful. Having said that, its trustworthiness has been tested against other near contemporary accounts and it is known to be chronologically correct in its timeline.[34] There are some who have insisted that Snorri's account cannot be relied upon because Snorri confused the use of cavalry and missiles with the Normans at Hastings. Additionally, some historians have a hard time believing that the Anglo-Saxons used horses as cavalry in warfare at all. We know that Edmund Ironside used horses, and evidence of this can be found in the *ASC*. Horses are documented as being used at Hereford as cavalry, and there are other instances that can be called upon, such as from the poem of Brunanburgh, and Ecgfrith's defeat of the Picts in the seventh century.[35] Whether Snorri was conflating tactics used by William at Hastings is a moot point. However, seeing as Harold and his huscarls were mounted already, remaining so for the initial attack makes sense. Staying mounted would give them the advantage. Harold had witnessed this style of warfare in Normandy during the Breton campaign with William.

When Harold Godwinson and his vast army of infantry and cavalry arrived, the saga states that Hardrada was riding around his lines, inspecting them, on a huge black horse that stumbled underneath him, throwing him forward over his horse's head. He jumped up quickly and quipped that a 'fall meant fortune was on its way'.

Harold Godwinson asks who this man was and is promptly told that he was King Harald of Norway. Our English Harold then rode with twenty huscarls up to the Norwegian lines. The saga reports that even the horses were mailed, an assumption of the times in which the saga was written. Harold calls out, 'Is Earl Tostig in this army?'

Tostig replied, 'There is no denying it. You can find him here.'

The English Harold says, 'Your brother, King Harold sends his greetings, and a message that you can have peace and the whole of Northumbria as well. Rather than you refuse, he is prepared to give you one third of his kingdom. Earl Tostig replies, 'This is very different to all the hostility and humiliation he offered me last winter. If he had made this offer then, many men would still be alive, and England would be in a much better state. If I accept this offer now, what will he offer King Harald Sigurdson for all his effort?' The rider, (Harold G) says, 'He has already declared how much ground he is to grant him: seven feet of ground, or as much more as he is taller than other men.'[36]

Tostig replied:

> 'Go now and tell King Harold to make ready for battle. The Norwegians will never say that Earl Tostig abandoned King Harald Sigurdson to join his enemies when he came west to fight in England. We are united in our aim: either we die with honour, or else conquer this land.'

When the English horsemen turned away to join their lines, King Harald asked, 'Who was that man who spoke so well?' and was told that it was King Harold Godwinson. He retorted that he should have been told who he was for he should not have come so close to their lines and get away. He turned to his men, and said heartily, 'Such a little man, who stood so proud in his stirrups!'[37]

We are told that Hardrada wore a blue tunic and his coat of mail was called Emma; it was so long it reached below his knee, and was so strong that no weapon could pierce it. He even found time to compose his own poetry!

> We go forward
> Into battle
> Without armour
> Against blue blades.

> Helmets glitter.
> My coat of mail
> And all our armour
> Are at the ships.[38]

Then the battle began.

The Raven Falls and the Golden Warrior Rises

The battle was fought on Monday 25 September.[39]

Harald's Saga states that the English are said to have made a cavalry charge, but what about the bridge that the *C* chronicle mentions?[40]

'Harold, king of the English, came upon them *beyond the bridge* by surprise; and there they joined battle and were fighting very hard and long during the day; and there Harold, king of Norway, was killed and Earl Tostig and countless people with them, both Northman and English. And the Northmen fled from the English.'

The *E* chronicle says simply that Harald and Tostig were slaughtered, and 'Harold courageously overcame all that raiding army.' The saga describes Hardrada being 'struck in the throat by an arrow'.[41] Tostig, we are told, was found among the dead, identified by a wart between his shoulder blades. *D* chronicle refers to King Harold as 'our king' who 'came upon the Northmen by surprise and encountered them *beyond York* at Stamford Bridge...and there was that day, a very hard fight on both sides'. Notice in *C* they 'came upon them *beyond the bridge*' suggesting that Hardrada's army were on the other side of the battle flats across the river. *C* comes to an end when the Northmen flee from the English.

The following remainder of the entry in *C* was added by someone whose first language was not English later in the twelfth century, and tells us about the iconic story about the lone *berserker* who defended the bridge singlehandedly so that no one could cross the bridge.[42] He picked off each man who came forth to fight him, with his broad axe. Not even a bow and arrow could kill him! After failing to exterminate the man, someone had the remarkable idea to sneak under the bridge to stab him under his mail coat. Having immobilised the man, Harold and his troops were able to cross the bridge and made there a great slaughter of both Norwegians and Tostig's Flemings.[43]

All this seems like something you'd expect from a saga rather than the usually concise *ASC*. It is intriguing to wonder why a later scribe felt the need to insert it into the chronicle at all, especially since there is no other earlier contemporary evidence anywhere for it. The much later source written by Henry of Huntingdon also mentions it, stating that the daring Viking 'worthy of eternal fame' killed forty Englishmen with his trusty axe, holding the bridge against the English advance until 3 o'clock in the afternoon. This happened after the two sides had fought fiercely from dawn, the overwhelming forces of the English pushing back the Norwegians beyond the river. This suggests that Hardrada's army had already crossed the bridge and were on their way to York, as *Harald's Saga* suggested they would be. Huntingdon's pitch was that the English waited for forty men to be killed by an axe wielding berserker before doing anything decisive to get rid of him. Eventually spurred into action, an Englishman speared him in the private parts from underneath the bridge. So, the English were able to cross and killed King Harald and his ally Tostig and 'laid low the whole of the Norwegian line, either with their arms or with fire'.[44]

But were the troops able to cross the bridge still mounted, or did they cross on foot? Neither Huntingdon nor the *ASC* state that Harold's army was mounted. The cavalry charge mentioned by the saga is not specific about the bridge, although there is a chapter headlined Stamford Bridge written in the saga. The Norwegians met the charge without flinching and the English had no easy time of it because of the arrow shots, so they rode around them in a circle, skirmishing to begin with. They kept charging the Viking circle and falling back, making no headway.[45] The English attack in a weak manner goading the enemy into breaching their own defences, so the English could ride them down from all sides, showering them with spears and arrows, echoing what happened later at Hastings with the Norman cavalry.[46] Suddenly, Hardrada makes a charge into the thickest part of the clash, rushing ahead of his troops who make way for him, and fighting two-handed. The English were about to be routed, immortalised in the words of Arnor the Jarls' poet:

> Norway's king had nothing
> To shield his breast in battle;
> And yet his war-seasoned
> Heart never wavered.
> Norway's warriors were watching
> The blood-dripping sword
> Of their courageous leader
> Cutting down his enemies.

Then as he rushed toward the foe, cutting through the enemy, Hardrada was struck in the throat by an arrow. Those of his chosen men who had rushed with him, fell also, and the battle raged on under the royal standard, taken over by Earl Tostig. A lull occurred in the fighting as the men formed up around their new leader. The English took a break. Mighty Harald was fallen, and the poet Thjodolf lamented 'We are all imperilled.'[47]

King Harold took the opportunity to offer quarter to his brother and all the surviving Norwegians. The poet Arnor waxes lyrical that the Norwegians shout back that they would rather die than beg for mercy from the English.[48]

Orri's Battle

Then came the storm of Eystein Orri. The most beloved of King Harald's men and betrothed of his daughter, Maria, arrived at this point from the ships with all the men he had. Hardrada had left a third of his force back at Riccall to look after his sea vessels along with Prince Olaf and the Orkney earls Paul, and Erland. They had run all the way in the late September heat, weighed down by their mail, depleted of energy and devastated to learn of their lord's death. This caused them to fall in a state of madness, overcome by battle lust. Eystein grabbed the shaft of Hardrada's banner and he and his fellows fought like madmen. The English fell in great numbers. But the Norwegians, already exhausted from their harrowing journey, threw off their mail so they could fight without the burden of their armour. Some collapsed where they stood and almost all the leading Norwegians died there, though some ran for it, heading for their boats. The carnage ended after dark.[49]

D reports that after a hard day's fight for both sides, Harald, called 'Fine-Hair' in error, and Earl Tostig died. The English chased the survivors, fiercely attacking them until they came to their ships. Some drowned, some were burned, and there were very few left alive, until the English had the place of slaughter. King Harold, we are told, gave safe-conduct to Prince Olaf, the Norwegian's bishop and to the earls of Orkney, and to all those who had been left at the ships. Most likely the sons of Tostig, Skule and Ketil, were among those pardoned by Harold.[50] Oaths were sworn to King Harold and the earls gave hostages and pledged to keep the peace and friendship with this land.[51] The king allowed them all to go home with just the amount of ships needed to take them which was as low as twenty-four, indicating that many of the Norse lost their lives.[52]

And whilst these things were happening, William's French fleet landed in Pevensey.[53] The Bastard had come at last.

CHAPTER TWENTY-THREE
England is Mine

The Crossing

Before he embarked on the early evening of 29 September, William sought out the church of St. Valéry to leave gifts of thanks. It was the feast of St. Michaelmas; a holy day.[1] He had been waiting in *St. Valéry sur Somme* for a fortnight for the weathervane on the church to change direction, appealing to God for favourable winds to cross the Channel, even parading the holy relics of the saint about the town to show the extent of his faith.[2] And, of course, the south winds came at last. On the day, William would have to wait until sunset to embark, for he needed the tide to be high in order to complete the monumental task of boarding the horses by ramps along the shore.[3]

The departure at five o'clock in the evening must have been a sight to marvel, with William, proudly leading the fleet at the prow of the *Mora*, the ship gifted to him by his wife, Duchess Matilda.[4] On the sternpost was a figure of a boy with an ivory trumpet and a lantern was hung on the masthead as a guiding light to the other ships. We can see the artist's interpretation on the Bayeux Tapestry.[5] The *Carmen* gives an animated description of a large instrumental band playing as the *Mora* sailed swiftly out to sea with the rest of the fleet struggling to keep up with William's greater pace.[6]

During the night they dropped anchor. When the dark skies began to lighten, William ordered that the sail be set and raced ahead again.[7] As the next morning dawned, William and his companions found themselves alone, the fleet far behind. Perhaps William had taken the more skilled sailors for himself, or the ship his wife had commissioned for him was of advanced technology. William was disconcerted, wondering what had happened to the rest of his army. He decided to order breakfast and wine as a distraction whilst they waited for the rest of the fleet to catch up. Gradually, to his relief, mastheads began to appear. All was well. William and his fleet set out once more towards the shores of Sussex.[8]

The Landing

The *Carmen* mentions that the fleet pulled onto the safe beachhead when the hour was at the third of the day (9 am) and a blazing comet filled the sky, a portent for the English of their coming defeat at the hands of the invaders.[9] William, it was said, tripped over as he stepped onto the English shore. In an entirely later fabricated anecdote, he landed on his hands and it was reported that a great cry went up amongst his men that it was a bad omen, but William, never daunted by superstitious thinking, jumped up with handfuls of sand and yelled, 'See, my lords, by the splendour of God, I have taken possession of England with both my hands. It is now mine, and what is mine is yours.'[10]

The number of soldiers, ships, and horses that William brought with him has been questioned by many. Modern historians believe that there was somewhere in the region of 7,000-12,000 men, divided into units of cavalry, archers, crossbowmen, foot soldiers and mounted archers, as well as noncombatants. A list of ships can be found in Van Houts, *The Ship List of William the Conqueror*: fourteen vassals were to provide a total of 776 ships and 280 knights, though William claimed that he had a thousand vessels available to him.[11] William of Poitiers has Duke William reply to Edward's royal standard-bearer, Robert FitzWymarch, that if he had only 10,000 men instead of the 60,000 he had brought with him, he would still be confident of being victorious.[12] Of course this is an exaggeration, and something like the first figures mentioned would be more realistic, given the population for the time and the amount of professional fighting men. Barlow suggests that 500 ships could have easily transported 20,000 with their horses, equipment and luggage.[13] He points to evidence based on excavated Viking ships of the period: up to forty or fifty men could have been held within them.

It is not sure for certain that William had been aiming for Pevensey but as Barlow recounts, the Norman abbeys of Fécamp and Grestain had properties in that area of Sussex. That and the ready-made defences of the old Roman Fortress of Anderida made it a good place to land where now stands Pevensey Castle. The shape of the shoreline was very different then than today.[14] The boats could have come ashore closer then to the stone stronghold, which was still fairly substantial, and required little improvement to make it safe for them to shelter in.[15] Once the arriving fleet had brought their ships to the shore to unload, they could make their camp, steal a cow from some poor hapless Englishman and have kebabs on the beach, as we see in Wilson's Bayeux Tapestry.[16] At some point, the Normans made for the market-town of Hastings and assembled their first castle on English soil, a portable building, on a promontory giving them strong visual access up and down the coast and out across the hills, inland. William would have known that Hastings was where the road to London began. The chronicles state that their first fortification was in Pevensey and second at Hastings.[17] The town's garrison was undoubtedly overwhelmed quickly. Its inhabitants either submitted, escaped, or were executed if they resisted.

Guy describes in the *Carmen*, that William's men go out to devastate and burn the surrounding lands, a punishment, we are told, the 'stupid people deserve' because they rejected William as their king. An Englishman hiding under a rock, watched the horror unfold: the slaughter of the 'perfidious' people, forced out of their homes whilst their children looked on, shedding tears.[18] The Englishman jumped on his horse and hastened to meet with the king returning from his victory at Stamford with great booty. He caught his breath and informed the king that the intruders were driving the people from their homes with fire and had 'taken captive boys and girls, even widows, and all the cattle. Upon hearing this, Harold, apparently, hissed in anger.[19]

Preface to Battle

Both Freeman and Stenton favour John of Worcester's assertion that on 1 October, the king was still in York when he received word that William had landed.[20] Orderic has him in London. According to Paul Hill, a march of 190 miles at a standard of 20 miles per day would have brought him to London by 10 October.[21] However, Freeman has him in York on the 1 October, and in London on the 5 October, which would have him travelling at a faster rate than 20 miles a day, more like 50, which seems feasible on horseback if they were to exchange horses halfway.[22]

Orderic gives us what Barlow calls a 'fictitious' account about occurrences in London. As more reports about the damage being done in Sussex were received, Harold became increasingly agitated. His mother, Gytha and brother Gyrth begged him to rest after his recent travails of marching north and back and fighting a battle in which his brother was killed. Orderic refers to him as the 'English tyrant', and in the same paragraph also calls him brave, strong, handsome, pleasant in speech, and decent to his friends.[23] William had brought over a mighty army in more ships than Hardrada had brought, and already he had erected two fortifications on the coast in Harold's hereditary lands. There was cavalry, infantry, bowmen, slingers, and engineers. One can imagine Harold pacing, hardly able to sit still. Who would not be agitated when your kingdom was being invaded by a determined pretender intent on seizing what was not his to seize? They were ravaging his lands and his people. In one story, Harold heard that his own manor of Crowhurst, close to where the Normans had landed, was being burned, and his faithful reeve had been hung from the gable of his longhall.[24] It was personal, designed to enrage and provoke.

According to Orderic Harold's brother, Gyrth, offered to lead the fyrd into battle in his stead, so Harold could not perjure himself. The king was furious at the suggestion, and when his mother clung to him, desperate to keep him from leaving, he was said to have kicked her away giving us an idea of his distraught state of mind.

We do not know where Orderic got this anecdote from, it is not repeated anywhere else. Orderic was able to draw on previous writings by English chroniclers.[25] Was it another tale to tarnish Harold's reputation further, that he was not only a murderer, a robber, a tyrant, but also a man who would kick his mother? On the face of it, that Harold was enraged and lashing out at those he loved, could be seen as a mark of his passion for his countrymen. Everything that he had done so far was testimony that he took his duties as king seriously. He was angry with himself for having let down those he was sworn to protect. And he had failed one of the rudimental duties of a king and allowed invaders to breach his shores. The Bayeux Tapestry shows us the scenes. We see livestock commandeered by the enemy; a wealthy woman, escaping from a burning house fleeing with her infant. This scene is thought to have been a representation of Harold's Eadgifu and their youngest child, Ulf. The manor set on fire could be Crowhurst, not far from the battleground, within William's reach.[26] Some historians see this as an explanation as to how Ulf was taken as hostage and why Eadgifu was there on the battlefield searching for her husband's corpse.[27] Were they both in William's custody before the battle? It is not mentioned anywhere in the sources. The Bayeux Tapestry is the only evidence we have, and it is sketchy and ambiguous at best. Would Harold had left his wife and child near the Sussex coast at this time? If they were in William's custody, it would explain why Harold wanted to get to William as quickly as possible. The later tradition of Waltham contradicts this theory and has it that Eadgifu was brought from Waltham to identify Harold's body, so there would need to be an intensive exploration of the theory.

William's plan to provoke Harold into leaving London before he had gathered all his army, appears to have had the desired effect. If he could lure the English out prematurely, William would reduce Harold's advantage, or at least even out the sides. Apart from Crowhurst in East Sussex, much of Harold's personal lands were to the west, but the lands ravaged by William, had been part of his inherited earldom for years.

The days between Stamford and Hastings are difficult to follow, as the English sources are quiet on what happened, but we can piece together the timeline by looking at the circumstances. It seems reasonable to believe that Harold was still in York when William landed in Pevensey. After recovering from battle, he would need to appraise the situation in the north and organise what was left of the northern militia. He acted quickly, preparing his surviving troops to march south and summonsing any local units fit and willing to accompany them. Edwin and Morcar's forces were in disarray, their losses at Fulford heavy. Waltheof's may have been in the same condition. Harold left Marleswein, previously appointed as sheriff of Lincolnshire, as *dux* in the north to support the young earls as they recovered. Harold would expect the northerners to meet up with the main army in London when they could and if Edgar was with Harold, he may have left him with Edwin and Morcar for safe keeping should he somehow fall into William's clutches.[28] The young ætheling was certainly with the brothers in London after Hastings, when they and the archbishops pledged their allegiance to him.[29]

As Harold had done on the journey north from London, Harold sent riders out to all the shires, calling out the thegns and their men, the five-hide men who owed military service. These were not peasants with pitch-forks but professional and semi-professional warriors.[30] But despite the speed with which Harold administered the call-to-arms to the shires, and the swiftness with which he travelled, there was no time for the men of the furthest shires to have received them and reach him in time to travel to Sussex with him. [31] No prior precedent had ever been set for the mobilisation of a national army in the defence of a realm and, as Stenton points out, by the time Harold arrived in London, he had no more than half the army he could expect to call up, including his own huscarls, plus the royal household guard that he had inherited through his kingship, and the huscarls of his brothers, Gyrth and Leofwin.

Before arriving in London, local tradition would have us believe that Harold stopped at Waltham where he prayed in the Church of the Holy Cross and rested for a while. It was there, nearby in Nazeing, that Eadgifu lived and where they may have spent their last night together. When he arrived in London, waiting for the rest of his *fyrd*, he called a council of war. Harold knew that many of his powerful men in England had just been killed in two battles, and only half his army was assembled, but he was keen to meet William as soon as possible.[32] Harold addressed his captains and comrades, disclosing to them the terrible ravaging, the impoverishment of his people, and despoilment of their kingdom occurring in Sussex.[33] Having heard enough, a great roar spilled from them that they would rather fight than put their necks under the yoke of another king. Harold, warmed by the response, first suggests they use diplomacy to avoid bloodshed and send envoys to the enemy, to request that they return home.[34] One has to wonder why the English were so eager to fight for Harold if he was such a despot.

On the 12 October, a specially chosen monk was sent to confer on Harold's behalf with the duke. He rode with alacrity all the way to Hastings with the king's letter hidden beneath a black cloak.[35] The message he was charged with advised William to desist in ruining the kingdom and to release the prisoners and anything else he had taken by force. Among other things, the missive also warned William that if he refused to leave or delayed making restitution, Harold would declare war on him and disclosed that he had the preposterous amount of 120,0000 men thirsting for battle.[36] The true number available to Harold was likely to have been around 14,000, based on a figure of 70,000 hides, and accounting for the roughly one man per five hides that the king was permitted to call upon in times of need.[37] Added to this were the royal huscarls and the huscarls of his earls, so likely another 1,500 or so more.

William was not deterred by the threat and he sent back Harold's monk accompanied by a monk of his own and an admonishment for the king, essentially telling him he was not going anywhere. Harold, William proclaimed, had wrongfully violated the oath to uphold his claim to the throne, for which the duke insisted he was entitled to by the 'death of his forbears'. England was his, and he meant to take it. He reminded Harold that he had sworn to be his vassal, and that if he would admit his crime, he would promptly forgive his faults and grant him the lands that had once belonged to his father.[38] Obviously Harold was not impressed about being granted lands that had been his for more than a decade. Guy's continuous claims that William was entitled to the English throne by hereditary right is a theme throughout the *Carmen*. Guy does not appear to have been privy to the background of William's flimsy relationship with Edward, and William's lack of any English link to the crown. Perhaps his concern was not for the English audience who might read his account, but rather for those on the Continent who dared to scorn his master's actions in invading another king's realm.

Poitiers' sympathy for Tostig left him disappointed that it was not Harold who had died at the Battle of Stamford, even though he had rid William of two determined rivals. Tostig was not the only family member that was Harold's enemy, as Poitiers asserts, his sister Queen Edith, 'so unlike him in morals, had been unable to bear weapons against him, fought him with prayers and counsel, for he was a man soiled with lascivious behaviour, a cruel murderer, an avaricious plunderer, and an enemy of the good and just.'.[39] Poitiers purports the falsehood that Edith so wanted William to rule the kingdom, that her husband, King Edward, had adopted him as his son.[40]

Even the half-Norman, half Breton, Robert FitzWymarc, related to both Edward and William, could not deter William from his mission. The king's standard-bearer sent a messenger to warn William that Harold had just defeated the great army of Norwegians, and that William had neither the strength nor the man-power to beat him. He suggested he not emerge from his fortifications for now, nor offer battle, for Harold was on his way with a large, powerful army which would make his own seem like wretched dogs.[41] To this warning William replied that he would not hide in a ditch, but would fight Harold as soon as possible, adding that even if he had only 10,000 men and not the (clearly hyperbole) 60,000 that he had brought with him, he would be just as confident of his victory.[42]

A few days later, according to Poitiers, William met the monk who had been sent to convey a message from Harold. The rhetoric that Poitiers puts into the mouth of William in reply to the message is an embellishment of Guy's earlier version. Poitiers, writing some years after Guy, has William announce that it was neither unjustly nor rashly that he had entered these lands that King Edward, as Harold had advised him, wanted him to rule, on account of the great honours and numerous benefits that I and my forebears had conferred on him and his brother. This had been sworn to him by the important nobles of the land. Not only that, it was he whom Edward trusted most in all of his bloodline to help him while he lived and govern his kingdom when he passed.' The next day he sent his own envoy to Harold, offering to settle the dispute by lawful due process, or by judicial combat between them. Harold refused, stating that he was on his way to win victory against him.[43]

Neither the *Carmen,* nor the work of William of Jumièges mention the pledge that was supposedly made by Stigand, Godwin, Leofric, and Siward. Nor is it documented in the English chronicles. Poitiers, however, to bolster William's claim has him declare that all of the aforementioned men had given their assurance that they would uphold his right to England after the death of Edward with a handfast oath, and even gave him the son and grandson of Godwin as hostages of good will. Finally, to seal the pact, Edward sent Harold to Normandy to confirm what all these important English men had 'sworn to him in his absence'. As we have already discussed we see that Poitiers elaborates on earlier rhetoric and uses fiction to persuade the reader that his version of the conquest is a truthful and honest account. Poitiers knew that in order to quieten those who were of the opinion that William's invasion and slaughter of England's king was unjust, he would need to fictionalise the truth.

The Danes for one, whose king, Swein, was Harold's cousin and had been brought up with him. After the Conquest, he supported the English rebels who fought against William and even invaded himself at one point, though the mission was unsuccessful. His sons also invade in 1075 and plan another coup in 1085 with the Flemish Count Robert, though it never materialised.[44] But later, if Adam of Bremen is anything to go by, Swein's intentions were more of a selfish nature, looking for booty or land, rather than for revenge for his cousin. However, another source written by an English monk living in Odense called Ælnoth, writing his biography of King Cnut IV of Denmark, makes this statement: 'the English, whose dukes, counts, lords, noblemen and other people of high rank had either been killed, or imprisoned, or deprived of their father's honours, wealth, dignity or inheritance or expelled abroad, or left behind and forced into public slavery, were not able to bear the tyranny of the Romans and the French and declined to seek foreign help.'[45] Van Houts wrote in her conclusion that William's contemporaries expressed at least as much condemnation of his actions in England as they expressed admiration for the military victory and reform of the English church.[46] News of the Norman victory led to widespread Continental consideration for their own affairs. The German chroniclers were in fear of Norman aggression. Flemish monks condemned it, even though many of their countrymen had fought for William. And Pope Gregory, in a letter to William, wrote of the harassment he experienced supporting his cause when he was a cardinal under Alexander's rule, suggesting that there was opposition to the invasion even in the papal court.[47]

Poitiers had to convince these doubters of the veracity of every word he wrote, and is fully aware that he employed both lies or a twisted version of the truth. To further ensure that his statements are believed, in chapter four of his *Gesta*, Poitiers opening statement reveals his intention to show how the crimes of Godwin and Harold, led to William's vengeance and victory at Hastings.[48] Manufacturing a new reputation that he had never had before, Harold, is presented as the spawn of evil, making William look like a saint, virtuously fighting for what was rightfully his, and won by the Grace of God.

CHAPTER TWENTY-FOUR

Battle for England

Guy d'Amiens, author of the *Carmen,* does not name the site of the battle, but various sources report that it took place 8 or 9 miles from Hastings.

There were two hills, a mile and a half apart that bookended the valley.[1] The marshy slope that trailed into the saddle of land from the ridge Harold had chosen to station his men on, was supposedly called *Senlac.* It was believed to be derived from the Anglo-Saxon name, *Sandlacu,* meaning a sandy stream in modern English.[2] The hills were named as Telham and Caldbec.[3] The land was marshy, and the origin of the name *Senlac* is shrouded in mystery. Tradition has it that the original meaning was later changed to *Sanguelac,* translated from the French to mean 'bloody lake'. Senlac was said to only come into use when Orderic Vitalis started writing in 1140.[4] Before that, chroniclers seem to have called it plain old Battle Hill. Barlow suggests that the area was uncultivated and therefore unnamed.[5]

Harold left London for Sussex on 11 October. He met the muster at the Hoary Apple Tree situated on Caldbec Hill the day before battle, approaching via the road from Rochester with the men from the west joining them from a prehistoric pathway that linked London to Lewes road.[6] William's scouts spotted Harold's army approaching. *Carmen* states that Harold wanted to attack the Norman camp at night. William sent this message to Harold boldly stating, via an envoy, 'Fitting greetings, O king from the duke, whom you force unjustly to do wrong. And this is so, because, as very many bear witness…that King Edward with the consent of his people and the advice of his nobles, promised and decreed that William should be his heir; and you supported him. The ring and sword granted him, and, as you know, sent to him through you, stand witness to this…Observe your oaths if you want to be saved.' Harold retorted, 'Get you behind me, you fool! Tomorrow it will be seen by the judgement of the Lord of the kingdom which party has right on his side, for the sacred hand of the Lord will make a just award.'[7] Poitiers, following the Carmen, also reports on Harold's plan for a night attack and a naval blockade which seems unlikely due to the time Harold had to organise the ships.[8]

Some of William's troops were out foraging and needed to be brought back as he summonsed them to arm. Whilst this was going on, William attended mass with his closest followers, and took the Eucharist in the village church where he had created his headquarters.[9] The holy relics that Harold had sworn his oath on were blessed before hanging them around his neck.[10] Then he and his companions pray for victory. The duke, now confident, is ready for war. Not even putting his hauberk on the wrong way around, a sign of bad luck, could diminish his poise and assurance. He simply laughed and turned it around.[11]

William set out from his camp inside Hastings at daybreak, Saturday 14 October.[12] His position was dangerous. He desperately needed to engage the English before the rest of Harold's army arrived. His plan, clear by his actions, was to draw him away from his base in London without his army's full compliment. William's strategy for England was not explained by any contemporary source, but it was obvious his conquest would require Harold's death, whether on the battlefield, or in captivity.[13]

A night attack such as the one suggested by Guy seems unlikely. When Harold reached the mustering point on Friday 13 October, he and his men would have been exhausted. Not only that, marshalling a large army in the dark would have had its difficulties, and probably nigh on impossible.

The Armies' Positions

Harold's decision to station his troops on the high ground of the ridge that summitted the valley said to be *Senlac*, meant that the steep gradient would reduce the impact of the charge on his troops. Harold knew the area well, for it was a local meeting point for the neighbouring levies who met annually to train, hone their skills or muster for war. He would have known the advantages of the terrain. The ground was around 235 feet higher than the bottom of the slope and behind the ridge on Caldbec was open heathland with the woods situated at the edge of the hill. A good escape route if it were needed. Historian, David Howarth, compares Harold's choice of position to Wellington's at Waterloo where the ground was very similar.[14] The ridge itself intercepted the road out of Hastings on Battle Hill. It was a strategic point, and Harold's aim was to stop the enemy from getting to London. As William and his troops came over Telham Hill, they seem to have been taken by surprise. The forest was glittering with spears as the English advanced out of the woods in mass formation.[15] Harold marshalled his best troops, huscarls and the more experienced warriors in the front lines along on the ridge, reinforcing the flanks behind them with the lesser thegns and five-hide men. He established his standards, the royal Dragon of Wessex and his personal banner, the Fighting Man, on the highest point. When this was done, he called for all the other flags to be joined with his.[16]

According to Wace, the English chanted, '*Oli Crosse!*' (Holy Cross!) and '*Godemite!*' (God Almighty) and '*Ut, ut!*' (Out, out), beating their shields and making as much noise to frighten the enemy host.[17] The war cry of the Normans, was '*Dex Aei!*' (God give us strength!)[18] The noise must have been incredible. Peter Merren suggests the English stood in ranks, with the elite well-armed, thegns and huscarls, standing in the front lines. The men of Middlesex served under the staller, Esegar; the men of Berkshire and Huntingdonshire, under their lord, thegn Ælfric. If the king's brothers were there, so would be the men of East Anglia, Cambridge, Essex, Kent, as well as Sussex and no doubt Hampshire, with Ælfwig, abbot of Winchester and Leofric, abbot of Peterborough, who died later of his wounds.[19] Wace also mentions men from up and down the country, including the West Country, Somerset, and Devonshire and even 'Eoforwic' (York) is mentioned, with the men of London being the first to turn up. But evidently none were able to come from beyond the Humber, for they were too weakened by 'Tostig and his Danes'.[20] Harold's own personal bodyguard, men who had known and fought with him since he first held office, surrounded the ground where his standard stood. The royal standard of Wessex. Harold's valiant huscarls were to die defending it and their king to the death. There are many versions of how he perished, but most agree that it happened toward the end of daylight, on the battlefield. Jumièges is the only source to mention Harold died in the first assault of the battle. However, the scribe contradicts himself by stating that the English took flight at dusk after hearing of his death.[21] It was unlikely that had Harold died so early on, and the English did not hear of it until sunset.

The shieldwall is often referred to in the *Carmen* as a 'dense wood'. According to the author, 'the English spurn the solace of horses, trusting in their strength as they stand fast on foot, counting it the highest honour to die in arms that their native soil may not pass under another yoke, leaving their horses in the care of ceorls, the lesser men of societal rank, to be looked after'.[22] The monk who had intercepted Harold on his supposed night attack had returned to William to reassure him that he had nothing to worry about, for he had seen the English combing their long hair and were nothing but reluctant girls, scared at the sound of thunder.[23] But their long hair was now tucked away inside their mail headgear and helm, and it was unlikely anyone could tell the elite French from the elite English, despite what Wace had said about peasants fighting with pitchforks and hatchets. Swinging their fierce axes above their heads, the English warriors would certainly not appear like reticent females.

If Harold had reconnoitred the ground the night before battle, it would have been a very different landscape he beheld from what we see today. The undulating hill tops and ridges, filled with streams feeding into the River Brede, created deep ravines called gills. The slope of the battlefield, called a saddle, is less severe today compared to what it would have been in 1066. The hill behind Telham, Blackhorse Hill, was 460 feet at its highest point and descended to 218 feet at the foot of Telham. It then ascended to 275 feet which was where Harold stationed his army.[24] Both edges of the ridge, almost 2000 feet across the concave-shaped slope, were incredibly steep. Harold knew that the sheer gradients of the slopes that edged the ridge would protect his English shieldwall on both sides, as long as it held the ridge. The enemy would have a lot of difficulty getting up the verges, especially the cavalry, and there was no option except to make frontal attacks on the English lines.[25]

The Battle Begins

The composition of William's army as described by Guy, was formed into three divisions.[26] The French were stationed on the left, the Normans led by William in the middle, and the Bretons on the right flank. Each division was made up of archers, infantry, and cavalry to the rear. Most historians agree that the battle was fought on 14 October 1066, and started at the third hour of the day, 9 am, and continued until nightfall. Barlow states that Harold's army took the Normans by surprise.[27] Guy reports that the horns sounded and the battle started before William had time to organise his cavalry. We are told that he had to send in his infantry without cavalry cover, though this seems unlikely as the English troops on the ridge were stationary, expecting the enemy to come to them. The start of the battle was up to William. He could have sent in his troops at any time when he was ready.

The duke's strategy was to send his troops up the slope and to break through the solid wall of shields. Guy tells us that the limewood boards of the English phalanx were easily penetrable and describes a clash at close quarters. 'Helmeted soldiers rush to crash shields against shields. Both sides brandishing their spears at each other. The English, apparently, fought fiercely, unafraid of the enemy.[28]

At this juncture in the *Carmen*, Guy decides to throw a little entertainment in for the reader with the daring of Taillefer, the juggler knight. Flinging his sword up high in the air and catching it as it falls, he shouted encouragement to his comrades. An enraged English warrior attacks him and brave Taillefer turned on the Englishman and lopped off his head, raising the grisly prize to show his companions that he had the first kill.[29]

The narrative switches to the Norman archers, 'transfixing' the enemy with their darts. Crossbowmen, 'strike and destroy shields'. The left and right flanks attacked both wings of the shieldwall, and William, riding at the centre, harasses the English vanguard. 'The serried mass of the English stand rooted to the ground, meeting javelin with javelin, sword with sword'. The dying, unable to fall, being so tightly packed, were held up in death by their shoulder companions: 'the dead do not make space for the living, for every corpse, although lifeless, stands as though unharmed and keeps his place'.[30]

Carmen, is vague in its chronology of battle, and it was as though different scenes, though described separately, occurred simultaneously. It appeared that the first feigned retreat came after that first clash, with Guy describing the flight of the French, fleeing as though vigorously repelled. According to Barlow, the French were surprised by the vehemence of the so-called reluctant English warriors and retreated in fear as the fierce axe warriors brandished their deadly blades.[31] In that moment, William saw how this could be used to his advantage. The feigned retreat is a well-known tactic that had been used throughout history in order to draw the enemy into a place of danger where they could be routed. It is possible Harold would have known of this strategy and knew that his troops must hold the lines if they were to be victorious. He would need to ensure that all his commanders knew that they were clear in their orders.

Sadly, Harold was let down by those less disciplined among the flanks. During one of the feigned retreats the English believed they had broken the enemy, and rushed after the fleeing infantry and cavalry. According to Guy, with the breach in the English lines, the dead were released, opening the wall up to the enemy. William's Bretons cleared the battlefield of its foe, as they ran from their lines to attack the 'fleeing' enemy. On the English right flank, large gaps formed in the wall as the undisciplined leave their ranks to be slaughtered by the French. The remaining English pack themselves in tighter than before and bravely fight on. The English, we are told, are superior in numbers, and their losses not yet significant. Beating back the foe, the English are ferocious in their rejoinder, and 'force them to flee'.[32]

Seeing his people beaten and retreating, William rebuked and struck them. Holding them back with his lance, he removed his helmet, shouted insults at them, warning them of the peril of trying to escape. His brother, Bishop Odo of Bayeux, exhorts them to stay with their commander, as we see in panel sixty-eight on the Bayeux Tapestry. The young men of the fleeing army, having been harangued so, are ashamed and turned back to re-enter the fray. Poitiers tells us that they believe that their duke had been killed.[33] Their valour returned, they attack the enemy unmercifully, the duke delivering the first blow. Drawing his sword, he sliced helmets and shields. Even his horse is a hero, leaving corpses in its wake.[34] And the English, we are told, quiver at the sight of the duke.

It is here that Gyrth and Leofwin were said to have been slaughtered, though the latter brother is not mentioned in the *Carmen*. The Bayeux Tapestry shows the brothers' death on panels 67 and 68 and name them both. We are told by Guy, that Gyrth, not frightened by the 'lion's face', brandished his spear. From afar, he hurled it, with his 'quick strong arm, wounding the duke's mount, and forcing him to fight on foot'. William rushed at Gyrth, tears him 'limb from limb', exclaiming, 'Take this trophy you have won from us. Since my steed has perished, as a footman I give you this trophy back'.[35]

Guy applauded the duke's battle prowess. He beheads, dismembers, and devours with Herculean strength; his sword, smothered with brains and blood, despatched many souls to hell.[36] We learn from the author that William was unseated several times from his horse. The first by Gyrth and the second by an Englishman known as the son of Helloc who received the same treatment for his crime as Gyrth did.[37] On the Bayeux Tapestry in panels 67 and 68, it is Gyrth and Leofwin who are shown being killed, but it is impossible to reconcile the 'son of Helloc' with Harold's younger brother Leofwin.

Count Eustace, 'the scion of a noble dynasty' who had caused all the trouble with Harold's father in 1051, dismounted and turned over his horse to William, taking the horse of one of his knights for himself. The count and duke form a tag team and clear the field of English troops. A good number hesitate to fight them, desert, or are destroyed. Thus, we learn that the English shieldwall begins to reduce. The French start plundering the corpses before the battle is even won. This is shown in the borders of the Bayeux Tapestry. The duke, determined to kill Harold, scanned the battleground for him. He spotted him on top of the ridge, fighting ferociously for his life, boldly cutting down those attacking him. The duke gathered his best knights together, Eustace, Hugh, and a knight called Gilfard. They charge to Harold's position, cutting a swathe across the field spurring up to the ridge. There was the king, the object of William's ire, surrounded by his huscarls valiantly protecting him. Anyone in the way of the French soldiers' way was slaughtered until they reached their prey.

Guy solemnly tells us:

> The first of the four pierced his (Harold) shield and chest with his lance, drenching the ground with his gushing stream of blood; the second cut off his head with his sword, below the protection of his helm; the third pierced the innards of his belly with his lance; and the fourth cut off his thigh and carried it some distance away. The earth held the body that they had in this way destroyed.[38]

Thus, Harold was slain. When the English hear, those still fighting lost heart. Defeated, they begged for quarter. Those who could, tried to escape into the woods. Harold's royal bodyguard fell with him around his standard.[39] Daylight was fading. God had granted William the victory and the field.

The Malfosse

Evening had fallen. The English, having lost their king and many other great men, were not able hold out. Exhausted, they knew there was no one coming to their aid.

The Normans were invigorated by the death of the usurper and collapse of the English lines. The duke's fury was implacable. He spared no one who came before him. The defeated warriors fled swiftly, jumping on horseback, some by foot. Some travelled via roads, some over open country. Eventually they collapsed in their own blood. Those disabled by battle attempted to drag themselves to safety, crawling and leaving tell-tale tracks of themselves with their blood and gore. Others made it into the forest only to die, their corpses blocking the routes in for those who come after. The Normans carried out their pursuit, slaughtering their prey. Eagerly they cut them down, slashed at their 'guilty backs', putting the last touches to the victory.[40]

According to Poitiers, during the chase, the Normans encountered a number of Englishmen making a last stand by an old rampart or entrenchment, protected by ditches. A few of the less wounded may have been suddenly energised by its discovery. They may also have been late arriving, possibly Edwin and Morcar's troops. William called out for Eustace who was retreating and ordered him not to withdraw. Eustace argued for a retreat and no sooner had he uttered these cowardly words, he was struck between the shoulders an almighty blow that caused blood to stream from his nose and mouth. He was carried away badly wounded. The duke charged at the men, and many fell on such unfavourable ground. Of course, the duke was unscathed.[41]

Orderic, who also followed Jumièges in claiming Harold was slain in the first assault, was the first to mention the ditch of doom, which the *Battle Abbey Chronicle*, c. 1180, referred to as the *Malfosse*.[42] 'When thus the Normans saw the English fleeing, they pursued them obstinately through the night till Sunday, to their own harm. For high grass concealed an ancient rampart and as the Normans, fully armed on their horses rode up against it, they fell, one on top of another, thus crushing each other to death' and causing an apocryphal amount of 15000 men to die.[43] Some believe that the *Malfosse* is represented in panel 66 of the Bayeux Tapestry, where you can see the horses tumbling into one another.

The *AC* describes the incident more succinctly: with Harold and his men laid low, those around them began to flee and it is here that 'where the fighting was going on, lamentably stretching for some considerable distance, yawned an immense great ditch'. The monk described the ditch as a cleft in the land, hollowed out by storms and overgrown within by brambles and thistles, so it covered the ditch and could not be seen until it was too late. As the French on horse came upon it unknown, the impetus of their charge flung them headlong into the gully where they were pounded to death. The scribe mentions that in his day, they called this the *Malfosse*.[44]

In the aftermath of the battle, the duke took rest on the battlefield whilst the dead lay about him. Hugh of Ponthieu led the evening pursuit, hunting and killing fugitives into the night. *Carmen* makes no mention of the *Malfosse* or Eustace getting carried off wounded. When the dawn arrived, the duke buried his brave dead in a mass grave. The English were left to be eaten by carrion.[45] Harold's 'mangled' body was wrapped in purple linen and taken to William's camp at Hastings to bury. Gytha, Harold's mother, requested that he release her son's body and offered his weight in gold. William was enraged at this insult, and refused, ordering his dead opponent be buried on the summit of a cliff, so he might guard the shore in death, as he had in life.

CHAPTER TWENTY-FIVE

The Killing of Harold, and his Last Resting Place

> He was the 'darling of the clergy, the strength of his soldiers, the shield of the defenceless'
>
> *Waltham Chronicle*

The only thing we can say with certainty about the death of Harold was that he was slaughtered on the battlefield during the violent melee around the king's standard. But in what manner was he killed? The earliest detailed evidence comes from Guy's poem. *Carmen* tells us he was hunted by a Franco-Norman hit squad. Immobilised, cut down, he was eviscerated, decapitated, and castrated.[1] Poitiers reveals nothing about Harold's death itself, preferring to laud William's valour and deeds during the battle and his pursuit of the fugitives. When he returned to the battlefield, Harold's body was found with his brothers'. Jumièges is confused, and contradictory and later traditions speak of death by arrow. The Bayeux Tapestry shows a man under the text, 'HAROLD' with a feathered bolt in his hand possibly pulling it out of his eye. The fact he is directly under his name suggests that he was undeniably the king. But next to him, under the text, 'is killed', is another, smaller man, mown down by a horseman whose sword wounds the man's leg.[2] These two images have caused mystification amongst historians as both images appear to represent the death of Harold.

Beside the arrow in his eye, the first Harold also holds a javelin in his other hand, hidden behind his shield. Perhaps the arrow was added later, to fit with the claims of chroniclers, such as Malmesbury, who was the first to mention the arrow, aside from one other Italian chronicler in 1080 which turned out to be a later insertion in the fourteenth century.[3] Malmesbury declared Harold was pierced in the brain by an arrow, and then hacked in the leg, just as the tapestry portrays.[4] Henry of Huntingdon has an arrow hit him in the eye, reporting that the duke ordered his archers to shoot high, so that when the arrows fell, they would drop from above, smiting the enemy.[5] Baudri, abbot of Bourgueil, writes similarly that Harold was hit by an arrow with 'deadly doom'.[6] It is possible that the two men on the Bayeux Tapestry are representing the same Harold, and the reader is supposed to view them as two separate scenes. The second Harold, cut down by the horseman, is shown losing his axe and has no shield, which is plausible if he had been wielding the two-handed axe. The two men's facial features are almost identical; however, their legs are not! One explanation for the puzzlement could be that at the time of the Bayeux

Tapestry's creation, Harold's manner of death was commonly known and there was no need to be so specific. Yet, which was the real Harold? And just what was the intention of the Bayeux Tapestry's artist?

Andrew Bridgeford, who wrote the *1066 : The Hidden History of the Bayeux Tapestry*, draws attention to the fact that this part of the embroidery was heavily restored in the nineteenth century.[7] The author asks, 'Did the restorers faithfully follow the evidence of the original stitch holes or did they do a bit of embroidering of their own?'. In 1729, Antoine Benoit's drawing of this scene, said to have been the earliest rendition, the figure underneath 'HAROLD' was not pulling out an arrow, but holding on to a spear or javelin shaft which oddly bears no tip. This throws some light onto the arrow story which is not mentioned until Malmesbury. Thus, the idea that the figure was originally throwing a javelin and not pulling an arrow out of his face seems plausible, backed up by no mention of an arrow wound in Guy's Carmen. And though Guy was not an eyewitness, he would have had access to plenty who had been there, one of which was a kinsman of his.[8]

A summary of the contemporary sources in rough chronological order, starts with the *Anglo-Saxon Chronicle*, which tells us simply that 'the king fought very hard against him with those men who wanted to support him, and there was great slaughter on both sides.[9] There was killed Earl Harold and his brothers, Earls Gyrth and Leofwin, and many good men fell during the battle'.[10] Written in 1067, the Carmen impresses upon the reader that Harold's killing was a *fait accompli*. It would have been far too dangerous for him to be kept alive, even in captivity, for he would have been the focus of future rebellions. None-the-less, William was to be plagued by constant uprisings in the first five years of his reign. The last thing he would have wanted was Harold alive.[11]

William de Jumièges, writing shortly after *Carmen*, claims Harold was killed in the first assault, pierced by many wounds. Hardly likely. Harold would not have been accessible so early on, barricaded behind his human palisade. William of Poitiers avoids implicating his master in Harold's ignominious slaying by not mentioning it at all. To do so would have diminished Poitiers efforts to make William seem like a saint and Harold a tyrant. And finally, in the Bayeux Tapestry, created between 1070 and 1080, Harold looks to have been laid low by an arrow, before being hacked to the ground with a sword.

The *Carmen* was first spoken of in the record by Orderic's mention of an untitled poem about the Battle of Senlac, which was written by Guy, Bishop of Amiens.[12] The unnamed poem appeared lost until its discovery in 1826, in the Royal Library in Brussels by the Hanoverian historian, Georg Heinrich Pertz. Almost immediately Pertz identified it as the long-lost poem mentioned by Orderic Vitalis in his *Historia*.[13] Unlike Poitiers work, whose attitude was Norman, Guy's viewpoint is very different. The bishop was French, from the aristocracy of Ponthieu. Hugh of Ponthieu, a member of the hit squad that cut down Harold, was his nephew. The men who he names in the poem as heroes are all French, apart from William of Normandy. Guy was often at the French court until his death in 1073, and noted to have been there twice in 1066, and in August of 1067.[14] It is possible that his nephew, Hugh of Ponthieu, had been his source for the events that took place on and off the battlefield. But other than to revere and commemorate his French compatriots as the stars of the Norman invasion against the perfidious English, it is difficult to pinpoint its actual purpose, though perhaps he wanted to ensure Norman gratitude for their noteworthy contribution to William's success.

Despite the *Carmen*'s bias toward Guy's countrymen, it seems that there can be little doubt that it is the closest we will ever come to learning how Harold died.

Search for Harold's Last Resting Place

The exploration for our king's last resting place has fascinated many people for centuries.

There are three main sites that still claim to be the burial site of Harold. They are the Holy Cross and St. Lawrence Church at Waltham Abbey, the Holy Trinity church at Bosham in West Sussex, and St. Michaels, Bishops Stortford in Hertfordshire. Guy d'Amiens in the *Carmen* purports his resting place was a cliff under a cairn in Hastings, marked with a mocking epithet.[15] Poitiers, though omitting the act of Harold's death from his work, names the relation of Harold who was entrusted with his corpse as the half-Norman, half-English, William Malet. Duke William, jesting that Harold was not worthy of a burial such as his mother, Gytha, desired for him, when so many of his compatriots lay unburied on the battleground, ordered Malet to bury Harold on the seashore. It was better that he be placed as guardian of the shore as he had done so in life in his madness and avarice.[16] Poitiers justifies the regicide of an anointed king, by savagely denouncing him and proposing Harold's death as proof he unlawfully seized the crown.[17] In order to depict the duke as a civilised and magnanimous Christian prince, Poitiers' William is merciful, unlike Guy's, and at least allowed the English to bury their dead.

But is it likely that William, a devout and pious man, would risk his reputation by denying the anointed Harold a Christian burial in a tomb made ready for his eventual death in the church he had prepared for himself? And what of the other candidates? Holy Trinity at Bosham and St. Michaels in Bishops Stortford?

Let us explore the possibilities.

Bosham: Church of the Holy Trinity

Although the importance of Bosham in Harold's life cannot be mistaken, it does not seem to have been brought under the radar of Harold's possible burial places until the 1950s. Harold's strong association with the church has long been embedded in the history of Bosham, as has the supposed burial of Cnut's 8-year-old daughter. Therefore, it is not surprising when they discovered the mysterious coffins, Harold and Cnut's daughter came to mind. The whereabouts of King Harold's remains seem to have been hidden from the general public by William, who did not want his grave to become a focus for martyrdom. Having him buried in Bosham underneath the chancel in the Holy Trinity would not necessarily have escaped the attention of the populace, given that the manor was the Godwinson's family home. Neither would burying him under a pile of stones with his name inscribed upon it stop it from becoming a national place of pilgrimage for a much-loved king. If it was the case that William wanted to avoid a focal point for potential insurgences, it did not prevent them from igniting all over the country in the first years after his victory at Hastings.

Though the mystery of Harold's burial place continues to confound us, it is the presence of a stone coffin that was first found in 1954 that brought the possibility of it being his to light. The church was already aware of a stone sarcophagus in 1865 containing the remains of a little girl thought to be Cnut's daughter. As prementioned in an earlier chapter, the 8-year-old child was thought to have slipped and drowned in the mill run in 1020. It still flows today past the church to the mill along the edge of the inlet at Bosham. But when they decided to do some work on the flooring in 1954, 'To the great astonishment' of the excavators, close to the little girl's coffin they found a second, beautifully carved Saxon coffin, previously undiscovered. This contained the remains of a 'stockily built man' with evidence of an arthritic hip joint. Much speculation ensued as to who this was and the suggestion that it was Godwin the great Earl of Wessex himself was dismissed, for the Anglo-Saxon Chronicle clearly states that Godwin died and was buried at Winchester in 1053.[18] According to Geoffrey W. Marwood, this superbly carved coffin was made of Horsham stone, containing the thigh and pelvic bones of a powerfully built man of about 5ft 6ins in height, aged over 60 years and with traces of arthritis. Whoever was buried here must have been a person of great importance to have been placed in such a prominent position in the church next to a king's daughter, as only nobles were buried inside the church. It is also probable that the coffin was opened at a much earlier date and the contents vandalised, as there was no trace of a skull and the remaining bones showed signs of fractures which would not have occurred with natural decomposition.[19]

Harold's body has not been sighted in hundreds of years. Traditionalists believe that he is interred at Waltham Abbey in Essex, and with good reason. But amateur historian John Pollock believes a forgotten body underneath a parish church in West Sussex holds the secret of where Harold's body lies. Following his research, a parochial church council in 2003 applied for human remains buried below the chancel arch at the Holy Trinity church in Bosham, to be unearthed.[20] Mr Pollock, who lived in the village, said: 'I am absolutely convinced that it is Harold in there.' The church already claims to be the resting place of King Cnut's daughter and the village is awash with seafaring tales and medieval myths ranging from a spooky bell heard at sea to hidden tunnels under the streets.[21] Pollock felt at the time, that he would be able to use more advanced scientific technology to examine the surroundings of the sarcophagus to ascertain if the stone dates back to the eleventh century.

One of the factors that Mr Pollock and his supporters were hoping would help them win the application from the Chichester Diocese, was the historical value of Bosham and its church. There has been a religious centre for hundreds of years prior to 1066, it is the oldest Christian site in Sussex. Bosham Church itself dates back to Saxon times and the lower stages of the tower and the first third of the chancel have survived from this period. The chancel arch was built in the eleventh century shortly after the Norman Conquest of 1066.[22] The church and the manor house of Bosham, which was situated next door to the church, appears on panels three and four of the Bayeux Tapestry. To add to the enigma of Bosham's history, the most significant events occurred in the eleventh century, starting with King Cnut and the death of his daughter in 1020, and the legend of him sitting before the sea, commanding it not to touch his feet.[23] It was in Bosham that King Harold's father, Earl Godwin, made his home with Gytha, where they brought up their six sons and three daughters. It was also the place where the brazen Swegn Godwinson lured his cousin Beorn to his death. And It was from Bosham that Harold left for Normandy on that fateful journey to meet Duke William, praying in the very church which stands there today for a safe journey, followed by a hearty feast in his manor house.[24] Why should he not be buried there?

The idea of Bosham being Harold's final resting place is not implausible in itself. But it would not have been likely that Gytha, who may have resided there pre-October 1066, would have been there long enough after Hastings to have overseen a burial there for her son, for William of Normandy was to inherit Harold's manor there and it is doubtful he would have allowed his enemy's mother to carry on residing there. The church estates had been awarded to the Norman churchman, Osbern FitzOsbern by Edward the Confessor, his kinsman. Osbern, was still in situ after the Norman Conquest. It is not beyond the realms of possibility that later in his reign, William thought to remove Harold's remains where he knew the loyalty of Osbern would secure the secret of the dead king's presence. However, the details of the bones in the coffin do not suggest he was a man in his forties, but one at least twenty years older. The arthritic hip does not correlate with a man as robust as Harold was, and he was described by many contemporary writers as very tall. A man of 5'6 would not have been considered tall even in the eleventh century.

Unfortunately, despite Mr Pollock's efforts, his hopes that a more accurate dating of the sarcophagus and bones could be attained, were dashed, for the church council declined the application which meant that we shall not ever know who this man is. One thing we can be sure of is that the mystery of this man's identity remains just that, a mystery.

St. Michaels, Bishop Stortford

This beautiful fifteenth-century church in the heart of the town, is positioned behind the high street on Windhill. For the last nine years, it has been the focal point for those who believe that Harold was buried in a sealed crypt in the church of St. Michaels. In 2014, an article appeared in the Daily Mail newspaper: 'Two amateur historians claim the remains of King Harold, who was shot through the eye at the Battle of Hastings in 1066, lie under an ancient parish church. Cousins Terry Muff and Kevin McKenzie, who claim to be distantly related to the last Saxon king, have spent years researching the mystery of his fate after his death. They are convinced his body was carried to Bishops Stortford, in Hertfordshire, by his grieving lover 'Edith the Fair' and buried at St. Michaels' Church. They say there are four surviving, intact Norman stone coffins that haven't been seen since the 19th century in a vault under the church. The pair are now calling on the vicar to open the vault and say they also expect to find the bones of his partner and his two brothers. Mr Muff, a retired police detective, said:

> King Harold II, his long-term wife and lover Edith the Fair and his two brothers, Leofwine and Gyrth, all, in fact, lie in a long-forgotten vault at St. Michael's Church. There are four surviving, intact Norman stone coffins which have not even been seen since the 19th century. It is our firm belief that, once an archaeological investigation is undertaken, at the very least, we will find King Harold's wife, Edith the Fair, who was venerated as a medieval saint, and very probably also King Harold and his two brothers.[25]

The two men, Kevin McKenzie and his cousin Terry Muff are part of a dedicated team of interested people who believe that the vaults beneath the church hold the secret of where Harold's remains are buried; not only Harold but also his wife who they refer to as Edith the Fair, and those of his brothers, Gyrth and Leofwine. The aim of the *Finding Harold Project* is to campaign for a limited, non-intrusive archaeological investigation of the vault which lies under the west end of the nave of St. Michael's Church. This would be unlikely to damage the structure of the vaults, nor would it disturb any of the contents of vaults themselves. The team are also interested in ensuring the maintenance and care of the structure so that it is properly preserved as part of English heritage, as stated on their social media page.[26] There has been a religious site where St. Michaels church now stands since at least the seventh century when Christianity was being established in England. St. Michael's Church as seen today, was largely built in the early fifteenth century in the style called Perpendicular. The oldest item in the church is the font which dates from the mid twelfth century. There does not appear to be any Saxon or early Norman work left to be seen. The church that exists currently appears to have been built on the site of the old Saxon church. In pre-conquest times it was customary for the church to be built in proximity to the manor estate. A few miles outside the manor was the forest of Hatfield which was owned by Harold. Like many men of his age, he was greatly interested in hunting and hawking. In the submission of their case made to the Consistory Court of St. Albans, McKenzie and Muff claimed that as the substantial estate in Hatfield Forest was owned by Harold, there can be no doubt that he would have resided at this estate often, being a keen huntsman.[27]

Harold's link to St. Michaels of Bishops Stortford was through his wife known as *Eddeva Pulchrima,* the Latin version for her Anglo-Saxon name which was Eadgifu the most beautiful. She was also known as *dives* meaning rich. As mentioned when discussing her in Chapter Seven, her name was often conflated with the name Eadgyth, Edith, or Edita. According to Domesday, she was the owner of the manor Stortford before the conquest. Stortford tradition has her selling the land to the Bishop of London in 1060, however, according to historian Ann Williams, this was likely to have been after the conquest as she is shown holding it in Domesday 'TRE'. St. Michael's tradition claims that 'Edith the Fair' secretly removed Harold's body from Waltham to Bishops Stortford for the purpose of burial in the old Saxon church that stood on Windhill, over which the new church is positioned. The tale tells us she then fled to Chester to live out her life in obscurity. In 1086, upon her death, permission was given for her to be buried alongside Harold in Bishops Stortford.[28] This legend, however, seems to have been conflated with Harold's second wife, Aldith, as the woman who fled to Chester. Throughout these legends, the real Eadgifu (Harold's first wife) was often referred to erroneously as Edith/Ealdgytha/Aldith. Nonetheless, she had no connection to Chester at all, unlike Aldith, the woman Harold married when he became king. Chester was an important strategic trading port in Mercia, and Aldith was Mercian. We know that she was taken there after the death of Harold by her brothers.[29]

It appears that there has been a tradition that Eadgifu was buried in St. Michael's, going back to Tudor times, confirmed by John Leland who was a sixteenth-century English poet and antiquarian, specialising in local history. His theory we will challenge shortly.[30] This local concept was reinforced in 1831 when men, working in the centre of the nave, unearthed a pudding stone coffin assumed to contain Eadgifu's remains. The tomb was re-sealed after the work was completed, remaining so until Reverend Francis Rhodes, father of Cecil Rhodes, arrived in 1850. St. Michael's new vicar gave permission to a parishioner to open a family vault beneath the nave and during the excavation, by chance revealed a further vault containing three other pudding stone coffins of early Anglo-Norman origin. Reverend Rhodes was obviously quite taken by the tradition of King Harold's coffin being secreted within the vaults of his church and allowed the opening of the largest of the coffins. Inside, the remains of a man of great stature was revealed, but Ailey, the author of this account, found it surprising that no mention was made as to whether or not the newly discovered skeleton was fully intact or damaged in any way as Harold's body would most likely have been.

It does not appear that the other two coffins were opened, although Rhodes was said to have later stated that they held the remains of both Harold's wives, the queen 'Ealdgyth' and 'Edith the Fair'. Ailey concluded that though never proven, it remains a possibility that Harold lies buried in St. Michael's Church.[31]

Other than oral tradition and Leland's statement that a saint called 'Aldgytha' was buried in in the church, solid evidence has never been fully forthcoming and the document submitted to the court by Mr McKenzie and Mr Muff appears to rely on circumstantial evidence which cannot be reconciled. Nevertheless, the discovery of the Norman puddingstone coffin obviously caused a lot of excitement. Although they never opened Eadgifu's tomb, it was just naturally assumed it was hers. And still, no one has been able to produce unassailable proof that this was the place that Harold had been taken to be buried.

It is Mr McKenzie's belief that if not Harold, then at least Eadgifu, and possibly Harold's brothers, were buried in Bishops Stortford. Could there be another conflation of Eadgifu, Harold's handfasted wife and the wife he married in the year of his kingship? As mentioned previously, the name Ealdgytha/Aldith was a completely different name to Eadgifu or Eadgyth, though for some historians, they are mere variants of the equivalent name. But if the name of the saint John Leland was talking about *was* Aldgytha, then it would be easy to see why people believed that the wife of Harold was buried in Stortford because Aldith *was* the name of his second wife. The other problematic issue is the reference to the woman buried there as a saint. There are no mentions of a 'Saint Eadgifu' in the list of Anglo-Saxon saints, that can be found anywhere, nor is there any St. Edith's known to have lived in the eleventh century. Nor are there listed any saints known as Aldgytha.

Like the story of Harold, there is little evidence to prove Eadgifu Swanneck was buried here, apart from the circumstantial evidence that she owned a manor in Stortford and Harold had large estates nearby. As the cousins state, Harold was always believed to have been buried at Waltham Holy Cross, but some years ago, the tomb which purported to be his, was opened and found to be empty.[32]

The mystery of Leland's saint deepens when we note a quote by Mrs Matthew Hall, author of *Lives of the Queens of England before the Norman Conquest*, as cited by McKenzie and Muff.[33] She herself cites Leland:

> One single line, however, preserved in Leland, informs us that the widow of Harold, after having lived through the greater part of the reign of William the Conqueror, deprived of regal dignity, stripped of lands and estates, the survivor of her parents, of two husbands and brothers,

and of her namesake, Editha the Good, the widow of Edward, chose a life of vicissitude and trial, in piety and peace, and was buried and worshipped as a saint, at Stortford, in Hertfordshire.

Worshipped as a saint perhaps, but not actually canonised. And Eadgifu was not known to have wed two husbands, but Aldith had. She was the wife of Gruffudd of Wales before marrying Harold. Eadgifu was likely to have survived her parents, as she had inherited her father's land and perhaps her mother's, but we know not of any brothers. Aldith had survived both parents and at least two of her brothers and had fled to Chester, which the Stortford tradition claimed that Harold's first wife had done. Due to this confusion, it still cannot be precisely claimed that Eadgifu is the woman buried in the vault. Nor can we assert that Harold's other wife is buried there despite the tradition, declared by Reverend Rhodes. Regardless of the links Leland made to Aldith, believing she was Harold's first wife, it is difficult to reconcile her with Bishop Stortford. She had no connections to the place. Having fled to Chester, it seems incongruent for her to be buried at Stortford.

Adding further to the muddle, the claim was also made by Hugh Candidus, Chronicler of Peterborough, that it was at Bishops Stortford where 'Saint Aldgyth' died.[34] It is difficult to find any knowledge of such a saint. Mr McKenzie and Mr Muff also admit that there is some conflation that led nineteenth century historians to believe that the woman in the vaults was Harold's second wife and not Eadgifu, though in their document, she is referred to as 'his devoted first wife, Ealdgyth *Swann hnesce*', which means Ealdgyth the gentle swan, not swan neck. They suggest that the couple were unable to marry religiously, due to consanguinity, which was prohibited to the church, and that the couple were both of the Royal House of Wessex.[35] Eadgifu, they reckon, was a lady of royal blood, believing her to be a granddaughter of Æthelred. Would not such a lady and her family have wished for a wedding formally blessed before God? We have already established in Chapter One, any link to the blood of Wessex in Harold's case cannot be proved. And as for Eadgifu being of royal blood, this is based erroneously on her being the daughter of Wulfgyth, said to be a daughter of Æthelred, another completely different woman named Ealdgyth.[36]

There is no doubting that Eadgifu, the landholder of Bishop's Stortford whose manor most likely lay close to the old Saxon church, was the first wife of Harold. But to establish whether or not Harold was buried there, one has to also be convinced that the body in the coffin under the vaults *is* Eadgifu. Sadly, we cannot substantiate proof that Eadgifu is buried there let alone Harold, no documented extant contemporary source mentions that she is there. And if we cannot be certain that she is there, we cannot in all probability agree that the legend of her bringing him to St. Michael's from Waltham was fulfilled.

The Church of the Holy Cross

Malmesbury was not writing in the interest of Waltham when he recorded that Duke William released Harold's body to his mother,[37] declining the large sums of gold offered for him, which he scorned as insulting.[38] Once obtained, Lady Gytha buried his body at Waltham. Wace also believed that Harold was buried at Waltham, but knew not who bore him there.[39] Considering the earlier tradition that both Guy and Poitiers relate that

Harold was left under a pile of rocks, the great Victorian historian, Edward Freeman, is convinced that Harold was at first buried on the Hastings clifftop and then moved to Waltham for a Christian burial.[40]

The Holy Cross at Waltham was the earliest of the churches to have claimed ownership of King Harold. Remembering the chronicle was written by a former secular priest in c.1177 post Waltham's takeover by Augustinian canons, we should consider that the anonymous author, had access to earlier archives.[41] Entering the establishment as a child, he would have known men who were of an age to remember the political circumstances that brought about the downfall of the Anglo-Saxon regime in 1066. He must also have had access to either a verbal narrative of what happened to the collegiate's revered founder (Harold) or documents that told of the consecration of Waltham, and Harold's final burial in Waltham. We know that he had heard much from Turkil the sacristan, who had been there at the time of the Norman Conquest.

The author of the *Waltham Chronicle* spoke of 'the most saintly king' Harold, who had not ruled for long, being tricked by the 'perfidious Normans', because he had refused to marry the daughter of William of Normandy. The narrator speaks briefly of the northern battle against the Norse, which he referred to as 'Battlebridge', where he incorrectly states that 'Harold, with his brother Tostig, slaughtered and overcame his enemies'.[42] The chronicle tells us that following his victory in the north, the king and a few companions journeyed south and rested at Waltham. When the king heard about the Normans' landing, he wanted to engage them at once in battle, but was advised by his companions to wait for Tostig, Gyrth, and Bondig, and the rest to return home (from Stamford Bridge).[43] We are told that the king was headstrong and trusted too much in his own courage instead of that of a full army. Unfortunately, the omens were not with him.[44]

Such tragic stories are never replete without a passage of mystical foreshadowing, probably inserted in hindsight to explain the disaster of 1066. The writer tells us that he heard this tale from Turkil, who claimed to have witnessed it. The story goes that Harold, praying before the holy cross that he cherished because it had once saved his life, vowed to God if he allowed him to win this war, he would make many endowments to the church and would serve God as a slave would serve his master. But as he lowered himself to lay in the shape of a cross, the head of the crucifix bowed as if in sorrow, a portent of what was about to happen. It was because of this apparent 'omen' the canons sent two of the elder brethren, Osgod Cnoppe, and Æthelric Childemaister to join the king's retinue. They were to have responsibility for the king's body, should things turn out badly.[45]

The Legend

The claim that King Harold went straight to Hastings from Waltham is unlikely. Other sources believe that he was in London before he trekked down to Caldbeck Hill where he met with his army. Nonetheless, the Waltham writer stated that 'alas, he went (despite being advised against it until the rest of his army had arrived) thronged by a small company of men, too boldly and too rashly to advance his cause, trusting more in his own personal strength than that of his men'. The chronicler refers to Prudentius' *Psychomachia*, 'God breaks all who are proud'.[46] The reference to pride infers that Harold's arrogance had been the cause of his downfall. 'And man's bodily habitation does not last long if God is not its foundation'.[47] The source does not spend any time describing the battle. It says little about their patron's death itself, but it does labour the point that Harold had been beaten by a much larger army than his own. The leading men 'fall this side and that', and the fierce Norman race, 'no strangers to stubborn resistance', penetrate the English ranks, thirsting above all for the blood of the king. The old canon, freely writes of his disdain for the Normans, calling them a 'savage' race, which he is able to do because he writes long after the Conqueror is dead. He elevates King Harold as the 'darling of the clergy, the strength of his soldiers, the shield of the defenceless' and among other such tributes, the 'pearl of princes' was slain by his fierce foe. The lament continues for three long paragraphs until the following poem ends that chapter.

> Alas, o king, you fall to a fierce foe, a duke and future king,
> Equal to him in combat, each a valiant knight.
> Firmin the Just's day
> For then you were the victor,
> Not so Calixtus' day
> So may both saints implore eternal rest for you,
> And all that worships God thus pray to Him.[48]

The next chapter describes the canons' request for Harold's body, how they sought, found, and buried him. Its mention of the 'bad omen', the bowing of the rood's head, is written as if the scribe felt the need to remind readers that it was entirely to blame for the downfall of the English. It speaks of the sorrow of canons, Osgod and Æthelric, who followed the king to his doom so they might witness his terrible demise. And it was in the aftermath of battle the two canons approached the duke nervously, humbling themselves before his feet.[49] Respectfully, they explain what the king had done for them and their establishment. 'Master we ask and urge you through the grace of God and for the salvation of all the souls who have lost their lives in this present cause of yours, to allow us at your good pleasure, to remove without hindrance the body of our lord, the king, the founder of our church, together with the bodies of the men who have chosen to be buried among us.' Duke William, so moved by their tearful entreaties, replied, 'Your king neglected his good faith, yet, though now he has paid the due penalty for his sin, he does not deserve to be deprived of the benefit of burial.' William also promised that out of respect for him and the men who had died in his cause he will establish a church and monastic community of 100 monks, who will 'pray unceasingly for the salvation of those men's souls and in this church will exalt your king himself above all others and, out of respect for him, to enrich the place with large endowments.'[50]

The brethren, consoled by the duke's comforting promises, offer the duke 10 gold marks for the use of his men to assist them in returning Harold's body without impediment, happy in the gift of his body so they can inter him in the place he founded for himself, in a tomb that in their time will be a perpetual memorial for their descendants.[51]

And so, their requests granted, the 10 marks declined, the monks search for the body of their king. Turning the corpses this way and that, they were unable to recognise him. Presumably this was the morning after battle, the king had been dead for over twelve hours. The monks decided that the only solution was for Osgod to ride and fetch the woman that the dead king had loved, named by the scribe as 'Edith Swannehals'.[52]

As she had been the concubine of Harold, she knew the marks on the king's body better than anyone, being admitted to a greater intimacy of his person.[53]

Journeyed back to Waltham and returned with Eadgifu. It is over 70 miles from Battle to Waltham Abbey, Osgod would have done nearly 150 miles, probably on horseback, and given that this was usually 20 to 25 miles per day, it would have taken him approximately six days depending on how good a horseman he was. By the time he returned, what was left of Harold's remains would be in a far worse state of decomposition.

Eadgifu was able to recognise him we are told, pointing him out by the marks known to her. His corpse, referred to as 'mangled', was placed on a bier by the canons. The author describes a company of armoured Norman warriors who accompanied them in fellowship with a large number of English survivors (perhaps latecomers to the battle) as far as 'Battlebridge', a place in Essex that straddles the River Couch. Harold was brought to Waltham and buried with great honour at the east end of the choir, where, 'without any doubt he has lain at rest until the present day'.[54] The old canon scathingly denied the story that was also circulating, that Harold had survived the battle and dwelled in a cave before dying in Chester. This suggests that the story of Harold the Hermit was known before the *Vita Haroldi*, also written by a canon of Waltham, was composed. The Waltham scribe declares the veracity of Harold's burial because he remembers being present when he was translated for a third time, which, as the author tells us, it occurred either because of the building of the new church, or because the brethren, out of devotion, were showing reverence to the body. He claims to have heard old men testify that they had seen with their own eyes and touched with their own hands the wounds on the very bones of their king.

Although previously rumoured in the chronicle, the *Vita Haroldi* was not composed until twenty-five years later. Bordering upon delusional in much of its content, its theme that Harold survived the battle appears to have been known for some time. Freeman refers to the account as food for the mythologist rather than the historian. The *Haroldi's* historical value is lacking, though the episode where he fell ill as a young man, recovered and resolved to build his church of the Holy Cross, is worthy of note though only appears to be known to Waltham. The legend of Harold's survival became fashionable in the twelfth century.[55] Harold, states the anonymous scribe of the *Haroldi*, escaped from battle, pierced with many wounds and the loss of an eye.[56] Found on the battlefield among the dead by a Saracen woman, he is concealed in Winchester for two years. Once recovered she took him on a pilgrimage to Jerusalem, then brought him back to England where he lived as a hermit in a cave, then after being turned down by European rulers for aid to win his crown back and a series of other adventures, he eventually ends his days as an anchorite in Chester living in virtuous piety.[57]

Eadgifu Swanneck has a whole chapter to herself in the *Haroldi*. The scribe wrote that hearing of the king's death, the canons sent a certain woman of 'shrewd intelligence' to where he had fallen, 'so that she might carry away the limbs of their dead lord, to be buried reverently in their church'. They believed her sex would be an object of compassion to the cruel Norman officers in authority, and that she was more fitted to carry out the search because she would more easily identify his body, and 'would handle his remains more tenderly, because she deeply loved him and knew him well, having been frequently present in the secret places of his chamber.[58] But we are told the woman (Eadgifu) unable to find the right corpse, chose what was in fact another man's unrecognisable corpse that the canons were said to have reverently received as Harold's and interred in their church, without question. Those who stole away the real king from the battlefield, seriously injured but not quite dead, were keen for this to be kept secret, in fear that the Normans would hear that he was alive. The *Haroldi* scribe was to vehemently deny that the king had been buried in Waltham. He has Gyrth survive to a ridiculously impossible age, testifying at the court of Henry II to his brother's life as a hermit. It can only be dismissed as total nonsense and is of no value whatsoever in the search for Harold's resting place.

But how do we reconcile the two versions of Harold's burial. Is it possible to accept Freeman's theory that Harold was buried first on the cliff then moved to Waltham?[59] According to Freeman, William Malet's connection to Harold is beyond doubt.[60] He was the man that the Conqueror entrusted to bury Harold in the first instance, hastily under a pile of stones, seemingly so that his body did not create a shrine and focus for English revenge. Guy, not mentioning Malet by name, reported that he was a half-Norman and half-English, companion of Harold. It was suggested that the use of the Latin *compater* meant that Malet and Harold had contracted some 'tie of spiritual brotherhood by standing as godfathers to the same child'. Freeman suggested that Malet may have had a connection to the House of Leofric, through his mother, though the connection is hard to fathom.

Evidence for both the clifftop burial and Waltham is certainly plausible but awkward to settle. Poitiers follows Guy's contemporary statement which was the earliest written detailed account of the burial and worthy of respect, as is Waltham's, though for different reasons. But if Harold was not buried at Waltham, how did the tale emerge? Osgod's journey to Waltham from the battlefield to fetch Eadgifu to identify Harold's body is problematic in that the Waltham Chronicle does not mention the time lapse which would have been significant, at least several days. However, it seems that Osgod returned with her without much delay. In reality, it would have taken roughly a week to get her to the battleground. The idea that Eadgifu was already there, or close by, seems more likely. Andrew Bridgeford's theory that the woman escaping from the burning house on the Bayeux Tapestry under the text *Hic Domus Incenditur*, was Eadgifu and her son Ulf, is worthy of note.[61] Ulf, the youngest of the couple's children, became William's captive.[62] Could there have been an attack on their house at Crowhurst, and were they taken into the custody of the duke?

The Bayeux Tapestry was very possibly conveying what had incensed Harold that he refused to heed his mother's pleas to wait and rest before confronting the Norman army. Villages close to Battle, Crowhurst, Whatlington, Netherfield, and Broomham, were all laid to waste according to the Domesday Book. But the image could have been representative of any noble woman, and it does seem rather risky for Eadgifu to be there with her young child when her husband was fighting an invasion on their doorstep. But if this was the case, it could explain how she came to be at the battle site so quickly; she was held hostage by William. Poitiers notes that Harold was in a hurry to get to the south when he heard his lands were being laid waste. Was he worried about Eadgifu? Had the family spent the summer at Crowhurst whilst he was campaigning along the coast? Was she still there when he left to go north?[63] This does not necessarily dismiss Countess Gytha from the tale, for she might well have been there too. But what do we make of the clifftop scenario?

Guy and Poitiers state that Harold was buried on the shore shortly after the battle. There the tale ended as far as they were concerned. Any later translation of his body was not in their interest. Waltham's version of his interment in the Holy Cross focusses only on local history.[64] The hurried burial on the shore would eventually be forgotten, making independent writers like Malmesbury and Wace concentrate on the Waltham story. William could have had a change of heart when he realised it would not benefit him to add to his list of sins which already included regicide. This is where the reconciliation of the two burials becomes awkward. The Waltham scribe implies Harold was taken there straight after he was found the day after battle which meant there would have been no time in bury him on the shore after being transported to the duke's camp in Hastings, as explained by Guy in his *Carmen*.

The confusion seems to stem from the fact that there were two petitions to William for Harold's remains. One by the canons, and one by his mother. The latter request was made once Harold's body had been sent from the battlefield to the camp at Hastings, which was then followed by the transportation of his body to Waltham. This leaves us to imagine that when the canons brought Eadgifu to the field to find her beloved Harold, it was under the instruction of William who was eager to have Harold's body in his possession.

This gives rise to two ideas, the first that once Eadgifu had found him, he must have denied her his remains; secondly, the canons later join with Countess Gytha to petition the duke again, which at this time he relents and agrees?[65] Freeman claimed that he had managed to conciliate the two burials in an order that made sense. The mistake made by Waltham's scribe, was the timing of the Waltham burial, and the circumstances in which Harold's body was found. Freeman believed that in William's haste to rid himself of a potential martyr's body, Harold *was* buried on the clifftop in the first instance. Later, perhaps around the time of his coronation, Gytha and her allies at Waltham made a second request which William, about to be crowned king of England, agreed to, as a gesture of goodwill.[66]

On the other hand, the different stories may all have just been variations on a theme which gave in 'to flights of fancy' as Ann Williams points out. For example, Poitiers claim that the Conqueror's suggestion that Harold be buried on the Saxon shore was said in jest, not to mention the fantastical tale of Harold's survival, penned by a delusional scribe of the Church of the Holy Cross, who was adamant that Harold was not buried in Waltham, but Chester.[67] The account of Harold's discovery by Eadgifu and conveyance to Waltham straight from the battlefield, envisioned by the anonymous scribe of the *Waltham Chronicle*, is a romantic one. Foes, brought together out of respect for a dead king, escort the funeral parade from the field of battle to his resting place, in which we can imagine was led by his weeping wife and mother, followed by a torch-lit train of mourners. It is a sentimental picture and one that is appealing, but for more than 70 miles seems doubtful.[68]

Harold's Last Resting Place

Whatever the truth of how Harold eventually made it to Waltham, there is no doubt that his last journey was the one to Waltham. And there can also be no doubt that he was meant to have been laid to rest in the church he commissioned, the church of the Holy Cross. According to William Winters, the last Anglo-Saxon king was said to have been interred roughly about 120 feet from the present east end of the church.[69] This part of the churchyard is now where the choir of Harold's church stood, and was once used as a garden by the Earl of Carlisle, and the builder of Abbey House, Sir Edward Denny. Today there is a stone slab commemorating Harold, 'This stone marks the position of the high altar behind which King Harold is said to have been buried 1066', and another block which says, 'Harold King of England. Obit 1066'. The author of *Waltham Chronicle* suggests that Harold was entombed near the high altar, signifying his status as king. He was said to have been translated three times, but it is not known whether his coffin is under the site of the stone slab outside the modern-day church or whether he was moved elsewhere.

My lovely guide, Tricia Gurnett of the King Harold Society, to whom I am grateful for spending time with, showed me around Waltham Abbey that chilly day in March, advised me that the King Harold memorial standing stone was scanned six years ago, about the time the stone underwent a restoration. It was examined using a radar to see if anything had been inside it when it was erected in the 1960s. It was found to be empty. Ms Gurnett also explained on good authority that no coffin or remains thought to be Harold's, have ever been found. As we know, Harold's body had been moved at least three times during the building work when his church gave way to the Norman building and then to the great Waltham Abbey of Henry II, but the remains of the king have since disappeared. With the amount of internments and the removal of remains to fit in new burials in over 900 years, it would be surprising if anything of him still remained.[70] Another scan of the churchyard was made in 2014, involving a theory by author Peter Burke and Oval films, but nothing ever seems to have emerged, not even the proposed documentary.[71] Whether or not he was moved from there at some later point to a different location we cannot know. Despite this he could still be there somewhere and whether or not he is, it does seem that this was his intended place of rest.

That Bosham is a candidate for Harold's burial is hardly surprising, it was after all his childhood home and probable place of birth. It is quite likely, one historian claims, that his mother would have wished for his body to have been buried in the home that she loved and suggests that Hastings was close to Bosham, therefore easier to get to than Waltham, but the actual distance is not much different between the two.[72]

Gytha would have known what her son's wishes were. As his mother, it is unlikely that she would have gone against the vision he had for himself. That he adored Waltham is evidenced by the care he took for it, his establishment of the collegiate, and his adornment of the church with many beautiful items and holy relics. With the battle over and England's fall evident, Gytha's time at Bosham was running short. Having been her son's property, it was now William's. The Holy Trinity Church next door to it was in the hands of Osbern as it had been before the conquest, but he was Norman and related to William. With all this in mind, Bosham seems doubtful.

There might have been a case for Bishops Stortford; some of the evidence produced by McKenzie and Muff is reasonable, such as the fact that Eadgifu and Harold both held land there, but this does not mean that their connections to the place were as strong as they were in the case of Waltham, which was mentioned by a variety of sources to have been the place that Harold's body was transferred. Harold's establishment of the church in Waltham offsets any idea of him being buried in St. Michael's unless he was moved there later, which is not impossible, but evidence is lacking. The claim that the cousins make about Bishop's Stortford being Eadgifu's home seems unusual, for it would seem more likely that the couple spent much of their time closer to Waltham, especially whilst it was under construction. If anything, local tradition has it that they lived at her home in

Nazeing. Eadgifu's association with the canons of The Holy Cross and her presence on the battlefield in the aftermath of the death of thousands of Englishmen and their king, is not denied by the Stortford legend. It is just whether or not Eadgifu decided to bring him 'home' to the manor in Hertfordshire or Waltham. Stortford is hardly connected with Harold, though Waltham is readily associated with him in various texts and was the place where he had prayed for his life twice. It seems natural that he would have wanted to be lain to rest in the church he had built in recognition of God's intervention in his illness. Throughout the construction of his church, Harold would have been there as much as he could, overseeing, and if Eadgifu's home was but 5 miles from the place, he could have easily gone between his manor at Waltham and Nazeing.

Stortford tradition implies that a man of tall stature was buried within the coffin found there, but this in no way lends itself to Harold who was said to have been dismembered and badly mangled. And it seems unusual that they did not open the other two coffins meant to contain both Harold's wives. How could they have known who they were if they had not opened them? And if they had opened them at any other time, no record has been found to date. Mr McKenzie and Mr Muff's case was not taken forward by the diocese, unfortunately, so for now, whose bodies lie in these four coffins cannot be confirmed. It is in hope I will wait for them to be identified one day.

With all this in mind, Freeman's case is perfectly rational. Harold may well have had two burials. The first was on unconsecrated ground on a cliff on Hastings shore and then perhaps two to three months later, around the time of his coronation, William relented, and allowed Harold's body to be transferred to Waltham. In doing so, we are able to reconcile Guy and Poitiers with the Waltham story. It is not necessarily what happened, but a reasonable attempt at describing what *might* have happened. If I had the power to choose I would go for the three-day escorted march from Battle directly to Waltham. It was how a brave king who died fighting for his life and country should have gone to the afterlife.

So, what kind of man was Harold Godwinson? As all medieval kings and leaders are, he was a complex individual, capable of good, competent kingship, responding efficiently in times of national crises; but like so many kings before and after him, he made mistakes and everyone will have their own opinion on his failure to secure the kingdom from the Norman invaders. It is hard to look at the distinct scenarios surrounding the events from the vantage point of a thousand years and say what he should have done when we weren't there. We know nothing of what went down that day, the mental and physical exhaustion, the trauma, and the loss of so many men. Imagine having to fight on when you know your friends, and brothers were dead, and that the fate of your family, your people, rested on your shoulders? Unless one has experienced the life of a soldier in any sort of war one cannot know. We can only envisage what we think we know happened.

THE END

Notes

Foreword

1. *The Laws od the Kings of England from Edmund to Henry I*, ed. A.J. Robertson (Cambridge, 1925, pp. 32-3 (IV Edgar clause 2a.2).

Chapter One

1. Anscombe, 'The Pedigree of Earl Godwin', pp. 129-50; Lundie W. Barlow, 'The Antecedents of Earl Godwine of Wessex', pp. 30-38.
2. Lundie Barlow is no relation to Frank Barlow. Frank Barlow, *The Godwins*, p. 25. For the family tree see p. 21.
3. I am grateful to Ann Williams for clarifying this with me in 2021. For Wulfnoth as a Sussex thegn. *The Anglo-Saxon Chronicles, E,* trans. Michael Swanton, p. 138.
4. Mason, *The House of Godwine*, p. 24. For John of Worcester see *The Chronicle of John of Worcester*, ed. and tr. Jennifer Bray and P. McGurk, pp. 460-61.
5. Barlow, *The Godwins*, p. 21.
6. Grills, *The Life and Times of Godwine*, p. 33.
7. I am grateful to Ann Williams for advising me in 2022; PASE is a structured database providing information on all recorded inhabitants from the late sixth century to the eleventh. Prosopography of Anglo-Saxon England: Home (pase.ac.uk).
8. Knowles, Brooke, and London, *The Heads of Religious Houses, England and Wales 940–1216*, p. 81.
9. Barlow, *The Godwins*, p. 24.
10. I am grateful for this clarification from Ann Williams 2022.
11. Knowles et al, *The Heads of Religious Houses*, p. 81.
12. *Knýtlinga Saga*, pp. 32-34.
13. *ASC, E,* p. 138.
14. Walker, *Harold the Last Anglo-Saxon King,* p. 3; *ASC, E,* p. 138.
15. Barlow, *The Godwins,* p. 24; *ASC, E,* p. 138, n7. The *F* chronicle names him as Earl Godwin's father.
16. Anscombe, 'The Pedigree of Earl Godwin', pp. 133-34; *ASC,* p. 138, n7.
17. Thank you to Ann Williams for clarifying, 07/01/2022.
18. Keynes, 'Æthelstan Ætheling [Athelstan the Atheling] (d. 1014)'.
19. Walker, *Harold the Last Anglo-Saxon King,* p. 2.
20. *ASC, E,* p. 138. A hide was a unit of land a family needed to sustain themselves. By the eleventh century, hides were calculated into hundreds which meant 100 hides made up the *hundred* which became the division of land within a county or shire. A hide was

roughly calculated at 120 acres, but not always necessarily so. The hide system was also used to account for military service as well as *feorm*, food owed to the lord. It was a complex system that was not static and often changed from shire to shire.

21. *ASC*, pp. 124-139.
22. Williams, *Æthelred the Unready: The Ill-counselled King*, p. 117.
23. For Wulfnoth's raiding of coastal lands see *ASC, E*, p. 138; for the collecting of provisions see, Key, *The House of Godwin*, p. 27.
24. *ASC, E*, p. 138.
25. Ibid, p. 138.
26. Ibid, p. 138
27. Ibid, p. 138-139.
28. John of Worcester, *Chronicle*, p. 461.
29. Walker, *Harold the Last Anglo-Saxon King*, p. 1.
30. John of Worcester, *Chronicle*, p. 461.
31. Ibid, p. 459.
32. Ibid, p. 459.
33. Ibid, pp. 459-461.
34. Grills, *The Life and Times of Godwine*, p. 27.
35. Tyson, *Godwin the Sea-lord*, 1.1.
36. *ASC, E*, p. 138.
37. Williams, *Æthelred the Unready*, p. 116.
38. Walker, *Harold the Last Anglo-Saxon King*, p. 3.
39. *Vita*, p. 22. For the rekindling of an old alliance and p. 24 for the marriage of Tostig and Judith.
40. Eric, 'Edward the Confessor and the Norman Succession', p. 209.
41. Grills, *The Life and Times of Godwine*, p. 33.
42. *Vita*, p. 24.
43. For Bruges see Tyson, *Godwin the Sea-lord*, 2.14. For Normandy and Scandinavia, thanks to Ann Williams for this clarification 06/01/2023.
44. Williams, *Æthelred the Unready*, p. 91.
44. Garmonsway, *Cnut and his Empire*, p. 6.
45. *ASC, D, E*, pp. 174-175.
46. According to Godwin's exploits abroad and his ability to impress, this would not be impossible.
47. Tyson, *Godwin the Sea-lord*, 2.15.

Chapter Two

1. *ASC*, p. 139.
2. Williams, *Æthelred the Unready*, p. 91. The Jomsvikings were supporters of Sweyn's father, Bluetooth whom Sweyn deposes.
3. Ibid, p. 143, does not mention Thorkell by name; *Encomium*, pp. 73-76 names him as Thorkell.
4. Tyson, *Godwin the Sea-lord*, 2.18; see also Mason, *The House of Godwine*, p. 25. Wulfnoth might have joined Thorkell, but states this is unlikely because of Godwin's future rise to a position of trust.
5. Barlow, *The Godwins*, p. 27; *Vita*, p. 5, discusses Godwin's qualities that drew Cnut toward him.

6. For *ship sokes* see, Lavelle, *Alfred's Wars Sources and Interpretations*, pp. 160-161.
7. *ASC*, p. 138.
8. Keynes, *Æthelstan*.
9. Tyson, *Godwin the Sea-lord*, 2.8. Simon Keynes points out that the location of Æthelingadene was in West Dean, however Tyson states that it was in East Sussex near the River Cuckmere however, her argument that Wulfnoth served under Æthelstan is plausible.
10. Keynes, *The Diplomas of King Æthelred the Unready 978–1016*, p. 267.
11. *ASC*, p. 144.
12. Ibid, p. 144, see also n10. See John of Worcester, *Chronicle*, p. 477 for an elaborate telling of Swegn death.
13. Ibid, p. 144; John of Worcester, *Chronicle*, p. 477 records that the Danish fleet wanted Cnut to be king.
14. Ibid, p. 145; John of Worcester agrees.
15. Ibid, p. 145.
16. Grills, *The Life and Times of Godwine*, p. 38.
17. Ibid. Grills suggests that he could well have learned the tactics and strategies he employed in Scandinavia fighting alongside the warrior sons of Æthelred.
18. Williams, *Æthelred the Unready*, p. 114.
19. Ibid, pp. 115-117.
20. Hagland and Watson, 'Fact or Folklore', pp. 328–33.
21. Grills, *The Life and Times of Godwine*, p. 34, suggests that the æthelings were related to the northern magnates (notably Siferth and Morcar) through their mother, Ælfgifu of York.
22. *ASC*, pp. 145-146.
23. *Encomium*, pp. 31-33.
24. *ASC*, p. 146.
25. Ibid, p. 148.
26. Ibid, pp. 146-149.
27. I am grateful for Ann Williams clarifying this with me, April 2022.
28. *ASC*, pp. 146-147.
29. Ibid, p. 148.
30. Ibid, p. 149.
31. Ibid, pp. 150-151.
32. Ibid.
33. Ibid, pp. 152-153. The *Magonsæte* was the name of the tribes in the lands bordering Wales.
34. *ASC*, pp. 152-153.
35. Grills, *The Life and Times of Godwine*, p. 38.
36. John of Worcester, *Chronicle*, p. 492.
37. Ibid, p. 493.
38. Bartlett, *King Cnut and the Viking Conquest of England*, p. 159.
39. Grills, *The Life and Times of Godwine*, p. 39.
40. *Encomium*, pp. 31-33.
41. *ASC*, E, pp. 174-177.
42. Ibid, p. 136.
43. Tyson, *Godwin the Sea-lord*, 1.3.
44. Eadmer, *Historia Novorum*, p. 5.

Chapter Three

1. *ASC, D, E*, pp. 154-155.
2. Ibid.
3. Garmonsway, *Cnut and his Empire*, p. 6.
4. Ibid, p. 21,
5. Anglo-Saxon Poem.
6. *Vita*, p. xxvii.
7. Ibid, p. 6. The author mistakenly refers to Godwin's wife as Cnut's sister, who was actually sister of Cnut's brother-in-law, Ulf.
8. Henry of Huntingdon, *The History of the English People, 1000–1154*, p. 16.
9. Keynes, *Cnut's Earls in the Reign of Cnut*, pp. 73, 84-86.
10. Henry of Huntingdon, *The History of the English People*, p. 16.
11. Ibid.
12. Ibid.
13. *Vita*, p. 6. 'Office bearer' could be associated with a position akin to *dux Anglorum*, deputy to the king of England or *sub-regulus*: second only to the king.
14. Grills, *The Life and Times of Godwine*, p. 58.
15. Ibid.
16. Saxo Grammaticus, *Danorum Regum Heroumque Historia*, p. 35.
17. *Vita*, p. 6.
18. William of Malmesbury, *Chronicle of the Kings of England from the Earliest Period to the Reign of King Stephen*, p. 123.
19. Lawson, *England's Viking King*, p. 93.
20. William of Malmesbury, *Chronicle of the Kings of England*, p. 123.
21. *Morkinskinna*, p. 113; *Fagrskinna*, p. 163.
22. Saxo Grammaticus, *Danorum Regum Heroumque Historia*, 10. XXII p. 142 and n167, pp. 214, 217.
23. Barlow, *The Godwins*, p. 31.
24. John of Worcester, *Chronicle*, p. 468.
25. Ibid.
26. Bennett Connolly, *Silk and the Sword*, p. 69.
27. Grills, *The Life and Times of Godwine*, p. 56.
28. *Knýtlinga Saga*, p. 29.
29. *Knýtlinga saga* tells the story of Godwin as a cowherd finds Cnut's brother-in-law, Ulf, wandering the countryside estranged from his unit, tells how the farmer's boy offers to help the dazed and battle-weary Dane and brings him home where he is looked after and given hospitality. When the Dane had recovered, he was given a horse to get home by Godwin's father and he offers to take the boy back with him and raise him up to greater things than he would be able to achieve as a farmer's boy. Thus, Godwin is rewarded by Cnut and made an earl, and given Ulf's sister's hand in marriage. The story is of course doubtful.
30. Grills, *The Life and Times of Godwine*, p. 32.
31. Ibid, p. 128.
32. Ibid, p. 56.

Chapter Four

1. Grills, *The Life and Times of Godwine*, p. 145.
2. *ASC, D,* p. 202.
3. Williams, 'The Spindle Side', pp. 109-20.
4. Bennett Connolly, *Silk and the Sword*, p. 72.
5. Williams, 'The Spindle Side', pp. 109-20; Bennett Connolly, *Silk and the Sword*, p. 72.
6. Eadmer, *Historia Novorum*, pp. 7-8.
7. *Hemingi*, vol. 1, pp. 275-276.
8. I am grateful to Joan Langhorne, archivist of Holy Trinity Church in Bosham for discussing the story of Cnut's daughter with me March 2023 and providing me with the explanation that its origin cannot be found and must be treated with caution as a tradition which belongs to the church's history and that there are no extant documents to hold fast with this tale. Mike@AbitaboutBritain, Bosham, *The King's Daughter and Harold*, 07/04/2017.
9. I am deeply grateful to Patricia Bracewell for clarifying this theory with me April 2022.
10. *ASC, D, E*, pp. 154-155.
11. *Encomium*, p. 33.
12. Ailred, Abbot of Rivaulx, *The Life of Saint Edward*, p. 8.
13. *Vita*, p. 6, says that Cnut appointed him as his office-bearer, *bailulus,* of almost all the whole kingdom.
14. Grills, *The Life and Times of Godwine*, p. 66.
15. *Vita.* p. 7.
16. Grills, *The Life and Times of Godwine*, p. 69.
17. Ibid, p. 72.
18. O'Brien, *Queen Emma and the Vikings*, p. 14.
19. Grills, *The Life and Times of Godwine*, p. 83.
20. Ibid.
21. *ASC, C, D,* pp. 158-59.
22. *ASC, C, D, E*, pp. 158-159.
23. Ibid.
24. Ibid.
25. Freeman, *The History of the Norman Conquest of England*, vol. 1, p. 538.
26. *Encomium*, p. 41.
27. Kings would not necessarily be consecrated immediately after ascension. The story of the archbishop refusing to consecrate Harefoot is not, to my knowledge, documented in any other extant manuscript and may have simply formed part of Emma's character assassination of Harold to further damn him as the murderer of her son, Alfred.
28. *Encomium*, p. 41.
29. Ibid.
30. John, *The Anglo Saxons*, chapt. 9, in Grills, *The Life and Times of Godwine*, p. 98.
31. Ibid. Curiously, *Encomium* leaves out what happened to Edward when he also ventured to England and mentions only what happened to Alfred. *Encomium*, p. 43.
32. Ibid.
33. William of Jumièges, *Gesta Normannorum*, p. 107.
34. *Encomium*, p. 43.
35. *ASC, C, D,* pp. 158-159; John of Worcester, *Chronicle*, p. 523.

36. John of Worcester, *Chronicle*, p. 523.
37. *Encomium*, p. 43.
38. Ibid.
39. John of Worcester, *Chronicle*, p. 523. The *Encomium* claims they were dragged out of their billets into the courtyard of the village to be 'decimated' like the Theban Legion of Christian Hagiography, except instead of sparing nine men out of ten, they spared one man in ten. *Encomium*, p. 45.
40. John of Worcester, *Chronicle*, p. 523.
41. *Encomium*, p. 45.
42. John of Worcester, *Chronicle*, p. 523.
43. *Gesta Normannorum Ducum*, pp. 104-107.
44. John of Worcester, *Chronicle*, p. 525.
45. *ASC, E*, p. 145.
46. Grills, *The Life and Times of Godwine*, p. 98.
47. *Encomium*, p. 45.
48. *ASC E*, p. 161.
49. *ACD*, pp. 158-161; *Encomium*, p. 47.
50. *Encomium*, p. 49.
51. Ibid.
52. *ASC, A*, p. 160.
53. Grills, *The Life and Times of Godwine*, p. 111.
54. John of Worcester, *Chronicle*, p. 531.
55. Stevenson, *The History of Ingulf*, p. 655.
56. Grills, *The Life and Times of Godwine*, p. 113.
57. John of Worcester, *Chronicle*, pp. 531-533.
58. John of Worcester, *Chronicle*, p. 531.
59. *ASC, E*, p. 161. A rowlock is a fitting on the gunwale of a boat which serves as a fulcrum for an oar and keeps it in place.
60. John of Worcester, *Chronicle*, p. 531.
61. Ibid, p. 533.
62. Ibid.
63. Ibid.
64. *ASC*, pp. 162-163. John of Worcester, *Chronicle*, p. 535. Freeman reports that he was a rapacious, brutal, and bloody tyrant, cited by Grills, *The Life and Times of Godwine*, p. 126.
65. *Vita*, p. 7.
66. Grills, *The Life and Times of Godwine*, p. 184.
67. *Encomium*, p. 53.
68. *ASC*, pp. 162-163.
69. Grills, *The Life and Times of Godwine*, p. 126.

Chapter Five

1. *Vita*, p. 12.
2. Ibid; Wilson, *The Bayeux Tapestry*, p. 1.
3. *Vita*, p. 12.

4. Ibid, p. 13.
5. Ibid, p. 14. This is interpolated by Osbert of Clare. As prior of Westminster Abbey, Osbert worked to strengthen the rights and prestige of his monastery. He championed Edward's sanctity. Bloch, *La vie de S. Edouard le Conffesseur par Osbert de Clare*, vol. 12, p. 12.
6. Hardy, 'The Translation of St. Mildred', pp. 380-381. In Grills, *The Life and Times of Godwine*, p. 142.
7. John of Worcester, *Chronicle*, p. 533.
8. *ASC*, pp. 162-163.
9. Ibid.
10. Grills, *The Life and Times of Godwine*, p. 137.
11. Adam of Bremen, *History of the Archbishops of Hamburgh*, bk.3 ch. X1V (13), pp. 124-125.
12. Ibid, pp. 135-136.
13. *Vita*, p. 11. It is not known whether the author was referring to Swein or Magnus, for the latter was king, having forced Swein out, at the time of Edward's coronation. Freeman, *The History of the Norman Conquest of England*, vol. 2, p. 18, believes it was Magnus, but Barlow believes it was more likely that the author was referring to Swein.
14. Licence, *Edward the Confessor Last of the Royal Blood*, p. 90.
15. Grills, *The Life and Times of Godwine*, p. 138.
16. *ASC, D*, p. 165.
17. *ASC, C, D*, pp. 164-165.
18. Hardy, *Lestorie des Engles solum la translacion maistre*, vol. 1, p. 381.
19. Barlow, *Edward the Confessor*, pp. 76-77.
20. Osbert of Clare, *Vita*, p. 14.
21. Stafford, *Queen Emma & Queen Edith, Queenship and Women's Power in Eleventh Century England*, p. 42.
22. Osbert of Clare, *Vita*, p. 14.
23. Grills, *The Life and Times of Godwine*, p. 128.
24. Snorri Sturluson, *St. Olaf's Saga*, p. 312, in Grills p. 128.
25. Osbert of Clare, *Vita*, p. 14.
26. *ASC, E*, p. 165.
27. Barlow, *Edward*, p. 65.
28. Osbert of Clare, *Vita*, p. 14.
29. Grills, *The Life and Times of Godwine*, 139.
30. William of Malmesbury, *Vita Wulfstani*, pp. 120-129.
31. Osbert of Clare, *Vita*, p. 15.
32. *Vita*, p. 79.
33. Strutt, *The Chronicle of England*, p. 97.
34. *Vita*, p. 28.
35. Licence, *Edward the Confessor*, p. 104.
36. Child Welfare Information Gateway, 'Parenting a Child Who Has Experienced Trauma'.
37. Walker, *Harold the Last Anglo-Saxon King*, p. 31.
38. Licence, *Edward the Confessor*, p. 91.

39. Grills, *The Life and Times of Godwine*, p. 44, mentions Cnut's sister Gytha who may well have been in the slave trade, but she was married to Cnut's friend, Eric.
40. From Ætheling Æthelstan's will we know that his grandmother had brought him up and had been custom since the tenth century, Stafford, *Queen Emma & Queen Edith*, p. 120.
41. Stafford, *Queen Emma & Queen Edith*, p. 120.
42. *Vita*, p. 54.
43. Grills, for Beorn, see p. 145; for all the sons of Ulf see p. 137.
44. Licence, *Edward the Confessor*, p. 102n79.
45. Barlow, *Godwins*, p. 166.
46. Grills, *The Life and Times of Godwine*, p. 145.
47. Ibid, p. 144.

Chapter Six

1. *Vita*, pp. 31-33.
2. Ibid, p. 15.
3. Grills, *The Life and Times of Godwine*, pp. 128, 147.
4. Ibid, p. 144.
5. John of Worcester, *Chronicle*, pp. 532.
6. Rex, *The Last English King: The Life of Harold II*, p. 31, suggests 1020. Walker, *Harold the Last Anglo-Saxon King*, p. 23, suggests he was around 25 when he was promoted as earl; Grills, *The Life and Times of Godwine*, p. 135 suggests 1026.
7. Hart, *The Danelaw*, table 5.2, p. 195.
8. Grills, *The Life and Times of Godwine*, p. 84.
9. Rex, *The Last English King*, p. 31.
10. Whitelock, *Anglo Saxon Wills*, pp. 80-85, 192-197.
11. Rex, *The Last English King*, p. 33.
12. Ibid.
13. Round, 'The Third Penny', pp. 62-64.
14. Trevelyan, *History of England*, p. 92.
15. Stenton, *Anglo-Saxon England*, p. 495n1.
16. Ibid.
17. My gratitude to Ann Williams for clarifying.
18. Stenton, *Anglo-Saxon England*, p. 495.
19. Abrams, 'Edward the Elder's Danelaw', p. 128.
20. Wood, *Domesday*, p. 130.
21. Harthacnut died at Tovi the Proud's wedding.
22. Licence, *Edward the Confessor*, p. 103.
23. *ASC C, E*, pp. 164-165.
24. Ibid.
25. See also John of Worcester, *Chronicle*, p. 543.
26. Licence, *Edward the Confessor*, p. 109.
27. Ibid.

28. Ibid.
29. Herman the Archdeacon and Goscelin of St. Bertin, *Miracles of St. Edmund*, ed. and tr. Licence, *Edward the Confessor*, pp. 37, 57.
30. *ASC C, D*, pp. 167-168; John of Worcester, *Chronicle*, p. 551.
31. *ASC, C, D*, pp. 184-185.
32. Refers Saxons on the Continent.
33. *Vita Haroldi*, see p. 112 for Harold's lawful crowning, and for Godwin's marriage to sister of Cnut and Harold being brother of the queen, p. 113.
34. Ibid, pp. 113-116.
35. Ibid, p. 116.
36. Ibid, p. 117.
37. Ibid, p. 118.
38. Ibid.
39. Snorri Sturluson, *King Harold's Saga (Heimskringla)*, vol. 3, p. 168; *Waltham Chronicle*, pp. 26-27.
40. *Vita Haroldi*, pp. 118-119.
41. *ASC, C, D*, p. 166-167.
42. *Vita Haroldi*, p. 119.
43. *Waltham Chronicle*, p. 23.
44. *Vita Haroldi*, p. 120.
45. Walker, *Harold the Last Anglo-Saxon King*, p. 137.
46. *Vita*, p. 31.
47. Rex, *The Last English King*, p. 31.
48. Eadmer, *Historia Novorum*, pp. 7-8.
49. Snorri Sturluson, *King Harald's Saga*, p. 150.
50. *Waltham Chronicle*, p. xxxiii.
51. Walker, *Harold the Last Anglo-Saxon King*, p. 138.
52. Ibid.
53. *Vita*, p. 30-31.
54. Ibid, p. 31.
55. Snorri Sturluson, *Harald's Saga*, p. 150.
56. Rogers, 'The Waltham Abbey Relic-list', p. 167.
57. Williams, 'The Spindle Side', p. 1.
58. Walker, *Harold the Last Anglo-Saxon King*, p. 120.

Chapter Seven

1. *Waltham Chronicle*, p. 55.
2. Williams, 'The Spindle Side', pp. 9, 11.
3. Sharpe, *King Harold's Daughter*, p. 21.
4. Fell, *Women in Anglo Saxon England*, page 89.
5. Flint, *Edith the Fair Visionary of Walsingham*, p. 101.
6. Ibid, p. 35.
7. The Shrine of Our Lady of Walsingham, 'The Story So Far'.
8. Dickinson, 'The Shrine of Our Lady of Walsingham,' p. xviii.

9. Flint, *Edith the Fair*, p. xviii.
10. Barlow, *Godwins*, p. 78.
11. S 1535, *The Electronic Sawyer, Online Catalogue of AngloSaxon Charters*, accessed on 09/10/2023 https://esawyer.lib.cam.ac.uk/charter/1535.html.
12. Williams, 'The Spindle Side', p. 11.
13. Ibid.
14. Clarke, *The English Nobility under Edward the Confessor*, pp. 273-279; Searle, *Women and the Legitimization of Succession at the Norman Conquest*, p. 176.
15. *GND*, pp. 161-163.
16. Williams, 'The Spindle Side', p. 11.
17. Ælfgifu of Northampton's relationship with Cnut was *more Danico*.
18. *Waltham Chronicle*, p. 54n1.
19. William of Poitiers, *Gesta*.
20. *Vita Haroldi*, p. 116.
21. I am grateful to Ann Williams.
22. Walker, *Harold the Last Anglo-Saxon King*, p. 69.
23. Ibid, p. 147.
24. Ibid, p. 146.
25. Walker, *Harold the Last Anglo-Saxon King*, p. 69.
26. Fell, *Women in Anglo Saxon England*, p. 97.
27. Walker, *Harold the Last Anglo-Saxon King*, p. 147.
28. Ibid.
29. *Waltham Chronicle*, p. 54.
30. *Vita Haroldi*, pp. 187-188.
31. Freeman, *The History of the Norman Conquest of England*, vol. 3, pp. 754-757.
32. Walker, *Harold the Last Anglo-Saxon King*, p. 150.
33. Thank you to Tricia Gurnett from the King Harold Society for clarifying.
34. *Waltham Chronicle*, p. xlvii.
35. Ibid.
36. *Vita Haroldi*, p. 119; *Waltham Chronicle*, p. xlvii.
37. For 1044–1045, see *ASC, C, D, E*, pp. 164-165.
38. Ibid, *E*, pp. 166-167.
39. Ibid, *C*, p. 166.
40. Ibid, *D*, p. 167.
41. Ibid, *C*, p. 166.
42. *Vita Haroldi*, p. 118.
43. *Waltham Chronicle*, p. xx.
44. Ibid, p. 27.
45. *Waltham Chronicle*, p. xix.
46. *Waltham Chronicle*, p. xx.
47. Ibid, p. xxiv, n2.
48. Napier, *The Old English Version of the Enlarged Rule of Chrodegang with the Latin Original*, cap. 11.
49. Ibid, caps. 8, 44.
50. Ibid, cap. 25.
51. *Waltham Chronicle*, p. xxiii.

52. Knowles, *Monastic Order in England*, p. 463.
53. *Waltham Chronicle,* p. xxiii.
54. *Waltham Chronicle,* p. xxiii.

Chapter Eight

1. *ASC, C,* p. 171.
2. John of Worcester, *Chronicle,* p. 548.
3. *Vita,* p. 16.
4. Grills, *The Life and Times of Godwine,* p. 129.
5. *Vita,* p. xv.
6. Ibid, p. 15-16.
7. Ibid, p. 16.
8. Ibid.
9. Grills, *The Life and Times of Godwine,* p. 184.
10. Hearne, *Hemingi,* pp. 275-276.
11. Now in Oxford since 1974.
12. It is not certain when Hrani died, but he was last recorded by John of Worcester as acting with Godwin, Siward, and Leofric in Worcester on behalf of Harthacnut in 1041.
13. Hearne, *Hemingi* pp. 275-276. Swegn repeats the allegation after he became earl.
14. Mason, *The House of Godwine,* p. 57.
15. Ker, 'Hemming's Cartulary: A Description of Two Worcester Cartularies, eds Cotton Tiberius A. xiii', pp. 49-75.
16. Licence, *Edward the Confessor,* p. 103.
17. Key, *The House of Godwin* p. 106.
18. Barlow, *Godwins,* p. 33.
19. Ibid.
20. Grills, *The Life and Times of Godwine,* p. 148.
21. John of Worcester, *Chronicle,* p. 549.
22. Grills, *The Life and Times of Godwine,* p. 148.
23. Thank you to Ann Williams, for the clarification.
24. Janet Nelson, 'The First Use of the Second Anglo-Saxon Ordo', p. 122.
25. Whitehead, *Mercia: The Rise and Fall of a Kingdom,* p. 86.
26. Licence, *Edward the Confessor,* p. 11.
27. Grills, *The Life and Times of Godwine,* 149.
28. Ibid.
29. Licence, *Edward the Confessor,* p. 111.
30. *ASC C,* p. 16.
31. John of Worcester, *Chronicle,* p. 549, named her as Eadgifu.
32. *The Domesday Book.* I am grateful to Sharon Bennett Connolly, 23/06/2022.
33. Ann Williams, *Kingship and Government in Pre-Conquest England c. 500–1066,* p. 101n51.
34. John of Worcester, *Chronicle,* p. 549.
35. Ibid.
36. *Hemingi,* pp. 275-276; Grills, *The Life and Times of Godwine,* p. 129.

37. Grills, *The Life and Times of Godwine*, p. 149.
38. Eadmer, *Historia Novorum*, p. 6.
39. Grills, *The Life and Times of Godwine*, pp. 149-150.
40. Barlow, *Edward*, p. 91.
41. Swein Estridson was commonly known by his mother's name which shows general contempt for his father, Ulf.
42. Grills, *The Life and Times of Godwine*, p. 152.
43. Magnus' was the son of Harald Sigurdson's (Hardrada) half-brother Olaf. Grills, *The Life and Times of Godwine*, p. 153, cites Snorri Sturluson: they had met at the Swedish court.
44. Grills, *The Life and Times of Godwine*, p. 153.
45. Ibid.
46. Ibid.
47. *ASC, D*, p. 167.
48. *ASC*, pp. 164-165.
49. John of Worcester, p. *Chronicle*, p. 545.
50. Theodoricus Monachus, *Historia de Antiquitate Regum Norwegiensiem*, p. 44.
51. Grills, *The Life and Times of Godwine*, p. 154
52. Ibid, p. 154.
53. *ASC, D*, p. 167.
54. John of Worcester, *Chronicle*, p. 549.
55. *ASC, D*, p. 169.

Chapter Nine

1. Barlow, *Edward*, pp. 97-98.
2. *ASC, E*, p. 168.
3. Mason, *The House of Godwine*, p. 55.
4. Licence, *Edward the Confessor*, p. 121.
5. *ASC, C*, p. 168.
6. Licence, *Edward the Confessor*, p. 121.
7. *ASC D, E*, pp. 168-167.
8. South Wales.
9. John of Worcester, *Chronicle*, p. 551.
10. *ASC, E*, p. 168.
11. *ASC, C, D*, pp. 168-169. The North Mouth is identified as Wantsum Channel.
12. *ASC, C, D*, pp. 168-169.
13. *Chronicle C*, correctly says Essex, (the Naze) and *D* incorrectly, Sussex.
14. John of Worcester says only 2 were left, *Chronicle*, p. 551.
15. *ASC*, pp. 184-185.
16. John of Worcester, *Chronicle*, pp. 549, 551.
17. *ASC, D*, p. 170.
18. *ASC E, C*, p. 168.
19. *ASC, C*, p. 168.
20. John of Worcester, *Chronicle*, p. 551.
21. Adam of Bremen, pp. 154-155, in Licence, *Edward the Confessor*, p. 123.

22. *ASC C, E,* pp. 168-169.
23. *ASC, C,* p. 171.
24. Grills, *The Life and Times of Godwine,* p. 158.
25. Licence, *Edward the Confessor,* p. 124; Grills, *The Life and Times of Godwine,* p. 157.
26. John of Worcester, *Chronicle,* p. 551.
27. *ASC C, E,* pp. 168-169; John of Worcester, *Chronicle,* p. 551.
28. Douglas, *William the Conqueror,* p. 76.
29. Bates, *William the Conqueror,* p. 100.
30. Licence, *Edward the Confessor,* p. 120.
31. *ASC, C, E,* pp. 168-169.
32. Mason, *The House of Godwine,* p. 55.
33. John of Worcester, *Chronicle,* p. 551.
34. Mason, *The House of Godwine,* p. 55.
35. Grills, *The Life and Times of Godwine,* p. 159.
36. Walker, *Harold the Last Anglo-Saxon King,* p. 25.
37. Fryde et al, *Handbook of British Chronology,* p. 214.
38. Mason, *The House of Godwine,* p. 58.
39. *ASC,* pp. 170-171.
40. Mason, *The House of Godwine,* p. 58.
41. *Vita,* p. 17.
42. John of Worcester, *Chronicle,* pp. 552- 553; *ASC, E, C, D,* pp. 174-176.
43. Walker, *Harold the Last Anglo-Saxon King,* p. 31.
44. Freeman, *The History of the Norman Conquest of England,* vol 2, p. 70n2.
45. Walker, *Harold the Last Anglo-Saxon King,* p. 32.
46. *Vita,* p. 19.
47. Ibid.
48. Williams, 'Spoliation of Worcester', pp. 368-388; Williams, 'Cockles amongst the wheat', pp. 12-14.
49. Stafford, *Queen Emma & Queen Edith* p. 139.
50. *Vita,* p. 19.
51. Ibid.
52. Mason, *The House of Godwine,* p. 59.
53. *Vita,* p. 21.
54. Grills, *The Life and Times of Godwine,* p. 155.
55. *Vita,* p. 24.
56. *ASC, E,* p. 172.
57. Ibid, E, pp. 172-173.
58. Ibid.
59. Ibid, p. 173.
60. Ibid, *E,* pp. 173, 175.
61. John of Worcester, *Chronicle,* p. 559.
62. *ASC, E,* p. 174.
63. Ibid.
64. Ibid, *E,* p. 173.
65. Ibid, *D,* p. 175.
66. John of Worcester, *Chronicle,* p. 559.

67. *ASC, D*, p. 175.
68. Ibid, *E*, p. 174.
69. Ibid, *D*, p. 175.
70. John of Worcester, *Chronicle*, p. 561.
71. Ibid.
72. DeVries, *The Norwegian Invasion of England in 1066*, p. 127.
73. *ASC, D*, p. 175.
74. Ibid, *C, E*, pp. 174, 176.
75. Ibid, *D*, p. 175.
76. *Vita Haroldi*, p. 118.
77. *ASC, E*, p. 176.
78. *Vita*, pp. 21-22.
79. Ibid, p. 22.
80. Licence, *Edward the Confessor*, p. 140.
81. *Vita*, p. 22; *ASC, E*, p. 176, reports that Earls Godwin and Swein rode to Bosham. John of Worcester states that Godwin, Swein, and Gyrth went into Thorney where a ship had been prepared for them, *Chronicle*, p. 561.
82. John of Worcester, *Chronicle*, p. 563.
83. *ASC, D*, p. 175.
84. *Vita*, p. 23.
85. *ASC, D*, p. 176, does not mention the archbishop's hunt of Earl Godwin just as the *Vita* does not mention the pursuit of Harold and Leofwin.
86. Ibid, *E*, p. 175.
87. *Vita*, p. 21.
88. Ibid, p. 22.
89. Ibid, p. 23.
90. *ASC, D, E*, p. 176, names the nunnery as Wherwell where Edward's half-sister was abbess. John of Worcester, *Chronicle*, p. 563, states she was sent packing on foot with just one handmaid.
91. John of Worcester, *Chronicle*, p. 563.
92. *Vita*, p. 23.
93. Ibid, p. 23.
94. *ASC, D*, p. 176.

Chapter Ten

1. *ASC, D*, p. 176.
2. Symeon of Durham, *Historia Regum*, p. 168.
3. John of Worcester, *Chronicle*, p. 563.
4. Wace, *His Chronicle of the Norman Conquest from the Roman de Rou*, tr. Edgar Taylor, pp. 66-67.
5. Rex, *The Last English King*, pp. 136-137, discusses the absurd assertions employed by the Norman Chroniclers to emphasise William's claim to the throne.
6. Wace, *Chronicle*, p. 67.
7. Licence, *Edward the Confessor*, p. 144,
8. Ibid.

9. Orderic Vitalis, *Historica Ecclesiastic*, pp. 184-187, 214.
10. Guy, Bishop of Amiens, *Carmen de Haestingae Proelio*, p. xiii.
11. Ibid, pp. xl-xliii.
12. Ibid, p. 19.
13. *GND,* vol. 2, p. 158.
14. William of Poitiers, *Gesta,* pp. 19, 121. Also see p. xx for the date.
15. Licence, *Edward the Confessor*, pp. 146-147.
16. Ibid, p. 147.
17. Ibid.
18. *Vita*, p. 23, this is in contrast with the *ASC,* who states that Edith was banished to Edward's sister's abbey of Wherwell.
19. Licence, *Edward the Confessor*, p. 147.
20. Abels, 'Royal Succession and the Growth of Political Stability in Ninth Century Wessex', p. 92.
21. William of Jumièges' tale that Edward offered the throne to William through Archbishop Robert as his narrative to justify the Conqueror's invasion, and this was widely accepted in the Normano sphere and followed by such writers as Poitiers and Vitalis.
22. *Vita*, pp. 20-21.
23. *GND*, pp. 159-160, no date is given but likely to be between 1051-1052.
24. *Vita*, p. 23.
25. Licence, *Edward the Confessor*, p. 144.
26. Bates, *William the Conqueror*, p.183.
27. Ronay, *The Lost King of England*, p. 71.
28. *ASC, C, D*, pp. 184-185.
29. Bates, *William the Conqueror*, p. 113.
30. Licence, *Edward the Confessor*, p. 147.
31. Wace, *Chronicle*, p. 67.

Chapter Eleven

1. *ASC, D*, p. 176.
2. *Vita*, p. 26.
3. Ibid.
4. Ibid.
5. Barlow, *Edward*, p. 94.
6. Ann Williams, *Land, Power and Politics: The Family and Career of Odda of Deerhurst*, p. 1.
7. *ASC, D, E*, p. 176.
8. Grills, *The Life and Times of Godwine*, p. 184.
9. Ibid, *D*, p. 203.
10. *The Annals of Tigernach*, vol. 2, pp. 376-402.
11. Walker, *Harold the Last Anglo-Saxon King*, p. 33.
12. *Historia Ecclesie*, p. 196.

Notes

13. *ASC, D*, p. 176 identifies 'Gruffudd' as Gruffudd ap Llywelyn; Licence, *Edward the Confessor*, p. 149, as Gruffudd ap Rhydderch, seems more likely.
14. *ASC, D*, p. 176.
15. *ASC, D*, pp. 178-179.
16. *ASC, E*, p. 177.
17. Grills, *The Life and Times of Godwine*, p. 191.
18. *ASC, C*, p. 182; John of Worcester, *Chronicle*, p. 571.
19. *Vita*, p 26.
20. *ASC, E*, p. 177.
21. *ASC, E*, p. 177.
22. *ASC, D*, p. 179.
23. *ASC, C*, p. 178.
24. *ASC, C,D*, pp. 178-179.
25. *ASC, E*, p. 177.
26. Grills, *The Life and Times of Godwine*, p. 192.
27. *AFC, F,* pp. 177-179.
28. *ASC, E*, p. 178.
29. Ibid.
30. Ibid.
31. Grills, *The Life and Times of Godwine*, p. 193.
32. Ibid.
33. Ibid.
34. Corner, *Porlock in Those Days*, p. 22.
35. *ASC, E*, p. 178.
36. *Vita*, pp. 26-27.
37. *ASC, D*, p. 179.
38. Grills, *The Life and Times of Godwine*, p. 194.
39. Ibid, p. 195.
40. *Vita*, pp. 26-27.
41. *ASC, C, D,* pp. 180-181.
42. *Vita*, p. 27.
43. Douglas *William the Conqueror*, pp. 63–64.
44. *Vita*, p. 27.
45. *ASC, E*, p. 180.
46. *Vita*, p. 27.
47. Ibid.
48. *ASC, D*, p. 181.
49. *Vita*, p. 27.
50. Ibid.
51. Ibid, pp. 27-28.
52. *ASC, C, D,* pp. 180-181.
53. Ibid.
54. John of Worcester, *Chronicle*, p. 571.
55. *ASC, C, D, E,* pp. 180-181.
56. *ASC, E*, pp. 181-183.
57. Ibid, p. 183.

58. *Vita*, p. 27.
59. Licence, *Edward the Confessor*, p. 154
60. Robertson, *Anglo-Saxon*, pp. 456-458.
61. Williams, *Odda*, p. 2.
62. *ASC, E*, p. 181.
63. John of Worcester, *Chronicle*, p. 561.
64. Ibid, p. 571.
65. Grills, *The Life and Times of Godwine*, p. 199.
66. Ibid.
67. *ASC, C*, p. 182; John of Worcester, *Chronicle*, p. 571.
68. Grills, *The Life and Times of Godwine*, p. 199.

Chapter Twelve

1. Breeze, *The Anglo-Saxon Chronicle for 1053 and the killing of Rhys ap Rhydderch*, pp. 168–169.
2. John of Worcester, *Chronicle*, p. 173.
3. *ASC C, D, E*, pp. 182-185.
4. *Vita*, p. 30.
5. *Vita*, pp. 30-31.
6. William of Malmesbury, *Vita Wulfstani*, p. 121.
7. Key, *The House of Godwin* p. 148.
8. Walker, *Harold the Last Anglo-Saxon King*, p. 61.
9. Rex, *The Last English King*, p. 89
10. Walker, *Harold the Last Anglo-Saxon King*, p. 84.
11. Ibid, p. 69.
12. Ibid, p. 62.
13. Ibid.
14. *Domesday Book Sussex*, 1,1.
15. Davies and Davies, *The Last King of Wales*, kindle edition, loc. 888.
16. *ASC, C, D*, pp. 184-185.
17. *ASC, C, D, E*, pp. 184-187; John of Worcester, states that Alfgar was 'guiltless', *Chronicle*, p. 577.
18. Davies and Davies, *The Last King of Wales*, loc. 952.
19. *ASC, C, D*, pp. 184-185.
20. John of Worcester, *Chronicle*, p. 529.
21. *ASC, C*, p. 184.
22. John of Worcester, *Chronicle*, p. 577.
23. Ibid.
24. *ASC, C, D, E*, pp. 184-187.
25. Ibid, *C*, p. 186.
26. John of Worcester, *Chronicle*, p. 577, refers to him as 'timidus'.
27. *The Last King of Wales*, loc. 1020.
28. *ASC, C, D*, pp. 186 and 187.
29. John of Worcester, *Chronicle*, p. 579.
30. Walker, *Harold the Last Anglo-Saxon King*, p. 90.

31. Davies and Davies, *The Last King of Wales*, loc. 167.
32. Gerald of Wales, *The Description of Wales*, p. 220.
33. *Sermo Lupi ad Anglos*, p. 59.
34. *ASC, C*, pp. 186-187; John of Worcester, *Chronicle*, p. 579.
35. Davies and Davies, *The Last King of Wales*, loc. 913.
36. Ibid.
37. Ibid, loc. 939.
38. Ibid, loc. 913.
39. Ibid, loc.939.
40. Ibid, loc. 979.
41. Ibid.
42. Ibid.
43. *Brut y Tywysogion, Peniarth*, MS. 20T, s.a. 1056.
44. Davies and Davies, *The Last King of Wales*, loc. 1005.
45. John of Worcester, *Chronicle*, p. 579.
46. *Domesday Book*, 'Herefordshire' folio, in Davies and Davies, *The Last King of Wales*, loc. 979.
47. *ASC, C*, p. 186.
48. John of Worcester, *Chronicle*, p. 579.
49. Ibid, pp. 579-581.
50. Thorpe, *Laws and Institutes*, vol. 2, pp. 254-255, 294-295.
51. DeVries, *The Norwegian Invasion of England in 1066*, p. 138.
52. *ASC, C, D*, pp. 186-187.
53. Petts, *The Early Medieval Church in Wales*, p. 170.
54. Davies and Davies, *The Last King of Wales*, loc. 1144.
55. Stenton, *Anglo-Saxon England*, p 573.
56. *ASC C*, p. 186.
57. Davies and Davies, *The Last King of Wales*, loc. 1172.
58. Stenton, *Anglo-Saxon England*, p. 574.

Chapter Thirteen

1. *ASC C, D*, p. 186.
2. Williams, 'The King's Nephew', pp. 327-340.
3. DeVries, *The Norwegian Invasion of England in 1066*, p. 140,
4. *ASC, C, D*, pp. 186-187.
5. *ASC, C, D*, pp. 184-185.
6. Licence, *Edward the Confessor*, p. 175.
7. Ronay, *The Lost King of England*, pp. 80-81.
8. Walker, *Harold the Last Anglo-Saxon King*, p. 92.
9. Ibid; Rogers, 'The Waltham Abbey Relic-list', p. 167.
10. *Vita*, p. 33.
11. Walker, *Harold the Last Anglo-Saxon King*, p. 93.
12. Ibid.
13. Barlow, *Godwins*, p. 81, followed by Walker, *Harold the Last Anglo-Saxon King*, p. 93.

14. *Vita*, p. 33.
15. Walker, *Harold the Last Anglo-Saxon King*, p. 93.
16. *Vita*, p. 33.
17. Ibid, p. 34.
18. Mason, *The House of Godwine*, p. 93.
19. Barlow, *Edward*, p. 218.
20. Wolf, 'Who was Agatha the Ancestress of Scottish and English Kings?', p. 1.
21. Licence, *Edward the Confessor*, p. 175.
22. Ronay, *The Lost King of England*, pp. 83-88.
23. *ASC, D, E*, pp. 187-188.
24. Ibid, *D*, p. 188.
25. Ibid, *E*, p. 188.
26. Licence, *Edward the Confessor*, p. 188.
27. John of Worcester, *Chronicle*, p. 583.
28. Barlow, *Edward*, p. 217.
29. Mason, *The House of Godwine*, p. 92.
30. Ibid, p. 93.
31. *Vita*, p. lxvi.
32. John of Worcester, *Chronicle*, p. 585.
33. Mason, *The House of Godwine*, p. 93.
34. Walker, *Harold the Last Anglo-Saxon King*, p. 95.
35. *ASC, D*, p. 199.
36. *ASC, D*, p. 188.
37. *Vita*, p. 33n2.
38. DeVries, *The Norwegian Invasion of England in 1066*, p. 140.
39. *ASC, D*, p. 188.
40. John of Worcester, *Chronicle*, p. 585.
41. Davies and Davies, *The Last King of Wales*, loc. 1212.
42. *Brut y Tywysogyon, Red Book of Hergest Version*, s.a. 1058.
43. *The Annals of Tigernach*, s. a. 1058.
44. Davies and Davies, *The Last King of Wales*, loc. 1212.
45. Ibid.
46. Licence, *Edward the Confessor*, p. 191.
47. Barlow, *Edward*, p. 209.
48. *ASC, E, F*, p. 188. See Licence, *Edward the Confessor*, pp. 192-193, for more on this theory.
49. *Vita*, p. 43.

Chapter Fourteen

1. *Vita*, p. 40.
2. *ASC*, p. 189.
3. Symeon of Durham, *Historia Regum*, p. 174, also gives the date of 1059; *Vita* p. 43.
4. *Waltham Chronicle*, p. 31.
5. Rogers, 'The Waltham Abbey Relic-list', p. 167.
6. *Waltham Chronicle*, p. 35.

Notes

7. Ibid, p. 35.
8. Ibid.
9. Ibid, pp. 36-37.
10. Ibid.
11. Ibid.
12. *Vita*, p. 34.
13. Ibid.
14. Barlow, *Godwins*, p. 89.
15. *Vita*, p. 34n5.
16. Ibid, p. 34. Bray and McGurk state in John of Worcester, p. 587n9 that this is also mentioned in *Vita Wulfstani*, pp. 16-17.
17. Barlow, *Godwins*, p. 89.
18. *Vita*, p. 34.
19. Barlow, *Godwins*, p. 89.
20. *Vita*, p. 35.
21. Barlow, *Godwins*, p. 89.
22. *Vita*, p. 35.
23. Whitehead, *The Rise and Fall of a Kingdom*, p. 210.
24. John of Worcester, *Chronicle*, p. 589.
25. *ASC, D*, p, 191.
26. Barlow, *Godwins*, p. 90.
27. *Vita*, p. 43.
28. Ibid, p. 57.
29. *ASC, D*, p. 191; John of Worcester, *Chronicle*, p. 593; Rex, *The Last English King*, p. 97.
30. John of Worcester, *Chronicle*, p. 593.
31. Charles-Edwards et al, *The Welsh King and his Court*, pp. 19, 27; literally the head of the household; *pen* meaning head and *teulu* meaning household.
32. John of Worcester, *Chronicle*, p. 593.
33. *ASC*, p. 191; John of Worcester, 1063.
34. Davies and Davies, *The Last King of Wales,* loc. 2066.
35. Maund, 'The Welsh Alliances of Earl Alfgar of Mercia', pp. 183-184; Barlow, *Edward*, p. 120.
36. Walker, *Harold the Last Anglo-Saxon King*, p. 119.
37. Stenton, *Anglo-Saxon England*, p. 576.
38. *Vita*, p. 42.
39. Gerald of Wales, Book ii, ch 3, cited by Rex, *The Last English King*, p. 97.
40. Ibid.
41. Davies and Davies, *The Last King of Wales*, loc. 1836. See loc. 2038 for the death of Alfgar.
42. Ibid, loc. 2156.
43. Powel, *The Historie of Cambria*, p. 101, in Davies and Davies, *The Last King of Wales,* loc. 2156.
44. Ibid, 2156.
45. Ibid, 2272.
46. *ASC, D*, p. 191.
47. *ASC, E*, p. 190.

48. John of Worcester, *Chronicle*, p. 597.
49. Davies and Davies, *The Last King of Wales*, loc. 2286 for examples of *teulus* abandoning their lord in literature.
50. Hudson, *The Destruction of Gruffudd ap* Llywelyn, pp. 331-350, in Ibid, loc. 2299.
51. Davies and Davies, *The Last King of Wales*, loc. 2299.
52. For more on this, see Ibid.
53. Davies and Davies, *The Last King of Wales*, loc 1822.
54. Davies, 'The Last King of Wales', 09/12/2012, https://www.iwa.wales/agenda/2012/08/the-last-king-of-wales/ .
55. Gerald of Wales, *Opera*, vol. 4, pp. 217-218.
56. John of Salisbury, *Policraticus*, vol. 2, p. 19.
57. John of Worcester, *Chronicle*, p. 593.
58. *Vita*, p. 42.
59. Davies and Davies, *The Last King of Wales*, loc. 2066.
60. Ibid, *loc.* 2130, to read more.
61. Jones, 'The Life of Saint Gwynllyw', https://www.maryjones.us/ctexts/gwynllyw.html, accessed 21/11/2023.
62. Davies and Davies, *The Last King of Wales*, loc. 2142.
63. Ibid, 2272.
64. *Brut* (Pen. 20), *s.a.* 1063.
65. Davies and Davies, *The Last King of Wales*, loc, 2396.
66. *Vita*, 42.
67. Stenton, *Anglo-Saxon England*, pp. 214–215.
68. F.M. Powicke, *The Thirteenth Century, 1216– 1307*, pp. 688-689.
69. Davies and Davies, *The Last King of Wales*, loc. 2549.

Chapter Fifteen

1. Douglas *William the Conqueror*, p. 15 also see n2 below, and p. 379.
2. Ibid, p. 379.
3. Ibid, p. 32.
4. Douglas and Greenway, *English Historical Documents*, vol. 2, p. 69.
5. Douglas *William the Conqueror*, p. 37.
6. Orderic Vitalis, *Historia Ecclesiastica*, vol. 3, p. 229.
7. *GND*, p. 93; Douglas *William the Conqueror*, p. 40; Bates, *William the Conqueror*, p. 62.
8. *GND*, Orderic interpolation, p. 95.
9. Ibid.
10. *GND*, p. 103; Douglas and Greenway, *English Historical Documents*, vol. 2, p. 51.
11. Douglas *William the Conqueror*, p. 119.
12. William of Poitiers, *Gesta*, pp.11-13.
13. Ibid.
14. Ibid, p. 81; also p. 80n2; Douglas, *William the Conqueror*, p. 51.
15. Elizabeth Searle, *Predatory Kinship and the Creation of Norman Power, 840–1066*, pp. 196-198.
16. Douglas *William the Conqueror*, p. 53.
17. *Vita*, p. 6.

18. Latin for 'under-king'.
19. Rex, *The Last English King*, p. 133.
20. Ibid, p. 132.
21. Wace, *Chronicle*, pp. 75-76.
22. Rex, *The Last English King*, pp. 134-35.
23. *GND*, p. 161.
24. Rex, *The Last English King*, p. 137.
25. Ibid., p. 295n18.
26. Ibid, p. 138.
27. Wilson, *The Bayeux Tapestry*, pl. 7.
28. William of Poitiers, *Gesta*, p. 71.
29. Rex, *The Last English King*, p. 138.
30. Ibid.
31. William of Poitiers, *Gesta*, p. 71.
32. *Code of Canon Law*; Stenton, *Anglo-Saxon England*, p. 578, thought Harold could withdraw from the oath later, claiming duress.
33. Corroborated by Bridgeford, *1066: The Hidden History of the Bayeux Tapestry*, pp. 67-68.
34. Rex, *The Last English King*, p. 138.
35. Ibid, p. 142.
36. *GND*, pp. 159-161.
37. Lawson, The Battle of Hastings 1066; Wace, *Chronicle*, p. 83, has the oathtaking at Bayeux, p. 83.
38. William of Poitiers, *Gesta*, p. 121.
39. *ASC, C, D, E, F*, pp. 180-181.
40. *ASC, E, F*, p. 183.
41. Eadmer, *Historia Novorum*, p. 6.
42. Walker, *Harold the Last Anglo-Saxon King*, p. 57.
43. *ASC, C, D, E*, pp. 182-183.
44. Ibid; *Vita*, p. 28; Walker, *Harold the Last Anglo-Saxon King*, p. 55.
45. Barlow, *Edward*, p. 303.

Chapter Sixteen

1. Bridgeford, *The Hidden History of the Bayeux Tapestry*, p. 23.
2. Ibid.
3. *ASC, E*, pp. 172-181.
4. Eadmer, *Historia Novorum*, p. 6.
5. Bridgeford, *The Hidden History of the Bayeux Tapestry*, p. 1.
6. Ibid, p. 3.
7. Rex, *The Last English King*, p. 146; Bridgeford, *The Hidden History of the Bayeux Tapestry*, p. 51.
8. Bridgeford, *The Hidden History of the Bayeux Tapestry*, p. 23.
9. Eadmer, *Historia Novorum*, p. 6. It is dubious that the dialogues are *verbatim*, however chroniclers were attempting to give an impression of what was likely to have been said.
10. Ibid.

11. William of Poitiers, *Gesta*, p. 69.
12. Eadmer, p. 7.
13. Ibid.
14. Ibid, pp. 7-8.
15. Ibid.
16. Wace, *Chronicle*, p. 72.
17. Eadmer, *Historia Novorum*, p. 7.
18. Rex, *The Last English King*, p. 137.
19. Eadmer, *Historia Novorum*, p. 7.
20. William of Poitiers, *Gesta*, p. 71.
21. Wilson, *The Bayeux Tapestry*, pl 24.
22. Douglas, *William the Conqueror*, p. 78.
23. Bridgeford, *The Hidden History of the Bayeux Tapestry*, p. 86.
24. Ibid.
25. Wilson, *The Bayeux Tapestry*, pl 26.
26. Ibid.
27. Eadmer, *Historia Novorum*, p. 8.
28. Ibid, p. viii.
29. Ibid, p. viii-ix.
30. Ibid, p. x.
31. Walker, *Harold the Last Anglo-Saxon King*, p. 108. Æthelric, deposed in 1070, died sometime after 1076. It is not likely that Eadmer, born two years after Æthelric was promoted to Selsey, had been able to speak with the bishop before he died in 1076. Walker's assertion that Eadmer himself admitted that he had got the information for his writings straight from Æthelric was incorrect, Walker, p. 230; In his *Life of Dunstan*, Eadmer states that he had conferred with a cleric named Æthelred, who had in turn been a follower of Æthelric. Eadmer, *Lives and Miracles of Saints*, p. 47.
32. Eadmer, *Historia Novorum*, p. 7.
33. Wilson, *The Bayeux Tapestry*, pl 28.
34. Ibid.
35. Ibid, p. 197.
36. Bridgeford, *The Hidden History of the Bayeux Tapestry*, p. 59.
37. Ibid, p. 161.
38. Eadmer, *Historia Novorum*, p. 9.

Chapter Seventeen

1. Barlow, *Godwins*, p. 115.
2. *ASC, C, D, E,* pp. 190-191; John of Worcester, *Chronicle*, p. 597.
3. *ASC, C,* p. 192.
4. *Vita,* p. 50n2.
5. *ASC C, D,* pp. 190-191; John of Worcester, *Chronicle*, p. 597.
6. Williams, 'Thegnly Piety and Ecclesiastical Patronage in the Late Old English Kingdom, pp. xxiv, 10-11.
7. John of Worcester, *Chronicle*, p. 599.
8. Covered in Fletcher, *Bloodfeud in Anglo-Saxon England*.
9. Ibid, p. 147.

10. Ibid, p. 147, states somewhere between 1041 and 1055.
11. Ibid, p. 158.
12. *ASC C, D,* pp. 184-185.
13. *Vita,* p. 43.
14. Symeon of Durham, *Historia Regum,* vol. 2, pp. 174-175.
15. Kapelle, *The Norman conquest of the North*, pp. 91-93.
16. Fletcher, *Bloodfeud in Anglo-Saxon England*, p. 151.
17. Walker, *Harold the Last Anglo-Saxon King*, p. 120.
18. Geffrei Gaimar, *Lestorie des Engles solum la translacion maistre*, pp. 218-219, 5153-5182.
19. *Vita,* pp. 35-36.
20. Walker, *Harold the Last Anglo-Saxon King*, p. 122.
21. John of Worcester, *Chronicle*, p. 597.
22. *ASC,* pp. 190-192; *Vita,* p. 50 n4; John of Worcester, *Chronicle*, p. 599; see Fletcher, *Bloodfeud in Anglo-Saxon England*, p. 158 for blood connections.
23. Fletcher, *Bloodfeud in Anglo-Saxon England*, p. 159.
24. John of Worcester, *Chronicle*, p. 599; Fletcher, *Bloodfeud in Anglo-Saxon England*, p. 160.
25. Fletcher, *Bloodfeud in Anglo-Saxon England*, pp. 146-160.
26. Ibid, p. 146.
27. *ASC, D,* p. 191.
28. *ASC D, E,* pp. 190-193.
29. John of Worcester, *Chronicle*, p. 599, omits any mention of Morcar.
30. *ASC, D,* p. 194.
31. *ASC, C,* p. 192.
32. *ASC, D, E,* pp. 192-193; is omitted by *C.*
33. John of Worcester, *Chronicle*, p. 599.
34. *Vita,* p. 51.
35. Ibid.
36. Ibid.
37. Ibid, p. 52.
38. Ibid, p. 53; a dig at Harold's oath made to William in Normandy.
39. Ibid.
40. Ibid.
41. *ASC, D, E,* pp. 192-193.
42. Davis, 'East Anglia and the Danelaw', p. 38.
43. Hill, *The Road to Hastings*, p. 145.
44. Walker, *Harold the Last Anglo-Saxon King*, p. 118.
45. Ibid, p. 117.
46. Williams, *Kingship and Government*, p. 148.
47. *Vita,* p. 50n4.

Chapter Eighteen

1. *Vita,* pp. lxvi, p. lxxix.
2. Ibid, p. 53.
3. Ibid.

4. Ibid.
5. Orderic in *GND,* p. 169.
6. *Vita*, p. 54.
7. Ibid, p. 55.
8. Walker, *Harold the Last Anglo-Saxon King*, p. 128.
9. Barlow, *Godwins,* p. 124.
10. Walker, *Harold the Last Anglo-Saxon King*, p. 130.
11. Ibid, p. 131.
12. *ASC*, pp. 181-182.
13. Thanks to Ann Williams, for clarifying, 30/11/2023.
14. Barlow, *Godwins,* p. 82.
15. Ibid, p. 175.
16. William of Poitiers, *Gesta*, p. 133.
17. Walker, *Harold the Last Anglo-Saxon King*, p. 132.
18. Ibid.
19. *Vita*, p. 72.
20. Ibid, p. 73.
21. Ibid, p. 74.
22. *Vita*, pp. 75-76.
23. Ibid.
24. Ibid.
25. Mason, *The House of Godwine*, p. 133.
26. Ibid, pp. 133-134; *Vita*, p. 77.
27. Wilson, *The Bayeux Tapestry*, p. 30.
28. *Vita,* pp. 79-80.
29. John of Worcester, *Chronicle*, p. 601.
30. Wilson, *The Bayeux Tapestry*, pl 31.
31. William of Poitiers, *Gesta*, p. 100, states that Harold received an 'impious consecration from Stigand who had been deprived of his priestly office by the pope'.
32. Walker discusses in more detail, *Harold the Last Anglo-Saxon King*, p. 156.
33. *ASC*, pp. 194-195.
34. *Waltham Chronicle,* p. 45.
35. William of Malmesbury, *Vita Wulfstani*, p. 141.
36. Ibid.
37. Henry of Huntingdon, *The History of the English People,* p. 24. Perhaps a conflation of *D* chronicle suggesting Ealdred wanted to elevate Edgar.
38. *ASC, C, D,* pp. 180-181.

Chapter Nineteen

1. Walker, *Harold the Last Anglo-Saxon King*, p. 133.
2. *ASC, C, D*, pp. 194-195.
3. John of Worcester, *Chronicle* p. 601.
4. William of Malmesbury, *Vita Wulfstani*, ed. Darlington, pp. 22-23.
5. Walker suggests the Northumbrians believed that Tostig would be reinstated, *Harold the Last Anglo-Saxon King*, p. 157; Lawson, *Hastings,* p. 32.

6. Licence, *Edward the Confessor*, p. 45, believes that Edgar was exiled; Sharon Bennett Connolly, 21/05/2023, anecdotally.
7. Barlow, *Godwins*, p. 127.
8. William of Malmesbury, *Vita Wulfstani*, pp. 22-23.
9. Walker, *Harold the Last Anglo-Saxon King*, p. 132.
10. Ibid, p. 157.
11. Ibid.
12. William of Malmesbury, *Vita Wulfstani*, pp. 22-23.
13. Barlow, *Godwins*, p. 124, for acquiring landholdings, p. 128 for marriage; Walker, *Harold the Last Anglo-Saxon King*, pp. 157-158.
14. *GND*, pp. 161, 163.
15. Barlow, *Godwins*, p. 87.
16. Ibid, pp. 128, 170.
17. Walker, *Harold the Last Anglo-Saxon King* p. 160.
18. Ibid, p. 158.
19. Ibid, p. 162.
20. Ibid, p. 159.
21. Wilson, *The Bayeux Tapestry*, pls. 33, 34, 35.

Chapter Twenty

1. Wace, *Chronicle*, pp. 93-94.
2. Ibid, pp. 95-96.
3. Ibid, p. 96.
4. *GND,* p. 161.
5. William of Poitiers, *Gesta*, p. 101.
6. William of Jumièges, *Gesta Normannorum*, p. 161.
7. Wace, *Chronicle*, p. 97.
8. Ibid, p. 98.
9. Ibid.
10. Ibid, p. 98.
11. Ibid, p. 98n7.
12. William of Poitiers, *Gesta*, p. 101.
13. Orderic Vitalis, *Historic Ecclesiastica,* ed. Chibnall, pp. 142-143; William of Jumièges, *Gesta Normannorum*, p. 101n5.
14. Bates, *William the Conqueror*, p. 219; Douglas, *William the Conqueror*, p. 184.
15. William of Poitiers, *Gesta*, p. 105.
16. Orderic Vitalis, *Historic Ecclesiastica,* ed Chibnall, p. 143.
17. Morton, *Pope Alexander II and the Norman Conquest*. Armstrong, 'The Norman Conquest of England, the Papacy, and the Papal Banner', p. 47.
18. Douglas, *William the Conqueror*, p. 187.
19. William of Malmesbury, *Vita Wulfstani*, p. 151.
20. Mason, *The House of Godwine*, p. 144.
21. William of Poitiers, *Gesta*, p. 105.
22. Orderic Vitalis, *Historic Ecclesiatica,* ed. Chibnall, p. 143.
23. William of Malmesbury, *Vita Wulfstani*, p. 151.

24. Douglas, *William the Conqueror*, p. 187.
25. Armstrong, 'The Norman Conquest of England', p. 50.
26. Ibid, p. 47.
27. Ibid, pp. 47-48.
28. William of Poitiers, *Gesta*, p. 126.
29. Ibid, p. 153.
30. Armstrong, 'The Norman Conquest of England', pp. 47-48n6.
31. Ibid, pp. 48n7, 49n12.
32. Ibid, p. 48.
33. Morton, *Pope Alexander II and the Norman Conquest* pp. 362-368, in Armstrong, 'The Norman Conquest of England', p. 48.
34. Armstrong, 'The Norman Conquest of England', p. 48.
35. William of Poitiers, *Gesta*, pp. 100–103.
36. Ibid.
37. Ibid, pp. 104–107.
38. Armstrong, 'The Norman Conquest of England', p. 61.
39. Morton, *Pope Alexander II and the Norman Conquest*, p. 366, in Armstrong, 'The Norman Conquest of England', p. 48; Cowdrey, *Pope Gregory VII*, p. 59.
40. Armstrong, 'The Norman Conquest of England', p. 40.
41. William of Poitiers, *Gesta*, pp. 152-155.
42. Armstrong, 'The Norman Conquest of England', p. 62.
43. Ibid, p. 63.
44. Orderic Vitalis, *Historic Ecclesiastica*, ed. Prévost and Delisle, pp. 236-237.
45. Armstrong, 'The Norman Conquest of England', p. 64.
46. Bates, *William the Conqueror*, p. 336; Lanfranc was an Italian-born jurist who renounced his career for a life as a cleric, eventually coming to England become Archbishop of Canterbury in 1070.
47. Armstrong, 'The Norman Conquest of England', p. 64n114; Orderic Vitalis, *Historic Ecclesiastica*, ed. Prévost and Delisle, pp. 236–237; Bates, *William the Conqueror*, p. 336. Plate 7 is of William's second coronation with two of the papal legates and the papal banner sent by Pope Alexander in 1070, in the late eleventh century Ramsey Benedictional.
48. Armstrong, 'The Norman Conquest of England', p. 67.
49. Ibid, p. 50.
50. Licence, *Edward the Confessor*, p. 15.
51. Ibid, p. 16.
52. Garnett, *The Norman Conquest*, p. 43.

Chapter Twenty-one

1. DeVries, *The Norwegian Invasion of England in 1066*, p. 231; Jones, *The Forgotten Battle of 1066 Fulford*, p. 121.
2. Walker, *Harold the Last Anglo-Saxon King*, p. 157.
3. Orderic Vitalis, *Historic Ecclesiastica*, ed. Chibnall, p. 139, accuses Harold of depriving Tostig of his earldom and exiling him. He also claimed Tostig as the eldest brother.

4. Ibid, p. 141 states erroneously that they had become good friends by marrying two sisters.
5. Ibid.
6. Orderic Vitalis, *Historic Ecclesiastica*, ed. Chibnall, pp. 143-145; Jones, p. 123. The Scandinavian sagas mention that Tostig goes to Norway to visit Harald Sigurdsson (Hardrada). Orderic fails to mention Swein, but some of the more detailed sagas recall that Tostig visits his cousin Swein.
7. Snorri Sturluson, *King Harald's Saga*, pp. 136-138. The saga also has a chapter on Tostig's visit to Swein, pp. 135-136.
8. Ibid, pp 48-63.
9. Barlow, *Godwins*, p. 136.
10. Orderic Vitalis, *Historic Ecclesiastica*, ed. Chibnall, p. 145.
11. Ibid.
12. *ASC, C, D*, pp. 194-195.
13. John of Worcester, *Chronicle*, p. 601.
14. *ASC, C, D*, pp. 194-195.
15. *ASC, C, D*, pp. 196-197; John of Worcester, *Chronicle*, p. 601.
16. *ASC*, p. 197.
17. Geffrei Gaimar, *Lestorie des Engles solum la translacion maistre*, pp. 218-219, 5153-5182.
18. *ASC, C, E, D*, pp. 196-197.
19. *Brunemue*: possibly the Burnhams in Norfolk.
20. Jones, *The Forgotten Battle of 1066 Fulford*, p. 126.

Chapter Twenty-Two

1. *ASC, C*, p. 196.
2. Ibid, *D*, p. 197.
3. Ibid, *C*, p. 196.
4. Ibid, *E*, p. 197n14.
5. Walker, *Harold the Last Anglo-Saxon King*, p. 170.
6. Williams and Martin, *Domesday Book: A Complete Translation*, vol. 3, p. 979.
7. *Chronica de Johannis de Oxenedes*, p. 293, in Barlow, *Godwins*, p. 135; Williams, *The Estates of Harold Godwinson*, pp. 179-80. Eadgifu Swanneck was said to be a benefactor of the Abbey of St. Bennet.
8. Walker, *Harold the Last Anglo-Saxon King*, pp. 170-171.
9. *ASC, C*, p. 196; John of Worcester, *Chronicle*, p. 603, claims 500+ ships.
10. *ASC, C, D*, pp. 196-197.
11. *ASC, E*, p. 197.
12. John of Worcester, *Chronicle*, p. 603; Symeon of Durham, *Historia Regum*, vol. 2, p. 180.
13. *ASC, C*, p. 196.
14. Ibid.
15. John of Worcester, *Chronicle*, p. 603.
16. *Domesday*, p. 786.
17. van Houts, *The Normans in Britain*, p. 145.

18. Snorri Sturluson, *King Harald's Saga*, pp. 141-142.
19. Ibid, pp. 142-143.
20. Composed by the poet, Stein Herdisaran. Snorri Sturluson, *King Harald's Saga*, p. 144.
21. Ibid, p. 143n1; John of Worcester, *Chronicle*, p. 603.
22. Ibid, p. 145.
23. *ASC, C*, p. 197; John of Worcester, *Chronicle*, p. 603.
24. Snorri Sturluson, *King Harald's Saga*, p. 146.
25. *ASC, C*, p. 197.
26. Ibid.
27. *ASC C, D, E*, pp. 197-198.
28. Snorri Sturluson, *King Harald's Saga*, p. 146.
29. Ibid, pp. 146-147.
30. Ibid, p. 147.
31. Ibid.
32. Ibid, p. 148.
33. *ASC, C*, p. 198.
34. Jakobsson, *The Early Kings of Norway*, pp. 4-6.
35. I am grateful to Paul Mortimer for clarifying this for me, 08/12/2022.
36. Snorri Sturluson, *King Harald's Saga*, p. 149.
37. Ibid, pp. 150-151.
38. John of Worcester, *Chronicle*, p. 603.
39. *ASC, C*, p. 198.
40. Snorri Sturluson, *King Harald's Saga*, p. 152.
41. *ASC, C*, p. 198n5.
42. Ibid.
43. Henry of Huntingdon, *The History of the English People*, p. 25.
44. Snorri Sturluson, *King Harald's Saga*, p. 151.
45. Snorri Sturluson, *King Harald's Saga*, p. 152n1.
46. Snorri Sturluson, *King Harald's Saga*, p. 152.
47. Ibid, pp. 152-153.
48. Ibid, pp. 153-154.
49. The *C*, p. 198, tells us Harold allowed *Hardrada's* son Olaf to go free. For Tostig's sons, see *Vita*, p. lxxvi.
50. John of Worcester, *Chronicle*, p. 605.
51. *ASC, D*, p. 199; John of Worcester says 20 ships.
52. John of Worcester, *Chronicle*, p. 605.
53. *ASC., D*, p. 199.

Chapter Twenty-Three

1. Guy, Bishop of Amiens, *Carmen de Haestingae Proelio*, p. 7.
2. William of Poitiers, *Gesta*, p. 111.
3. Ibid.
4. van Houts, *The Ship List of William the Conqueror*, p. 179; William of Poitiers, *Gesta*, p. 107n2.
5. Wilson, *The Bayeux Tapestry*, pl. 42.

6. William of Poitiers, *Gesta*, p. 113. For the band, see Guy, Bishop of Amiens, *Carmen de Haestingae Proelio*, pp. 7, 9.
7. Guy, Bishop of Amiens, *Carmen de Haestingae Proelio*, p. 9; William of Poitiers, Gesta, p. 113.
8. Ibid.
9. Halley's Comet hung around until July 1066.
10. Aubrey, *The National and Domestic History of England*, p. 139.
11. Elisabeth van Houts, 'The Ship List of William the Conqueror', *Anglo-Norman Studies* 10 (1987), pp. 159-183.
12. William of Poitiers, *Gesta*, p. 117.
13. Guy, Bishop of Amiens, *Carmen de Haestingae Proelio*, p. lxvi.
14. Hill, p. 167.
15. Guy, Bishop of Amiens, *Carmen de Haestingae Proelio*, p. 11n3.
16. Wilson, *The Bayeux Tapestry*, pl. 46.
17. *ASC, D,* p. 199; William of Poitiers, *Gesta* p. 115.
18. Guy, Bishop of Amiens, *Carmen de Haestingae Proelio*, p. 11.
19. Ibid.
20. Freeman, *The History of the Norman Conquest of England*, vol. 3, p. 746; John of Worcester, *Chronicle*, p. 605; Stenton, *Anglo-Saxon England*, p. 592.
21. Hill, 'The Debate Concerning the Remains found in Bosham Church', p. 170.
22. Freeman, *The History of the Norman Conquest of England*, vol. 3, p. 746.
23. Orderic Vitalis, *Historic Ecclesiastica*, ed. Chibnall, p. 17.
24. Marren, *The Battles of York, Stamford Bridge, and Hastings*, p. 98.
25. van Houts, 'Orderic', p. xxi.
26. Bridgeford, *The Hidden History of the Bayeux Tapestry*, pp. 132-133.
27. Wilson, *The Bayeux Tapestry*, pls. 45, 46, 50.
28. Many thanks to Sharon Bennet-Connolly, 21/05/2023.
29. *ASC, D, E,* p. 199.
30. Many thanks to Roland Williamson, 09/09/2016.
31. Stenton, *Anglo-Saxon England*, p. 592.
32. John of Worcester, *Chronicle*, p. 605.
33. Guy, Bishop of Amiens, *Carmen de Haestingae Proelio*, p. 13.
34. Ibid, p. 13.
35. Ibid, p. 15.
36. Ibid.
37. Barlow, *Edward*, p. 171.
38. Guy, Bishop of Amiens, *Carmen de Haestingae Proelio*, pp. 15-16.
39. William of Poitiers, *Gesta*, p. 115.
40. Stafford, *Queen Emma & Queen Edith*, p. 275.
41. William of Poitiers, *Gesta*, p. 117.
42. Ibid, p. 121.
43. Ibid.
44. van Houts, 'The Norman Conquest through European Eyes', p. 22.
45. Ibid, p. 3.
46. Ibid p. 10.
47. Ibid, p. 9.
48. William of Poitiers, *Gesta*, p. 5n5.

Chapter Twenty-four

1. Marren, *The Battles of York, Stamford Bridge, and Hastings*, p. 101.
2. Orderic, ed. Chibnall, p. 173n3.
3. Howarth, *The Year of The Conquest*, pp. 167, 169.
4. Ibid.
5. Guy, Bishop of Amiens, *Carmen de Haestingae Proelio* p. lxxvii.
6. Gravett, *The Fall of Saxon England*, pp. 50-51.
7. Guy, Bishop of Amiens, *Carmen de Haestingae Proelio*, p. 19.
8. William of Poitiers, *Gesta*, p. 125.
9. Ibid.
10. Ibid.
11. Ibid
12. As shown on the Bayeux Tapestry. Wilson, *The Bayeux Tapestry*, p. 152.
13. Guy, Bishop of Amiens, *Carmen de Haestingae Proelio*, p. lxxiv.
14. Howarth, *The Year of The Conquest*, p. 169.
15. Guy, Bishop of Amiens, *Carmen de Haestingae Proelio*, p. 23.
16. *Brevis Relatio de Guillelmo Nobilissimo comite Normanorum* p 32. It was the first literary account to refer to the location of Harold's Standard. Guy, Bishop of Amiens, *Carmen de Haestingae Proelio*, p. lxxix.
17. Wace, *Chronicle*, p. 184.
18. Ibid, p. 191.
19. Marren, *The Battles of York, Stamford Bridge, and Hastings*, p. 106.
20. Wace, *Chronicle*, p. 174.
21. *GND*, p. 169.
22. Guy, Bishop of Amiens, *Carmen de Haestingae Proelio*, p. 21.
23. Ibid.
24. Marren, *The Battles of York, Stamford Bridge, and Hastings*, p. 102.
25. Ibid, p. 103.
26. Guy, Bishop of Amiens, *Carmen de Haestingae Proelio*, p. 25.
27. Guy, Bishop of Amiens, *Carmen de Haestingae Proelio*, p. lxxvii, believed it was a tactical success.
28. Ibid, p. 25.
29. Ibid.
30. Ibid, p. 27.
31. Guy, Bishop of Amiens, *Carmen de Haestingae Proelio*, p 27n4.
32. Ibid, p. 27.
33. William of Poitiers, *Gesta*, p. 128.
34. Guy, Bishop of Amiens, *Carmen de Haestingae Proelio*, p. 29.
35. The precise meaning may be lost in the translation, but it could be that William attacks Gyrth with his own spear.
36. Ibid, pp. 29, 31.
37. Ibid, p. 31.
38. Ibid, p. 33.
39. Ibid, p. 33.
40. William of Poitiers, *Gesta*, p. 137.

41. Ibid, p. 139.
42. Orderic Vitalis, *Historic Ecclesiastica*, ed. Chibnall, p. 177. Also appears in *GND*, p. 169; Searle, *The Chronicle of Battle Abbey*, p. 39.
43. A ridiculous exaggeration.
44. *AC*, p. 39.
45. Guy, Bishop of Amiens, *Carmen de Haestingae Proelio*, p. 35.

Chapter Twenty-five

1. Guy, Bishop of Amiens, *Carmen de Haestingae Proelio*; Wilson, *The Bayeux Tapestry*, pl.71.
2. Wilson, *The Bayeux Tapestry*, pl. 71.
3. Foys, 'Shot Through the Eye and Who's to Blame'.
4. William of Malmesbury, *Vita Wulfstani*, pp. 151-153.
5. Henry of Huntingdon, *The History of the English People*, p. 27.
6. Brown, *The Bayeux Tapestry: History and Bibliography*, p. 174.
7. Bridgeford, *The Hidden History of the Bayeux Tapestry*, p. 14n16; Lawson, *Hastings* pp. 231.
8. For William of Malmesbury, *Vita Wulfstani*, p. 153; for Henry of Huntingdon, *The History of the English People,* see p. 27.
9. Suggests that not all wanted to support him, however that so many attended the battle, meant there was wide opposition to a Norman king.
10. *ASC, D*, p. 199. Chronicle, *E*, p. 198, says simply Harold fell with his brothers.
11. The fate of Walter de Mantes echoes Harold's.
12. Orderic Vitalis, *Historic Ecclesiastica*, ed. Chibnall, pp. 175, 177.
13. Guy, Bishop of Amiens, *Carmen de Haestingae Proelio*, p. xxv.
14. Ibid, p. xviii.
15. Guy, Bishop of Amiens, *Carmen de Haestingae Proelio*, p. 35.
16. Ibid, p. lxxxvi; Orderic Vitalis, *Historic Ecclesiastica*, ed. Chibnall, p. 179. Malet buries him on the shore, agreed by William of Poitiers, *Gesta*, p. 140.
17. William of Poitiers, *Gesta*, p. 140.
18. *ASC, C, D, E*, pp. 182-185; Hill, 'The Debate Concerning the Remains found in Bosham Church', 10/12/ 2003.
19. Marwood, *The Stone Coffins of Bosham Church*, p. 4.
20. Ibid
21. Ibid.
22. Joan Langhorne, anecdotally 21/01/ 2023. Many thanks for the clarification.
23. Henry of Huntingdon, *The History of the English People*, pp. 17-18.
24. Wilson, *The Bayeux Tapestry*, pl3.
25. Zolfag Harifard, 'Do King Harold's Remains lie Under a Hertfordshire Church?'
26. https://www.facebook.com/KingHaroldIIsburialsite.
27. McKenzie and Muff, *The Forgotten Vaults of the Godwins*, p. 6.
28. Paul Ailey, *King Harold, Bishops Stortford*.
29. John of Worcester, *Chronicle*, p. 605.
30. Tikkanen, 'John Leland, English Antiquarian'.

31. Ailey, *King Harold, Bishiops Stortford*.
32. McKenzie and Muff, *The Forgotten Vaults of the Godwins*, p. 1. I have not been able to clarify this statement with Waltham Abbey.
33. Hall, *Lives of the Queens of England Before the Norman Conquest*, vol. 2, p. 397, quoted by McKenzie and Muff, *The Forgotten Vaults of the Godwins*, p. 2.
34. Hugh Candidus, *The Peterborough Chronicle of Hugh Candidus*, pp. 30-32.
35. McKenzie and Muff, *The Forgotten Vaults of the Godwins*, p. 3.
36. Thanks to Ann Williams for the clarification.
37. Freeman, *The History of the Norman Conquest of England*, vol. 3, p. 773, for Malmesbury.
38. William of Malmesbury, *Vita Wulfstani*, p. 153.
39. Wace, *Chronicle*, p. 259.
40. Freeman, *The History of the Norman Conquest of England*, vol. 3, p. 783.
41. *Waltham Chronicle*, p. xxxii.
42. Ibid, p. 45.
43. The unreliability of some of the chronicle's information does not form any basis to dismiss the whole manuscript and therefore should still be discerned as evidence.
44. *Waltham Chronicle*, p. 47.
45. Ibid.
46. *Waltham Chronicle*, p. 48n1. The idea that Harold left London too early without an army strong enough in numbers is a popular one, though has little substance. It is true, on the other hand, that he could have increased his numbers had he waited longer, though Harold likely thought the situation was dire.
47. Ibid, p. 49.
48. *Waltham Chronicle*, p. 51; St. Firmin of Amiens feast day 25 September, the day of Stamford Bridge battle; Calixtus' day, October 14.
49. Ibid.
50. *Waltham Chronicle*, p. 53. The Battle Abbey Chronicle is one of two sources to have mentioned his decision made after the battle.
51. Ibid. There is some allusion to the duke offering to bury him in his new church, but the canons decline. 'No great king to be, grant the prayers of suppliants that your noble highness may rejoice in your victory.'
52. Ibid, p. 55, called Edith in error.
53. Ibid. Handfasted marriages were out of fashion at time of writing.
54. *Waltham Chronicle*, pp. 55-57.
55. William Winters, *The Burial of Harold at Waltham*, p. 1.
56. Ibid, p. 1. Winters quotes Geraldus Cambrensis.
57. *Vita Haroldi*, pp. 135-182.
58. Ibid, pp. 187-188.
59. Freeman, *The History of the Norman Conquest of England*, vol. 3 p. 783.
60. Ibid, p. 777.
61. Bridgeford, *The Hidden History of the Bayeux Tapestry*, p. 132; Wilson, *The Bayeux Tapestry*, p150.
62. Walker, *Harold the Last Anglo-Saxon King*, p. 197.
63. Bridgeford, *The Hidden History of the Bayeux Tapestry*, pp. 132-133.
64. Freeman, *The History of the Norman Conquest of England*, vol. 3, p. 783.
65. William of Malmesbury, *Vita Wulfstani*, p. 155.

66. Freeman, *The History of the Norman Conquest of England*, vol. 3, p. 784.
67. William, 'Art of Memory', loc. 320.
68. *Waltham Chronicle,* pp. 55, 57.
69. Winters, *The Burial of Harold at Waltham*, p. 17.
70. My gratitude to Tricia Gurnett, 1 March March and 14 August, 2023.
71. Levy, 'TV Hunt for Body of King Harold'.
72. Hollick, '1066 Where is Harold Buried?'.

Abbreviations

ASC	*The Anglo-Saxon Chronicles, E*
Brut (Pen. 20)	*Brut y Tywysogion, Peniarth*, MS. 20
Domesday	*Domesday Book: A Complete Translation*
Encomium	*Encomium Emmae Reginae*
Hemingi	*Hemingi Chartularium ecclesiae Wigorniensis*
Malmesbury	William of Malmesbury, *Chronicle of the Kings of England From the Earliest Period to the Reign of King Stephen*
Symeon	Symeon of Durham, *Symeonis Monachi Opera Omnia, Historia Regum*
Vita	*The Life of King Edward The Confessor*

Bibliography

Abels Richard, 'Royal Succession and the Growth of Political Stability in Ninth-Century Wessex'. *The Haskins Society Journal* 12 (2002): 83-98.

Abrams, Lesley. 'Edward the Elder's Danelaw'. In *Edward the Elder, 899–924*. Edited by N.J. Higham and D.H. Hill, 135–151 (Abingdon: Routledge, 2001).

Adam of Bremen. *History of the Archbishops of Hamburg, Bremen.* Translated by J. Tshan (New York: Columbia University Press,1959).

Ailred, Abbot of Rivaulx. *The Life of Saint Edward: King and Confessor*. Translated by J. Bertram (Kingdom: Saint Austin Press, 1997).

The Anglo-Saxon Chronicles, E. Translated by Michael Swanton (London: Phoenix Press, 2000).

The Annals of Tigernach. Translated by Whitley Stokes (Burnham-on-Sea: Llanerch Press, 1993).

Anscombe, A. 'The Pedigree of Earl Godwin'. *Transactions of the Royal Historical Society* 7 (1913): 129-50.

Armstrong, Dan. 'The Norman Conquest of England, the Papacy, and the Papal Banner'. *Haskins Society Journal* 32 (2021): 47-72.

Aubrey, William H.S. *The National and Domestic History of England* (London: James Hagger, 1867) 1867.

Barlow, Frank. *Edward the Confessor* (London: Yale University Press, 1997).

Barlow, Frank. *The Godwins: The Rise and Fall of a Noble Dynasty*. 2nd ed. (Edinburgh: Pearson Educational, 2004).

Barlow, Lundie W. 'The Antecedents of Earl Godwine of Wessex'. *New England Historical and Genealogical Register* 61 (1957): 30-38.

Bartlett, W.B. *King Cnut and the Viking Conquest of England* (Stroud: Amberley, 2018).

Bates, David. *William the Conqueror* (New Haven: Yale University Press, 2016).

Breeze, Andrew. 'The Anglo-Saxon Chronicle for 1053 and the Killing of Rhys ap Rhydderch'. *Radnorshire Society Transactions* 71 (2001): 168-169.

Brevis Relatio de Guillelmo Nobilissimo comite Normanorum. Edited by Elisabeth M.C. van Houts. Royal Historical Society Camden Fifth Series 10 (July 1997): 5-48.

Bridgeford, Andrew. *1066: The Hidden History of the Bayeux Tapestry* (London: Harper Perennial, 2004).

Brown, S.A. *The Bayeux Tapestry: History and Bibliography* (Woodbridge: Boydell, 1988).

Brut y Tywysogion, Peniarth, MS. 20. Edited and translated by T. Jones (Cardiff: Cardiff University of Wales, 1952).

Brut y Tywysogyon, or The Chronicle of the Princes, Red Book of Hergest Version. Edited and translated by T. Jones (Cardiff: Cardiff University of Wales, 1955).

Charles-Edwards, Thomas, Morfydd E. Owen, and Paul Russell (eds.). *The Welsh King and his Court* (Cardiff: University of Wales Press, 2000).
The Chronicle of Battle Abbey. Translated by Elizabeth Searle (Oxford: Clarendon Press, 1980).
Clarke, Peter A. *The English Nobility under Edward the Confessor* (Oxford: Oxford University Press 1994).
Connolly, Sharon Bennett. *Silk and the Sword* (Stroud: Amberley, 2018).
Corner, Dennis. *Porlock in Those Days* (Exmoor: Rare Books and Berry, 1992).
Cowdrey, H.E.J. *Pope Gregory VII, 1073–1085* (Oxford: Oxford University Press, 1998).
Davies, Sean. 'The Last King of Wales'. 09 December 2012. https://www.iwa.wales/agenda/2012/08/the-last-king-of-wales/.
Davies, Sean and Michael Davies. *The Last King of Wales: Gruffudd ap Llywelyn, c. 1013–1063.* Kindle edition (Cheltenham: The History Press, 2012).
Davis, R.H.C. 'East Anglia and the Danelaw'. *Transactions of the Royal Historical Society* 5 (1955): 23-39.
DeVries, Kelly. *The Norwegian Invasion of England in 1066* (Woodbridge: Boydell Press, 1999).
Douglas, David C. *William the Conqueror*. new edn. (London: Yale University Press, 1999).
Dickinson, J.C. *The Shrine of Our Lady of Walsingham* (Cambridge: Cambridge University Press, 1956).
The Domesday Book: A Complete Translation, vol. 1. Translated and edited by Ann Williams and G.H. Martin (London: The Folio Society, 2003).
The Domesday Book: A Complete Translation, vol. 3. Translated and edited by Ann Williams and G.H. Martin (London: The Folio Society, 2003).
Domesday Book: Sussex. Tranlated and edited by John Morris (London: Phillimore Ltd., 1976).
Douglas, D.C. and G.W. Greenaway. *English Historical Documents*. Vol. 2 (Oxford: Oxford University Press, 1953).
Eadmer. *Historia Novorum in Anglia (Eadmer's History of Recent Events in England)*. Translated by Geoffrey Bosanquet (Peterborough: Cresset Press, 1964).
Encomium Emmae. Edited by Alistair Campbell (Cambridge: Cambridge University Press, 1949).
Freeman, Edward Augustus. *The History of the Norman Conquest of England, Its Causes and its Results*. Vols. 1 and 2 (Oxford: Oxford University Press, 1877).
Fell, Christine. *Women in Anglo Saxon England* (Oxford: Blackwell, 1987).
Fletcher, Richard. *Bloodfeud in Anglo-Saxon England* (London: BCA, 2002).
Flint, Bill. *Edith the Fair Visionary of Walsingham* (Leominster: Gracewing, 2015).
Foys, Martin. 'Shot Through the Eye and Who's to Blame'. *History Today* 66, no. 10 (Oct. 2016). https://www.historytoday.com/shot-through-eye-and-who%E2%80%99s-blame.
Garmonsway. G. *Cnut and his Empire* (London: H.K. Lewis, 1963).
Garnett, George. *The Norman Conquest: A Very Short Introduction* (Oxford: Oxford University Press, 2009).
Geffrei Gaimar. *Lestorie des Engles solum la translacion maistre*. Edited by Thomas Duffus Hardy and Martin Charles Trice (London: Eyre and Spottiswoode, 1888).

Bibliography

Gesta Normannorum Ducum, of William of Jumièges, Orderic Vitalis and Robert of Torigny, Vol ii, Books v-vii. Edited and translated by Elisabeth C.M. van Houts (Oxford: Oxford Medieval Texts, 1995).

Gerald of Wales. *The Description of Wales*. Edited and translated by L. Thorpe (Harmondsworth: Penguin Classics, 1978).

Gravett, Christopher. *Hastings 1066: The Fall of Saxon England* (Oxford: Osprey, 2000).

Grills, Hubert. *The Life and Times of Godwine, Earl of Wessex* (Swaffham: Anglo-Saxon Books, 2009).

Guy, Bishop of Amiens. *The Carmen de Haestingae Proelio*. Edited and translated by Frank Barlow (Oxford: Clarendon Press, 1999).

Hagland, Jan Ragnar, and Bruce Watson. 'Fact or Folklore: The Viking Attack on London Bridge'. *London Archaeologist* 10, no. 12 (2005): 328–333.

Hardy, T. 'The Translation of St. Mildred, Catalogue of Materials, vol'. 1. In *The Life and Times of Godwine Earl of Wessex*. Edited by Hubert Grills, 380-381 (Norfolk: Anglo-Saxon Books: Norfolk).

Hart, C. *The Danelaw*. 1st ed. (London: Hambledon Continuum, 1992).

Hemingi Chartularium ecclesiae Wigorniensis. Edited by T. Hearne. Vol. 1 (Detroit: Gale Echo).

Henry of Huntingdon. *The History of the English People, 1000–1154*. Translated by Diana Greenway (Oxford: Oxford World's Classics, 2002).

Herman the Archdeacon and Goscelin of St. Bertin. *Miracles of St. Edmund*. Edited and translated by T. Licence (Oxford: OMT, 2014).

Hicks, Carola, ed. *England in the Eleventh Century* (Stamford: Paul Watkins, 1992).

Hill, Paul. *The Road to Hastings: The Politics of Power in Anglo-Saxon England* (Stroud: Tempus Publishing, 2005).

Historia Ecclesie Abbendonensis: The History of the Church of Abbingdon. Edited and translated by J. Hudson. Vol. 1 (Oxford: OMT, 2002–7).

Howarth, David. *1066: The Year of The Conquest* (New York: Viking Press, 1977).

Hugh Candidus. *The Peterborough Chronicle of Hugh Candidus*, Edited by W.T. Mellows (Peterborough: Peterborough Natural History, Scientific, and Archæological Society, 1941).

Jakobsson, Sverrir. 'The Early Kings of Norway: The Issue of Agnatic Succession, and the Settlement of Iceland'. *Viator* 47 (2016): 4-6.

John, Eric. 'Edward the Confessor and the Norman Succession'. *The English Historical Review* 94, no. 371 (1979): 241–267.

John of Worcester. *The Chronicle of John of Worcester*. Edited and translated by Jennifer Bray and P. McGurk (Oxford: Oxford University Press, 1995).

Jones, Charles. *The Forgotten Battle of 1066 Fulford* (Reading: Tempus Publishing, 2006).

Jones, Mary. 'The Life of Saint Gwynllyw: Of the Anchor Placed in the Church and not Seen, and of the Bloody Cheeses'. https://www.maryjones.us/ctexts/gwynllyw.html, accessed 21/11/2023.

John of Salisbury, *Policraticus*. Edited by C.C.J. Webb (Oxford: Oxford University Press, 1909).

Kapelle, William E. *The Norman Conquest of the North: The Region and its Transformation, 1000–1135* (London: Croom Helm, 1979).

Ker, N.R. 'Hemming's Cartulary: A Description of Two Worcester Cartularies in Cotton Tiberius A. xiii'. In *Studies in Medieval History Presented to Frederick Maurice Powicke*. Edited by R.W. Hunt et al, 45-75 (West Port: Greenwood Press, 1979).

Key, Michael John. *The House of Godwin: The Rise and Fall of an Anglo-Saxon Dynasty* (Stroud: Amberley Publishing, 2022).

Keynes, Simon. 'Æthelstan Ætheling [Athelstan the Atheling] (d. 1014)'. *Oxford Dictionary of National Biography* (Oxford: Oxford University Press, 2004). Online edition.

Keynes, Simon. *Cnut's Earls in the Reign of Cnut*. Edited by A. Rumble (Cambridge: Cambridge University Press, 1994).

Keynes, Simon. *The Diplomas of King Æthelred the Unready 978–1016* (Cambridge: Cambridge University Press, 1980).

Knowles, David, C.N.L. Brooke, and Vera C.M. London, eds. *The Heads of Religious Houses, England and Wales 940–1216* (Cambridge: Cambridge University Press, 2009).

Knowles, M.D. *Monastic Order in England*. 2nd ed. (Cambridge: Cambridge University Press, 1963).

Knýtlinga Saga: The History of the Kings of Denmark. Translated by H. Palsson, S.I. Tucker, and P. Edwards (Odense: Odense University, 1986).

Lavelle, Ryan. *Alfred's Wars Sources and Interpretations of Anglo-Saxon Warfare in the Viking Age* (Woodbridge: Boydell Press, 2010).

Lawson, M.K. *The Battle of Hastings 1066*. 3rd ed. (Cheltenham: History Press, 2016).

Lawson, M.K. *England's Viking King 1016–35* (Cheltenham: History Press, 2011).

Licence, Tom. *Edward the Confessor Last of the Royal Blood* (New Haven: Yale University Press, 2020).

Marren, Peter. *1066: The Battles of York, Stamford Bridge, and Hastings* (Barnsley: Pen & Sword, 2004).

Marwood, Geoffrey Wl. *The Stone Coffins of Bosham Church* (published by author, 1970).

Mason, Emma. *The House of Godwine: The History of a Dynasty* (London: Hambleden, 2004).

Mike@AbitaboutBritain, Bosham, 'The King's Daughter and Harold'.07 April 2017. https://bitaboutbritain.com/bosham-cnut-the-kings-daughter-and-harold/.

Morkinskinna. Translated and edited Theodore M. Anderson and Kari Ellen Gade (New York: Cornell University Press, 2000).

McKenzie, Keven P. and Terence G. G. Muff. *The Forgotten Vaults of the Godwins* (PDF, 2015).

Napier, A.S. *The Old English Version of the Enlarged Rule of Chrodegang with the Latin Original*. (Oxford: Early English Texts Society, 1916).

Nelson, Janet. 'The First Use of the Second Anglo-Saxon Ordo'. In *Myth, Rulership, Church and Charters*. Edited by Julia Barrow and Andrew Wareham, 117–126 (Ashgate: Aldershot, 2008).

O'Brien Harriet. *Queen Emma and the Vikings: The Woman Who Shaped the Events of 1066* (London: Bloomsbury, 2006).

Orderic Vitalis. *Historica Ecclesiastica*. Edited by Marjorie Chibnall. Vol. 2 (Oxford: Claredon Press, 1969).

Orderic Vitalis. *Historia Ecclesiastica*. Edited by A. Le. Prévost and L. Delisle. Vol. 2 (1838–1855).

Bibliography

Petts, D. *The Early Medieval Church in Wales* (Stroud: History Press, 2009).
Powicke, F.M. *The Thirteenth Century, 1216–1307* (Oxford: Clarendon Press, 1982).
Rex, Peter. *The Last English King, the Life of Harold II* (Chelmsford: The History Press, 2008).
Robertson, A.J. *Anglo-Saxon Charters* (Cambridge: Cambridge University Press, 1956).
Ronay, Gabriel. *The Lost King of England* (Suffolk: Boydell, 1989).
Round, J.H. 'The Third Penny'. *English Historical Review* 34 (1919): 62-64.
'S 1535'. *The Electronic Sawyer: Online Catalogue of AngloSaxon Charters*. https://esawyer.lib.cam.ac.uk/charter/1535.html, accessed 09/10/2023.
Saxo Grammaticus. *Danorum Regum Heroumque Historia*. Translated and edited by E. Christiensen (Oxford: British Archaeological Reports Oxford Ltd, 1980).
Searle, Eleanor. *Women and the Legitimization of Succession at the Norman Conquest* (Pasadena: California Institute of Technology, 2017).
Sermo Lupi ad Anglos. Edited by Dorothy Whitelock. 3rd ed. (Frome: Butler & Tanner Ltd, 1963).
Sharpe, Richard. *King Harold's Daughter* (Cambridge: Cambridge University Press, 2012).
Snorri Sturluson. *King Harold's Saga (Heimskringla)*. Edited by B. Aðaljardnson (Reyjavik: 1941–1951).
Snorri Sturluson. *King Harald's Saga, Heimskringla*. Translated by b Magnus Magnusson and Herman Palsson(Harmondsworth: Penguin Books, 1977).
Stafford, Pauline. *Queen Emma and Queen Edith: Queenship and Women's Power in Eleventh Century England* (Oxford: Blackwell Publishers, 2001).
Stenton, F.M. *Anglo-Saxon England* (Oxford: Clarendon Press, 1988).
'The Story So Far'. The Shrine of Our Lady of Walsingham. walsinghamanglican.org.uk, accessed on 09/10/2023.
Stevenson, J., ed. *The History of Ingulf: Church Historians of England, vol. ii, part ii* (London, 1854).
Strutt, J. *The Chronicle of England* (London: Thomas Jones, 1872).
Symeon of Durham. *Symeonis Monachi Opera Omnia, Historia Regum*. Edited by Thomas Arnold (London: Longman, 1885).
Tikkanen, Amy. 'John Leland, *English antiquarian*'. Encyclopedia Britannica online. https://www.britannica.com/biography/John-Leland accessed on the 11/08/2023.
Theodoricus Monachus. *Historia de Antiquitate Regum Norwegiensiem*. Translated by David McDougall and Ian McDougall (London: University College, 1998).
Thorpe, Benjamin. *Laws and Institutes*. Vol. 2 (Cambridge: Cambridge University Press, 2012).
Trevelyan, G.M. *History of England*. 1st. ed. (London: Longmans Green, 1926).
Tyson, Kathleen. *Godwin the Sea-lord*, 1.1. Academia, 2016. https://www.academia.edu/33173728/160907_Tyson_Godwin_the_Sea_Lord_pdf.
van Houts, Elisabeth. 'The Norman Conquest through European Eyes'. *The English Historical Review* 110 (Sept. 1995): 832–853.
van Houts, Elisabeth. *The Normans in Britain* (Manchester: Manchester University Press, 2013).
van Houts, Elisabeth. 'The Ship List of William the Conqueror'. *Anglo-Norman Studies* 10 (1987): 159-183.

Vita Edwardi Regis: The Life of King Edward The Confessor. Edited by Frank Barlow (London: Thomas Nelson and Sons, 1989).

Vita Haroldi. Edited and translated by W. de Gray Birch (London: Elliot Stock, 1885).

Wace. *His Chronicle of the Norman Conquest from the Roman de Rou.* Translated by Edgar Taylor (London: William Pickering, 1837).

Walker, W. Ian. *Harold the Last Anglo-Saxon King* (Stroud: Sutton Publishing, 2004).

The Waltham Chronicle. Edited and translated by L. Watkiss and M. Chibnall (Oxford: Oxford University Press, 1994).

Williams, Ann. 'Cockles Among the Wheat: Danes and English in the Western Midlands in the First Half of the Eleventh Century'. *Midland History* 11 (1986): 1-22.

Williams Ann. 'Land and power in the Eleventh century: the estates of Harold Godwineson'. *Anglo-Norman Studies* 3 (1981): 171-187.

Williams Ann. 'The King's Nephew: The Family and Career of Ralph, Earl of Hereford'. In *Medieval History.* Edited by C. Harper-Bill, C.J. Holdsworth, and J.L. Nelson, 327-343 (Woodbridge: Boydell, 1989).

Williams, Ann. *Kingship and Government in Pre-Conquest England c. 500-1066* (London: Palgrave Macmillan, 1999).

Williams, Ann. *Land, Power and Politics: the Family and Career of Odda of Deerhurst* (Deerhurst: The Deerhurst Lecture, 1997).

Whitehead, Annie. *Mercia: The Rise and Fall of a Kingdom* (Stroud: Amberley Publishing, 2018).

Williams, Ann. 'The Spindle Side: The Kinswomen of Earl Godwine of Wessex'. In *Approaches to History: Essays in Honour of Hirokazu Tsurushima.* Edited by Yukio Arai, Naoki Haruta, and David Roffe, 1-12 (Tokyo: Tosuishobou, 2022).

Williams, Ann. 'Spoliation of Worcester'. *Anglo-Norman Studies* 19 (1996): 383-408.

Williams, Ann. 'Thegnly Piety and Ecclesiastical Patronage in the Late Old English Kingdom'. *Anglo-Norman Studies* 26 (2002): 1-24.

William of Malmesbury. *Chronicle of the Kings of England From the Earliest Period to the Reign of King Stephen.* Translated by J.A. Giles (1847).

William of Poitiers. *The Gesta Guillelmi of William of Poitiers.* Edited by R.H.C. Davis and Marjorie Chibnall (Oxford: Clarendon Press, 2006).

Wilson, David M. *The Bayeux Tapestry* (London: Thames & Hudson, 2004).

Winters, William. *The Burial of Harold at Waltham.* Revised edn. (Waltham Abbey Historical Society, 1892).

Wolf, Armin. 'Who Was Agatha the Ancestress of Scottish and English Kings?'. *Foundation for Medieval Genealogy* (July 2011). https://fmg.ac/publications/journal/volume-3/file/295-agatha-4, accessed 2/4/22.

Wood, Michael. *Domesday: A Search for the Roots of England* (London: BBC Books, 1986).

William of Malmesbury. *Vita Wulfstani.* Edited by R.R. Darlington (London: Royal Historical Society, 1928).

Index

Adam of Bremen, 31, 68, 184
Adelard of Uhtrect, (also known as Ailard), physician and schoolmaster of Waltham Collegiate, 44, 52, 53
Aldith of Mercia (Ealdgyth), Queen of Wales, second wife of Harold Godwinson, 49, 50, 115, 116, 122, 158, 196, 197, 198
Alexander ii, Pope, 121, 162-166
Ælfgifu, daughter of Æthelred, 120, 144
Ælfgifu of Northampton, 10, 21, 22, 50, 155, 159
Ælfgifu of York, 3, 4, 10, 33
Ælfhelm of York, 3, 4 13, 78
Ælfheah, Archbishop of Canterbury, 7, 134
Ætheling, 4, 8, 24, 85, 86, 111-115, 151-152
Æthelingadene, 3, 8
Æthelmær of Mercia brother of Streona, 1, 2, 4
Æthelmær Cild, son of Aethelweard the Historian 1, 2
Æthelred, King of England, 1, 3, 4, 8, 9, 10, 13, 14, 21, 23, 30, 33, 48, 85, 151, 155
Æthelric, (also known as Alfric) monk of Canterbury, Bishop of Selsey, kinsman of Godwin, 71, 115, 140-141
Æthelric of Mercia, Father of Streona, 1, 2, 4
Æthelric, owned land in Kelvedon, 170
Æthelstan Ætheling, 2, 3, 5, 8, 9, 10, 12
Æthelstan, Bishop of Hereford, 70, 108
Æthelstan, son of Tovi the Proud, 31, 41, 94

Æthelweard of Mercia, brother of Streona, 4
Æthelweard, the Historian, 1, 2
Alfred Ætheling, 3, 9, 13, 23, 24, 25, 26, 28, 29, 32, 36, 38, 43, 73, 78, 86, 95, 155
Alfred the Great, x, 58
Anglo-Saxon Chronicle, x, xi, 2, 10, 24, 192, 194
Anscombe and Lundie Theory, 1, 2
Anselm, Archbishop of Canterbury, 135, 139

Baldwin IV, Count of Flanders, 6, 73
Baldwin V, Count of Flanders, 5, 13, 23, 25, 44, 52, 53, 63-67, 69, 73, 77, 81, 88, 112, 130, 146, 150, 167
Baltic Wars, see also Wends, 15, 18
Battle of Hastings, x, 43, 51, 56, 82, 127, 129, 132, 135, 163, 186-190, 195
Battle of Sherston, 2, 14
Battle of Stamford Bridge, 16, 46, 173-177, 180, 183, 199
Bayeux Tapestry, 20, 29, 45, 46, 83, 130, 132, 135, 136, 138, 140, 153, 154, 160, 163, 179, 180, 181, 188, 189, 190, 191, 192, 194
Benedict, Pope, 117, 120, 154
Beorn, Earl, son of Estrid, 17, 18, 35-36, 38, 39, 52, 53, 58, 66-69, 102, 195
Bernicia, 143, 148
Bondi, staller, 91, 159, 199
Bosham, Sussex, see also Holy Trinity Church, 20, 59, 60, 63, 66-68, 77, 103, 136, 140, 193-195, 204
Boulogne, 23, 69, 73, 74, 75, 81, 84, 86, 86, 94, 130, 135, 164

Brihtric, brother of Streona, 3-5, 8, 9, 13
Bruges, 6, 13, 25, 26, 42, 63, 64, 66, 67, 69, 70, 74, 77, 88, 89, 91
Burghred, 121, 145
Byrhtnoth, Ealdorman of East Anglia, 14, 40

Canterbury, xi, 50, 51, 71, 74, 75, 95, 106, 135, 139, 140, 141
Carmen de Hastingae Proelio, x, xi, 82, 83, 129, 132, 179, 183-193, 203
Cerdic, 36, 84, 85, 114
Christmas, 8, 39, 45
Cnut, King of Denmark, England, and Norway, 5, 6, 8, 9, 10, 11, 12, 13, 14, 15, 16, 17, 18, 20, 21, 22, 23, 28, 29, 30, 34, 35, 36, 43, 50
Cnut's daughter, died in Bosham, 59, 193-184
Compton, *(Cumtune),* land owned by Wulfnoth Cild, 3, 7, 9, 103
Copsige, Tostig's Deputy, 145, 148, 169, 171

Danelaw, 8, 12, 40, 147, 157
Danes, 3, 7, 10, 11, 14, 26, 35, 40-43, 51, 52, 65, 66, 106, 148, 152
Denmark, 10, 16-18, 21, 22, 26, 28, 30, 31, 35, 36, 38, 42, 43, 51, 52, 58, 63-65, 66-67, 69, 71, 116, 164, 167, 168, 184
Diarmait mac Mael na mBo, Lord of Leinster, 28, 122
Domesday Book, 40, 48, 49, 50, 102, 144, 202
Dover, 23, 27, 73-75, 77, 93, 131, 137
Drogo, Count of the Vexin, 69, 97, 127
Dublin, 28, 88, 89, 90, 116
Duncan I, 143, 144
Dux Anglorum, 38, 39, 129-131

Eadgifu, Abbess of Leominster, 53, 61-64, 102
Eadgifu, daughter of Earl Godwin, 19, 20, 103, 137
Eadgifu Swanneck, (also known as Eadgifu the Rich, Edith Swanneck) common-law wife of Harold Godwinson, see also Edith the Fair, 39, 48-51, 55-56, 100-104, 159, 181, 102, 196, 197, 198, 201-205
Eadric Streona, 1, 3, 7, 9-14, 24, 143, 151
Eadmer of Canterbury, x, 13, 20, 83, 133, 135-141
Ealdgyth, wife of Edmund Ironside and widow of Sigeferth, 9, 10, 111
East Anglia, 10, 14, 17, 21, 31, 35-40, 48, 50, 51, 52, 88, 89, 96, 102, 104, 108, 111, 115, 143, 186
Easter, 30, 39, 100, 157, 158, 165
Edeva Pulchra or *Dives,* see also Eadgifu Swanneck, 48
Edgar Ætheling, 35, 36, 113, 114, 115, 151, 152, 155, 156, 157-159, 182
Edgar the Peaceable, King of England, 12, 33, 62, 86
Edith, Queen of England, xi, 15, 16, 19, 29-35, 38, 39, 42, 43, 47, 49, 57, 60, 72, 77-79, 83-87, 104, 111, 142, 150, 152, 153, 183, 195
Edith the Fair, also known as Eadgifu Swanneck, 48, 49, 195, 196, 197
Edmund Ironside, King of England, 9, 10, 11, 12, 13, 85, 86, 175
Edmund, son of Edmund Ironside, 86, 111-113, 152
Edmund, son of Harold Godwinson, 51
Edward the Confessor, King of England, x, xi, 1, 3, 6, 9, 13, 15, 18, 19, 23, 24, 25, 27, 28, 29, 30, 31, 32, 33, 34, 35, 36, 38, 39, 41, 42, 43, 44, 130, 151, 152, 195
Edward the Exile, 85, 86, 111-114
Edwin, Earl of Mercia, 49, 72, 122, 145-148, 157, 158, 169, 171, 172, 182, 190
Eilaf, brother of Jarl Ulf, 6, 13, 17, 59, 111
Encomium Emmae Reginae, 12, 14, 23-25, 28, 30
Emma of Normandy, 3, 4, 12, 13, 21-26, 28, 30, 31, 32, 33, 34, 50, 81, 90, 114, 155, 159
Erik, Jarl of Northumbria (*Eiríkr Hákonarson*), 14, 16, 21

Index

Ermenfrid of Sion, 164, 165, 166
Esegar (Ansgar) the Staller, Portreeve of London, Sherrif of Middlesex, 10, 41, 91, 94, 159, 186
Essex, 11, 39, 40, 42, 50, 52, 55, 67, 91, 95, 170, 186, 194, 201
Estrid, Cnut's sister, 16, 17, 35
Eustace, Count of Boulogne, 23, 69, 73, 74, 130, 135
Eystein Orri, 173 see also Orri's Storm

Flanders, 5, 6, 23, 25, 28, 52, 63, 64, 65, 69, 70, 73, 81, 89, 91, 97, 102, 112, 132, 146, 150, 164, 167, 169, 173
Five Boroughs, 9, 10

Gaimar, x, 144, 169, 171
Gilbert, Archdeacon of Lisieux, 162, 164
Giso, Bishop of Wells, 120, 121, 159
Gloucestershire, 38, 58, 67, 75, 88, 96
Goda, sister of Edward (also known as Godgifu) 23, 69, 70, 73, 85, 97, 127
Godwin, Earl of Wessex, x; lineage, 1-7, 8-13, 15-17, 20-28, 29-36, 38, 39, 42, 43, 46, 47, 51, 52, 53, 57-79, 80-84, 88-97, 100-103, 114, 115, 119, 129, 132, 133, 135, 141, 155, 184, 194
Godwin Cild, son of Harold and Eadgifu, 49, 51
Godwinsons, the family, x, xi, 28, 33, 34, 35, 36, 38, 42, 43, 44, 46, 47, 150, 155, 171
Gospatric, son of Maldred, 121, 144, 147
Gospatric Uhtrædson, 142, 143, 144
Gruffudd ap Llywelyn King of Gwynedd and Wales, 45, 62, 66, 67, 104, 107-110, 115-118, 122-126, 129, 158-159
Gruffudd ap Rhydderch, 62, 66, 67, 90, 104, 107, 108
Gunhild, Harold's sister, 19, 20, 47, 51, 103
Gunhild, Harold's daughter, 49, 51
Gunhildr, daughter of Cnut, wife of Holy Roman Emperor, Henry III, 21, 44
Gunhildr, Cnut's niece, 31, 40, 41 42

Guy, Bishop of Amiens, x, 129, 162, 180, 183, 185-189, 182, 193, 198, 202, 203, 205
Guy, Count of Ponthieu, 130, 131, 133, 136
Gyrth Godwinson, Earl of East Anglia, 16, 19, 20, 35, 88 91, 103, 115, 117, 120, 150, 181, 182, 188, 189, 192, 195, 196, 199, 202
Gytha, Lady of Wessex, wife of Earl Godwin, 16-20, 35, 36, 43, 44, 46, 51, 57, 59, 60, 63, 66, 85, 88, 92, 95, 97, 100, 103, 150, 181, 190, 193, 194, 195, 198, 202-204
Gytha, daughter of Harold, 51, 55
Gytha, daughter of Osgod Clapa, 41, 44
Gytha, wife of Earl Ralph, 85, 115

Hakon, Cnut's deputy in Norway, 41, 59
Hakon, son of Swegn Godwinson, 63, 76, 97, 100, 133, 137
Harald Bluetooth, King of Denmark, 18
Harald Hardrada, 45, 46, 52, 64, 65, 113, 116, 150, 158, 167, 168, 171, 173, 175-178
Harold Godwinson II, Earl of East Anglia, Wessex, King of England, x-xii, 1, 2, 16-18, 19, 20, 27-28, 31, 34, 35, 38-44, 49, 92-94, 96-98 100, 101, 123, 142-147, 167-169, 170, 171, 180-184; abroad, 111-113, 117-118; appearance and character, 45-46; Battle of Hastings 185-190; Battle of Stamford 173-178; burial place, 193-205; conflict with Wales, 122-126; death of the Exile, 114; death of Harold, 191-193; Earl of East Anglia, 38-46; exile in Ireland, 47, 88-92; Earl of Wessex, 102-110; In Normandy, 129-132, 135-141; illness, 43, 44, 89; In Lord of Waltham 51-56, 119-120; King of England, 157-160, 162-166; relations with siblings, 46, 47; marriage to Eadgifu, 48-51; succession, 150-156;
Harold Harefoot, King of England, son of Cnut, 21-26, 32, 38, 50, 59, 77, 155

Harold, son of Earl Ralph, 85, 88
Harthacnut, King of England, 13, 17, 18, 21, 22, 25-31, 35, 38, 53, 70, 78, 116, 155, 168
Hemming, brother of Thorkell the Tall, 6, 13, 18
Hemming's Cartulary, 59, 63
Henry I, King of France, 44, 88, 94, 128, 134
Henry III, Holy Roman Emperor, 21, 44, 52, 53, 69, 111, 112, 164
Henry of Huntingdon, x, xi, 15, 39, 50, 132, 155, 159, 172, 176, 177, 191
Herefordshire, 36, 38, 75, 88, 90, 91, 96, 97
Hertfordshire, 35, 193, 195, 198, 205
Holy Trinity Church, Bosham, 20, 103, 136, 193-195, 204
Honorius, the Antipope, 164, 165
Hostages, 6, 13, 31, 36, 62, 76, 82, 83, 92, 93, 96 97, 100, 119, 123, 131, 132, 133, 134, 138, 139, 173, 174, 178, 184
House of Bamburgh, x, 142, 144, 145, 148
House of Wessex, 1, 31, 87, 198
Huscarls, 22, 27, 41, 45, 68, 109, 159, 168, 171, 175, 182, 183, 186, 189
Huntingdonshire, 35, 39, 50, 145

Ireland, 28, 47, 58, 67, 74, 89-93, 97, 98, 104, 105, 106, 122, 150
Isle of Ely, 13, 24, 166

John of Worcester, x, xi
Jomsvikings, 5, 7
Judith, wife of Tostig Godwinson, 28, 73, 77, 88, 120, 121, 146

Kent, 3, 11, 67, 86, 91, 93, 102, 103, 168, 170

Leo, Pope, 69, 72, 84
Leofric, Bishop of Exeter, 34
Leofric, Earl of Mercia, x, 22, 30, 39, 59, 62, 66, 70, 72, 75, 76, 88, 94, 95, 96, 103, 109, 114, 115, 132, 146, 184, 186

Leominster, 61-64, 72, 90
Lindsey, Lincolnshire, 8, 169
Leofwin (also known as Leofwine) Godwinson, Earl of Kent and Essex, 1, 16, 19, 28, 46, 195, 196
Leofwine, Ealdorman of Mercia, 14
London, 9, 10, 11, 22, 23, 24, 26, 35, 41, 76, 77, 94, 114, 131, 158, 165, 168, 170, 181, 182, 185, 186, 199
London Garrison, 10
Lord of Walsingham, 48
Lyfing, Bishop of Worcester, 26, 63

Macbeth, King of Scotland, 95, 104, 117, 143
Malcolm, 104, 105, 115, 117, 118, 121, 122, 143, 144, 145, 148, 169
Maldred, 143-147
Magonsæte, 11, 58
Magnus (the Good), King of Norway, 22, 25, 30, 31, 32, 35, 38, 41, 42, 51, 52, 58, 64, 65, 116, 168
Magnus, son of Harold, 51
Magnus, son of Harald Hardrada, 116, 117, 122, 125, 144, 158, 168
Malfosse, 189, 190
Malmesbury Abbey, 9, 10, 55
Marleswein, 159, 182
Matilda, Duchess of Normandy, 28, 130, 135, 179
Mercia, 14, 22, 39, 58, 59, 95, 96, 107, 109, 114, 115, 125, 129, 145, 129, 145, 196
Morcar, thegn of Five Boroughs, 9, 10
Morcar, Earl of Northumbria, 49, 72, 122, 145-148, 157, 158, 169, 171, 172, 182, 190

Nazeing, 51, 52, 56, 100, 182, 205
Nicholas ii, Pope, 119, 120, 121, 154
Norfolk, 39, 115, 171
Norman Conquest, x, xi, 31, 47, 49, 57, 135, 144, 155, 163, 192, 194, 195, 199
Normandy, 5, 9, 24, 28, 29, 34, 36, 44, 45, 49, 50, 63, 69, 73, 80, 81, 82, 83, 84, 86, 94, 97, 127-134, 136-141, 151, 155, 160, 162, 164, 165, 170, 171, 175, 184

Index

Normans, x, xi, 2, 60, 82, 84, 95, 101, 105, 124, 126, 130, 131, 138, 140, 152, 154, 156, 162, 163, 170, 175, 180, 181, 186, 187, 189, 190, 199, 200, 202
Northamptonshire, 35, 145, 147
Norway, 38, 65, 116, 168
Northumbria, 14, 22, 96, 104, 122, 142, 143, 145, 147, 148, 168, 169, 175

Odda, Earl of Somerset, 55, 88, 90, 91, 92, 93, 96, 104, 111, 115, 155
Odo, Bishop of Bayeux, 127, 135, 188
Orri's Storm, 177-178
Orderic Vitalis, x, xi, 82, 127, 135, 139, 163, 167, 172, 179, 181, 185, 190, 192
Osbert of Clare, 30, 32, 33, 57
Osgod Clapa, a jarl of East Anglia, 31, 38, 39, 41, 42, 53, 64, 67, 90, 115
Oxford, 9, 22, 59, 146, 147
Osbern Pentecost, 70, 88, 95

Penitential Ordinance, 163, 164, 165, 166

Ralph de Mantes, Earl of Hereford, 75, 85, 88, 90, 96, 105, 111, 137, 151
Rhuddlan, 45, 122
Richard I, Duke of Normandy, 14, 21, 127
Richard II, Duke of Normandy, 29, 128
Richard FitzScrob, 70, 95
River Couesnon, 45, 138
River Thames, 11, 16, 26, 50, 76, 93
Robert Champart, (also known as Robert of Jumièges) Archbishop of Canterbury and Bishop of London, 19, 34, 71, 72, 74, 77, 82, 83, 84, 90, 95, 115, 127, 128, 130, 131, 132, 133, 135, 137, 155
Robert I, Duke of Normandy, 29, 81, 97, 127
Robert Fitzwymarc, king Edward's Standard bearer, 153, 159, 180, 183
Roman de Rou, xi, 129, 130

Sandwich, 3, 10, 31, 41, 52, 66, 67, 68, 90, 91, 93, 168, 169, 170
Saxons, 107-108, 116

Scandinavian sagas, x, 171-173, 176
Sheppey, 10, 11, 93
Ships, 3, 4, 5, 6, 7, 9, 10, 13, 26, 27, 35, 41, 42, 52, 64, 66-70, 90-94, 104-107, 122, 164, 169, 171-174, 176-181, 185
Sigeferth of Five Boroughs, 9, 10, 111
Siward the Strong, Earl of Northumbria, x, 27, 30, 27, 30, 39, 55, 71-76, 94, 96, 104, 132, 143, 144, 145, 146
Snorri Sturluson, 9, 44, 174, 175
Somerset, 10, 38, 44, 58, 59, 88, 92, 121, 186
Spearhavoc, Bishop of London, 72, 90
St. Benet Holme, Norfolk, 48, 51, 171
St. Omer, Flanders, 20, 47, 55, 112, 117, 146, 150, 167
Stigand, Bishop of East Anglia and Winchester, Archbishop of Canterbury, 30, 77, 95, 117, 119, 132, 134, 139, 153, 154, 161, 163, 165, 184
St. Michaels, Bishops Stortford, 195, 196, 197, 198, 204
Suffolk, 39, 49, 50, 77
Sussex, 3, 5, 8, 45, 91, 95, 102, 103, 140, 168, 170, 179, 181, 182, 185, 186, 193, 194
Sweden, 17, 64, 112
Swein Cnutson, King of Norway, 21, 50
Swein Estridson, King of Denmark, 16, 18, 30, 31, 35, 36, 42, 52, 53, 58, 63-65, 68, 70, 85, 158, 167, 168
Swegn Godwinson, Earl of Hereford, Gloucestershire, Oxfordshire, Berkshire, Somerset, 16, 17, 18, 20, 34, 35, 36, 38, 39, 42, 46, 52, 53, 57, 58, 59-65, 66-76, 78, 79, 82, 88, 89, 91, 93, 95, 96, 97, 98, 101, 102, 105, 108, 132, 195
Sweyn Forkbeard, King of Norway and England, 6, 7, 8, 9, 14, 17, 18, 31 57

Thames, 11, 16, 26, 50, 76, 93
Thorkell the Tall (Þorketill inn hávi), 2, 3, 5, 6, 7, 10, 14, 17, 18, 21, 38, 40, 48
Thorgils Sprakaleggr, 16, 17, 20
Thurstan, 39, 41

Tostig Godwinson, 16, 18, 28, 34, 35, 38, 43, 46, 47
Tovi the Proud, 10, 31, 41, 44, 52, 53, 55, 85, 94, 115

Ulf, Bishop of Dorchester, 95, 96
Ulf, Godwin's brother-in-law, 2, 13, 16, 17, 18, 35, 38
Ulf, son of Harold Godwinson, 51, 181, 202
Ulfketel (Snillingr), 10, 11, 40
Ulfgeat, 4, 5, 13

Victor, Pope, 112, 115
Vikings 3, 4, 5, 6, 14, 125, 174
Vita Ædwardi Regis, xi, 5, 14, 15, 31
Vita Haroldi, 42, 43, 44, 45

Wace, xi, 129, 135, 137, 161-162, 198
Wales, 43-45, 62, 67, 105-107, 122-126, 129, 140, 142, 151
Walter, Bishop of Hereford, 120, 121
Walter, uncle of William of Normandy, 127, 128
Walter de Mantes, 85, 137
Waltham Chronicle, xi, 41, 43, 45
Waltham, Church of the Holy Cross (also Holy Rood), vii, 42, 44, 52, 54, 104, 112, 154, 181, 182, 193-199, 201-205; consecration, 119
Waltham Collegiate, 45, 51-55
Waltham, manor of, 31, 41, 44, 49, 52, 55, 56, 71, 91, 100, 102, 104, 119, 120, 199, 205

Waltheof, Earl of Northampton and Huntingdon, 49, 72, 122, 143-148, 157, 158, 159, 169, 171, 172
Welsh Marches, 39, 41
Wends, 9, 15-16, 21
Wessex, 1, 2, 12, 14, 15, 16, 31, 34, 39, 58, 67, 76, 85, 87, 88, 100, 101-104, 111, 167
William, Bishop of London, 90, 95, 96
William, Duke of Normandy, xi, xii, 2, 20, 28, 45, 46, 49, 50, 51, 63, 69, 73, 80-86, 94, 127-141, 144, 147, 150, 152, 154-156, 158, 160-165, 166-169, 170, 171, 175, 179-181, 182-198, 195, 197, 198-205
William of Jumièges, xi, 23, 82, 127, 184
William Fitz Osbern, 143, 161, 162, 128
William of Malmesbury, x, xi, 16, 33
William of Poitiers, xi, 47, 82
Wilton Abbey, 32, 33, 49
Winchester, 22, 24, 43
Witan, also council, 8, 12, 22, 26, 28
Witenagemót, 9, 71
Wulfgyth, 41, 49
Wulfheah, 4, 5, 13
Wulfnoth Godwinson, son of Earl Godwin, 19, 51, 76, 97, 100, 133, 137
Wulfnoth Cild, father of Earl Godwin, x, 1, 2, 3, 4, 5, 6, 7, 8, 13
Wulfwin the goldsmith, 50, 51